# ROMANS
## Where Life Begins

# ROMANS
## Where Life Begins

Roy L. Laurin

**KREGEL PUBLICATIONS**
Grand Rapids, Michigan 49501

*Romans: Where Life Begins,* by Roy L. Laurin.
Published 1988 by Kregel Publications, a division of
Kregel, Inc. All rights reserved.

**Library of Congress Cataloging-in-Publication Data**

Laurin, Roy L. (Roy Leonard), 1898–1966.
  Romans: Where Life Begins / Roy L. Laurin.
  Reprint. Originally published: Findlay, Ohio: Dunham
Pub. Co., © 1948.

  1. Bible. N.T. Romans—Criticism, interpretation, etc.
I. Title.
BS2665.L37      1988    227'.106—dc19          88-12130

ISBN    0-8254-3130-1 (pbk.)

5  6  7  8  9  Printing/Year  92  91  90  89  88

*Printed in the United States of America*

# CONTENTS

## *Section 1*
## THE SINNER IN REDEMPTION

## *Section 2*
## THE JEW IN REJECTION

**6** *Contents*

## *Section 3*
## THE CHRISTIAN IN EXPERIENCE

# PREFACE

ROMANS is where life begins experimentally. It begins historically at the Creation and spiritually at the Cross. Now we see its experimental appropriation and application in the life of individuals.

Romans is the record of Christianity's philosophy and doctrine. It sets forth the Christian's creed in a profound manner.

The ensuing study is not intended to be a critical or doctrinal treatment, but rather a devotional exposition with particular attention paid to the practical application of its teaching to ordinary everyday life.

This volume, a revision of a limited earlier edition, is offered with the prayerful hope that many more will find it useful in their personal study of the Epistle to the Romans.

Roy L. Laurin

# ACKNOWLEDGMENT

Acknowledgment for the stimulation of thought and helpful explanation as well as quoted material is given particularly to W. Griffith Thomas' three-volume exposition of Romans, published as part of "The Devotional Commentary."

Acknowledgment is also given to Bishop Moule and W. E. Vine.

The author also earnestly wishes to acknowledge helpful suggestions and material from sources which cannot now be identified because the material used in this volume was not gathered with any previous thought of publication.

# PREFACE

ROMANS is where life begins experimentally. It begins historically at the Creation and spiritually at the Cross. Now we see its experimental appropriation and application in the life of individuals.

Romans is the record of Christianity's philosophy and doctrine. It sets forth the Christian's creed in a profound manner.

The ensuing study is not intended to be a critical or doctrinal treatment, but rather a devotional exposition with particular attention paid to the practical application of its teaching to ordinary everyday life.

This volume, a revision of a limited earlier edition, is offered with the prayerful hope that many more will find it useful in their personal study of the Epistle to the Romans.

ROY L. LAURIN

# ACKNOWLEDGMENT

Acknowledgment for the stimulation of thought and helpful explanation as well as quoted material is given particularly to W. Griffith Thomas' three-volume exposition of Romans, published as part of "The Devotional Commentary."

Acknowledgment is also given to Bishop Moule and W. E. Vine.

The author also earnestly wishes to acknowledge helpful suggestions and material from sources which cannot now be identified because the material used in this volume was not gathered with any previous thought of publication.

# INTRODUCTION

The Epistle to the Romans is not a piece of casual correspondence between friends, but a document from an apostle of Christ, to a congregation of Christians.

The author's signature appears at its beginning and not at its close. In that signature lies the authority of all that follows, for the author is not writing as a free lance. He is not exploiting personal opinion. He is not advancing private theories. He writes as "a servant of Jesus Christ," and in that capacity he is a revelator of divine truths.

Paul wrote this letter about a quarter of a century after the crucifixion of Christ—the year 58 A. D. At the time he was the house guest of a man named Gaius, a wealthy citizen of the Grecian city of Corinth.

One of the most singular features of the letter was the manner of its postal service. When Paul signed this document and tied the sheets of papyri, on which it was inscribed, into a roll and wrapped them in a piece of oiled, animal skin, he gave them into the hands of a messenger. Paul was at least 1,500 miles from Rome. There were no railways, or stage lines, no transport planes; only intermittent shipping facilities. But, in the need of that moment, God supplied a postman who was in reality a postwoman. Her name was Phebe. She was probably the first postwoman in history.

Phebe was a widow of considerable wealth, we gather of considerable parts, who served as a deaconess in the Christian Church of Cenchrea some nine miles from Corinth. She was on her way to Rome on business, and into her hands was intrusted this important document. Did Phebe, the postwoman, know the importance of this document? Probably not, but God knew her trustworthiness. It is a tribute to womanhood that so important a document and so sacred a trust should have been put into feminine hands upon such a perilous journey.

Let us look into the leather bundle that Phebe has strapped to her person, and see what is written on the papyri strips.

As you read this letter you will be struck with a recurring phrase. Over and over again in its sixteen chapters, are the words "of God"—"of God"—"of God." You count them, a total of fifty-nine times, and are convinced that they must be significant. They are! They lay bare the purpose of the document, for around these two words the writer gathers the contents of his message.

This Roman Epistle is recognized as a masterpiece of rhetoric and logic on the subject of salvation in which the argument is reduced to two considerations: conception of a salvation which is of God. One is a justification by works, and the other a justification by faith.

When you have digested its contents, you find yourself standing before God with the security of your soul and the reality of eternity resting upon the virtue of

these two words: "of God." You further find yourself faced with a decision, the most momentous you
ever made, whether you will build the hope of your
life on a human philosophy of justification by works
or on a divine philosophy of justification by faith.

Throughout this letter you cannot escape the insist-
ence of these two words, "of God." They stare at
you from every page. They follow your conscience
in every chapter. They substantiate the argument of
the writer in every contention. And they authenticate
this letter as a revelation from God because it is "of
God."

Years ago, a trial was being conducted in one of
our courts. It was a case where a certain document
played the chief part. The original document was
held by the prosecution and a similar document, pur-
porting to be genuine, was held by the defense. The
prosecution felt that the defense document was a fraud,
but it seemed impossible to disprove its genuineness.

In arguing the case, the prosecuting attorney was
holding the defense document in his hand, and as he
held it to the light, he noticed its watermark. It
contained the name of a well-known papermaker. His
name had certain marks which denoted the year of
manufacture. A hurried communication was sent to
the paperhouse and it was found that this paper had
been made some years later than that on which the
document of the defense was professed to have been
drawn up. It was a fraud. The Bible in Romans is
truth-marked revelation. It pre-dates all man's best
efforts. It is "of God," and is genuine.

Here is a simple plan of division for the book.

I.   THE SINNER IN REDEMPTION. Chapters 1-8
II.  THE JEW IN REJECTION. Chapters 9-11.
III. THE CHRISTIAN IN EXPERIENCE. Chapters 12-16.

The book begins with man "in sin" and ends with man "in Christ."  It begins with a horrible portrayal of character in the rough and concludes with a list of noble men and women who were once sinners but are now saints.

# 1

# THE UNASHAMED MAN
## *Romans 1:1–17*

THE Unashamed Man is Paul, the writer of the Epistle to the Romans. He was not always as we find him in these writings. He was once the chief instigator against Christianity and the Christian communities. Now he becomes its chief exponent to the greatest city of his day, the city of Rome.

First of all, notice that the writer has four general things to say.

I. ABOUT HIMSELF. Verse 1.

"Paul, a servant of Jesus Christ, called to be an apostle, separated unto the gospel of God."

Four words classify and describe Paul and his mission in life.

1. As to His Character.

(1) *He is a "servant."*

This means a "bondservant." He regarded himself not merely an ally but rather the purchased possession of his Master. He had forsworn the title to his life and surrendered himself to a consuming passion—the service of Jesus Christ.

His avocation was making tents, but his vocation was

changing lives and homes and cities and nations by the preaching of the gospel.

Back of the commonplace term of a servant was a dignity of service that not only Paul possessed but that all Christians may possess if they are aware of their position. Paul who was a servant of Jesus Christ was also by that fact "an officer of the King." Would it make any difference in your attitude to your job and your situation and even your apparent plight if you looked at yourself as an "officer of the King"? Well, you are, if you are a Christian, and a servant of Jesus Christ. Talk like it. Look like it. Walk like it. Work like it. Live like it. And the royal bounty of your Master will be portioned out to you as the dividend of such a life.

(2) *He is an "apostle."*

Most people want the high place without first taking the low. Most people want the robes of honor without first wearing the coarse garments of humble service. But in God's order the "servant" precedes the "apostle."

Whether our service to God is rendered in the pulpit, in the choir, in the bedchamber, in the prayer closet, or the mission field, such service is an expression of the one will of the God who has purchased us to be His bondservants and given us our several tasks.

Those who give the cup of cold water should go about their duty with as much dignity as those do who give the cup of communion. Their service may be diverse in operation, but it has the similarity of a servant's task to a common Master.

The accuracy of a watch is not dependent on the beauty of its case, but on the precision of its parts. Hidden away in the movement of a good watch are jewel joints where the pinions swing on the face of jewels. There are many choice people who are like jewels in a watch. They are hidden and obscure, more valuable in their place than all the decorations and gems on the case. Are you a hidden jewel joint? All can not be as the hands of a watch in the public eye pointing out the time. Some are jewels on which the pinions of God's purposes swing with perfect precision. If you are one of these hidden ones thank God and be faithful.

2. As to His Career.

(1) *He is "called."*

This was the credential of Paul's service. Perhaps it has a more particular meaning in our day, for specific Christian service such as the ministry and missions. Without the "call" there is not much credential for a man being a public servant in things religious. If the church has a divine mission, then we must believe that it has divine direction, and in that case, the employment of its ministers must be in God's hands. But we have to lament the fact that so few bear any evidence either of a divine commission or a divine mission.

The apostle's call was an appointment to execute a commission so sacred and so important that every day and every act was lived and undertaken with this in view.

(2) *He is "separated."*

This was the strategy of Paul's service. It is not brilliance and genius that God needs in men nearly so much as He needs those who will stick to their task.

To be separated does not mean to be isolated. The

need is not for *isolation* but *insulation*. God does not propose to save men and then have them removed from the arena of life and sequestered from its earthly problems. But God does want His servants insulated. The purpose of insulation in electricity is to prevent the transfer or leakage of power by putting a non-conducting substance around the transmitting instrument. The Christian needs to be insulated against the disastrous and weakening effect of evil influences that surround him. His best insulation is a separation of motives, ideals, and purposes from the common run of living.

This means consecration plus concentration. And the triad for successful Christian living is completed when we think of this order: commission, consecration, concentration.

II.  ABOUT HIS MESSAGE.  Verses 2-6.

Paul speaks of his message as "the gospel of God." He immediately places it beyond the position of a novelty. It was not an expedient invention such as unbelieving intellectuals have tried to make out. They say that it was an emergency measure produced out of the tragic circumstances of the death of Jesus Christ. But such was not the case.

It was not the gospel of Paul, or of the disciples. It was "the gospel of God." Proof of this lies in the fact that it pre-dates its actual history and its ardent preachers by many hundreds of years, for the principles of the gospel, and the prophecies of the Saviour, were in existence through the entire Old Testament. Yes, and one can go back before history and find it in eternity, for Christ is declared to be "the Lamb of God slain from the foundation of the world."

We find out, as Paul challenges Rome with the claims and considerations of this message, that the gospel was both prophesied and personified. It was both written and revealed.

1. It Was Prophesied in the Old Testament. Verse 2.

"Which he had promised afore by his prophets in the holy scriptures."

Its prophecies were not only in words to be actually identified by chapter and verse, but in ceremony, ritual, travel and people.

It was written in the history of that era across the face of the deserts, the ruins of ancient cities, the splendor of great civilizations and in the fortunes and failures of a chosen nation.

Thus, the Old Testament is not only the documentary defense of the gospel, but equally as much the documentary evidence of the gospel.

2. It Was Personified in Jesus Christ. Verses 3, 4.

The promise became a person. The prophecy became a personality. The scripture became a character.

The world is asking anew in these crucial days, what is Christianity? Scholars try to define it but Scripture says "ecce Homo"—"behold the man"—for Christianity is Christ, a person.

This personification of the gospel and salvation in a man is after all one of the surest evidences of its divine origin. If man had invented it, he would have given good advice. But the gospel is not good advice, it is "good news," and it is such news, understandable and practical, because it is in a person.

If Christianity is a person and if this person is Jesus
Christ, then we will naturally ask: "Who is Jesus
Christ?" Jesus Christ is not in the past tense. All
other people are put in the past tense when they die,
but not Christ. He is our greatest contemporary.

If you establish the character of the person, you have
established the character of Christianity.

Notice three things said here of Christ which tell
us who He is.

(1) *His humanity.* Verse 3.

"Concerning his Son Jesus Christ our Lord,
which was made of the seed of David according
to the flesh."

The humanity of Jesus was by birth for the word
"made" means "born." His birth identifies Him with
a royal family, but it goes back beyond this lineage
to the beginning. The humanity of Christ was not
an historical coincidence or accident, it was the completion of a chain of genealogical and biological events.
The final link in that chain was Mary, who produced
her son in the capacity of "the seed of the woman,"
which was originally promised in Genesis 3:15.

(2) *His deity.* Verse 4.

"And declared to be the Son of God with power,
according to the spirit of holiness, by the resurrection from the dead."

This is a declaration of Christ's deity. The declaration is that of the Holy Spirit. And the proof of the
declaration is in the resurrection. Thus, the birth and
the burial of Jesus are linked together. He who was

divinely born, was divinely raised. He, who was born in a virgin womb was raised from a virgin tomb.

His was a birth which has no parallel in history. This makes Jesus Christ unique and at the same time approachable. Because of His deity He has power to aid you, and because of his humanity He has feeling to understand you.

When His deity is matched with His humanity, we have a faith that is neither antique, outworn by its age, nor obsolete, outgrown in its usefulness. We have a faith which is living and powerful and presently available to the moment's needs.

(3) *His availability.* Verse 5.

"By whom we have received grace and apostleship, for obedience to the faith among all nations, for his name."

III. About His Addressees. Verses 7-9.

God cared little for Rome's splendor and nothing for Caesar's conquests, nor for the nation's power, but in that city of splendor there was a people whom God loved. It was to these people that Paul wrote his Epistle. "To all that be in Rome, beloved of God" or as Weymouth puts it, "God's loved ones who are in Rome."

You will observe that Paul did not say "to all that be *of* Rome." It was not written to Romans, but to Christians. It was written to a company of Christian refugees gathered out of the empire for mutual protection and worship. And as long as they were *in* Rome, but not *of* Rome, they wielded a tremendous influence.

A brilliant historian, seeking to explain the tremendous influence of the church during the first two centuries of our era and the decline of that influence during the third and fourth centuries, made this illuminating comment: "During the first and second centuries *the church was in the world*; during the third and fourth, *the world was in the church*." Does that not speak of our condition now?

Here was this company unnoticed and probably unwanted and yet they held the fate of that empire in their hands. Does the world fully realize that its fate and its future are settled by the gospel which is today in the hands of the world's minority; or does the world take as little cognizance of the Christian as it has of other great movements and moments?

Not only was this company of Christians strategically placed at the heart of a great empire, but the message they had was strategic to the salvation and destiny of the world. The message of Paul may be summed in a single sentence—"The just shall live by faith." This message would have saved Rome from its subsequent decline and decay. If Rome had noticed this community of Christians and heeded its message, the course of history would have been changed.

Bad men soon become mad men when they throw off the restraints of God from their conscience. When Finland was raped and Poland bombed in the late war we could think of nothing but mad men off the leash and running amuck through the bloody streets of a vaunted civilization. At last the true stripe of ideologies of nationalism showed beneath the hypocritical garb that covered them. Let the rest of the world bear in mind that no nation can espouse anti-Christianity and remain either civilized or humane. Let us preserve what remnants of peace, liberty and freedom that yet remain to us by remembering that the Bible and its Christ are our last bulwarks. As Christians we can render no greater service to our nation than to proclaim and explain, to preach and practice the teachings of this Book of Books.

This message of God, through Paul, was not sent to the Emperor, for the agency of Rome's salvation was not in the government. It was not sent to the magistrates, for the agency of Rome's salvation was not in the courts. It was not sent to the teachers, for the agency of Rome's salvation was not in the schools. It was not sent to the philosophers, for the agency of Rome's salvation was not in the forum. Instead, it was sent to the church, for the agency of Rome's salvation was in the Christians. It is so today. But the Christian has got to do more than talk about it if he is to gain the recognition and respect to the world he would save. He has got to live it.

Three things are observed concerning these Christians in Rome and all others of their kind since then.

1. The True Character of Christians—Saints of God. Verse 7.

"To all that be in Rome, beloved of God, called to be saints: Grace to you and peace from God our Father, and the Lord Jesus Christ."

Saints are not a special class of ecclesiastical royalists. They are such as are born anew by the new birth. Their holiness is a newness of life and their sainthood is a recognition of divine relationship. Let

Christians *be* what they *are* and the world will have before nightfall a new brand of Christianity.

To these heavenly-atmosphered people, Paul gives a salute, "Grace to you and peace from God our Father, and the Lord Jesus Christ." When grace is had *from* heaven, peace is to be had *in* Rome.

2. The True Renown of Christians—Faith in God. Verse 8.

"I thank my God through Jesus Christ for you all, that your faith is spoken of throughout the whole world."

Paul said, "I thank my God." Here was a personal and possessive faith. Luther speaks of Christianity "as the religion of possessive pronouns." Anyone can say "God" but only a Christian can say "my God."

Here was a world-renowned church. Renowned not for its buildings, its wealth, or its memberships; but renowned for its faith.

Here was a church of faith in the midst of a city of force. This church overshadowed by the frightfulness of Roman might caught the eye of God who honored it for its faith. It was easy to have faith in Jerusalem where Jesus was present and teaching, but it was a different matter to have faith in Rome where Caesar was seeking victims for his Christian spectacles. But as the strongest oaks grow in the stiffest winds, so the strongest faith develops in the stoutest tests.

3. The True Life of Christians—Service for God. Verse 9.

"For God is my witness, whom I serve with my spirit in the gospel of his Son, that without ceasing I make mention of you always in my prayers."

A religion based upon faith must be proved by its life. Christian character must be demonstrated in Christian conduct. Worship must be followed by work. What justification have you given to your faith since you believed? The world waits for your works as much as God looks for your faith.

Paul was a man of purpose. He was not as so many are, aimless drifters and shiftless shirkers in the midst of whitened harvest fields that will spoil for want of workers. It is a good thing "to plan your work and then work your plan." It is a good thing to have some purpose in life. Otherwise you will finish life as a selfish consumer rather than a selfless producer.

IV. ABOUT HIS PURPOSES. Verses 10-17.

There are three things mentioned in these verses which define Paul's purpose in life.

1. A Divine Direction in Life. Verse 10.

"Making request, if by any means now at length I might have a prosperous journey by the will of God to come unto you."

Paul's purpose was to visit Rome "by the will of God." It was to be by God's will and not Paul's willfulness. Most of us live on the basis of human willfulness rather than the divine will.

But God's will is not always according to our desires. Paul prayed for "a prosperous journey" by which we presume he meant a pleasant and comfortable journey. But notice how God answered Paul's prayer. Paul went to Rome, finally, as a prisoner in chains. After praying this prayer for "a prosperous journey" he was persecuted by the Jews. He was

then taken into custody by the Roman officials. He
was then brought before Agrippa, afterwards before
Festus, and finally he was taken to Rome in chains.
On the way he suffered shipwreck, was bitten by a
venomous viper, but through all his various experiences, his prayer was answered, for he was brought
*to Rome.* He was not brought to Rome by Paul's will
for a prosperous journey, but it was by the will of God;
wherein all His divine purposes were accomplished
which later resulted in the gospel reaching the further-
most outposts of the empire. Had Paul gone as a private citizen and not as a prisoner, he would not have
been placed in that providential place whence the
whole household of Caesar was touched with the gospel.
God's prosperity may not be according to our estimates,
but it always brings the greatest blessing.

Your path to the ultimate prayerful goal of life
may be devious too. You may have had your shipwreck, being cast up on some strange island of circumstance. You may travel to your Rome in a wheelchair, or a bed, in an obscure place. But hold fast
in faith to the God who never fails. You will get to
Rome.

2. An Unselfish Interest in Others.   Verses 11-13.

"For I long to see you, that I may impart unto
you some spiritual gift, to the end ye may be established; That is, that I may be comforted together with you by the mutual faith both of you
and me.   Now I would not have you ignorant,
brethren, that oftentimes I purposed to come unto
you, (but was let hitherto,) that I might have
some fruit among you also, even as among other
Gentiles."

Prayer always leads to unselfishness. Paul prayed and when he got up from his knees, he put his prayer into deeds. He made himself available to God as the instrument through which God could answer his prayer. We have such a wrong conception of prayer. We like to disassociate ourselves entirely from it except to get its answers. But we do not want its responsibilities.

Paul saw in his visit the benefits of a "concurrent encouragement." He saw an opportunity to give. He saw in his visit an opportunity to impart some gift. If our relations with others were placed on this high level, it would produce a paradise. If we saw in our friends the opportunity of doing something rather than doing somebody, the law courts would go out of existence.

Paul saw another advantage resulting from his visit to Rome. He saw the beneficial effects of a "mutual faith." Christian faith leads normally to Christian fellowship, which in turn brings strength and encouragement. Where should such faith and fellowship be cultivated more profitably than in the home? Family faith is the most intimate and the most necessary that we know of. Cultivate it and nourish it and it will produce dividends of blessing in peace, happiness, and comfort.

Paul saw another result occurring from his visit to Rome. It was not only faith; not only fellowship, but fruit. This is suggested in the thirteenth verse, "Now I would not have you ignorant, brethren, that oftentimes I purposed to come unto you, (but was let hitherto,) that I might have some fruit among you also, even as among other Gentiles."

A fruitful life is as necessary as a life of faith. In fact, faith will normally lead to fruit. This life of fruitfulness is not restricted to any particular age except it be infancy. Old age may be as fruitful in its measure of opportunity as the age of youth. The ages of man have been facetiously catalogued thus: "The Tender Teens; The Torrid Twenties; The Thrilling Thirties; The Forceful Forties; The Fretful Fifties; The Sensible Sixties; The Serene Seventies; The Aching Eighties; The Nodding Nineties." But all ages have their measure of opportunities. Let us see that we use them.

3. A Compulsion in Life's Responsibilities. Verses 14-17.

"I am debtor both to the Greeks, and to the Barbarians; both to the wise, and to the unwise. So, as much as in me is, I am ready to preach the gospel to you that are in Rome also. For I am not ashamed of the gospel of Christ: for it is the power of God unto salvation to every one that believeth; to the Jew first, and also to the Greek. For therein is the righteousness of God revealed from faith to faith: as it is written, The just shall live by faith."

Here are found three significant "I am's."

(1) *I am debtor.*" Verse 14.

This is a life-changing idea. If it possesses you, it will transform your whole plan and purpose of life. We need a change from the creditor to the debtor idea. Many people take the creditor attitude. They say, "the world owes me something." According to them, the world owes them a living, happiness, and riches. The world does not owe anyone a living—you owe the world a life. In the beginning God set man to a task on the principle that he was a debtor, that he owed the world initiative, industry, management and culture for God "blessed them and God said unto them, be fruitful and multiply and replenish the earth and subdue it and have dominion. . . "

Why has the church largely lost the respect of the world? Because it has lost its debtor convictions. Evangelism has failed because the evangelist has ceased to be a debtor. He thinks on terms of what he will get, rather than what he can give. When we have humanity on our heart rather than money and pleasure, our world will be vastly different. Paul was just such a man and said, "I am a debtor."

(2) *"I am ready."* Verse 15.

If people are thinking wrongly of themselves, they are of time. It is what they will do with their to-morrows. Paul said, "I am ready." You can do much with five minutes today, but with a hundred years of yesterdays you can do nothing

What keeps people from being ready? Sometimes it is fear. Of John Knox, it was said that "he feared God so much he had no room to fear man." Paul's readiness was an eagerness to put his gospel to the severest test of its existence and he did not fear Rome.

In Rome, his readiness would meet *the greatest religious test* for it would come to grips with paganism.

In Rome, it would meet *the greatest political test* for it would come to grips with imperialism.

In Rome, it would meet *the greatest social test* for it would come to grips with a city's motley mob.

In Rome, it would meet *the greatest moral test* for it would come to grips with a nation's vast criminality.

(3) *"I am not ashamed."* Verses 16, 17.

The bold statement of the apostle was that he was "not ashamed," and he gives two reasons:

a. "For" the gospel is the power of God (Verse 16). There is something thrilling and substantial about power. There is no shame in the presence of strength. And before proud Rome with its vaunted might, the gospel was an overwhelming favorite, because it released to human need the power or "dynamite" of God.

b. "For" the gospel reveals the righteousness of God. (Verse 17). There was not only strength in the gospel, but virtue; not only power, but beauty. Here, at last, was the basis for the release of divine power into human affairs—the righteousness of God. This righteousness had been violated by sin, vindicated by the cross, revealed in the gospel and imparted by faith.

We have in these two verses, seven remarkable elements of the gospel. (Suggested by W. Griffith Thomas):

(a) The source of the gospel—"God."

(b) The nature of the gospel—"power."

To the Jews, the gospel was a "stumbling block" because they were proud; to the Greeks, the gospel was "foolishness" because they were wise; and to the Romans, it was "weakness" because Rome was the epitome of power. But here was power that mastered the powerful.

(c) The purpose of the gospel—"salvation."

Salvation is not outdated by civilization. Rome's civilization may have been an iron one and ours may be an atomic one, but a man may go to ruin as quickly in a modern automobile as in an ancient chariot.

(d) The scope of the gospel—"everyone."

There is no nationalism in Christianity. Neither the pigment of the skin nor the geography of the race are barriers. It belongs to "everyone" because it fits the need of all.

(e) The reception of the gospel—"believeth."

"Faith," a very simple soul said, one day "is the hand of the heart." It reaches for the greatest treasure and grasps the greatest prize.

(f) The efficiency of the gospel—"therein is the righteousness of God revealed."

God's righteousness is revealed in His Son. Perfection is in a person.

(g) The outcome of the gospel—"the just shall live by faith."

The Christian life begins in faith and continues in faith. It was born by faith and it lives by faith.

Here is one of the most significant statements of the Bible. In ordinary language righteousness means to be made right. There is much that is wrong with us and our world, and whatever rectifying of this wrong we will ever do, will neither be by law nor by creed, but by this sin-emancipating principle: "the just shall live by faith."

This final word: Thrice Paul hurled his words across the sea from Corinth to Rome, and said, "I am." He was effective in these because he linked his life and labors to the Christ who is the great "I Am." Without Him, you may want to be, you may intend to be, but with Him you are.

# 2

## THE INEXCUSABLE MAN
### Romans 1:18–32

THERE is a vast difference mechanically between the character of the world of the first century and our world of the twentieth century, but not morally. In ours, restraints may be more binding and acts of immoral violence kept within a minimum bound. There is a vast difference scientifically but not spiritually. Our spirituality may be more refined and it may have eliminated the crude and cruel deities of paganism, but it has not defined for us a personal and intimate knowledge of the true God. We have merely transferred our religious affections to different deities. Instead of the gods of the Pantheon, there are the gods of the mart and of the mind.

The book of Romans is not outdated by the centuries. It deals with a fundamental matter, which underlies the life and times of all the centuries. That fundamental matter is man's need of a righteousness which he does not naturally possess and which will make him both right with God as well as right with his fellowman. The means of conveyance for this righteousness is the gospel which Paul sets forth to proclaim to the Roman nation through the Roman Christians.

The presence of this gospel is in itself the evidence

of the need of the gospel. There is no purpose for it if there is no need for it. God is not superfluous and He would not have given this revelation without a reason.

Let us set down this premise as the place of beginning. If the gospel has a divine origin, it is because it has a human need. If God has revealed His righteousness, it is because man has displayed his unrighteousness. If God has sent His Son, it is because the world has shown its sin. Man's need of salvation is shown by the simple fact that there is a Saviour.

Man's sin is the measure of God's salvation. They are both universal. But while the measure of salvation is universal, the manner of salvation is individual.

The universality of the need of salvation is set forth in a threefold set of arguments in the first three chapters of Romans:

1. The Gentile Need. Chapter 1.

2. The Jewish Need. Chapter 2.

3. The Universal Need. Chapter 3.

In the face of these facts of the human need and the divine provision, all men of whatever condition or class are inexcusable. They are inexcusable in the twentieth century as well as in the first century. They are inexcusable in their science as in their paganism. They are inexcusable in America as in Africa. The inclusive verdict is that they are "without excuse."

The pattern of the argument on which this inexcusableness is convincingly established is threefold. Verses 17-32.

I. THE INEXCUSABLENESS OF MAN. Verses 17-20.

Man is inexcusable because:

1. The Righteousness of God Is Revealed in the Gospel. Verse 17.

> "For therein is the righteousness of God revealed from faith to faith: as it is written, The just shall live by faith."

We must be careful to observe that we are dealing here with a fundamental fact of salvation. The basis of that salvation is "the righteousness of God" which is contrary to the human philosophy of salvation resulting from the righteousness of man.

This righteousness is first revealed, then received. In the first place, we notice that this saving righteousness is *revealed*. It is not a human discovery. It did not come after centuries of slow search and gradual climb out of a religious darkness. But instead, it was a sudden burst of light. It was a sudden display of the right. It is a gospel effect and not an educational and scientific or historical effect. It has but one medium and one channel—the gospel—"for therein is the righteousness of God revealed." This saving righteousness is not revealed in astronomy or zoology or philosophy, for it is found neither in nature nor in the mind—but in the gospel.

In the second place, we notice it is something to be *received*, for it is "from faith to faith." In other words, it depends on faith and leads to greater faith. This faith is an act of reception so that the possession of a saving righteousness is not the result of our achievement, but of our acceptance.

After righteousness received, comes righteousness achieved. Many confuse the two and seek to establish their own righteousness by acts of goodness. It is not our acquired righteousness that saves, but Christ's. After the reception of this righteousness, it will normally result in our achieved righteousnesses. But in any case, these righteousnesses are the effect and result of the resident righteousness received through the gospel.

The Scriptures do not minimize human righteousness but human nature must be made right before it can produce what is righteous.

What is this righteousness which is revealed? The question is important. The righteousness which is revealed in the gospel is not a doctrine, or a plan or an idea, or a proposition. It is a Person. God does not only give an explanation of righteousness in the Scriptures; He gives a demonstration of it. It was in Christ, so that the essence of our appropriation is not to understand an intricate proposition but to follow Him. Its essence is in the advice given by His mother: "Whatsoever He saith unto you, do it." It is so because it was designed for a world of multiple classes, and multiplied conditions.

Man is inexcusable because:

2. The Wrath of God Is Revealed from Heaven. Verse 18.

"For the wrath of God is revealed from heaven against all ungodliness and unrighteousness of men, who hold the truth in unrighteousness."

The gospel does not shape itself to the contour of human desires, but rather to the principles of divine requirements.   For this reason, it is a revelation; not only of the mercy of God, but of the justice of God. There can be no mercy unless there is justice.   In any other case, it is a legal farce.

The fact is here stated that "the wrath of God is revealed."   It is not a future expectation but a present fact.

It is revealed in the records of the Scriptures—in the Flood, in Sodom, and in Jewish national disintegration. It is revealed in the laws of nature.   The Scriptures say, "Whatsoever a man soweth, that shall he also reap."   What does he reap?   He reaps the wrath of God in his ungodly sowing.   There is to be a judgment on sin, but we must never lose sight of the fact that there is also a present judgment by our sins.

Sin established a process of degeneration, for there is in every part of man and nature, a law of death. "We are wont to imagine that nature is full of life. In reality, it is full of death.   We cannot say it is natural for a plant to live.   Examine its nature fully, and you have to admit that its natural tendency is to die.   It is kept from dying by a mere temporary endowment which gives it an ephemeral dominion over the elements.   Withdraw this temporary endowment for a moment and its true nature is revealed.   Instead of overcoming nature, it is overcome.   The very things which appear to minister to its growth and beauty now turn against it.   The sun which warmed it, withers it; the air and rain which nourished it, rot it."

Into this universal process of degeneration, the gospel introduces a process of regeneration.   This salvation by regeneration, is a "deliverance from the downward bias of the Soul.   For in every man and woman there is a natural principle lowering them, deadening them, pulling them down by inches to the mere animal plane, blinding reason, searing conscience, paralyzing will." But God's salvation will stop this drifting process of the soul, turn it around and make it go the other way. But if we either reject or neglect this gospel provision, then we must expect in nature and in man the inevitable process of justice in judgment. This is both a law of God in the natural world, and a law of God in the spiritual world.

In the revelation of the gospel, we face an inevitable alternative. It is the wrath of righteousness. It is Christ as Judge—or Saviour. And all of this is in the very nature of justice, a thing demonstrable in the natural world outside us as well as in the spiritual world within us.

Let us be sure to hold these things in proportion. After all, the Saviour is not a being from whom to flee. He is one to whom to fly. The gospel appeal is love and not hate. The force is attraction and not repulsion. The means is faith and not fear.

Man is inexcusable because:

3. The Knowledge of God Is Revealed in Nature. Verses 19, 20.

This deals with that ubiquitous question "what about the man without a Bible?" The answer here is in effect—that all men have another Bible. It is bound with the covers of the day and the night. It has pages of atmosphere. Its print is the stars, plants, trees, flowers, animals, and man. The verdict is that the man without a Bible is "without excuse." He is "without excuse" because that which is knowable about God is evident in the world which is about man. He is "without excuse" because he has a revelation in nature as well as a revelation in Scripture.

Just how extensive is this revelation in nature? Suffice it to say that it is enough to bring all men the knowledge of God so as to make them "without excuse."

David Livingstone reported that he found primitive tribes in Africa, completely out of touch with civilization and possessing no knowledge of Scripture or civilized morality, who were conscious of being sinners. What they felt to be sinful paralleled exactly what the Bible reveals as sinful. So singular was this sense of sin in its correspondence to the Bible that it is difficult not to feel that God's moral law received by Moses on Sinai, is but the copy of a prior law which God wrote on the heart of the first Adam. Although marred by the fall it may still be traced in primitive men who have retained it from generation to generation.

But in order to be specific let us point out four things contained in these two verses to reveal the extent of this knowledge which the race has of God through the revelation in nature.

(1) *Where knowledge is revealed.* Verse 19.

"Because that which may be known of God is manifest in them; for God hath showed it unto them."

Two words stand out in this verse to heighten its statement of a universal fact. The first word is "manifest" and it means apparent. The second word is "showed" and it means enlightened. These two words are terms applied to the entire race. But they are here particularly and specifically applied to a certain class designated by the personal pronoun "them." It is "in them" that God has made certain things apparent and it is "unto them" that God has given a certain enlightenment. It refers to those of the previous verse where it speaks of the "unrighteousness of men, who hold the truth in unrighteousness." It is men who "through their wickedness suppress the truth." These men in particular and all men in general are without excuse because what is knowable about God has been displayed openly. Any one of the five physical senses will give any man or woman a knowledge of God to render them inexcusable for suppressing the truth.

It is by the world within, that we are able to apprehend the world that is without. And it is by this world without that God convinces us of the world above. And it is by this world above that God convicts all men of an inexcusable ignorance.

(2) *What knowledge has been revealed.* Verse 20.

"For the invisible things of him from the creation of the world are clearly seen, being understood by the things that are made, even his eternal power and Godhead; so that they are without excuse."

The simple proposition of this statement reveals that all men in all sections of the world are without excuse for ignorance because two invisible qualities of God, namely, His divine power and His divine nature, are revealed in the visible things of the created world.

In other words, the natural reveals the supernatural; the creation reveals the Creator; and the visible reveals the invisible. Therefore, it is not a question of theology, education, or religion. It is a question of eyesight, for if a person has eyesight or any other sense, he has enough God-sight to make him "without excuse."

There is no reasonable justification for atheism, agnosticism or skepticism. Nor is there any reasonable excuse for ignorance because God is revealed in everything around us we see, feel, taste, smell or hear.

(3) *When knowledge was revealed.* Verse 20.

". . . from the creation of the world."

It is as continuous as it is universal. It is as continuous as it is contiguous, for it lies next to the hands and feet, the eyes and ears of every human being of every generation from the beginning of the race to the present moment.

Not only is the knowledge of God revealed in the original acts of creation, but also in the continuous acts of divine Providence. There has not only been a revelation in creation, but also a revelation from creation which renders the men of earliest antiquity just as much "without excuse" as the person of modern life. The knowledge of God does not depend on the press or on the preacher. It depends on the human willingness to believe what one sees.

(4) *How knowledge has been revealed.* Verse 20.

". . . being understood by the things that are made."

God is to be understood by His works. This understanding may not be a full understanding of God, for remember we are dealing only with the revelation of God in nature besides which there is a revelation of God in Scripture. But it is such a knowledge as renders him "without excuse." For in the absence of the Scripture, God must judge him in the presence of nature.

These four facts of this knowledge of God revealed in nature bring us to a definite conclusion. The conclusion is that if God made us and all that is about us, then God has some claim upon us as His creatures.

The Bible tells us that God's claims upon us are twofold; first, the claim of creation and second, the claim of redemption. In the first instance, He made us, while in the second instance, He bought us. We are answerable and accountable to Him for our attitude to that twofold claim.

But what about the person who does not know about redemption? God's claim is then the claim of creation. Even then it is sufficient to render that man "without excuse," for in creation man may see somewhat of redemption. The way of salvation for any man is for that man to follow the light given to him. The world will be judged according to its deeds on the basis of its light. (Rom. 2:6). The world will never be judged on our neglect to make it a better light, but on what it has done with the light it has. We must always remember that whatever limitations surround others, or ourselves in understanding others that "the Judge of all the earth shall do right" (Gen. 18:25).

In the Old Testament before the gospel came, men were saved by faith through the light of ritual. In our day, wherever the gospel has not come, men may be saved by faith that comes through the light of nature's revelation. We do not say that all such are saved, but affirm that any may be if he obeys what light God gives him.

Whoever and wherever man is, whatever grade of

culture or civilization may exist, it is a universal duty enjoined by nature and Scripture to worship God.

Christ died for all the world, ignorant or enlightened, civilized or uncivilized. Whether the knowledge we have comes through nature or Scripture, all are held amenable to God. The extent to which this is carried out among men is for an allwise God to determine. Meanwhile, we are responsible to carry out a commission of evangelization to all the world. This evangelization is necessary and indispensable. It is so because whatever light through nature man may have, it is not the full light. God never intended that the riddle of the universe's where? why? and whence? should be understood by nature worship. This will come only through Scripture and the One who came in the full blaze of divine glory—Jesus Christ, the Light of the world.

For this reason, geology will not suffice. It is the gospel that alone satisfies. Nature says—God is; Scripture says—God is a Person. Nature says—God is Power; Scripture says—God is Love. Nature says—God is Perfect; Scripture says—God is Righteous. Nature says—God is seen by Force; Scripture says—God is had by Faith.

Following its arguments concerning the inexcusableness of all men, this Scripture deals next with the second of its propositions.

II. THE INEVITABLE CONSEQUENCE OF UNBELIEF. Verses 21-23.

Knowledge not only creates responsibility, it constitutes responsibility.

We have in this Scripture of three verses all the

vast and vicious effect of man's neglect of his knowledge of God. It is so whether that knowledge has come through nature or Scripture. But it is certain and it is inevitable.

It is revealed in three things:

1. The Degradation of Religion. Verse 21.

> "Because that, when they knew God, they glorified him not as God, neither were thankful; but became vain in their imaginations, and their foolish heart was darkened."

The first effect of disobedience to whatever knowledge we possess is its effect on our inner life. What was intended to reveal God, now actually obscures Him. The knowledge that should be light, now becomes darkness. What was to be wisdom, has now become folly.

It declares here that "when they knew God they glorified him not as God." When did man know God? Is it not popularly taught that man is gradually coming to know God through a process of religious evolution? What does it mean then when it says here, "when they knew God"? Does it mean what it says or is this a mistake? Paul is right when he declares that man once "knew God" but although knowing God man refused God's rights over him, and the result was a religious, intellectual and moral degeneration in which they "became vain in their imaginations and their foolish heart was darkened."

It is not true that in man's experience he commenced with an idol and ended with God. But rather man commenced with God and has ended with an idol. It matters not whether that idol is a piece of stone in Africa or a piece of gold in America; whether it is the bush gods of the jungle or the mental gods of the colleges.

The religious history of the race from the beginning is recorded in these brief verses. That history began with a clear and perfect knowledge of God. It has been degeneration instead of regeneration. It has been downward instead of upward. It has been away from God instead of toward God. The absence of truth has brought the presence of error and this in turn has led to the inevitable process of evil which has produced the successions of decay and decline in empires and degradation in individuals.

There was light which man received with his original creation. That original light was the divine image in which he was created. With the light came certain responsibilities, among them a negative and a positive command. The negative command in Genesis 2:16, 17 said, "Of every tree of the garden thou mayest freely eat: But of the tree of the knowledge of good and evil, thou shalt not eat." The positive command in Genesis 1:28 said, "Be fruitful, and multiply, and replenish the earth, and subdue it: and have dominion." The result of keeping the negative command would be spiritual life. The result of keeping the positive one would be physical life.

But early man turned from this light and consequently lost it and with it his spiritual life. With this loss a process of spiritual degeneration set in. Man, who was originally a theist now became a deist. He withdrew from the restraints of God upon his conscience. He went out and builded cities and civilizations, but they were void of the original knowledge of

God. From knowing God as a person with whom he walked and talked in the Garden, he made a god of his surroundings. Generation after generation this degeneration became deeper until, at last, we see in the savage the depths of the religious depravity of the race. We see the end of man's original intelligent, enlightened and personal fellowship with God in his revolting fetish and idol worship.

Originally, man was a monotheist—a worshiper of one God—the God of the Garden. Now, and since a time subsequent to the Garden, man is and has been in many parts of the world, a polytheist—a worshiper of many gods—the gods of the jungle.

There is no sign of idolatry in the Old Testament until we reach a time contiguous to Abraham where we find in the Chaldean life the corruption of religion in revolting idolatry. Modern archaeology reports this: "The outstanding feature of all this remote civilization in its relation to the Bible is the evidence it affords that monotheism (the belief in one Supreme God) preceded polytheism (the belief in many gods)."

It is the contention of some that man made God, reversing the scripture statement to read, so man created God in his own image, in the image of man created he Him. This inversion of Scripture is as false and wrong as any untruth can be. The fact is that being made in the image of God, man descended to the place where he has lost the reflection and revelation of that original image and is now groping in religious darkness. And so, in this scripture, we trace man's religious degradation to ingratitude and intellectual pride—"Because that, when they knew God, they glorified him not as God, neither were thankful; but became vain in their imaginations, and their foolish heart was darkened."

This testimony of the Scripture is verified in modern research. History and archaeology both reveal the religious fall of man. We trace it through the Vedic hymns of the Hindus; there are traces also in Egypt, in Babylon, in Greece, and in Rome. We see in the Sacred Record how man failed to regain the height from which he fell, even with the coming of the first Scriptures through Moses. It will never be fully accomplished until man is restored through the Lord Jesus Christ.

In Jesus Christ is the highest revelation of God, and through Him comes the righteousness of God. Thus, what was lost through the first Adam in religious experience is restored in the last Adam in spiritual life. What man lost in fellowship with a personal God and what he has tried to retrieve by centuries of fetishism, idolatry, and polytheism, is found in fellowship with the person of God's Son, Jesus Christ. What was lost by unbelief is restored by faith. What was lost through disobedience to God's spoken Word is restored by obedience to God's written Word. What man has tried to regain by religious achievement through law, through works, through worship, through penance, is gained by faith for "the just shall live by faith."

This is the essential difference between Christianity and philosophy, between the gospel and religion, as such. The one reveals God and the way to Him; while the other obscures God and the way to Him by the imaginations of vanity and the darkness of human speculations.

What has been revealed and what we have related of the supporting evidences of the religious degradation of man is a fact demonstrable in nature. There is a principle in nature that is known as the *Law of Reversion to Type*. Originally, man was created in God's image. In other words, he had a divine type. But he lost that type through sin. Without the sense of deity, the support of deity, and the sublimity of deity, he descended generation after generation until be became bestial in attitude and like the beasts he deified for worship. He who began as a nobleman in God's image became like an animal in his passions and habits.

If you allow a plant, which has passed through a process of development by cultivation, to grow alone it will gradually revert to its original type. Allow an animal or a bird to do it and the same thing will result. Allow a man to do it and his body will deteriorate into a bestial savage; his mind will degenerate into imbecility; his conscience into lawlessness and vice; his soul into godlessness and depravity. And the verdict of the laws of God in nature, as well as the laws of God in Scripture, declares that there must be a conversion to a higher type—in the image of Christ —or else there will be a reversion to a lower type.

Religion proves the need of redemption and history warns us against neglect, while biology declares the necessity of the new birth.

The inevitable consequence of unbelief not only leads to the degradation of religion and the turning of light to darkness and knowledge to ignorance, but it leads also to other consequences.

2. The Corruption of Intelligence.  Verse 22.

"Professing themselves to be wise, they became fools."

The corruption of intelligence that is spoken of here is specific.  It is the intelligence of the mind in respect to God.  Man has had a notable career in conquering the elements, in developing the sciences and creating the arts, but in religious science, he is but an infant.  His natural mind is described in the previous verse as becoming vain.  It literally means "in their reasonings or speculations they went astray."  Such is always the case.  The person who knows his responsibility to God and who does not glorify Him as God will be incapable of thinking right about God.

This was not always so.  Once man thought God's thoughts after Him.  Once he possessed a perfect intelligence.  With that intelligence he could have set himself to his divinely appointed task of being fruitful, of multiplying, of replenishing, of subduing, and of having dominion over the earth.  With that intelligence, he would have achieved an early dominion over the elements and the earth.  He would have discovered the laws of nature and life much sooner than Galileo and Newton.  He would have discovered the forces of electricity and radio sooner than Edison and De Forrest.  But instead, having lost the brilliance of his intelligence through the eclipse of his soul, he has had to slowly grope his way out of the primitive condition into which his fall in sin had plunged him.  But his complete restoration to a competent intelligence must wait his restoration to the divine image.  That restoration is commenced in Christ's redemption on the cross and is completed in Christ's return in glory.

But what we should particularly observe is the Bible's accurate account of man's history. It speaks here of the corruption of intelligence. The Bible record of earliest life declares man to have been perfect in intelligence. Adam was able to give all the beasts and birds of creation proper zoological names. In the seventh generation from Adam there is a man named Lamech whose three sons were the introducers of the earliest crafts and sciences. One son, Jabal, was the first agriculturalist; another son Jubal, was the father of music; the third son, Tubal-Cain, was the first metalurgist and industrialist.

In these respects, the Bible is found correct in recording man as an intelligent being at his creation. Wherever men delve into the ruins of the past they find evidences of their early intelligence and notice their later corruption. And the cause of his mental decline was his spiritual decline. The verdict is—"professing themselves to be wise, they became fools." This wisdom, with which they proposed to displace God and supplant Him by a personal divinity, they thought they would acquire from the tree of the knowledge of good and evil, for the suggestion was "in the day ye eat thereof, then your eyes shall be opened, and ye shall be as gods." But instead of becoming wise as they intended, they became foolish. Instead of becoming more divine, they became less human. Instead of doing away with God, God sent them away from Him. Such is the folly of sin.

The religious history of the world is exactly what is described here—"they became fools." It is a history of superstition, of bigotry, of ignorance, of degradation, of vice and of the grossest immorality and most ridiculous idolatry.

Man has lost his moral and intellectual and spiritual sense of God, because he has lost God. He will not find God until he finds the way back to God. The way back to God is not an intellectual way; it is not a religious way; it is not a moral way. You can not think your way back to God because human thought-life will not co-ordinate with divine thought-life, for "the carnal mind is enmity against God." You can not worship your way back to God because man is a spiritual rebel from God's presence. You can not moralize your way to God because character is vitiated with sin. You must be regenerated back to God through the process of a new life by a new birth. Thus, the way back to God is Jesus Christ who boldly declared Himself as such in these words: "I am the way, the truth and the life; no man cometh unto the Father, but by me." And so, it is more than a religious question, more than an intellectual question, more than a moral question. It is a biological one and Christ, who is the "Logos" or the "science" of God, supplied the new biology in these words: "But as many as received him, to them gave he power to become the sons of God, even to them that believe on his name: Which were born, not of blood, nor of the will of the flesh, nor of the will of man, but of God" (John 1:12, 13).

3. The Debasing of Deity. Verse 23.

"And changed the glory of the uncorruptible God into an image made like to corruptible man, and to birds, and to fourfooted beasts, and creeping things."

The religious history of mankind is the record of a corrupted God.

Man aspired to a great change—"to be as gods," but the result was that he changed his God for gods. He changed the glory of the person of God revealed in his garden fellowship, for the debasing images of his hands. The history of natural religion in relation to revealed religion is one of substitution. Man substituted gods for God. Cain substituted a sacrifice; Sarah substituted a son; Aaron substituted a calf; and all through history natural religion is an effort of substitution seeking justification by genius rather than by faith.

The process of man's debasing of God and substitution is accurately described here. First, he made God into an image like man. Then he fashioned God like birds, then like the quadruped animal, and finally in the lowest form of idolatry known to heathendom, the figure of reptiles.

The record of history is found to follow this pattern. There are the humanized gods of Assyria, Babylon, and Egypt, culminating in the Apollo of the Greeks. There is the eagle of the Romans, the bull of the Egyptians, and the serpent of the Assyrians. And when you examine the national arms of the nations of the world, their emblems are of beasts, birds or reptiles.

Man is religious, incurably so and invariably so, but if his religion is not pure in its knowledge of God in wisdom and righteousness and virtue, it becomes corrupt in its ignorance of God in bigotry and idolatry and immorality.

Wherever one traverses the geography of the globe, he finds religious men to whom there remains—in their darkened, superstitious and cramped souls—some remnants of a knowledge of God. These remnants of a knowledge of God are traceable to the Garden of Eden from whence his expulsion sent him on devious ways, collecting various gods. And now surrounded by the inventions of science, he has reached the pinnacle of religious deception and has deified reason.

How different the Bible's way to God and the achievement of the highest and best! It is not the way of the idolater. It is not the way of the thinker. It is not the way of the moralist. It is the way of faith. It is contact and fellowship with the person of the Son of God. It leads to light. It leads to love. It leads to purity and kindness and peace and joy. It encompasses every human need. It destinates the soul to eternity and promises the body a resurrection and glorious regeneration. And withal these things it puts upon the pilgrim's lips a thankful song.

III. THE DIVINE FORSAKING OF MAN.    Verses 24-32.

The human forsaking of God leads to the divine forsaking of man.

These verses are led off in verse 24 with the word "wherefore." What happens in the succeeding verses is the result of what happened in the previous verses. In the previous verses, men who possessed an originally perfect knowledge of God did not glorify God and the result was they forsook God and became "vain in their imaginations." They "changed the glory of the uncorruptible God into an image made like to corruptible man, and to birds, and four-footed beasts, and creeping things." And now comes this "wherefore." Because of this forsaking, comes another forsaking.

Because man gives up God, God gives up man. Because man debased God in idolatry, God permits man to debase himself in immorality.

Three times in these verses, it records an awful fact—a tragedy of tragedies. It records the fact three times that "God gave them up."

## 1. God Gave Them Up to Idolatry. Verses 24, 25.

"Wherefore God also gave them up to uncleanness, through the lusts of their own hearts, to dishonor their own bodies between themselves: Who changed the truth of God into a lie, and worshipped and served the creature more than the Creator, who is blessed forever. Amen."

## 2. God Gave Them Up to Sensuality. Verses 26, 27.

"For this cause God gave them up unto vile affections: for even their women did change the natural use into that which is against nature: And likewise also the men, leaving the natural use of women, burned in their lust one toward another; men with men working that which is unseemly, and receiving in themselves that recompence of their error which was meet."

## 3. God Gave Them Up to Depravity. Verses 28-32.

"And even as they did not like to retain God in their knowledge, God gave them over to a reprobate mind, to do those things which are not convenient; Being filled with all unrighteousness, fornication, wickedness, covetousness, maliciousness; full of envy, murder, debate, deceit, malignity; whisperers, backbiters, haters of God, despiteful, proud, boasters, inventors of evil things, disobedient to parents, Without understanding, covenant-breakers, without natural affection, implacable, unmerciful: Who knowing the judgment of God, that they which commit such things are worthy of death, not only do the same, but have pleasure in them that do them."

First, notice this statement repeated thrice: "God gave them up." The divine forsaking leads to human folly. What is portrayed in the category of sensuality and crime hereinafter is but the normal effect of natural religion. The religious history of the world is not a beautiful story. Read the records of natural religion and it is a record of vice, of crime, of sensuality of the grossest character. In fact, the worst thing in this world is perverted religion. What might have become the sweetest has become the bitterest. What should have been the purest has become the vilest. We remember an object lesson that came to us once when visiting a sugar mill outside of Honolulu. After the sugar had passed through its process of purification from the cane of the field to the unrefined product waiting its last stage of preparation, we saw car loads of a foul, reeking, rancid, putrid substance which was the residue of this sweet, clean sugar. Out of the sweet came a bitterness that was revolting when it became contaminated and corrupted. The heart that is meant to worship God and hold the divine image becomes a foul hold for the vilest and the foulest practices when it forsakes God.

The picture that is presented is not what all men and women are in actuality, but rather what they all may become. It is their human potential. A false worship will lead to a false life. No worship is better than a false one.

To reverence God is to respect yourself. God and man once had a common meeting-place. It was the fellowship of a perfect garden. That was destroyed and man banished. Through later years, the meeting-place was tabernacle and temple wherein through the figure and symbol of a sensible worship God met with man. It may surprise you to know that the common meeting-place of God and man in this day is not the flesh of the garden, nor the stone of the temple, but the spirit of regenerated lives. Our bodies are now intended to be God's meeting-place with man. If we reverence God in them, we will respect ourselves and the issue of such self-respect will be purity, beauty and all the train of strong and lovely virtues.

Again it says in verse 25 that man "changed the truth of God into a lie." There is no greater perversion than this. Among men it is slander; before God it is blasphemy. It is the blasphemous slandering of God. The history of natural religion has been such a history as this. It has been the lie of idolatry—that God could be manufactured by the hands. It has been the lie of philosophy—that God could be reproduced by the mind. It has been the lie of theology—that God could be reproduced by the heart. It has been the lie that a man can be justified by his own deeds. It has been the lie that a man can be justified by his own character. Against this lie, which has been perpetrated and perpetuated through the centuries, is the truth which was from the beginning. The truth found in God's clothing for Adam; God's sacrifice for Abel; God's substitute for Isaac—the truth, namely, that "the just shall live by faith." Trifle with this truth and the inescapable consequences of error, and evil will engulf your body and soul.

As we view a world not only of such potential evil as is described here, but see it in force today in crime, in war, and in a general wickedness that is true alike of both civilized and uncivilized, we wonder about God's omnipotence. And the question some ask is this: "If God is a God of both love and absolute power, why does He allow evil to exist?" The very fact that evil, human suffering, inequality, injustice, and war exist, indicates to some people that God is either not good or not powerful enough to make the world good. Why does not God enforce good in man? In the first place, He is not a policeman. God's original arrangement with man was a co-operative one. He said to the man He made: This is my world but your job. But man soon renounced this arrangement and became a reactionary, a revolutionist, and a rebel. And as long as man chooses to live apart from God, he will live in evil and suffering. The only remedy is a return to God. This will never be because God enforces it, for force does not change human nature. It will be at the completion of redemption when Christ returns at which time "the knowledge of the Lord shall cover the earth, as the waters cover the sea."

So long as man has given up God, God permits him to be handed over, selfbound, to the slavery of his own nature which leads, when unrestrained, to that vast area of criminality and godlessness depicted in this section of Scripture.

One of the most tragic expressions of Scripture is in the words found in verse 26: "Even their women did change." The last bulwark of any civilization is its womanhood. The standards which she either lifts or lowers determine the conditions of society. God intended that in her should be preserved the last virtues and the remaining strength of the race. But when she releases her affections to the natural propensities of the lower nature, it seals society's doom.

The final declaration of this section heads a category of sins and crimes that might have been transcribed from a police desk blotter. These are as modern as they are ancient. They belong to society as well as to savagery. They begin where our entire problem begins —man's forsaking of God. Verse 28. "And even as they did not like to retain God in their knowledge, God gave them over to a reprobate mind, to do those things which are not convenient."

Where do these come from? Out of the swamps of paganism? Out of the caves of savages? Not directly, only indirectly. They come from the source that Jesus identified as the source of all wrong. He said, "For from within, out of the heart of men, proceed evil thoughts, adulteries, fornications, murders, thefts, covetousness, wickedness, deceit, lasciviousness, an evil eye, blasphemy, pride, foolishness: All these evil things come from within, and defile the man" (Mark 7:21-23.)

And now we face a decision. We cannot have more righteousness in the world by having less Bible. We cannot have more peace by having less Christ. We must decide today what we will do with God's Book and God's Christ. If philosophy says man dies like a beast, then his temptation is to live like one. But if his philosophy is of this Book, it tells of a good life because it is a life that belongs to God. Let us put the Bible and its Christ in their rightful places in heart and home.

# 3

## THE JUDGED MAN
### *Romans 2:1–16*

I N THE face of gross sin in others, the reactionary
tendency may be to see none of it in ourself. But
the possibility of deceiving ourself regarding the ultimate issues of right and wrong is removed when we
face this Scripture.

In the first chapter of Romans we saw the natural
creation of the world and the natural character of
man. We also saw the presence of evil in the absence
of truth. Now in the second chapter, the matter of
universality is made a matter of individuality. God
speaks to the man and not to the race.

There is a tendency in most of us to condemn others
and condone ourself. This is abruptly arrested with a
rude awakening, for if God had us looking through a
telescope in the first chapter, while He swept the
whole panorama of racial evil; He now has us looking
through a microscope at our own intimate and personal
record.

It has been truly said that "the gospel can never
be proved except to a bad conscience." Proof of the
gospel is easiest seen when we have need for it and we
never have a sense of need for it until we have a true
sight of ourself.

In Chapter 1, the world stood in the presence of the justice of God.

In Chapter 2, the individual stands in the presence of the judgment of God.

In Chapter 3, we stand in the presence of the justification of God.

In this second chapter are to be found ten facts concerning the subject matter of judgment. They are such things as will convince us that life here and hereafter is regulated by a mind both just and righteous. Most people are mental cowards when they meet the word, "judgment." They are afraid of it. Probably because of an instinctive guilt. But it is here, and it must be faced with the facts, or it will be suffered by us.

In any world regulated by intelligence, there must be a place of compensation to keep both a natural and a moral balance. That compensation must be on the one hand gain and on the other hand loss—on the one hand reward and on the other hand retribution. It can be no less.

We see this law of compensation in nature. The flood and dust storms were retributive acts of nature because of the agricultural sins of man. When we chop down our forests; burn up the brush of the foothills; plow up the grass of the plains; we deprive nature a way of stopping the water and wind from accumulating too fast. Without these natural barriers, which we have destroyed, it then sweeps over our cities and causes wide devastation. Kill off the mountain lion which kill the deer, and you will increase the deer to such proportions that they will starve for lack of sufficient food. God, the Creator, has in all nature a perfect balance. Destroy it and it will destroy you. It is so in the moral world.

Let us look at it in these ten items of fact concerning judgment:

I. IT CONSIDERS PERSONAL GUILT. Verse 1.

> "Therefore thou art inexcusable, O man, whosoever thou art that judgest: for wherein thou judgest another, thou condemnest thyself; for thou that judgest doest the same things."

This verse tells us that when a person sits in judgment upon another person, he is only sitting in judgment upon himself because his judgment is by its very nature a reflection of his own guilt. This was nationally so of the Jew to whom it is a tacit reference. He assumed, because of his religious traditions, that he did not come under the need of the gospel, for his sin was not the sin of the Gentiles mentioned in the first chapter. But the fact is this, that if in the first chapter the Gentile is what he is in spite of or because of his paganism, then in the second chapter the Jew is what he is in spite of his Judaism. Whether he is a paganistic Gentile or a judaistic Jew, he needs the gospel which is designed for both Jew and Gentile. The priority mentioned is to the Jew first, not because of any nationalistic favoritism, but in the very need of the circumstances.

Some people have the habit of feeling superior to other people because they were reared or trained in more advantageous circumstances. It is not how you come but what you have become that matters. Sin is a matter of character regardless of nationality. It is a biological question rather than a theological one.

When we arrogantly classify others and exempt ourselves from the stigma of racial and personal sin, we are condemning ourself, and the thing we condemn ourself for is not the sin of judging but the sin of sinning, for "thou that judgest doest the same things."

There is but one time when we are permitted to sit in judgment—that is when we judge ourselves. "For if we would judge ourselves, we should not be judged." (I Cor. 11:31).

This is not only nationally true of the Jew; it is personally true of each of us. It has a practical bearing on human relations. It is not only a question between God and man, but also between man and man. The cantankerous spirit of judging and criticizing spoils more happiness probably, than anything else.

What should one do when judged and maliciously criticized? The first thing to do is to be sure you are right where being right counts—before God. If you are right in God's eyes, you can afford to be seen wrong in man's eyes. The next thing to do is to forget your critics. Henry Ward Beecher never uttered a truer saying in his life than this: "Life would be a perpetual flea hunt if a man were obliged to run down all the innuendos, inveracities, insinuations, and misrepresentations which are uttered against him."

If a person is honest with himself and God, he has no business worrying about malicious criticism. "If you worry about what people think of you, it means that you have more confidence in their opinions than in your own."

II. ITS ESTIMATE IS ALWAYS ACCORDING TO TRUTH. Verse 2.

"But we are sure that the judgment of God is according to truth against them which commit such things."

In the first verse, we see judgment by man while in the second verse we see judgment by God. What a difference there is! God's judgment is reliable and truthful, never to be repented of.

Judgment always presupposes a standard. But whose standard is it going to be? Yours or mine? Man's or God's? If there is to be a standard, it must be the standard of what we call "the norm." Therefore, it must be what it says here, "truth." Ignore this Book and you will be ignorant of the true standards of life. Reject this Book and you will reap the corrections of a negative judgment.

Phillips Brooks said, "The only way to get rid of a past is to get a future out of it." There is a future in every past. That future partakes of the character of the past. You cannot get a good future out of a bad past. Even a good present will never change a bad past, for a good present is never retroactive. You must obliterate the past if you would obtain a future out of it. No criminal can have a good future until the law has wiped out his past. God's way of wiping out the past is not the penance of the law but the processes of grace. Grace will draw its deft fingers over it and change it.

On the other hand, if we ignore the past, it will not ignore us because pasts have a faculty of futurizing themselves. The Bible says, "Some men's sins are open beforehand, going before to judgment; and some men they follow after" (I Tim. 5:24). They march step by step with our conscience. They haunt us in our dreams.

The only way to get a good future out of a bad past is to have the past judged which will prevent the future from being judged. The Cross of Christ was the potential judgment of all sin and every past. Identify yourself with it by faith, and you will find a good future out of a bad past.

But there is a present to think about. Is it what it ought to be? Do we live peacefully with ourselves and amicably with others? Or is it jangling and turmoil? It may be that "the treatment we receive from others is often the echo of the treatment we accord them. The estimate others have of us is the result of the exhibition we make of ourselves. We are holding ourselves up as a bulletin board for everyone to read—not as we would like to be, but as we are. There is one rule by which we can always hear the kind of echo we like to hear—the Golden Rule."

In the second verse, we saw that the standard of judgment was truth. This truth is revealed truth—not acquired truth. It is divine truth—not human truth. There is no escape from the truth and no exception to it. Such is no more possible here than it is possible that you can escape or be exempt from the truth of the multiplication table or the alphabet. If you disregard the laws of multiplication, how can you get the right sum. If you disregard the laws of the musical scale, how can you get the right melody? If you disregard the laws of chemistry, how can you get the right compounds? It is no more possible in the law of truth to have the right life if you disregard it.

III. It is Inescapable in its Effect. Verse 3.

> "And thinkest thou this, O man, that judgest
> them which do such things, and doeth the same,
> that thou shalt escape the judgment of God?"

We ought to think more often than we do about
the ancient, yet up-to-date law of the Bible found in
Ecclesiastes 11:1, "Cast thy bread upon the water;
for thou shalt find it after many days."

This means bad bread as well as good bread. There
will be a finding as certainly as there has been a casting. The one is as inevitable as the other has been
definite. But if there is a compensation for distribution, there is as certainly a compensation in retribution.
You cannot escape it. What you give, you get. This
judgment of God is both present and future. It is both
natural and spiritual. God's judgment is both judicial
and penal.

The judgment that comes upon sin is in the very
nature of sin itself. As Henry Drummond has observed: "The sentence is being gradually carried out
all along the path of life by ordinary processes which
enforce the verdict with the appalling faithfulness of
law . . . If it makes no impressions on a man to know
that God will visit his iniquities upon him, he cannot
blind himself to the fact that nature will. Do we not
all know what it is to be punished by nature for
disobeying her? We have looked around the wards of
a hospital, a prison, or a madhouse, and seen there
nature at work squaring her accounts with sin. And
we knew, as we looked, that if no Judge sat on the
throne of heaven at all, there was a judgment there,
where an inexorable nature was crying aloud for

justice and carrying out her heavy sentences for violated laws."

God's judgment follows two rules. The first rule is positive. "Whatsoever a man soweth, that shall he also reap." It has to do with sins of commission. The second rule is negative. "How shall we escape if we neglect so great salvation?" It has to do with the sins of omission.

In the second verse, we see the estimate of divine judgment. It is the estimate of God's truth. We stand or fall before God, not by what we think of ourself, but rather by what God thinks of us. In the third verse, we have the administration of judgment. Would it not be wise to inquire? Would it not be good to get measured? After all, it is not presumption that counts, but faith. It is not approximation that blesses, but appropriation. Suppose, now that we totally ignore the whole scheme of revelation and the whole scope of Christianity and say to ourself that we will go our own way. What then? Let God answer. "Thinkest thou this O man . . . that thou shalt escape the judgment of God?"

The indictment of sin was made on a racial and impartial basis in Chapter one, but here, in Chapter two, the responsibility for sin is put on an individual basis. But Scripture does not merely level an indictment and levy a responsibility; it offers a remedy. It is a remedy which is scaled to the proportions of universal manhood, of whatever stature, age, condition, color, or class. It is not a religious, legal, or philosophical remedy; it is the remedy of grace by faith, for "the just shall live by faith."

IV. It Considers God's Available Goodness.   Verse 4.

"Or despisest thou the riches of his goodness and forbearance and long-suffering; not knowing the goodness of God leadeth thee to repentance?"

We see a contrast between verse three and verse four.   In verse three, it speaks of the "judgment of God," while in verse four it speaks of the "goodness of God."   The judgment of God is an expression of justice, while the goodness of God is an expression of mercy. The judgment of God is the penalty for sin, while the goodness of God leads to the remedy for sin.   The goodness of God is a preventive for His judgment.

It declares here that goodness leads to repentance. Repentance is in no sense the means of our salvation. We are saved by faith and not repentance.   But if goodness is the expression of God's attitude to us in our sin, then repentance is an expression of our attitude to God in being willing to forsake sin.

We like the thought here that, "the goodness of God leadeth thee to repentance."   Weymouth renders it like this: "The goodness of God is gently drawing you." God is drawing us and not driving us.   He is using a cross and not a club.   The means is love and not force.   It is our privilege as a free moral agent to either accept or reject this goodness.   Though God made the earth, He could not save us unless we allowed Him to.   After all, the blackest sin in the category is not "righteousness violated but mercy despised."

It is difficult for human beings to space the distance involved in the consideration that the Bible gives to two worlds.   One world is the world of time.   The other world is the world of eternity.   There is a tie and an unseen bridge between these two worlds. This world is not a material world and the other one a spiritual world, for even now the material is supervised by the spiritual and the spiritual superimposed upon the material. In our present experience in life we discover that, "the visible is the ladder up to the invisible; the temporal is but the scaffolding of the eternal," and if we were only more sensible and more realistic, we would appreciate the further fact that, "the immaterial world is a firmer reality than the material." It is therefore quite impossible to divorce one world of time from another world of eternity or a mortal life from an immortal life. They merge in the mystery of a moment that exists somewhere after death. Their differences dissolve in the realm that is just a reach beyond our five senses. And for this reason, while the end of time may be the end of matter in its present form, it is not the end of mind. Nor is it the end of memory or emotion for the sufficient reason that life continues on the same level of its present quality in the next world. What we are here, we will be there. The one necessary requirement is that we have a life fitted for the new world. The only life is the Christ-life for "He that hath the Son hath life."

V. It is Future as Well as Present. Verse 5.

> "But, after thy hardness and impenitent heart, treasurest up unto thyself wrath against the day of wrath and revelation of the righteous judgment of God."

We are dealing here with the eternity of judgment. What is this judgment for? So far we notice the word sin has not occurred in this chapter. We can be sure it is intentionally omitted though tacitly included. The omission is to make the obligations biological and moral and social, and not merely theological. Its judgment is to be because of a misspent life. After all, sin is the fundamental cause of a misspent life. But we are not occupied now with the causes so much as the effects.

What are we here for? Why do we live? For what purpose did God create us and endow us with faculties and surround us with resources? Go back to the beginning and you will find the purpose. It was to govern under God. It was to be a co-operative enterprise. But we have fallen so far from that high view of life as to have lost ourselves in materialism and godlessness. Can one think for a moment that there would be war in Europe, crime in America, savagery in Africa, heathenism in Asia—if man had kept his original contract with God? Never!

Now we face the spectacle of the goodness of God drawing men to repentance. We find a Christ and a cross. We find a gospel overture. All of these are intended as the way back to the original plan of life. But instead of embracing it, there is hardness and impenitence of heart. What is to be the end of it? Is God going to lay down conditions of life and then laugh at them? If He did He would cease to be God.

Whatever judgment comes in the future is no more because of God's wrath than the present judgment is. It is distinctly phrased in these words: "But after thy hardness and impenitent heart treasurest up unto thyself wrath."

The wrath of God is not vindictive or arbitrary—it is described as "the revelation of the righteous judgment of God." It is the effect of law. It is the result of righteousness. It is not a burst of divine temper or a passion of rage as some foolishly imagine. It is a revelation of righteousness that comes because of a persistence in unrighteousness. It is the effect of efforts to hold a world in order. It is God's supreme effort to be God.

Man must bear the responsibility for his misspent life in the face of God's judgment, for the reason that he failed of that God-offered privilege of repentance that would have transferred the responsibility of his sin to Christ. The responsibility of our sin is ours until it becomes Christ's. He bore our sins that we need not bear their judgment. Sin was judged in Him, that it might not be judged in us. But if a man despises the riches of God's goodness, he is amassing in the treasury of his soul the riches of wrath.

Talk about the riches of wealth! None of it can be transferred to the world beyond us. But whoever we are, we are amassing memories, amassing character, amassing experience, amassing a life transferable from body to spirit, from time to eternity. We should give more than a passing care to the reckoning that must be made.

Whatever wrath the Scriptures speak of is never recorded until the Bible has laid down a veritable barrage of heart-melting words. It is only after it speaks of the riches of "goodness," the riches of "forbearance," and the riches of "long-suffering" that wrath is presented.

How long do we go until the cup of divine patience flows over? The length of "goodness," of "forbearance," and of "long-suffering," is a long way.

VI. It is Based on Divine Justice.   Verse 6.

"Who will render to every man according to his deeds."

Scripture is here considering a just judgment, not the divine provisions for eternal life.   It is not the method of obtaining eternal life, but the basis on which God is going to make an adequate and proper adjustment in lives as a prelude to the extensive life that follows this.

To that end the statement reads: "Who will render to every man according to his deeds."   It does not say "for" his deeds.   The distinction between "to" and "for" holds a difference worthy of consideration.   The whole scheme of the Christian philosophy of salvation and preparation for the world that is coming is not on the barter basis.   It is not a merit and demerit system of righteousness.   It is thoroughly ethical and particularly worthy of God.   Whatever judgment God makes, the justice of His judgment will be on the basis of our deeds.   The fundamental reason for this is because our conduct is the visible expression of our character; as what you do is the proof of what you are.

The principle upon which the eternal distinction between men is made is biological.   It is whether we have life or not—life that is scaled and fitted for the new world.   No person is going to be lost because he lied; but if lying is a habit of life, it is an index of character.   No person is going to be saved because he told the truth.   Titus 3:5 says: "Not by works of righteousness which we have done, but according to his mercy he saved us, by the washing of regeneration, and renewing of the Holy Ghost." Our entrance into heaven is gained through the possession of the life of Jesus Christ. But our standing is a matter of related life—"according to his deeds."

One could wish to soften the subject and cushion it with tenderness. But he must be honest and faithful. He must teach it as he finds it.

There lived a certain farmer who was a sceptic and a scoffer and disdained anything religious. He proceeded one year to prove, as he thought, the foolishness of believing in God. So he plowed his fields on Sunday, planted, cultivated, reaped and harvested on Sunday, and then gathering in his neighbors, one Sunday in October, he said: "See here! I plowed, planted, cultivated, reaped and harvested my crops on Sunday and they are quite as good as any of yours. There is no God, and keeping the Sabbath is a joke or else my crops would have failed."

Listening to his idiotic tirade was a godly neighbor, hardened morally as well as physically, and schooled in spirituality as well as agriculture. He waited until his scoffing neighbor had concluded his denunciation of God on the basis of his recent experiment and then solemnly said: "God does not always settle his accounts in October."

VII. It Has Rewards and Regrets. Verses 7-10.

"To them who by patient continuance in well doing seek for glory and honour and immortality eternal life: But unto them that are contentious and do not obey the truth, but obey unrighteousness, indignation and wrath, tribulation and anguish, upon every soul of man that doeth evil;

of the Jew first, and also to the Gentile: But glory, honour, and peace, to every man that worketh good; to the Jew first, and also to the Gentile."

There is immediately set forth in verses 7 and 8 the contrasting causes. On the one hand it is "continuance," and on the other hand it is "contentious." One brings reward and the other regret.

"Continuance" means "persistent right doing." It means the kind of life which is the result of a righteous character. "Contentious" means "self-willed." It is more than a fractious and unkind conduct. It refers to the first sin ever committed, the sin of self-will. It is a certain disposition against God and divine standards.

The result of "continuance" or persistent right living is to be "glory and honor and immortality, and eternal life." This comes not in payment of a certain kind of conduct, but as the effect of a certain kind of character. The character is the result of a certain kind of life. The life is the result of a certain kind of birth. The birth is the result of a certain kind of faith. The faith is the heart of this message to the Romans, namely, "the just shall live by faith."

The result of being "contentious" in those who "do not obey the truth but obey unrighteousness" is "indignation and wrath." This also is the effect of a certain kind of character which is the result of the lack of a certain kind of life which goes back to the lack of a certain kind of faith. For here, the lack is in those who "do not obey the truth"; without the truth they are without the faith. Their lives are the expression of the lack of character; hence, the regrets.

In verses 9 and 10, it declares that both regret and reward are not a matter of nationality or even religion. In the one case, the regrets are to "the Jew first and also to the Gentile." In the other case, the rewards are similarly to "the Jew first and also to the Gentile."

If the Jew has had (and he has) a priority of privilege, he will also have a priority of responsibility. There are times when advantage becomes disadvantage. Think of the vast privileges that came to the Jewish nation from Abraham to Christ. They are to be judged on the use or abuse of their privileges. Think of the vast privileges now enjoyed by modern men who surfeit their souls with light and truth. Each will be judged on the use or abuse of his privileges.

Some further mention should be made of the expression "to the Jew first." It occurs previously in Chapter one where the gospel is declared to be "the power of God unto salvation to everyone that believeth; to the Jew first and also to the Greek." Here a distinct priority is stated. The purpose being this: since the preparation for the gospel and the Messiah of the gospel was distinctly Jewish, the intention of God was that it should reach the Jew first. For what reason? Certainly not for racial preference, for in the matter of salvation God is no respecter of persons or races. The Jew was offered the advantages of the gospel in order that he might become the first propagator of the gospel. It is so here in the book of Romans. But since the writing of this letter Paul adopted a new preaching policy expressed in Acts 28:28 where Paul declares to the Jews, "Be it known therefore unto you, that the salvation of God is sent unto the Gentiles, and that they will hear it." This latter statement in

Acts was given three to five years after the one in Romans. The Jew forfeited his prior rights to gospel privilege by this persistent rejection. Since that time, the gospel is to be extended to all men with an equal emphasis and invitation.

But while we are saying this in respect to proper exegesis of the Scriptures, let us speak a word for the Jew of today for whose national plight we have the greatest sympathy. A current writer suggests this: "To love the Negro in Africa and exploit him in our own town, or to sympathize with the Jew in Germany and despise him in our own street is worse than meaningless." No Christian is Christ-like when he permits a nationalistic hatred to possess him. We have a mission to the Jew. It is both evangelistic and humanitarian. Let us mind it and do it.

VIII. It is Impartial in its Scrutiny. Verse 11.

"For there is no respect of persons with God."

This statement actually means that there "is no acceptance of the face." God scrutinizes the soul. The circumstances of birth or training are no credentials of favor. In the crucible of the judgment moment, God will not say, "Who are you?" He will say, "What have you done with the life I gave you?" If character is born now in the cradle of a Bible faith, it will stand the testing of the crucible of judgment. After all, eternity is a matter of eternal life. If we are fitted with that life, we are fitted for that eternity. And so, it is a question of spiritual biology. Do we have that life?

The feature of judgment which is being discussed

at this point in the chapter is not the effects of judgment which come in our present life, but those effects which are future. It is the future adjustment with which God must balance the accounts of human history. There must be, so to speak, a final balancing of the budget. God will do it equitably and ethically and when it is done, society will be prepared for a new and an eternal era of existence, not only without the presence of sin and its multiplying attributes but the effects of sin and its damning and increasing liabilities. There will not only be a new heaven atmospherically, not only a new earth geologically; not only a new race biologically, but there will be a new basis of life ethically and judicially for God says, "Behold I make all things new."

In that case, something must be done with all the defects of character, all the violations of divine law, all the criminal acts and all the vileness of sin. That adjudication will come at the judgment. Now we are told how it will come.

IX. It is Universal in its Scope. Verses 12-15.

"For as many as have sinned without law shall also perish without law; and as many as have sinned in the law shall be judged by the law; (For not the hearers of the law are just before God, but the doers of the law shall be justified. For when the Gentiles, which have not the law, do by nature the things contained in the law, these, having not the law, are a law unto themselves: which show the work of the law written in their hearts, their conscience also bearing witness, and their thoughts the mean while accusing or else excusing one another)."

The clue to these four verses is in the little word "for." It occurs three times.

In verse 12—"*For* as many as have sinned without law . . ."

In verse 13—"*For* not the hearers of the law . . ."

In verse 14—"*For* when the Gentiles which have not the law . . ."

In each case it has to do with the law and the relation of three kinds of action to that law.

1. In verse 12 it deals with those who have sinned either in or out of the law. Back in the first chapter it spoke of man's inexcusableness before God because of the revelation of God in nature. Here, however, it is not nature but reason. It is not an external witness either of Scripture or nature, but an internal witness of reason and intuition.

Upon both a verdict of guilty will be pronounced and a sentence of judgment executed. To the man without law, who did not respect the internal witness of God will come "perishing." To the man within the law, who did not respect its external witness, will come "judging." In either case, a man is to be judged on the basis of what light he has. The man without an external revelation, such as the Law of Moses, will never be penalized because he did not know. On the other hand, the man who had the Law of Moses will never be saved because he had it. Instead he will be judged by its standards.

Let us keep clearly before us that Scripture here is not dealing with the subject of salvation but judgment. It is not telling us how we are going to be saved but how we are going to be judged. Although verse 13 says, "For not the hearers of the law are just before God, but the doers of the law shall be justified," the fact remains eternally true that the function of the Law is not to justify but to judge. The Law has been a standard and not a salvation. It has pointed out the need of salvation but never provided the remedy of salvation. The Israelites were measured by the tables of the Law, but saved by the altars of sacrifice.

In both cases, the man without "law" and the man within "the law" had a definite responsibility to God. That responsibility was on the basis of what he had done with what he had.

2. In verse 13 it deals with those exclusively within the Law. And it suggests that the important thing is not hearing the Law read, but doing the Law's teachings. We must observe that the Law—and here it means the Mosaic Law or the external law of revelation—is never satisfied by mere approval and applause. It must be obeyed. It is no use to extol the Law in principle and violate it in practice. We cannot be indifferent to it.

3. In verses 14 and 15, it has something to say about those who do not have the Law.

Neither having the Law nor hearing the Law are sufficient recommendations to God. The argument that is presented here is directed to the Jew who both had and heard. It is argued by Paul that if having a law saves the Jews then the Gentiles will be saved also, a thing which to the Jew was unthinkable.

The Gentiles, Paul argues, had a law in their hearts. It was intuition and reason. If the Gentile respects the law of his reason, he is as much entitled to salvation as the Jew, if he respected the Law of revelation, if salvation would come via the Law. But it is not salvation that comes, only responsibility and accountability.

This settles the question, we think, on the basis of treatment for those who do not have or have never heard the Law or the gospel. Their treatment will never be by a Law they did not have or never heard. They will never be judged by the Jewish revelation or the Christian revelation. Their judgment will be on the basis of their own light which is the inner revelation of intelligence or intuition.

While the New Testament specifically declares that salvation never comes apart from Christ, some people may actually embrace and trust Christ who have never heard of Him. Having never heard of the gospel, he may loathe his sin and truly repent of it and trust in God, such as Abraham did twenty centuries before Christ. To Abraham, this pre-advent faith was "counted unto him for righteousness." And not only of Abraham was this true, but all the Old Testament worthies who "died in faith, not having received the promises, but having seen them afar off, and were persuaded . . ."

It is most evident from Scripture that men will be judged according to the knowledge of God which they possess and never according to any higher standard they do not possess. But for all who live outside the realm of revealed Christianity there are two sources of light. First, the Light of Nature in which the arbiter is experience. Second, the Light of Reason in which the arbiter is conscience.

X. ITS STANDARD IS IN THE GOSPEL. Verse 16.

"In the day when God shall judge the secrets of men by Jesus Christ according to my gospel."

The whole subject matter of judgment in these verses was begun with the law (Verse 12), and ends with the gospel (Verse 16). After all, the whole essence of judgment will not be whether a man has kept certain legal restrictions, but has he a new life fitted for the new world? Life never comes out of law. Life can only come from life and in this case it is Jesus Christ.

The Law was fulfilled in the gospel because the Law is fulfilled by the gospel. It is not now the Law question but the life question. It is not now the sin question but the Son question. Christianity reduces the religious quest of man down to the terms of biology and birth. It does not say you must be regulated, but it does say "ye must be born again."

Even the gospel has elements of judgment for by it God will judge "the secrets of men." Think of the secrets that are to be exposed when the records of life are opened. All the hidden thoughts and deeds tucked away in the minds of men will come to light by the blazing light of perfect righteousness which will x-ray the whole panorama of memory.

There is offered us in the gospel the establishment of life upon a sure foundation, removed from the uncertainty of natural culture or the restrictions of legalism. It is a new life founded upon a new Lord —the Lord Jesus Christ.

# 4

## THE BOASTING MAN
### *Romans 2:17–29*

THERE are comparatively few people who are interested in a theological or a moral precept. Those who are, are what we term religious technicians who are interested in them for more or less professional reasons. But this is not generally true of the average person who lives with life's problems from morning to night. The reason that this average person is not so interested is largely due to the fact that through the years of the existence of such concepts and precepts they have collected the parasites and barnacles of religious hypocrisy and cant. On the other hand, we know of no one, unless he be thoroughly reprobate, who is not interested in a personal example and demonstration of Christian living. If Christian ministers fail to reach the average man, it is because too often he brings his tools into the pulpit and flings sentences full of religious language or talks with a stilted speech. If Christian laymen fail to impress the work-a-day world with their Christian experience, it is because they have tried to make their Monday Christianity different from their Sunday Christianity.

We strike at the heart of all hypocrisy, a religious failure, when we remind you that Christianity is the possession of a life and the creation of an organism.

We make it too much the mechanism of an organization. A Christian truly begun is born; and a Christian truly continuing is living the normal expressions of this inner life. In other words, he is an organism and an organism is "anything which carries out the functions of life." A flower is a plant organism that carries out the functions of plant life. A sheep is an animal organism that carries out the functions of animal life. An eagle is a bird organism that carries out the functions of bird life. And in the highest of all realms of existence and experience, a Christian is a spiritual organism who carries out the functions of spiritual life. But we have mechanized and ritualized and secularized the Christian life into such an incongruous thing that the average man wants none of it. He sees no sense to it—no meaning in it; he sees no difference from what he already has in it.

Paul is striking at this problem of religious insincerity when he deals with this fourth hypothetical man—the Boasting Man.

In the first half of this second chapter he deals with the religious man's unrighteousness. In the second half he deals with the religious man's self-righteousness. Which is the greater of the two is not determined, but both are to be abominated and abhorred. In the first half of this second chapter, Paul deals with the man who considered himself beyond the reach of judgment. In the second half he deals with the man who has a religious heritage which was not supported by righteous living. In other words, he is dealing with a religious profession which does not have a correspondingly proper religious performance.

I. THE CLAIMS OF PRIVILEGE BY THE RELIGIOUS PROFESSOR.
  Verses 17-20.

Whatever assumption a man makes before God must be justified by his life before man. Words are not enough to verify a profession of Christianity. It requires works to fit and substantiate the words. This is, in substance, the burden of this whole section.

The religious man of whom Paul is speaking was boastful of his orthodoxy. His whole defense was his intense orthodoxy. His proud boast was in his precise religious behaviour. We believe in orthodoxy if by orthodoxy one means what the Scriptures teach. But there are many different kinds of orthodoxy in the world at this moment. These various orthodoxies are what are doing more harm than all the heresies hell ever invented. People are not only troubled with heresies but with the confusion of orthodoxies. The criteria of faith are not in theology but in the Word of God. So long as we subscribe to that kind of orthodoxy, we are well started toward a right life.

The thing we ought to stop and ask ourselves is this: What are we orthodox for? Lots of people are orthodox just because it is their opinion, and we venture to assert, with the Bible as support, that an opinionated orthodoxy is a diabolical heterodoxy. Orthodoxy is more than opinion. It is not an end but a means to an end. The Scriptures are a source of life as well as light. You can be thoroughly orthodox and yet be spiritually dead. You can have light without life. A scripturally orthodox faith leads to a new species of life which in turn leads to a production of fruit after its kind.

Carlyle cried out: "Produce! Produce! Were it but the pitifullest infinitesimal fraction of a product, produce it, in God's name." And the trouble with this boasting man was exactly this—he possessed a correct orthodoxy that satisfied his intellect but did not touch his life. It gave him a subject to talk about but left him without an object to live for.

We like the distinction that is aptly made of the difference between the form of truth in the Bible and the form in theology. "In theology truth is propositional—tied up in neat parcels, systematized and arranged in logical order . . . But truth in the Bible is a fountain. It is diffused nutriment. So diffused that no one can put himself off with the form. It is reached not by thinking but by doing. (If you want to know the Bible, do it.) Truth in the Bible is an orchard rather than a museum."—Sir Henry Drummond.

We are at the place where the claims of the boasting religious man are to be reviewed. Ten claims are made for him by Paul because these were the things which were made by his own lips as he strutted down the avenue of self-content and of self-appointed importance. But it was not this man's claims that established his credit, as we shall see, for God made counterclaims that he could not stand up to.

Listen to this religious man's boasting as he lays claim to ten separate items of religious privilege and preferment.

1. The Claim of a Name. Verse 17.

"Behold, thou art called a Jew."

It was a racial and nationalistic claim that was

presumed to carry the credentials of divine privilege. But personal qualifications never pass through the blood. They are not hereditary. They are personally acquired in our own individual rights.

2. The Claim of a Document. Verse 17.

". . . and restest in the law."

He took refuge in the Law of Moses as if the possession of the document was his protection. His protection was not in having the Law but in keeping it.

3. The Claim of a Deity. Verse 17.

". . . and makest thy boast of God."

It was his assumption that Jehovah was his private property, and belonged to no other nationals. The fact was that his prior knowledge of God was a trust that it might be given to the whole world. He was hugging God to his bosom when he should have been flinging His name to, and living His life before, the whole world.

Do you think there is any cause for shame among Christians on this same score? We are gloating over our God and denying the knowledge of Him to one billion people.

4. The Claim of a Knowledge. Verse 18.

"And knowest His will."

Here was the greater condemnation because he claimed to know, not in the general terms of a casual religious experience, but the heart of the divine will.

5. The Claim of Discernment. Verse 18.

". . . and approvest the things that are more excellent."

He pretended to be skilled in moral problems with the ability to make distinction between right and wrong.

6. The Claim of Specialized Knowledge. Verse 18.

". . . being instructed out of the law."

In other words, he had been catechized with a meticulous regularity and felt the superiority of instruction. But a high standard of instruction always demands a high standard of living.

7. The Claim of Leadership. Verse 19.

"And art confident that thou thyself art a guide of the blind."

He professed the exalted place of one who showed the way. But it is not sufficient to point out the way. One must lead the way. In the path to life, Jesus said, "follow me." When he said "go" He also promised His presence.

8. The Claim of a Light Giver. Verse 19.

". . . a light of them which are in darkness."

It is true that revelation came through a Jewish source. Every spiritual heritage that the Christian world enjoys is from the Jew. He gave us the prophets. He gave us our Psalms. He gave us our Bible and our Christ. But possessing that light, he did not receive it for himself alone but for the world. Neither did we. As Christians, we not only have light but we are the light. Christ is revealed light while the Christian is reflected light.

Whatever sense of spiritual security we may have can only come when the reflection of light has taken place. It does not matter how large or small the reflector may be. Be sure it is clean and be sure it faces the Light.

9. The Claim of Educator. Verse 20.

"An instructor of the foolish."

Religious instruction makes the highest demands upon the instructor. A person may teach mathematics or languages and escape scrutiny so far as the effect of his teaching on his life is concerned. But the instructor in spiritual things is required to possess a practice equivalent to his teaching. For this reason Christian service is literally an awe-full responsibility. The message is measured by the messenger. He teaches equally as much by example as by exhortation.

10. The Claim of Maturity. Verse 20.

". . . a teacher of babes, which hast the form of knowledge and of the truth in the law."

Here was a man who held the form of religious knowledge in which he was comparable to the man of whom Paul wrote in II Timothy 3:5. "Having a form of godliness, but denying the power thereof." Christianity comes in the form of knowledge that it might be understood. But it is in its very nature a force of divine power that it might be used in the life situations that constantly confront humanity. A river is a form of liquid beauty so long as it is allowed to run in its natural water-course. Build a dam across that water-course and harness it to generators, and it becomes a force of electric energy that transforms industries and communities.

We have been content entirely too long to hold Christianity as a form; to repeat it, to visualize it, and to sing it. Let it become a force to transform ourselves and our materialized civilization and it will perform its God-given intention.

We have reviewed the ten claims to privilege and preferment of the religious man, and when we have finished, we discover that the pagan Gentile and the religious Jew have both followed an identical pattern of delinquency. As we review the sins of the Gentile found in chapter one, and the sins of the Jew found in chapter two, they are reduced to the same sins for each man.

In either case, the claims of culture, civilization or religion are not the sources by which they are to be justified. One is not to be preferred above the other; nor is one to be condemned more than the other. Sin is equally offensive whether it is a religious sin or a materialistic sin; whether it is a pagan sin or a Jewish sin; an intelligent sin or an ignorant sin.

This man's record of religious boasting sets in bold relief the great peril of being religious without being redeemed. Here was a hypothetical man typical of a vast company whose ancestors had been custodians of the Old Testament faith. For generations, the symbols of redemption and the truths of redemption had passed through their hands not only in sacrifice but in Scripture. And now they were in danger of missing its entire significance.

It is our danger today. It is the danger of reducing Christianity to a tradition, a collection of phrases, or a statement, and missing its whole meaning which is a historic redemption that leads to a personal regeneration.

Against these claims of privilege made by this boasting man, God lays certain counterclaims.

II. CLAIMS OF RESPONSIBILITY UPON THE RELIGIOUS PRO-
FESSOR. Verses 21-24.

The claim was profession; the counterclaim was the
demand of possession. The claim was teaching; the
counterclaim was the demand of practice. The claim
was religion; the counterclaim was the demand of
reality.

Here was a man who boasted of his superior religious
experience. But when a man really has God he will
not need to boast of the fact. It will become self-
evident and will be seen in the concurrent evidence of
a godly life.

The Pharisee made his boast of God when he went
up to pray: "I thank thee that I am not as other men."
Yet God heard the publican who confessed his un-
worthiness and he "went down to his house justified."
The rich made their boast of God when they came
to the temple with their gold. Yet Jesus took notice
only of the widow with her mite.

There is the lip side of religion and the life side.
Paul now presents the counterclaims of the life side.
He submits the test of reality. In other words, he
says to this boasting man, does your practice parallel
your preaching; or is your preaching in one direction
and your practice in another? Lip and life, preaching
and practice—they must be parallel. There are degrees
of inconsistency in the best of saints, and yet the
general course of a genuine Christian experience will
harmonize with its profession.

Here is seen, in its most corrupting form, the results of spiritual pride; spiritual degeneracy. It is a
danger that is greatest to those who pride themselves

in orthodoxy, in regularity, and loyalty to religious order.

The Scriptures speak of judgment beginning first at the house of God. Instead of crusades of social action, outside, the best preparation the Christian community can make for a useful service to the world is a self-instituted crusade of self-inspection and self-correction. Let us have a house cleaning and a heart cleaning, and bring to the world the name of God untarnished and unsullied by an inconsistent practice.

Here are the counterclaims Paul addresses to those of religious privilege and preferment at Rome:

1. The Counterclaim of Practice. Verse 21.

> "Thou therefore which teachest another, teachest thou not thyself? thou that preachest a man should not steal, dost thou steal?"

Paul is saying to this boasting man if all of the ten claims he makes are an estimate of his position, then what about his practice?

Teaching always increases the responsibility of the teacher. To teach means not only an idea which is to be passed on, but a test of that idea in the laboratory of personal experience. It is to be able to say accept it because I have proved it. The teacher must not only be a purveyor of knowledge, but an assayist and a prover of truth by his own experience and practice.

2. The Counterclaim of Purity. Verse 22.

> "Thou that sayest a man should not commit adultery, dost thou commit adultery?"

The greatest evidence of a true gospel is a pure life proceeding from that gospel. The greatest vindication of the truth of our faith is the purity of our life. For as one has said—"thou must thyself be true, if thou the truth wouldst teach."

3. The Counterclaim of Sanctity. Verse 22.

". . . thou that abhorrest idols, dost thou commit sacrilege?"

This last phrase literally means: "Dost thou plunder or rob temples?" Whatever the historical and contemporary implication of this charge might have been upon the local Jew, it certainly has a different meaning for us. We know only one man who plundered temples and he was a man who made a practice of stealing little bells used in the services of European cathedrals.

The reference here is to the temple of truth we call the house of God. It does not have the same significance as the original Temple of Solomon, but it is to us a place synonymous with truth, reverence, and God. Religious professors purloin its treasures of truth by inconsistent living. They rob it of its sanctity by their unchastity. They rob it of its truth by their doubts and untruthfulness. They rob it of its reverence by their irreligious lives. And the end of this plundering of the temple of truth is the effect it has on those who do not go to church. Because the church-goer has violated in his practice what he has professed in his worship, the nonchurch-goer says there is nothing there to be desired. There is no truth, sanctity, or reverence. It has been robbed of these sacred things by the vain professor of religion.

Religious racketeering is not a new thing. It is the pillaging of sacred things for personal gain. It is as ancient as it is modern. But as surely as there are religious racketeers so surely are there Christian apologists. Do not permit the persuading influence to come from the evil side, but from the good side. Do not reject the gospel because of its abuse. Accept it because of those whose lives are holy credentials of a divine faith.

4. The Counterclaim of Honor. Verse 23.

"Thou that makest thy boast of the law, through breaking the law dishonorest thou God?"

By being legal in letter but illegal in life, the boasting man was bringing dishonor upon God. God is honored by a holy life and dishonored by its opposite. This puts a pointed question before each of us. Are we, zealous to have people believe as we do, careful to live so they will want to live as we do? We who put the measuring line of orthodoxy on faith, do we put the same exacting standards on life and practice? We who sing on Sunday, "Holy, holy, holy; Lord God Almighty," do we live so as to honor that holy One through the week?

God is best honored by the life rather than the lip. If life is a companionship and a communion with Him it must be expressed in a life which will not tarnish the name of God.

God is anxious to win others through us. The greatest attracting force is a Christ-like life. Do we in that case cause the world to expect that a Christian is a person to be implicitly trusted in business? Are they led to believe that a Christian is worthy of a friendship? Are they led to believe that a Christian's tongue and temper bear the evidences of Christ's conquest; that the Christian merchant has a just and honest standard; that the Christian craftsman has put honor in his task; that the Christian employer acts like he has a Master in heaven; that the Christian employee has more than a selfish interest in service; that a Christian's time, talents and treasure are under the jurisdiction of a consecrated steward? The world is expecting, let us give it no cause to suspect us of inveracity of lip or insincerity of life.

Verse 24 remains now as a summary of the foregoing counterclaims and Paul lays these words upon the religious professor: "For the name of God is blasphemed among the Gentiles through you, as it is written."

Failing in these things of practice, of purity, of sanctity, and of honor we shall cause the name of God to be blasphemed. In the lives of God's professed people, there is at stake the honor and character of God. Men's opinions of the God we profess are based not upon our theological propositions but upon our conduct. Who will ever tell how much of the agnosticism and infidelity and current indifference that exists are due to the sins of those who bear His name? It is a thought of sufficient solemnity to give all of us pause in our religious exercises to consider how much is due to our own personal delinquencies.

In verse 24, it further indicts the insincere religious man for his boasting. His boasting of God was in effect a blasphemy upon God. So it declares, "For the name of God is blasphemed among the Gentiles through you."

When there is disparagement between religious profession and practice, praise becomes profanity; blessing becomes cursing; and profession becomes hypocrisy. Comfort is brought to the cause of the enemy when a Christian professor gives the lie to his life by insincerity.

Let us pause a moment in our religious enthusiasm for the letter of the Law, for strictness of order, for sectarian contentions, for pharisaical distinctions, and ask what effect our lives are having on the world which is watching us.

When the case of the religious boaster, whose proud boasts become the boomerangs of blasphemy, is summed up, it is the case of a person who knew the Law and not the Law Giver. He has a parallel in the New Testament in the man who tries to live the Sermon on the Mount but does not know the Sermonizer of the Mount. If we were more thoughtful of our influence upon the lives of others, we would consider ourself and our life in an altogether different manner.

There now follows in this section of our study a consideration of the outward and inward marks of our religious sincerity or profession.

III. THE EXTERNAL SPHERE IN RELIGIOUS REALITY. Verses 25-27.

"For circumcision verily profiteth, if thou keep the law: but if thou be a breaker of the law, thy circumcision is made uncircumcision. Therefore if the uncircumcision keep the righteousness of the law, shall not his uncircumcision be counted for circumcision? And shall not uncircumcision which is by nature, if it fulfil the law, judge thee, who by the letter and circumcision dost transgress the law?"

The mark boasted of by this religious man before us was the flesh mark of a religious rite. He claimed it as a mark of religious superiority. He claimed it as a distinction of great merit. By it he thought himself set aside in a select class. But his was a great delusion. The fact was that the religious rite he boasted of was nullified by his bad life; and for him, in God's sight, it was as if he had never been so marked. In this manner bad living defeats the purpose of a religious profession because bad practice nullifies profession. What counts is consistent practice.

We are not to minimize this rite of the Old Testament any more than we should the New Testament rites of baptism and the Lord's Supper. But these things are ritualistic hypocrisies if they are not followed by a life which corresponds to their high profession. Whether it is Jew or Christian and whether it be circumcision or baptism, these were, in their proper sphere, intended to be seals of certain blessings and not blank checks of license to practice whatever pleased fancy. They were and are the Christian soldier's initiation which declares him now under orders to a higher obedience. It is our abuse of these that nullifies their very value, for their value is not a rite value but a life value.

After all, we must not put "the holy bath and the holy meal in the place of spiritual regeneration and spiritual communion." Neither must we fall into the subtle tendency to substitute the outward for the inward; the mechanical for the spiritual; or the symbol for the actual.

Once more we have the appearance of the problem discussed before upon two previous occasions. It is the problem of the man without a written law and is referred to in verses 26 and 27. "Therefore if the uncircumcision keep the righteousness of the law, shall not his uncircumcision be counted for circumcision? And shall not uncircumcision which is by nature, if it fulfil the law, judge thee, who by the letter and circumcision dost transgress the law?"

In the eyes of God, this man, who, without possessing the written Law, makes his life conform to what he believes is right, will be accepted. While the man, who, possessing the written Law, violates it and nullifies it, will be rejected. It is not having the law letter that counts with God. It is keeping the law spirit. Anything less than this would be unworthy of God. He could not be God and require more. He would not be God and require less.

This religious man claimed a flesh-mark as the highest evidence of his religious excellence. He is justly refuted and disillusioned. It is not the highest evidence. It had its place in an old regime. But whatever place it had was not the highest place. And whatever carry-overs we undertake to Christianity in an effort to make external marks the highest evidence are equally refuted by the same argument.

If this and other marks like it are not the highest evidences of religious reality, what are?

Six marks are submitted:

1. The Spirit Mark.

"The Spirit itself beareth witness with our spirit, that we are the children of God" (Rom. 8:16).

This is the mark upon our spirits. It establishes an affinity between the divine Spirit and the human spirit. It brings the authentication of divine life into our lives. We know we are truly Christian because of the inner witness of life.

2. The Word Mark.

"Being born again, not of corruptible seed, but of incorruptible, by the word of God, which liveth and abideth forever" (I Pet. 1:23).

This is the mark upon our minds. We know that our experience is genuine because its birth is true to the biology of the Bible. We know that all the functions of a normal spiritual birth were completed. When we have considered every detail of our Christianity, we know it to be so because God has said so. Therefore, we can say, "I know whom I have believed."

3. The Life Mark.

"Therefore if any man be in Christ, he is a new creature: old things are passed away; behold, all things are become new" (II Cor. 5:17).

This is the mark upon our lives. Here we prove something by being someone. What we are after profession is different from what we were before profession. It is the difference of creation. Once it was an old creature: now it is a new creature.

4. The Service Mark.

"But be ye doers of the word, and not hearers only" (Jas. 1:22).

This is the mark upon our hands. It is the legitimate expectation that doing should follow hearing; that there is a time for real Christian action. That time comes when a person believes with all his heart. His hands react with a holy service. True piety is not found in folded hands but in hands full of living and fruitful service. Hands that bless the most are not held over those in need, but held under them and extended toward them with intention to aid and to succor.

5. The Love Mark.

"By this shall all men know that ye are my disciples, if ye have love one to another" (John 13:35).

This is the mark upon our hearts. Where love is to be most expected, it is often least found—in the home and in the church. Jesus did not say the test would be creed for the mind or ritual for the hand but love for the heart.

6. The Lip Mark.

"Whosoever shall confess that Jesus is the Son of God, God dwelleth in him, and he in God" (I John 4:15).

This is the mark upon our lips. It is true that there is false confession, but when there are the supporting claims of spirit, mind, life, hands, and heart, then we may be certainly assured that the lip mark is genuine.

IV. THE INTERNAL SPHERE IN RELIGIOUS REALITY. Verses 28, 29.

"For he is not a Jew, which is one outwardly; neither is that circumcision, which is outward in the flesh: But he is a Jew, which is one inwardly; and circumcision is that of the heart, in the spirit, and not in the letter; whose praise is not of men, but of God."

We have been considering up to this point the Christian's world life substantiating and validating his worship life. Now we consider the matter in reverse, which while it sounds like a paradox, is nevertheless true. Paul inspects the reality of the inner life in respect to the unreality of the outer life.

This tells us that outward profession, dress or ceremonialism is not the final proof of religious reality. After all, the inner test is what counts, for in so far as New Testament Christianity is concerned it is not something you put on, nor something you dress up in, nor something you act out as an actor in a play. It is something which begins within. It is life, and life is always an inner manifestation. You do not hang oranges on trees—you get them from what is inside the tree.

It is not by natural birth but by spiritual birth that Christian reality comes. It is not by outward religion but by inward redemption. Its reduction to simple terms puts the matter this way—has God moved into your heart? God must be in the heart if godliness is to be in the life.

There is a breakdown in the practical effects of our modern Christian experience because the outward and the inward are not in right relation. We do not have sufficient inward life to meet the outward testings.

There is a story of an old gentleman who watched a small boy struggling with a very large apple. Finally he said, "Too much apple, isn't it sonny?" The little fellow with his mouth full of apple and his hand full of more apple replied, "No sir, mister, not enough boy." Our problem is not that there is too much world, too much temptation, too much habit, too much sin, and too much evil, but there is not enough Christianity. An old divine said, "There is enough religion in the world to sink it, and I fear not enough Christianity to save it." What we must be sure about is that we have enough Christianity. By that is meant an inner spiritual experience of birth, of growth, and of competence to meet the grave spiritual and moral life problems that face us on the outside.

# 5

## THE GUILTY MAN

### Romans 3:1-31

IN MODERN warfare the first thrusts of mechanized power units which carry an attacking army into enemy territory so that it captures strategic locations, are followed by what is called "mopping up" operations. In these operations, the details of conquest are attended to and every part of the conquered territory is brought under the control of the invader.

While the full implication of this analogy is not apparent here, we can best explain the contents of this third chapter, particularly its first part, as Paul's "mopping up" operations. The strategic centers of opinion have been conquered. Gentile paganism and Judaism have both been proved inadequate. All men, regardless of their natural condition and their native religion, have fallen under the indictment of sin and are shown to be in need of the gospel. Now Paul recapitulates the main features, and proceeds to bring the whole detailed realm of human character and conduct under the specific need of the remedy provided in the gospel, before he presents the main feature of his message.

We understand that Paul is dealing primarily with the Jew, for he begins by posing a question which some Jewish arguer might ask—"What advantage then hath the Jew?" But while he may be dealing primarily with the Jew, he is not dealing in any final or restricted sense with a Jewish question. This is as much a Gentile question for after all, it is a question which either has been or will be asked by every religious or moral person. That question is: What advantage is it to be religious? Paul has conclusively proved that the nationalistic Gentile and the nationalistic Jew, the racial Gentile and the racial Jew, and the Paganistic Gentile and the Judaistic Jew are all guilty of sin. Now in that case the Jew arises to ask, what advantage is there in being a Jew? That question is in many minds today. Does the religious man have any advantage over the non-religious man? Does the moral man have any advantage over the immoral man?

Let us remember that the gospel presents a plan of life. If it is a plan worthy of a divine planner, it must be both ethical and equitable. If it requires one thing of one, it must require the same thing of another. It must be as impartial as the laws of nature. But the Jewish man took the attitude that since he had received the revealed message of the Old Testament, he was exempt from the needs and conditions of the New Testament message. He forgot that the Old Testament was not complete without the New Testament; that the lamb upon the Old Testament altars was but the promise of the Lamb on the New Testament cross; that the Old Testament Messiah was the New Testament Christ; that the just lived by faith whether in Abraham's day or Paul's day.

The laws of life in the gospel are as rigid as the laws of electricity in nature. The blessings of this new life are available and discoverable only by those who follow directions. It makes no difference how earnestly we may search for them, they come by one means—"the just shall live by faith."

Let us look now at the contents of this section.

I. WHAT ADVANTAGE THEN HATH THE JEW?   Verses 1-8.

In chapters one and two we saw man's relationship to the doing of evil. There neither nationality nor religion proved to be any exception. Now in this third chapter we see God's relationship to the person who has committed evil.

There are seven specific items found in the first eight verses:

1. The People of God. Verse 1.

"What advantage then hath the Jew? or what profit is there of circumcision?"

The Jew who hears the gospel's claims is saying— What advantage is there in my national position and what profit is there in keeping the commandments? If I am a sinner equal with the Gentile and in need of salvation like the Gentile, what have been the benefits and privileges of being a Jew?

We must never lose sight of the fact that these people were the people of God. They were chosen for a definite and specific reason. That is remarkably revealed in their history. In the beginning there were two distinct lines of descent from Adam. One line was through Cain and it was non-religious. The other line was through Seth and it was definitely religious. Its genealogies are carefully preserved. Its record is marked by fidelity to God. Through them came specific revelations. This line issued at last in Abraham. From Abraham there were also two lines of descent. One line was through Ishmael and it was definitely pagan. The other line was through Isaac and became, in his twelve grandsons, the foundations of the Jewish nation. The history of this nation has been unlike any other nation. It is not noted for its commerce, great cities or wars. It is noted for its priests and prophets. Through it has come a Book and a Man. That Book is the Bible, and that Man is Jesus Christ. These two have blessed the world as nothing else before or since. They, under God, are the product of the Jewish nation who have every right to be known as "the people of God."

But the Jewish nation is not merely a nation with a past. It has a future—a glorious future. If it has shown the individual the way to life through a Book and a Man, it will also show the world the way to perfect government through One who will be its King. Today the plight of the Jew is one of extreme pity, but he has a better future in spite of the intense spirit of anti-semitism that prevails.

2. The Oracles of God. Verse 2.

"Much every way: chiefly, because that unto them were committed the oracles of God."

The question has been asked—"What advantage then hath the Jew?" The answer is "much every way." There were many advantages. One was birth, for a Jew was born into the covenants of blessing and in the land of blessing. Another was the advantage of priority for the redemption of the world came through this nation. But the apostle says, "chiefly, because that unto them were committed the oracles of God."

This means the Old Testament Scriptures. An oracle was, properly speaking, the message or voice of God. It was every bit of that to the Jew. It was a revelation through the Old Testament Scriptures. Herein lay the great advantage of being a Jew—the advantage of being the writer, the custodian, and the possessor of the sacred Scriptures. It was the advantage of a preview of world dominion and world redemption. It was the advantage of the first glimpse of a gigantic plan of the ages. It was the honor of belonging to a nation chosen to be the channel through which that message might come to the world. But while it was an honor and a privilege, it was also a great responsibility. Having this foreview and this prior knowledge, the Jew was to be held peculiarly accountable for any misuse and abuse he made of his privilege. The blessing that would come out of his advantage would not be in having the oracles of God as a national heirloom, but in using them as a God-given trust.

Let us turn this question upon ourselves and Christendom. What advantage hath the Christian? The answer is the same—"Much every way." We too are a people of a Book. The Scriptures of both Old and New Testaments have been committed to us not only as custodians but as evangelists and teachers. From these Scriptures we have had a priority of knowledge. We have laid the foundations of civilization. We have founded our nation. We have taken the Bible throughout much of the world. And yet we have conspicuously failed not only to appreciate our advantages but to appropriate them. With them in our possession for centuries, we still find millions without their knowledge. The world waits the threatened collapse of civilization; not for lack of science or money or learning, but for lack of God in our commonwealths.

Someone has said that "fifteen minutes a day devoted to one definite study will make one a master in a dozen years." Think of that simple recipe in relation to the Bible. Will we dare devote fifteen minutes to this Book, not only to its truths, but also to its life? If we will dare such a thing, we will become mastered by the Son of God and masters of a new life.

3. The Faithfulness of God. Verse 3.

"For what if some did not believe? shall their unbelief make the faith of God without effect?"

In this verse, the phrase "the faith of God" literally means "the faithfulness of God." Weymouth translates it like this—"What if some Jews proved unfaithful? shall their unfaithfulness nullify God's faithfulness?"

Does it mean, the apostle is arguing, that because some Jews proved unfaithful to their trust and did not capitalize on their advantages that God is going to set aside His Word and let every man's independent idea prevail? Will a Jew find himself on the right side of destiny merely because of the national company he keeps? Will a religious man find himself on the right side of destiny because he was religious? Will a moral man find himself on the right side of destiny because he was moral? Is the law of life set by the individual or by God? That is exactly what it means when it says, "shall their unbelief make the faith of God without effect?"

There is one thing that can be counted on with precise regularity and perpetual continuity. It is God's faithfulness to His own promises, His own standards, His own laws, and His own words. What He has said He will do. What He has promised He will fulfill. What He has ordered He will perform. God is God, and keeping His Word in faithfulness is God-like.

Our viewpoint depends upon our point of view. "When we look into the heavens on a clear night we imagine that we see countless numbers of stars, but science says no. We see only a few thousand in reality, six thousand to be exact. That is the highest number human eyes unaided by powerful instruments are capable of seeing. The average number we can see on average nights is forty-five hundred. On the other hand, the big telescopes reveal millions. According to Nature Magazine more than 100,000,000 stars are within reach of the Yerkes Observatory reflector which is forty inches. More than 1,500,000,000 stars can be recorded photographically with the giant one-hundred-inch reflector at Mount Wilson Observatory. Many times more than this is revealed by the new two-hundred-inch reflector on Mount Palomar. Apparently there is no limit to the number of stars, nor to the marvels of the universe."

It is so with our mental point of view as well as our optical point of view. The Bible increases the breadth and depth of our appreciation and understanding of the here and the hereafter. If you want your viewpoint right, get the right point of view.

We began to investigate the seven items found in the first eight verses of this third chapter concerning God's relation to the person who has committed evil.

Here is the fourth of these seven things:

4. The Truthfulness of God. Verse 4.

> "God forbid: yea, let God be true, but every man a liar; as it is written, That thou mightest be justified in thy saying, and mightest overcome when thou art judged."

If, according to the suggestion of the previous verse, God altered His word, it would destroy the whole realm of truth. But such could never be, for Paul says, "God forbid: yea, let God be true but every man a liar." What does He mean? Does He want every human being to become an assassin of truth? No, of course not. He is saying here that although all men should be proved false, God will always be found true. His character never changes. His word never fails.

If God has proved Himself to be so meticulously accurate and precise in nature, as He has in the planetary movements, we would most certainly expect to find it so in His character. There is a truthfulness about God that we can trust. We may cast ourself upon Him with perfect assurance.

God is to be vindicated by His Word and not by our circumstance. Our circumstance may be entirely contrary to our plans but not God's purpose. In His purpose "all things work together for good." In His purpose there is the far view which we do not see by our short-sightedness. Trust Him because He will not fail. He will not because He cannot, since He is God.

5. The Righteousness of God.  Verse 5.

"But if our unrighteousness commend the righteousness of God, what shall we say?  Is God unrighteous who taketh vengeance?  (I speak as a
man.)"

The very unrighteousness of man enhances the
righteousness of God.  All the evil record of human
sinfulness sets in bold relief the holy and unimpeachable character of God.  But if that is the case, will not
that very perfection in God lead Him to a benevolent
attitude to man?  Will not God forego any promised
punishment upon evil doing man?  Will not the very
purity of His character lend itself to a merciful treatment of the offender?  Paul says, I argue this as
man to man.  I speak as a man might speak in reasoning human affairs.

But the very righteousness of God constitutes His
rightness.  The very maintenance of the universe
depends not on His omnipotence alone nor on His
omniscience alone, but on His righteousness.  Because
He is righteous He is right.  He is right with nature
and He is right with man.  Therefore, He will be
right in the exercise of whatever judgment is necessary to bring into adjustment a badly balanced world
of sin and evil.

Get on God's side and you will be on the right side.
In the darkest hour of the Civil War someone asked
Abraham Lincoln whether he thought God was "on
our side."  After a thoughtful pause, the President
said: "I don't know.  I haven't thought of that.  What
I am really anxious to know is whether we are on
God's side."

It seems that much of our religious effort through the centuries has been an attempt to get God on our side. The cross put an end to all this religious coaxing and teasing. By the simple process of an act of faith it puts us on God's side. When that is true, we are not only on the right side but the last side. It is not only right but eternal.

6. The Judgment of God. Verse 6.

> "God forbid: for then how shall God judge the world?"

To the suggestion just offered that possibly God might reconsider some of His laws and refrain from judgment, Paul figuratively throws up his hands. He is actually saying "away with the thought." It is utterly impossible that God could look upon any kind or form of sin and retain His divine integrity.

Some were saying in Paul's day that since God's pardon of man's sins so beautifully enhanced His righteousness it would be for His greater glory to pardon all sins apart from the gospel. To this Paul says, "God forbid." It cannot be if God is to be. He cannot righteously overlook the Jewish man's sin because he is a Jew. He cannot righteously overlook the religious man's sin because he is religious. He cannot righteously overlook the moral man's sin because he is moral. God must be consistent with His character and His Word, both of which are revealed in Scripture and nature.

7. The Glory of God. Verses 7, 8.

> "For if the truth of God hath more abounded through my lie unto his glory; why yet am I also judged as a sinner? And not rather, (as we be

slanderously reported, and as some affirm that we say,) Let us do evil, that good may come? whose damnation is just."

It speaks in verse 7 of "the truth of God," but this is subordinate to the main idea of God's glory. There had been those who contended in the early days of the Church that since God's treatment of sin in pardoning the sinner enhanced His glory, in that case they ought the more to sin since sinning brought both good and glory. Some even charged Paul with preaching this sort of thing. He disavows it. He condemns it and justly so. Sin is sin in any case. Its nature cannot be changed by its use. If God reverses its consequences by His grace, it is not because of the sin or the sinner, but of God's providence. You can not have more good by creating more evil. You can not have more holiness by committing more sin. You can not have more peace by waging more war.

And this same principle is applicable in our own world both personal and public. You can not get good out of evil. A fortune built on dishonesty will never produce personal peace or happiness. A life built on lies and falsehood will never stand. A world order established by military aggression will never last. The first world war was fought to make the world safe for democracy, but within twenty years after its peace articles were signed, 354,000,000 out of Europe's 550,000,000 were living under dictatorships. Democracy had been banished from four-fifths of continental Europe because men worked on the principle that war could produce peace. Today's Europe proves it cannot. It is utterly impossible to get a good effect out of a bad cause. And what is true in the nations is true of the individual.

There needs to be a new conscience about this very matter in our times. We speak not now of the world in general, but of the Christian in particular. There is no valid holiness which leaves out truthfulness. There is no true Christianity which is not built on decency and honesty. Anything else than the highest is a cheap fraud and a hypocritical sham. We need a new generation of Christian leaders and Christian laymen who will live above the level that is reached by the accusing finger which says with prophetic accuracy, "Thou art the man." Our cause would prosper much faster if our Christianity were more pure.

Besides this, let none of us forget that it is one of the foundation facts of the universe that man is personally responsible to a personal God. Whatever actions we have engaged in will be reviewed in His presence. We may escape public notice and public shame here but never hereafter.

In the light of all this and particularly these seven facts about God's relation to the one who commits evil, what is the secret of successful living? You notice we do not say the secret of escaping judgment. That is a low view of life. That is the cheap attitude of getting by. Let us not think of getting by or of getting off, but rather of getting on. There is but one sure way— obedience to God through an act of faith and a life of faith. All life in the natural world or the spiritual world is made fruitful by obedience.

Obedience is not the mark of a slave. It is instead the mark of a master and a leader. The great leaders

of the world have never been their own masters.
Obedience is God's way to power. In health it is
obedience to the laws of the physical. In spiritual
health it is obedience to the laws of the Spirit. If
any of us ever attain a commanding hold in life, it
will be because we, in our lives, are subject to the
will of God above us. In this manner the obedient
will be obeyed; the conquered will be the conqueror;
the follower will become the leader; and the Lord's
bond-slave will become the master.

II. WHAT THEN, ARE WE BETTER THAN THEY? Verses 9-26.

Here is the question—"What then, are we better
than they?"

Here are two prominent pronouns "we" and "they."
"We" undoubtedly speaks of the Jewish position, and
"they" of the Gentile position. It is here an inquiry
into any supposed superiority that the Jew may have
over the Gentile because of his nation and his religion.
Paul, of course, is posing the question in order to
answer it, and as he answers it we observe a very
definite message to mankind in general, regardless of
nationality.

The answer to this question follows immediately.
"No, in no wise: for we have before proved both Jews
and Gentiles, that they are all under sin."

In the answer to the question there is a sweeping
verdict of guilt placed alike on Jew and Gentile.
Paul sweeps away supposed nationalistic superiority
and religious preference and ceremonial perfection;
and in the name of the all-wise Judge puts guilt where
guilt belongs. Guilt is a matter of human nature. It

comes out of the character with which we were born
and not the conditions in which we live. Guilt of
conscience is not only an item of revelation; it is a part
of intuition. It comes through the light of reason as
well as revelation. And the universal effort of man
to be religious is in itself an admission of guilt and
an effort toward divine appeasement.

1. The Verdict Stated. Verse 9.

If the conviction is ever entertained by any of us that
we are better before God on the basis of our own
merits, we are being tremendously deceived. We
may be better socially, culturally, educationally, and
financially, but all these are artificial veneers, which,
when stripped off, reveal us to be on an equal footing
before God. That footing is character and the apostolic
judgment of the universal character of man is this:

"We have before proved both Jews and Gentiles,
that they are all under sin."

Notice three things:

(1) *The Character of the Verdict—"sin."*

This is the first time the word "sin" occurs in
Romans. But it is not the first time its effects are
seen. The awful racial and individual results have
been witnessed through the centuries of human history.

One need not seek for another cause for the world's
woes than this cause. It is a word that cannot be
pronounced except one imitate the hiss of the serpent,
"s-s-s-s-s-sin." The gospel of Christ holds its only
remedy and consequently the only hope for adjusting
the maladjustments of life.

(2) *The Dominion of the Verdict—"under."*

Men are not merely sinners by name. Sin brings
more than a classification. It brings a conquest. It

brings dominion. Sin is more than a synonym for evil. Its effects are the symptoms of disease.

Sin is a great power controling man and it is such a power as he cannot escape either by his own choice or volition. It is a power from which he must be redeemed and regenerated. Historically all men have been redeemed. That occurred at Calvary nineteen centuries ago. But it remains for him to be experimentally regenerated and thus delivered from the reigning power of sin. This regeneration comes by our choice through an act of faith in the Son of God. From that initial act of faith, each subsequent step is an act in faith which gives us mastery and dominion in the realm of personality within and world-problems without.

(3) *The Extent of the Verdict—"all."*

The extension of this dominion knows neither the barriers of time, space, race, culture, or condition. It is as universal as man. It is as human as humanity.

We have next in this section (as Dr. Griffith Thomas suggests) "Sin in Human Character" and "Sin in Human Conduct."

2. Sin in Human Character. Verses 10-12.

"As it is written, There is none righteous, no, not one: There is none that understandeth, there is none that seeketh after God. They are all gone out of the way, they are together become unprofitable: there is none that doeth good, no, not one."

The depth and breadth of the sinfulness of human character is defined by the word "none" which is repeated four times. And this, you will remember, is an extension of the extent of sin's dominion that "all" are "under sin."

(1) *"There is none righteous."*

Man is not now being viewed by the relative standards of human beings, for by such standards there are many righteous people. He is viewed here by the absolute and impeccable standard of divine righteousness. Before such there is no human righteousness.

Dare a man or woman seek refuge in the Law? Such were folly for the Law could not make anyone righteous. It could only make one's unrighteousness more apparent. The Law was given to measure us, and its verdict was "guilty."

(2) *"There is none that understandeth."*

The apostle is not trying to prove the imbecility of humanity. He is not talking now of the learning of mathematics or arts or science. It is such understanding as comprehends God. Men know more about the stars in the skies than they do about the God who made them. And so Paul argues elsewhere. "Where is the wise? where is the scribe? where is the disputer of this world? hath not God made foolish the wisdom of this world? For after that in the wisdom of God the world by wisdom knew not God, it pleased God by the foolishness of preaching to save them that believe" (I Cor. 1:20, 21).

Man needs the understanding of faith and not the understanding of facts in order to understand God upon the terms of a mutual acquaintance.

(3) *"There is none that seeketh after God."*

Notice that it says "after God." Paul is not attempting to disprove the existence of natural religion. Man universal is an incurably religious person. Religion is man's search for God, while Christianity is God's search for man. It is incontestably true that man is a religious seeker, but the implication here is that his search has been both misguided and misdirected. The true fact of the religious history of the world is this: God is not concealed, but man is lost. Humanity is not holiness in human flesh, for "the carnal mind is enmity against God, for it is not subject to the law of God, neither indeed can be." Therefore, it is not circumcision or catechism that human nature needs, but regeneration.

Divinity does not lie just underneath the epidermis. Man is not a god in disguise.

(4) *"There is none that doeth good."*

Surely Paul is too inclusive in this indictment. "Isn't Red Cross work 'good'?" "Isn't social service work 'good'?" "Isn't charitable work 'good'?" Yes, of course, all of these things are good in their sphere. Paul is not speaking of that sphere, but of things that commend themselves to God to attain a personal righteousness. Before God the work partakes of the quality of the worker. Therefore, if there is none righteous before God on the basis of natural character, there is nothing good as the result of natural conduct.

3. Sin in Human Conduct. Verses 13-18.

"Their throat is an open sepulchre; with their tongues they have used deceit; the poison of asps is under their lips; Whose mouth is full of cursing and bitterness: Their feet are swift to shed blood: Destruction and misery are in their ways: And the way of peace have they not known: There is no fear of God before their eyes."

The sinful conduct which proceeds from the sinful character is discussed under an anatomy of evil.

It speaks of:

(1) *Their throat.* Verse 13.

Their throat is described as an open sepulchre. It is likened unto a grave containing the unsealed remains of death. What a commentary this is on man's anatomy of sin. The throat of a sinner is a place of vileness and viciousness.

(2) *Their tongue.* Verse 13.

The character of the natural tongue is deceitful. Think of all the spawn of the news sources of the world today. The foreign policy of totalitarian governments was based on this very word "deceit."

(3) *Their lips.* Verse 13.

The asp is an adder whose poison is contained in a small sac concealed at the root of the tongue. When the fangs pierce the flesh of its victim, the poison is injected into the flesh by hypodermic process through the hollow fang, from the poison sac under the tongue. The poison of this asp or adder is so active that it is fatal almost the instant of contact and that without remedy. Such is the powerful descriptive of an unregenerate tongue.

(4) *Their mouth.* Verse 14.

It is full of blasphemy.

(5) *Their feet.* Verses 15, 16.

What an up-to-date description this is. Bloodshed never traveled as swiftly as it does today. It has the wheels of the motor car and the wings of the airplane. The armadas of death and destruction and misery have been unleashed upon civilization with an unprecedented **fury.**

(6) *Their mind.* Verse 17.

Peace is a quality of mind and heart. It is not merely a part of the molecules of the brain, it is a part of nature. But where there is sin, there is no peace. And so long as we remain aloof from the cross of Christ, we shall continue to be a world without peace.

(7) *Their eyes.* Verse 18.

Here is a sinful arrogance that plumbs the deepest depths of human depravity. The "fear of God" does not mean the fear of fright but the fear of faith. Fear means a "reverential trust." This is what the nations need.

Paul pauses now in his panoramic summary of man's sin and summons that man inside the hall of divine justice. There in the awe-full splendor and the hushed solemnity of the divine presence, the sinner stands to be measured not now by the defects of human character and the defections of human conduct, but by the standard of the divine law. By every conceivable contrast and comparison; by every standard of measurement and calculation, man stands guilty. It is futile for him to appear otherwise. It is folly for him to try to escape the conclusions of history, of experience, and of Scripture. He stands in need. The question is —in need of what?

If we are to do something about our world situation, we must do something for man. Unless the builder grows, the building is in vain. After all, what is wrong with the world is that which is wrong with men in the world. If we are ever to make our world right, we must make our manhood and womanhood right.

4. The Law and Man's Unrighteousness. Verses 19, 20.

The purpose of the Law is set forth in very specific terms. It was never offered at any time as a panacea for the world's ills. Rather, it was given as a diagnosis of the world's ills, and Paul says in verse 19:

> "Now we know that what things soever the law saith, it saith to them who are under the law: that every mouth may be stopped, and all the world may become guilty before God."

In substance he says this: the condemnation of the Law rests on those who depend on the Law. Therefore, no one can escape the condemnation of guilt or the sense of need for the Law gives a revelation of man's unrighteousness, just as much as it gives by its standard of perfection, a revelation of God's righteousness.

Paul then goes on to set forth the two sides of the Law in verse 20.

(1) *Its negative side.*

> "By the deeds of the law there shall no flesh be justified in His sight."

It is impossible to be made right or righteous by the Law. It is almost entirely negative for it shows what man is not, without supplying that lack which it reveals. It requires the positive gospel to follow the negative Law to complete the remedy God intends to offer.

(2) *Its positive side.*

> "By the law is the knowledge of sin."

The Law cannot save because this is not its office. Its office, as expressed here, is to give the knowledge to man that he is a sinner. It is a micrometer of character. It is a moral mirror. It condemns but does not convert. It challenges but does not change. It points the finger but does not distribute mercy. The Law is a preparation for the gospel which is a provision. The Law is the Great Restrainer while Love is the Great Redeemer. The Law-Giver now becomes the Love-Giver.

There is no life in the Law. There is death, for its pronouncement was—"thou shalt die."

Let no one presumptuously say: "My religion is the Ten Commandments." If he does, he lays himself open for an awful condemnation. Before he sets out to keep the commandments his great need is to know the Commander. It is life that the world needs, and when it has life it will have the intuitive desire and the spiritual power to keep any regulation of propriety that God may require.

5. The Gospel and God's Righteousness. Verses 21-26.

If the Law measured man's unrighteousness, we find that the gospel manifests God's righteousness.

We find ourselves at the moment with a tremendous deflation. All the cherished defenses of human ingenuity have crumbled. All the historic hiding places of a guilty conscience have vanished. We find ourselves faced with the inevitable conviction that there is no salvation in character, neither is there any salvation in the Law. If this is so, then where and how is there any salvation? It is a tremendous question. Will we rush off in despair and dissipate our energies in a futile search in the maze of tradition? Or, will we wait long enough for an answer? God has been faithful in revealing the facts of guilt; will He not be

equally faithful in revealing the facts of grace? Yes,
He will, and He does it quickly.

We are at the turning point of this Epistle. Here is
the hinge upon which the contents of this letter swing
from the records of sin to the revelations of salvation.
We turn from man's unrighteousness to God's righteousness. There now follow seven facts of His righteousness as they are found in the message of the
Christian gospel.

(1) *Righteousness manifested.* Verse 21.

"But now the righteousness of God without the
law is manifested. . ."

There is an epochal change to be noted here. Paul
says "but now," and in these words he contrasts the
days previous and the days present. He speaks of the
Law which was and the gospel which is. He is
contrasting man's wrongness and God's rightness. He
is setting in view a new age in God's treatment of the
world's problem.

The world's problem is not primarily the problem of
war but of peace. It is not the problem of crime but
of character. It is not the problem of pollution but of
purity. It is not the problem of religion but of
righteousness. If the world has peace, there can be no
war. If the world has the right character, there can
be no crime. If the world has purity, there can be
no pollution. If the world has righteousness, the
essence of the religious search is finished. And it is
the provision of this righteousness that is offered to
the world through the gospel by God.

The word "righteousness" should be divested of all
the mechanical misconceptions which have been given

it. It means "rightness." In other words, when a man is righteous, he is right. When man is right, the world will be right. See how strategic the gospel is to modern life! In this important day of the world-changing discoveries a new heralding of the gospel needs to be given. If we would declare a moratorium on ecclesiasticism and give ourselves to a simple and sincere exploitation of the possibilities of the gospel, we could stop humanity's plunge toward the brink of disaster.

Notice that this righteousness, or rightness, which all humanity needs is found apart from the Law and is imparted by the gospel. God now deals with the world on a different basis. It is grace and love and faith through the Cross of Christ. It is distinct and separate from law and works.

(2) *Righteousness witnessed.* Verse 21.

". . . being witnessed by the law and the prophets."

This is nothing new. It was not invented by Paul and introduced as an innovation. Here is something which bears the stamp of "the law and the prophets." It is certified by the Old Testament as well as the New Testament. After all, the Old and New Testaments are not antagonists. What is enfolded in the Old Testament is unfolded in the New Testament. What is concealed in the Old Testament is revealed in the New Testament. The New Testament consummates what the Old Testament commences.

Truth is of such a nature that it is beyond invention. Strictly speaking, there can be no new discovery of truth. New religions are not new at all. Every modern religious vagary has had an ancient counterpart. Whatever spiritual truth there is to know is traceable to this Book of books. God will never be revealed more fully than He is in the Bible. Proof of this is that man has yet to write a better Bible. God will never be revealed more beautifully than He was in Jesus Christ. Proof of this is that man has yet to produce a better man.

(3) *Righteousness obtained.* Verse 22.

"Even the righteousness of God which is by faith of Jesus Christ unto all and upon all them that believe: for there is no difference."

If there is a universal need of righteousness or rightness, there is also to be found in its provision, a universal way for its possession. It does not come to the American in one way and to the African in another; to the European in one way and the Asiatic in another. The possession of it is as universally the same as the need of it.

How is it obtained? The answer is in two words, "by faith." Thus, it is seen as a gift to be received and not a reward to be achieved. It is something to obtain and not something to attain. There is a conspicuous place in Christian experience for works as well as faith, but always after and never before or with. There is an equally conspicuous place for attainment and achievement. But such things which include all the nobilities of grace and godliness are the consequence of faith and new life. After them the whole realm of the conquests of noble Christian character open up in a never ceasing vista of enchantment and challenge. But we must be sure to be well started. It is "by faith."

(4) *Righteousness needed.* Verse 23.

"For all have sinned, and come short of the glory of God."

The little three-lettered word "all" measures the vast need of humanity. Its measurement is not only of the exterior but of the interior. It is the quantity of our need as well as the quality of our need.

Man's sin has caused him to come short of God's glory, and coming short of the divine glory, he has lost his human glory. A gory mankind instead of a glorious mankind has been history's story of the human race. Its root cause has been sin and its original lack is the loss of the glory of God to dignify and stabilize life. Recover this and we take that long step which makes the difference between war and peace, failure and success.

(5) *Righteousness provided.* Verse 24.

"Being justified freely by his grace through the redemption that is in Christ Jesus."

If the need is so extensive, so deep in human character as well as so broad in human conduct, then there must be an adequate provision. That provision is in the redemption of Christ. God's righteousness is provided in Christ's redemption.

The needed righteousness or rightness of human beings is not distilled out of one's personal devotion; nor achieved out of one's personal actions. It is provided. It is provided historically. It is experienced personally. There is a point in history which is marked by a fact—that fact is the cross which tells of God's righteousness provided. There is also a point in experience which is marked by faith which brings that rightness into the realm of one's life and reality. Do we know both the fact and the faith? Do we know both the history and the experience?

(6) *Righteousness declared.* Verse 25.

"Whom God hath set forth to be a propitiation through faith in his blood, to declare his righteousness for the remission of sins that are past, through the forbearance of God."

The effect of Christ's redemption was retroactive. That is, it had relation to men and women of a prior time, for in the declaration of His righteousness in Christ, God considered those who lived before the cross, who by faith embraced the coming Messiah of the cross.

This takes care of that complaint so frequently voiced, "Why did not Christ come sooner?" The fact is He did come sooner. He came to Adam in the coats of skins; He came to Abel in the acceptable offering; He came to Abraham in the substituted ram; He came to Israel in tabernacle and temple; and for all who would, He was found in prospect for we read: "These all died in faith, not having received promises, but having seen them afar off, and were persuaded of them, and embraced them, and confessed that they were strangers and pilgrims on the earth" (Heb. 11:13).

Faith was the condition of their salvation, and it is the condition of ours. Their faith was prospective while ours is retrospective. Theirs looked ahead to the cross as prophecy while ours looks back upon the cross as history.

(7) *Righteousness satisfied.* Verse 26.

"To declare, I say, at this time his righteousness:

that he might be just, and the justifier of him which believeth in Jesus."

Righteousness is satisfied, not only in the act of justifying the sinner, but by that very act it is also the justification of the Justifier. God is set forth in all His divine justness by the fact that he justifies the sinner through the redemption of the Redeemer.

Anything less than the cross as the historic redemption; anything less than the blood of Christ as the means of redemption; anything less than the faith of the sinner as the appropriation of redemption; anything less than the justification of the sinner as an act of God's justice and mercy would be less than God-like. Here and now, upon the historic ground of Calvary's redemption stands God panoplied in all the glories of deity and set forth in all the loveliness of virtue. Geology may reveal a God of power and precision, but the gospel reveals a God of mercy and beauty.

III. WHERE IS BOASTING THEN? Verses 27-31.

"Where is boasting then? It is excluded. By what law? of works? Nay: but by the law of faith. Therefore we conclude that a man is justified by faith without the deeds of the law. Is he the God of the Jews only? is he not also of the Gentiles? Yes, of the Gentiles also: Seeing it is one God, which shall justify the circumcision by faith, and uncircumcision through faith. Do we then make void the law through faith? God forbid: yea, we establish the law."

There can be no boasting if man reviews his record. That record is written in black ink in chapter one of Romans. There can be no boasting if man remembers the Law, for the Law measures him with a relentless impartiality. There can be no boasting if man considers the cross, where the love of God is incarnate and the mercy of God is manifest. All boasting ceases where reason and remembrance hold sway.

Upon what grounds dare one boast of his fitness and preparedness before God? There are two grounds used by men and they are suggested in verse 27—First, on the ground of God's Law; second, on the ground of man's works. Both are summarily declared inadequate.

Fitness is found on one ground alone, "by the law of faith." It is not because of the performance of deeds prescribed, but rather the performance of faith prescribed. Notice it says, "by the law of faith." Not a faith which is law, but a law which is faith.

There is now set forth a grand conclusion to the whole matter under discussion. It has been a question of man's need of an adequate righteousness in the face of a record of historical and personal unrighteousness. The need has been universal and now the means is declared to be as universally necessary as the need. In other words, it is not one thing for the Gentile and another for Jew. Neither is it one thing for the ancient pagan and another for the modern sophisticate. Verse 28 states it that this one thing is "faith." "Therefore we conclude that a man is justified by faith without the deeds of the law."

There is no retreat from this divinely pegged position. There is no redress from this divinely stated condition. It is absolute and final. Whoso defies it with an assault of superstition, reason, or whatever weapon he may choose, is doomed to be an eternal loser. The conclusion is true for three reasons:

1. God Will Admit No Racial Advantages. Verse 29.

It is the same for Jew as well as for Gentile. In this matter we must remember that "there can be no stepchildren in the family of God."

2. God Demands Faith Irrespective of Other Claims. Verse 30.

Special claims of preferment are not allowable in the presence of faith. Righteousness comes solely and wholly by faith without any consideration of works. It is for the Jew "by faith" since he must come this exclusive way. It is for the Gentile "through faith" since he must come the same way.

3. God Has Established the Law Through Faith. Verse 31.

The law of faith does not violate the Law of Moses. It establishes it not through my act in keeping it, but through God's act in fulfilling it. That law was fulfilled in Christ and all of its benefits accrue to us through our faith, which, operating on the basis of a spiritual law, links us with all the treasury of divine resources.

The law of faith does infinitely more than the Law of Moses. The Law may make me conscious of sin, but faith makes me the companion of One who conquers me and whose love controls me. He who was my Creator is now my companion.

Could an organ forbid its maker to play upon it? Then we have no reasonable right to forbid Christ to sit at the manuals of our wills, emotions, and intellects, and play the multiple chords of music.

# 6
## THE JUSTIFIED MAN
### Romans 4:1–25

IN THE early stages of World War II the British
government turned over to the United States for
safe keeping, one of the most precious pieces of paper
possessed by any people. It is one of four copies of
the historic Magna Charta signed by King John of
Runnymede in 1215 A. D. The Magna Charta is a
document of epochal political and social significance in
the history of man. It is the model of all principles of
liberty and freedom. It sets forth the principles of
such liberty and freedom as the birthright of the nations. This document was deposited with fitting ceremony in the Congressional Library where it rested
opposite our own Constitution and Declaration of
Independence under constant guard.

The reverence of this Magna Charta of political and
Social freedom is not nearly so vital as the reverence
of the Magna Charta of the Bible. Not only the Bible
as a whole, which is the world's Magna Charta of
spiritual freedom, but that Magna Charta to which
we are now being introduced in this fourth chapter
of Romans. It is the great Bill of Rights, the Declaration of Independence, the Magna Charta of life, namely, "the just shall live by faith."

This truth is, all other things being equal, the most important item of the whole Bible. It is epochal to the whole realm of truth. It is pivotal to the experience of all personal truth. From false conceptions of it, all heresy begins. And in half-truths about it, all fanaticism is bred.

It is difficult to keep from being theological when one deals with so profound a matter as justification. But, after all, simplicity is the greatest profundity. An effort will be made to be simple but not childish, for with some, you know, simplicity is synonymous to childishness. Jesus was always simple enough to be understood but so profound as never to be exhausted.

The immediate purpose of the chapter is to declare the principles of the new life in Christ. We call it Christian experience. The ultimate purpose of the chapter, however, is the production of new men and women.

A very few years ago, a Wall Street financier left a fortune of $50,000,000 which he designed to be spent "to make a nobler race of men." The effort is utterly futile. No fortune, however large, can ever produce noble men. It may provide some ennobling agencies, but ennoblement by this process is at best only a cultural veneer. Nobility cannot be bought. It is the result of birth. By birth we do not mean the nobility of dukes and grandees, for this kind of nobility is only artificial. There is a nobility of birth, however, that will ensure us not only a "nobler race of men" but what is better, a race of noble men. Such a race as this must be Bible-born. The Bible is a book which produces new men. It produces a nobility of character. It is the character of the "divine nature." "Whereby are given unto us exceeding great and precious promises; that by these ye might be partakers of the divine nature" (II Pet. 1:4). This new nature of nobility has an ethical and spiritual foundation. It is justification by faith.

At the close of the third chapter of Romans, the force of the revelation is on the matter of faith. It is there the "law of faith." Here at the beginning of the fourth chapter, it is what faith produces, namely, justification.

The great truth of justification is presented not by principle but by personality. It is not laid down by "thus and so," but acted out and lived out in a great man's life. We see it in the laboratory of experience rather than the classroom of ethics. We see it produced in actual life and that life is not in a monastery but on the busy thoroughfare of daily experience. It is in the life of Abraham.

This chapter of the Justified Man may be most conveniently divided into three sections.

## I. How ARE WE JUSTIFIED? Verses 1-8.

We have before us this great word, "justification." What does it mean? If we said that justification is a legal act of God declaring the guilty guiltless that would be a good definition. It is the complete acquittal of the guilty sinner. And in that you can see that the course of our inspection in this art gallery has been in perfect order. We have looked at the Inexcusable Man, the Judged Man, the Boasting Man, the Guilty Man, and now all the conditions of character and conduct are met in the remedy offered in justification.

Justification is a part of the whole process of the new birth. Mr. Moody put this process into six words:

1. Repentance—a change of mind.
   A new mind about God.
2. Conversion—a change of life.
   A new life from God.
3. Regeneration—a change of nature.
   A new heart from God.
4. Justification—a change of state.
   A new standing before God.
5. Adoption—a change of family.
   A new relationship toward God.
6. Sanctification—a change of service.
   A new condition with God.

Justification indicates the new standing which the sinner has before God. It can be put this way. To be justified is to be considered by God just-as-if-I'd never sinned. This is more than euphony. It is a spiritual reality, for when a guilty sinner comes to God and is justified, he is henceforth thought of and seen by his heavenly Father just as if he had never sinned. What a glorious condition that is.

To the inquiring guilty man, haunted by an evil conscience, who would ask, how may I be justified so as to become just as if I'd never sinned, comes an answer out of history. It is found in Abraham's experience.

But near Abraham there lived a great philosopher and saint by the name of Job. Of all the problems of philosophy he was concerned about, the one about justification was his greatest concern. He asked, "How then can man be justified with God?" (Job 25:4). In Job's day his contemporaries were seeking justification at shrines of idolatry and bloody altars of human sacrifice. It was plain that this did not satisfy or justify.

Now let us take the eight verses of this section carefully in hand and follow our question through them. The question is, "How are we justified?" Here we find a contrast between works and faith as principles of justification. It is a contrast found in one man's experience—Abraham.

1. The Experience. Verses 1-3.

"What shall we say then that Abraham our father, as pertaining to the flesh, hath found? For if Abraham were justified by works, he hath whereof to glory; but not before God. For what saith the scriptures? Abraham believed God, and it was counted unto him for righteousness."

The answer is quick and decisive.

(1) *It is not works.* Verse 2.

(2) *It is by faith.* Verse 3.

2. The Explanation. Verses 4-8.

"Now to him that worketh is the reward not reckoned of grace, but of debt. But to him that worketh not, but believeth on him that justifieth the ungodly, his faith is counted for righteousness. Even as David also describeth the blessedness of the man, unto whom God imputeth righteousness without works. Saying, Blessed are they whose iniquities are forgiven, and whose sins are covered. Blessed is the man to whom the Lord will not impute sin."

(1) *Works recognize a debt.* Verse 4.

If our philosophy of salvation is one of works it is based upon the principle of debt. But who sets the amount of the debt? We determine the amount of the works which we think are sufficient. But the debt is of such a nature that no work or collection of works could dissipate it.

We must never lose sight of the fact that salvation is a problem of life and not labor. It is biology and not effort. We labor not to become alive, but because we have life and wish to sustain it. Thus, labor is not the cause of life but its effect. The great difference between law and grace is the difference between labor and life.

As one has said,

> "I will not work my soul to save,
> For that my Lord hath done;
> But I will work like any slave,
> For love of God's dear Son."

The ideal of the Christian life is far removed from the idea that it involves some mystical salvation of the soul that gives a smug complacency about heaven. It is a glorious fellowship of service where heart beats with heart and hand is put to hand. This labor of service here is not ended with an eternal ease but continues in the other life. Heaven will be a place of pleasant occupation.

(2) *Faith recognizes a favor.* Verse 5.

Salvation is not an artificial religious creation that has been conceived by man and which can only be received after certain artificial conditions are met. Wages are an artificial creation of economics and man must meet the conditions of labor. But salvation is a form of life. It is spiritual life. To have this life, you do not go through any artificial movements. It is fulfilled. It is received. It is born. It is not manufactured. It is not earned.

The simple condition for the possession and experience of this new life is faith. Faith is the link between the material and the immaterial; between the known and the unknown.

The moment a person exercises faith in Jesus Christ, that moment his faith satisfies the conditions of God. It immediately brings to his cause all of the righteousness of Christ which is the ground of all salvation.

This verse declares that "his faith is counted for righteousness." There are no less than eight times in this chapter when the words, "counted," "imputed," or "reckoned" occur. In each case they mean "to place to our credit." When God justifies a person, He does so by placing to his credit all of the righteousness of Christ. This balances the moral and spiritual budget for us. We are now possessed of sufficient working capital of character to proceed to the business of living. Up to this point, salvation was God's responsibility. From this point it continues to be God's responsibility except that we are responsible for the right use of our lives and the wise investment of our capital of character.

When it says that "faith is counted for righteousness," it does not infer that faith is righteousness. Faith brings righteousness. Faith and righteousness are not equivalents. Righteousness is the ground of our justification, while faith is the means of our justification. We are never saved or justified by or because of our faith, but rather through our faith so that the saving element is always the grace of God and never the meritorious faith of man.

In verse 6 it speaks of "imputed righteousness," while in verse 8 it speaks of "imputed sin." Sin is imputed or "placed to our credit" because of nature. Righteousness is imputed because of a new nature. Sin is the result of the inherited Adamic nature; righteousness is the result of Christ.

This was never more beautifully stated than by that great apostle of justification by faith who set the world aflame with the great message of the Reformation, Martin Luther. He said, "Lord Jesus, thou art my righteousness and I am thy sin: Thou hast taken what was mine and given me what was Thine."

Now the sum of the matter assembled in this contrast between works and faith as the means of justification, is, that the one and only condition is faith. It is so because the ethics of God require it. It is so because the universal state of man requires it. But the faith that is required to bring me to such a place of advantage is but the beginning of a great and an expanding experience. It puts into us the impetus of a new and greater life. It enlarges the horizon of our hopes. It broadens the area of our labors.

It has been well said that, "it is vanity to desire to live long and not to care to live well." Let us dare to—"Do more than exist, live; do more than touch, feel; do more than look, observe; do more than read; absorb; do more than hear, listen; do more than listen, understand; do more than think, ponder; do more than talk, say something."

It is the greatest moment in any man's life when God becomes a reality to him. Such a moment is that man's moment of beginning. That kind of a moment came to a great man named Abraham one night when he stood beneath a brilliantly starlit sky and found God in a new way. Abraham had just come from a victorious battle that saw him and a handful of his servants drive off the invading army of four Eastern kings. It was Abraham's most dangerous moment. Flushed with victory, he could have considered himself Palestine's permanent protector and missed the far-reaching effects of a great mission. That greater mission was to the world. And so, that night, God bade him look at the stars. They were beyond count. Then God said in token of Abraham's great mission to the world, "So shall thy seed be." He was to be the spiritual father of the world. Multitudes would follow in his train. He would be more powerful than all the monarchs of Assyria, Babylonia, Egypt, Greece, or Rome.

That night Abraham accepted the challenge of God. He refused the confinements of Palestine. His would be a mission to the world. And Abraham "believed God and it was counted to him for righteousness." It was then at the door of his tent, as his God-directed gaze swept the innumerable stars of the sky, that Abraham was justified by faith. He was not kneeling in a church. He was not bowing before an idol. He was not on a painful pilgrimage to some holy shrine. He was just believing God. It is done in the miracle of a moment. It is the changing of our status in the eyes of God that begins the changing of our stature by the means of grace.

Here lies the secret of all religion. It is in faith. It is not in search or effort or torture. It is just to believe. Not to believe anything, but to believe God. Here lies the secret of large living. That night Abraham was changed from a sheep magnate to a master of men. He became a great leader. The change came through faith. All of Abraham's great achievements were through the conquering power of his faith.

II. WHO ARE JUSTIFIED? Verses 9-17.

Since Abraham was so wondrously justified, is it not true then that this blessing may belong to the Jews only? This was the question Paul was asking because there were many of them who were thinking it.

Men have tried over and over again to put labels on God's packages; fences around God's gardens; and "no trespass" signs in God's pastures. If it has not been Jewish restrictions, then it has been sectarian restrictions. Here we find it in one of its narrowest and most depressing efforts. It was the effort to limit the blessing of justification to Abraham's natural descendants and make it totally dependent upon and available through a religious rite. God is not as provincial as we.

There follows in the ensuing verses, from the first appearance of this threat of bigotry, a most adequate answer and an expanding vision of world-wide service.

1. It Was Not Dependent on Rite. Verses 9-12.

"Cometh this blessedness then upon the circumcision only, or upon the uncircumcision also? for we say that faith was reckoned to Abraham for righteousness. How was it then reckoned? when he was in circumcision, or in uncircumcision?

Not in circumcision, but in uncircumcision. And he received the sign of circumcision, a seal of the righteousness of the faith which he had yet being uncircumcised: that he might be the father of all them that believe, though they be not circumcised; that righteousness might be imputed unto them also: And the father of circumcision to them who are not of the circumcision only, but who also walk in the steps of that faith of our father Abraham, which he had being yet uncircumcised."

Justification which constitutes a new standing before God was not dependent on the keeping of a physical rite or observance. It was not tied to something ritualistic. In Abraham's case we find that he observed the rites. He was careful to be as proper as God wished him and commanded him to be. But we must not mistake the shadow for the substance, nor magnify the symbol over the actual.

While it is true that Abraham fulfilled all the conditions of the rite, it is equally true that the rite did not bring Abraham justification. This is proved by the statement in verses 10 and 11: "How was it then reckoned? when he was in circumcision, or in uncircumcision? Not in circumcision, but in uncircumcision. And he received the sign of circumcision, a seal of the righteousness of the faith which he had yet being uncircumcised; that he might be the father of all them that believe, though they be not circumcised; that righteousness might be imputed unto them also."

This shows that Abraham's justification took place fourteen years before the rite was performed. For that reason the rite itself had nothing to do with his acceptance with God. But the rite was in no sense a futile and empty religious observance. It had a purpose. That purpose is found in two words spoken of in verse 11—"sign" and "seal." The sign was a testimony and the seal was a ratification. The benefit was in the obedience. The purpose of a seal is to give the mark of genuineness to a document. There is no value in the seal apart from the thing that it authenticates. The important thing is what is inside the document. But in the case of these people, they were magnifying the seal and neglecting the substance which the seal was to validate.

Another thing to be remembered here is the fact that a seal is always affixed after the document is written and completed, to confirm the genuineness of what is written.

In the case of New Testament Christian experience, there is a seal of genuineness. It is not a flesh mark but a spirit mark. It comes at the moment of justification after one has accepted by faith the provisions of the gospel. At that moment, after he has believed, the seal is affixed and the transaction declared legal and valid. At that moment the believer is "sealed with that holy Spirit of promise, which is the earnest (pledge money) of our inheritance (a guarantee) until the redemption of the purchased possession" (Eph. 1:13, 14).

Every Christian, truly regenerated and justified, has such a seal affixed. It gives to him security and certainty. It is the advance of eternity that is paid down at the first moment of faith. It is the pledge of complete redemption. It is the certainty that God will claim His new creation.

But there is a difference for in the Old Testament rite the seal was performed by man while in the New Testament operation of faith the sealing is affixed by God. It is a divine work giving a divine security to the believer. Because he did not make the seal, he cannot break the seal.

In this way we see that the rite referred to in Abraham's life confirmed his justification although it did not confer that justification.

What has all this to do with those who live today? Simply this. Every human being is in need of a personal rightness before God. If we consult our conscience, it tells us of that need. If we consult the history of mankind, it tells us of that need. If we consult Scripture, is also tells us of that need. It has been further revealed that the individual is incapable of presenting a personal righteousness of his own achievement. And so he has but one way open for him to establish a right relationship with God. That way is the way of faith. It is the way of faith because faith is the law of life. It is the law which brings to us the unimpeachable righteousness of Jesus Christ. This is placed to our credit with it all the powers and forces of a new existence.

2. It Was Not Dependent on Law. Verses 13-17.

"For the promise, that he should be the heir of the world, was not to Abraham, or to his seed, through the law, but through the righteousness of faith. For if they which are of the law be heirs, faith is made void, and the promise made of none effect: Because the law worketh wrath: for where no law is, there is no transgression. Therefore it is of faith, that it might be by grace; to the end the promise might be sure to all the seed; not to that only which is of the law, but to that also which is of the faith of Abraham; who is the father of us all, (As it is written, I have made thee a father of many nations,) before him whom he believed, even God, who quickeneth the dead, and calleth those things which be not as though they were."

Here again the blessings of justification were not made conditional upon the keeping of an external law. The Law had its purpose. It was, however, a God-given purpose and not, as it has been so often made out to be, for a man-made purpose.

The Law did not provide anything. Its purpose was to pronounce, as it declares in verse 15, "the law worketh wrath." The Law brought men under condemnation and never offered justification. This was so even in the heyday of the Mosaic institutions. It was so, as we saw in Abraham's case, long before the Law came into existence. It is so now, long after the Law has gone out of dispensational order.

The age-old and the age-long means of justification is as declared in verse 16, "grace." Here is the key word of the Christian gospel. It is a gospel of grace. It is not a gospel of race. It does not depend upon natural birth but spiritual birth. It is not a matter of a national heritage, but of spiritual inheritance. It is not something we are born into, but something we must be born-again into. It is not a gospel of place. It does not depend on the excellence of our advantages nor upon our achievements. It is in its very essence the gift and bestowment of a new life which brings us into the experience of new things. It is a gospel of grace. Grace means "graciousness." It is the graciousness of God in His attempt to meet the predicament of man. Grace does for us what we could not do for ourselves. It indicates a means of salvation through God's unmerited favor and not man's meritorious effort. There is a large and conspicuous place for man's efforts, but it is always after grace and never before.

Grace is not something which appears new in the New Testament. It is as old as the Old Testament. It was grace in Abraham's days as it plainly states here. It was grace in David's day for he exclaimed, "He hath not dealt with us after our sins; nor rewarded us according to our iniquities. For as the heaven is high above the earth, so great is his mercy toward them that fear him. As far as the east is from the west, so far hath he removed our transgressions from us" (Psa. 103:10-12). This is the operation of grace which reveals an age-old pattern of salvation. It was not one thing for one age and something else for another. As there is a community of circumstances maintaining through all the ages, so there is an identical treatment of these circumstances. The sinner is met on the same ground in all ages. And when the gospel is heralded after the cross, it is found to have followed the divine pattern from the very beginning. The Cross is seen to be the pivot of the ages. It is the pivot to which all ancient life moved. It is the place from which all modern life must move.

Christianity still remains a gospel of grace. Modern science has not changed it nor out-moded it. Modern man has not progressed beyond its need. It is the hope of humanity of all ages.

There is an example in these verses before us of

the narrowness of man when he deals with the great subject under discussion. He invariably narrows salvation to some sectarian consideration. The Jews were notorious in this thing. They shut it up to physical rites. They made it a nationalistic property. They raised high fences of Rabbinical Law about it. But in the midst of the attempt made in Paul's day and refuted, as it was by him, in this letter, we see what God intended the extent of salvation to be.

Abraham was more than a patriarch. He was one of the great personality pivots of the ages. His seed was to be as numerous as the stars. This, of course, meant his spiritual seed and referred to the vast kingdom of faith that would come into being from that day henceforth. But this kingdom was not to exist in some scattered and inorganic form. It was to become a great force and exist in a great government and have dominion in an actual manner over the affairs of the world. This idea is bound to revolutionize our thinking about the world. It is going to halt our pessimism for instead of wars every quarter of a century, there is coming an era of permanent peace. Instead of a life lived under the constant handicap of natural calamity, there is coming an age of physical perfection. Instead of a life under the dominion of unregenerate men, there is coming an age of justice, equality, and freedom. The coming age is the age of the coming Kingdom.

In verse 11 it speaks of Abraham as "the father of all them that believe." He is not merely the father of a physical progeny. He is the father of all who have been or will be justified by faith, apart from the consideration of ritual, race or law. This links the be-

lievers of the Old Testament with the believers of the
New Testament, and the place of their union is the
Cross of Christ.

In verse 13 it speaks of Abraham as "heir of the
world." He is linked to an association far beyond the
blood ties of Israel. He belongs to an area of life
far beyond the boundaries of Palestine. What a program this unfolds! It is unfolded, bear in mind, from
one man's particular experience of God. It was based
on his justification. Thus the fortunes of this world
are tied up to the principles of justification. In Adam,
God commenced a great world kingdom, but Adam lost
his franchise of government because he sought a salvation by works. Abraham received his kingdom on
the night of his justification because he found a salvation by faith. Thus, the very destiny of the world is
linked with the Bible's plan of salvation. How thrilling
to be a part of such a magnificent plan as this. We,
too, as Abraham's spiritual children, are "heirs of the
world." We are in the legal line of a great inheritance
that will bring us one day into the sphere of world-
dominion. We shall have a part in world-government.
We shall be members of a great world-commonwealth.

It is in God's plan that the eventual rule and dominion of the world shall be vested in the spiritual
children of Abraham in whom the new kingdom of
God was reconstituted. We who belong to Christ
belong to the world-wide family of faith into whose
hands will be committed the dominion of the world.

There will be an end to despotism some day. It
will not be achieved by ballot-box or peace treaty.
It will come when the Kingdom of God comes into
force and authority. That Kingdom is hidden in the

hearts of believers now. It will be manifest at the coming of the King, and with it will come the long waited release of earth and humanity from its bondage.

But what we are to particularly notice here is that God's plan for a world-wide Kingdom of actual earthly dominion and actual human government is that it is conceived in His plan for the redemption of the individual. In other words, His plans for things international are tied up to the Cross of Christ. Both begin with justification. Both are spiritual. Both are born of faith. The Kingdom in the world and the Kingdom in us is the result of redemption and new birth.

The Kingdom of God was not invented at some church convention and adopted as some pet religious scheme. It is God's plan of the ages. It begins in justification and it ends in glorification. It was promised in one man—Abraham. It will be produced by one Man—Christ.

Woodrow Wilson said at one of the crises of his life, "I would rather fail in a cause that I know some day will triumph, than win in a cause that I know some day will fail." The triumph of wrong seems to be everywhere about us, but if you are the child of a Bible-born faith, yours is a cause that will triumph after all else fails. You can afford to wait in faith and calmness. While catastrophes of every kind crash about you and work their ruthless way through life, smashing cherished dreams, just remember that the verdict is not yet in. God has not yet had His say. The great offensive of righteousness has not yet commenced. It stands poised in His well-planned purpose and when it comes, your faith will be vindicated. There is but one thing to do until that time comes.

Do not simply wait, work. Do not merely believe something, do something. Do not merely say something, be someone.

There lies hidden in the apparent commonplace of the incident before us one of the most thrilling accounts in all the Bible. It is the story of one man's faith. Faith is not some feeling you pluck out of the air and use as an Aladdin's Lamp to rub yourself into some easy and miraculous way of life. Faith is a law which, when fulfilled, enables you to live the usual life in an unusual way. Faith is something you do which is based upon something God has said.

Abraham's great experience commenced with what God had said about Abraham becoming "a father of many nations." The manner of its accomplishment was beyond natural and human expectation. But Abraham fixed his faith upon the divine promise and moved out into the stream of events which at last saw the fulfillment of his hope.

If Abraham is to become the father of a great spiritual progeny, both Jewish and Christian, then how fitting that his life is to become for us the great example of faith.

The real heroes of the world today are not the heroes of force but of faith. When once the decision to die has been made by the soldier in battle, death is a normal event. But the child of faith who fights a battle of health, or of poverty or of obscurity is a real hero. In those battles one must die every day. One must fight alone. One must see the apparent hopeless outlook. In those situations, the cripple, the invalid, the housewife, the aged, the unemployed, the handicapped, the obscure, have the opportunity of becoming heroes and heroines of faith with far greater glory accruing to their name, and success to their cause than any soldier who ever took the field of battle.

Remember this, the greatest blessings and the largest contributions have been made to the world and life by the heroes of faith. Choose to become such a blesser of the world. For your example and encouragement, you have before you the story of Abraham's conquest by faith.

III. WHEN ARE WE JUSTIFIED? Verses 17-25.

There are six things spoken of in connection with the faith that brought Abraham justification.

1. The Reckoning of Faith. Verse 17.

"(As it is written, I have made thee a father of many nations,) before him whom be believed, even God, who quickeneth the dead, and calleth those things which be not as though they were."

It says here, "before him whom he believed, even God." Abraham's faith was in a person. It was not what human faith is, belief in some idea or scheme. Abraham had faith in God; therefore, he could have the utmost confidence in his cause and the course of his life.

There is danger in modern religious experience of being sidetracked from the primary purpose. Christianity is the revelation of a person. Christianity is the experience of a person. Christianity is the fellowship of a person. It is not merely singing songs and folding hands. "This is life eternal that they might know thee, the only true God, and Jesus Christ whom thou hast sent" (John 17:3).

Because Abraham believed in a person, his faith could reckon "those things which be not as though they were." It might take years for it to come to pass, but faith reckons it accomplished now.

2. The Basis of Faith. Verse 18.

"Who against hope believed in hope, that he might become the father of many nations, according to that which was spoken, So shall thy seed be."

We notice that Abraham's remarkable faith which is described in the words, "Who against hope believed in hope," is based on what God has said, for it was "according to that which was spoken."

The measure of a person's faith is the measure of their faith in God's Word. Outside of the realm of the Bible, faith is only presumption and conviction is only conjecture.

It was under "utterly hopeless circumstances that Abraham hopefully believed." But whatever hope he exercised in the midst of hopelessness was because his faith had the foundation of God's Word.

3. The Consideration of Faith. Verses 19, 20.

"And being not weak in faith, he considered not his own body now dead, when he was about an hundred years old, neither yet the deadness of Sarah's womb: He staggered not at the promise of God through unbelief; but was strong in faith, giving glory to God."

The strength of Abraham's faith was the strength of God's ability. It was not how intense Abraham concentrated on his problem. He was perfectly relaxed. Its strength was in God's almighty power.

Faith considers. It does not close its eyes to reality. It does not seek to evaporate difficulties by piously ignoring them. Faith does not minimize difficulties; it magnifies God. To all natural appearances and probabilities, there was not a solitary chance for the achievement of his goal. But in the midst of this consideration faith "staggered not" but was "strong." And because of this, faith makes the impossible possible; faith makes the mortal immortal; faith makes the ordinary extraordinary.

When faith is the dominating force of our lives, it changes the very quality of our labors and makes them fit into the great scheme of God for eternity. For when one lives and labors by faith, "it is as noble an achievement to light a kitchen fire as to enlighten a darkened soul if that is the thing God has for us to do."

After all, what is the difference between great men and ordinary men? It is the daring of faith which determines to leave the ordinary paths and go all the way with God. The thing that makes the difference is faith added to mediocrity; faith added to sincerity; faith added to ignorance; faith added to the commonplace.

4. The Persuasion of Faith. Verse 21.

"And being fully persuaded that, what he had promised, he was able also to perform."

Faith gave a great persuasion that God "was able." This persuasion gave to this man's faith the quality of a divine ability. Reason says God is able to do the natural things, but faith says God is able to do the supernatural. And here faith turned into action all the forces of the divine ability and saw it achieve what experience and intelligence said could not be done.

5. The Effect of Faith. Verses 22-24.

"And therefore it was imputed to him for righteousness. Now it was not written for his sake alone, that it was imputed to him; But for us also, to whom it shall be imputed, if we believe on him that raised up Jesus our Lord from the dead."

Faith brought righteousness. And what happened to Abraham opens up a great sphere of life for us, because it is "for us also, to whom it shall be imputed, if we believe."

Faith creates what amounts to a sort of spiritual bank account. It creates spiritual capital. This is put to our credit. We may draw on it whenever we will. No wonder, then, that so many are bankrupt and impoverished spiritually. They have never laid up this spiritual credit to their account against the time of their need. Just as surely as you live, so surely will come the time of your need; and in that time you will have need of spiritual credit.

6. The Justification of Faith. Verse 25.

"Who was delivered for our offenses, and was raised again for our justification."

The final and net result of faith is the full and complete justification of the one who exercises it. It is not only vindication before man, as to the success of life's venture, but a full and complete acquittal before God. Thus, there is victory, glorious and complete, upon life's two fronts—the human and the divine;

the earthly and the heavenly; the natural and the spiritual.

In concluding his treatment of Abraham's triumph of faith, Paul points out that Abraham's faith had to do with a redemption that was future while our faith has to do with a redemption that is past. Abraham's faith was prophetic while our faith is historic. Abraham believed God for a posterity to follow him while we recognize One who has preceded us. Our faith is to be in Jesus Christ, "who was delivered up for our offenses, and was raised again for our justification."

Notice the phrases, "delivered up" and "raised again." Christ was delivered to death but raised to life. He was delivered for offenses we had committed and raised to bestow a righteousness we did not have. He was delivered to deliver us from a past life, and He was raised to raise us to a new life. The Christ "delivered" was negative while the Christ "raised" is positive. The Christ "delivered" means death to an old life. The Christ "raised" means life in a new sphere. The disciples of the Christ "delivered" faced a tomb. The disciples of the Christ "raised" faced triumph. The Christ "delivered" says, "Come unto me all ye that labor and are heavy laden and I will give you rest." The Christ "raised" says, "Go ye into all the world and preach the gospel to every creature."

To believe God is to behave like He wants you. To believe God is to act upon God's commands. Faith is the great challenge of the impossible. It is the daring of doing.

# 7

## THE RECONCILED MAN
### *Romans 5:1–11*

THE Bible is the great pattern book of life. In it
life is laid out in its best style and form. It goes
back to the beginnings of life and reveals what is
wrong. It leads us to the Cross where we have a
new beginning. It then stretches our view out into a
great panorama of prospect as we see what life will
become. But in doing all this, it has not neglected to
show us the secret of life for the present. For this
purpose, the Bible is not merely a pattern book. It
does not leave us with great outlines and neglect the
substance of life itself. The Bible not only supplies
an explanation of life, but it furnishes an experience.
It not only supplies a pattern of life, but it furnishes
the power. It is, therefore, the great power book of
life, and in the wake of our use of it flows all the
beautiful and lasting effects of life in its best form.

This is what we see as we turn to the fifth chapter
of Romans. We see the practical effects of this new
life as they flow directly from justification. Justification is more than a Bible name. It is an experience
that leads to ever greater and expanding experiences.
You may have contented yourself with the ecclesiastical
blessings of the Church or the small effects of a narrow
religious experience, but not until you know what

justification is will you know what the real Christian life is.

Many times we have wrapped the truths of God in too many explanations so that people, having contented themselves with the explanation, have missed the experience. When you go to your grocers for bread, you do not want that bread wrapped up in sheet after sheet of waxed paper. One is sufficient to protect it. Nor do we need or want these great truths wrapped up in wordy explanations that obscure the truth itself.

In this fifth chapter are to be found the practical effects of faith. In chapter four there was shown the necessity of faith while in chapter five there are shown the effects of faith.

These effects of faith in this fifth chapter are revealed in a twofold sense.

I. THE EFFECT TO THE INDIVIDUAL. Verse 1-11.

Two decades ago, the average span of life was thirty years. Today it has been lengthened to sixty years and beyond through the greater understanding of the human body and the environment in which that body lives. This is a very notable thing. But what is more important to man than his physical existence is his spiritual existence. His life is more essential than his living. It is not so much how long he lived as how well. The quantity of years is not nearly so desirable as the quality of life. And yet, the almost universal emphasis is on the animal aspect of life. Let us give more attention to God's plan of life and God's pattern of life. This will not merely improve the species but it will renew it. It will not merely lengthen the span of years in time, but it will put eternity into our years. The beginning of all these things is in the Bible's justification by faith.

This chapter opens with a magnificient statement: "Therefore being justified by faith, we have peace with God through our Lord Jesus Christ." Lift out the word, "therefore," and the words, "we have," and you have accentuated both the cause and the effect of Christian experience.

The cause is "being justified by faith." The effect is "peace." You cannot have this blessed effect without this beginning cause. Anything less than this may be religious but it is not Christian. It may be human but it is not divine. It may be ethical but it is not the gospel. Let us be sure we begin with the proper cause and we are certain to end with the proper effect, "peace."

An outline of the ensuing verses reveals three things as the result of our justification.

1. Peace of Heart. Verses 1, 2.

> "Therefore being justified by faith, we have peace with God through our Lord Jesus Christ: By whom also we have access by faith into this grace wherein we stand, and rejoice in hope of the glory of God."

The first great effect of a genuine Christian experience is the sensation of peace. It is found not only in the tranquility that comes to our emotions and the relaxing of the tension caused by a guilty conscience and the sweet release from the sense of a guilt, but in a new relationship with God.

It is said here that "we have peace with God." This

is the very first effect of salvation. It is so because the natural life is enmity against God. The normal relationship with God is not peace but war; it is not friendship but estrangement. Sin has set up two separate spheres of existence, and the only bridge between the two is the Cross.

It was David who gave us one of our first glimpses into this state of affairs when he cried out in the throes of his repentance, "Against Thee, Thee only have I sinned." He saw that first of all sin was not a social crime, not a civil crime, but a spiritual crime. For this reason no one can have peace in the heart until and unless he has peace with God. Salvation is something more than an ethical problem. It is something more than settling a score with a bad past. It is business which a person has with God. That business can only be transacted upon the principles and with the parties stated in the gospel.

It not only states here that peace is "with God," but the further fact that this peace with God is "through our Lord Jesus Christ." We do not have peace with God through our ethical efforts or through our religious righteousness or through our moral manners. Peace is not an effort but an effect. It is the effect of Christ's person and work. You do not get peace because you feed the hungry or give to the Red Cross. All of these are the legitimate obligations of a genuine spiritual experience, but the acquisition of peace is not an achievement of effort. It is the effect of the linking of our faith with the person and work of the Lord Jesus Christ.

You have heard well-meaning people ask, "Have you made your peace with God?" Peace is not a reward, it is a gift. Peace is not made by us for it was made once for all by Christ who "made peace by the blood of His Cross." If man has peace, it is because he signs an armistice of repentance and accepts the terms of God which are unconditional surrender. And when we surrender and lay down the carnal instruments of our conflict, we find "peace."

The world is periodically at war because it is at variance with God. There has never been consecutive and consistent peace on earth because there has never been a vital recognition of God. Nations have only been nominally Christian. Or, whenever you have national espousals of anti-Christian philosophy, you have its consequences in war and bloodshed.

Germany in the last war was a most conspicuous example of that fact. Germany was the scene of the highest and the lowest in Christian truth. It was in Germany where Luther raised the torch of justification by faith and lit the fires of revival throughout the world. But it was in that same Germany that there occurred the corruption of Christianity some 150 years ago through the rationalists. The recent Germanic gods, that drank the blood of innocents, were but the natural result of her rationalistic conceptions of over a century and a half ago.

Wherever peace is lacking in individuals, its cause is traceable to the root of all human ill—sin. How few there are who know the content of one of language's most beautiful words—peace! Hollywood is the symbol of the world's great futility. Through it the world seeks what it will never find. Peace is not pleasure. Peace is not amusement. Peace is not diversion. Peace is not fun. Peace is spiritual life received through a spiritual birth under the auspices of a spiritual law.

There is another thing that further explains the possession of peace. It is in the second verse where it says in continuation of verse one, "By whom also we have access by faith into this grace wherein we stand, and rejoice in the hope of the glory of God." In verse one it is said, "we have peace," while in verse two it says, "we have access." In other words, we have peace through Christ because through Him we have access to God and His great love. To "have access" is to have had an introduction, or, as it literally means, "free admission" to God's presence. This is an exclusive feature of the gospel and a thing that shuts all men up to the necessity for Christ. He said, "I am the way, the truth and the life, no man cometh unto the Father but by me." The source of our peace is on the strength of His introduction.

2. Purpose in Life. Verses 3-5.

"And not only so, but we glory in tribulations also: knowing that tribulation worketh patience; And patience, experience; and experience hope; and hope maketh not ashamed; because the love of God is shed abroad in our hearts by the Holy Ghost which is given unto us."

It can be said exclusively of the Christian, because of the new adjustment of his life with the eternal purposes of God and the eternal person of God, that he alone of all men has a real purpose in life. In him there is now a meaning for tribulation. Before, these experiences were the effects of nature that must be endured; but now, they become the instruments of nobility and enrichment that are to be accepted and used for better things.

Paul begins by saying, "we glory in tribulations also." This would sound like, and surely be, a form of emotional insanity, if it were not for Paul's pattern of thought. He saw himself and his fellow Christians as life companions of God. He understood that justification placed him and them in a new category. They had an introduction to God and consequently an initiation into a new life. In that new life God resolved all of the seeming misfortunes and experiences and calamities of the natural world into a source of good. Whatever was bad became good. Whatever was wrong became right. Whatever was tragic became triumphant.

Paul did not merely endure these experiences, he enjoyed them. He did not suffer them, he gloried in them. The specific thing that Paul gloried in is described as "tribulations." This word is derived from the Latin word, "tribulum," which was the threshing instrument wherewith the Roman farmer separated the grain from the husks. And acting in exactly the same capacity are the adversities of life such as sorrow, disease, distress, invalidism, poverty, reverses, and so on. These are the tribuli of the Great Winnower of our souls by which He separates the chaff of sinfulness and selfishness from the corn of the spiritual nature.

In the economy of God, His dealings include tribulation as well as justification. Justification is something done for us while patience and experience and hope are something done in us. Justification gives peace but it cannot give patience. This comes only in the experiences of life itself. And when we have a well-grounded hope, as we do in grace, these experiences of the :"tribuli" do not destroy our peace with God; they only serve to make it more sure. As the storms which rage in the branches of the tree agitate the roots and send them deeper and firmer into the soil, so is the action of the "tribuli" upon the soul.

Another thing that we must not miss here is the process of tribulation. It says that "tribulation worketh." That is to say, tribulation works out. It works out what God works in. The proof of character is in conduct. God gives us a new character; hence, we should have a new conduct. It is the same thought expressed in Philippians 2:12,13, "Work out your own salvation with fear and tremblng. For it is God which worketh in you." Tribulation not only works out but it develops. It develops and enlarges and matures the elements of the new character.

Yes, tribulation "worketh." What it does, it does on purpose. It is not fate but faith. It is not accident but appointment. The farmer does not flail his wheat just for the sake of beating the stalks of the shock. He has a purpose and the purpose is to get the grain. The purpose of the tribulum in life is the perfection of life. And this purpose is that expressed in Romans 8:28, "All things work together for good," but they are things in the lives of those who are in God's purpose.

We sometimes wish to hasten the purpose of God and speed up the work of the tribulum, but they are of such a character as must run their course.

Now we observe the threefold effect of tribulation:

    (1) *Patience.* Verse 3.

    "Tribulation worketh patience."

This means that tribulation develops steadfastness, fortitude, and endurance. Patience is more than a gentle meekness. It is a spiritual stoicism that makes one strong.

Tribulation may come upon us like a great pressure, but remember, power is developed out of pressure. It is the pressure of steam that makes power for the locomotive. It is the pressure of the water of a dam that gives power for the turbines. Pressure not only gives power but perfume, for when you crush a flower, it releases the perfume locked up in the cells of the petal.

It is truly said that "tribulation is a way to triumph. The valley-way opens in the highway . . . Crowns are cast in crucibles. Chains of character that wind about the feet of God are forged in earthly flames . . . Scars are the price of scepters." Yes, "these are they that have come out of the great tribulation."

(2) *Experience.* Verse 4.

"And patience, experience. . ."

Experience has a beautiful meaning, "ripeness of character." Fruit is of no use until it is ripe. It is so with character. The best apples are they which the sub-frosty mornings have touched. The leaves are never brilliant in their multi-colored beauty until the frost has come. And the good office of patience through tribulation is that it ripens character. It is a ripeness that would not come in the seclusion of ease or comfort.

The Greek equivalent of the word, "experience," is used but twice in the entire New Testament. Once it is translated, "experience," and once it is translated, "experiment." But the meanings are identical, for tribulations are experiments in life that develop experience.

The purpose for which we conduct experiments is to establish proof and to produce reality. If you were to invent a household utility, it would have to be submitted to the National Underwriters' Laboratory for testing. Here it would be subjected to every conceivable scientific tribulation. Out of their experiments would come experience. And out of the experience comes assurance and confidence. And in similar fashion, patience, through tribulation, develops proof of the reality of our experience and proves the genuineness of our faith.

(3) *Hope*. Verse 4.

". . . and experience, hope."

The lasting effect of this kind of hope, which is worked out by experience through patience and tribulation, is that it "maketh not ashamed because the love of God is shed abroad in our hearts by the Holy Ghost which is given us."

The Christian's hope will not disappoint. This is so because it is necessarily founded in the integrity of God. It is linked to His character. It is so because He stands behind the events of our lives. This hope will not disappoint because "the love of God is shed abroad in our hearts." The love of God in our hearts is a pledge by Him of the love he holds in His heart for us. If we have His love we also have His keeping. If we have His love we also have His security. If we have His love we also have His care. Therefore, its presence is God's pledge that the ultimate outlook will be both good and glorious. It makes no difference what the present reckoning may be; the outcome is a matter of divine integrity.

Another thing that appears here is the Holy Spirit's place. This is the first time the Holy Spirit is mentioned in the book of Romans. His mention, you notice, is not in a strange and technical connection. It is in that intimate sense of possession. The Holy Spirit belongs to every believer at the moment of the new birth. The Holy Spirit is personal to every Christian. The believer does not have to ask for Him but act upon Him. The believer does not have to pray for Him but praise God that he has Him. It is here stated that the Holy Spirit comes as a gift and that that gift is a present fact—"which is given unto us."

Do we appreciate the strong implication of this whole matter? It is this, that life has a purpose and that purpose is God's. It is being worked out of the seeming afflictions and adversities of life. Its final outcome is a pledge of God in love. That love is now on deposit in our hearts and it is there, not as an uncertain emotion, but as a divine communication through the Third person of the Trinity.

3. Prospect of Salvation. Verses 6-11.

The salvation that is in prospect here is not merely that which affects the soul and which is the believer's present experience of faith. It goes beyond this to include all of life and all of time and eternity. In fact, it means the completion of our salvation to embrace every detail of God's great plan.

We now come to the basic foundation of the whole Christian structure. It rests in the person and work of Christ. Our participation in Him as a matter of faith, results in our participation in all the benefits

of His great life and work. It is, in short, His work
of salvation.

Notice three things about this prospect.

(1) *We are saved from sin.* Verse 6-8.

"For when we were yet without strength, in due
time Christ died for the ungodly. For scarcely
for a righteous man will one die: yet peradventure
for a good man some would even dare to die. But
God commendeth his love toward us, in that,
while we were yet sinners, Christ died for us."

This is the past salvation.

a. The necessity—"When we were yet without
strength."

The death of Christ is set forth as an absolute
necessity. It says in verse six that "when we were yet
without strength, in due time, Christ died." Here is
what is properly called "the moral prostration of humanity." It was "without strength." Figuratively
speaking, it could not lift a finger to save itself.

b. The time—"in due time."

In "due time" means at the appointed time or at
the right historical moment. It is elsewhere stated by
Paul that "when the fulness of the time was come,
God sent forth his Son, made of a woman, made under
the law" (Gal. 4:4).

Christ came when the age-old efforts had completely exhausted humanity. Every religious and
philosophical experiment had failed. We must remember that up to the time of Christ's appearance
we have the appearance of every great religion, save
one, and every great philosophy. Christ's coming was
in "due time." He found humanity prostrated by its

efforts of self-salvation. Had Christ not come in this "due time," and at this proper historical moment, it would have resulted in the complete destruction of civilization. Christ's coming innoculated the race with a new life. The presence of a "third sex" of Christians proved to be the salt that saved from complete corruption.

The same thing will be repeated once more. The complete moral prostration of society is going to occur again. In spite of our vaunted progress and our so-called invincible science, humanity will be brought to the brink of another precipice of self-destruction. In that crisis, Christ will come in another "due time" to save it from utter destruction.

c. The means—"Christ died."

Here you will notice that our salvation demanded Christ's death. Three times in the brief compass of these verses, it speaks of Christ's death. We were not saved by His life or His moral precepts or His beautiful example. It was His death. His death was required as the legitimate penalty for sin, a condition which must be fulfilled before the world could have a new basis of life.

d. The subject—"For the ungodly."

For whom did Christ die? It states here "the ungodly." He did not die for nice people, or good people, or righteous people, but ungodly people. This ungodliness is what has been previously proved as the natural character of the race. It reveals the need of Christ's death, for if we were naturally godly there would have been no need of the extreme measures required for our salvation in His death.

Another thing that appears in connection with our salvation is the depth of the divine love that both prompted it and accomplished it. Notice what it says in verses 7, 8, "For scarcely for a righteous man will one die: yet peradventure for a good man some would even dare to die. But God commendeth his love toward us, in that, while we were yet sinners, Christ died for us."

There are three kinds of men mentioned in these two verses. It speaks of righteous men, good men, and sinful men. There have been cases, Paul argues, when men have died for other men. But when that was so they were either righteous men or good men. They were men who were considered worthy of the sacrifice of one's life. But this was not so in the case of Christ. He died for ungodly men. It was "while we were yet sinners, Christ died for us." It is human to die for good men. It is divine to die for evil men.

(2) *We are saved from wrath.* Verse 9.

"Much more then, being now justified by his blood, we shall be saved from wrath through him."

This is the future of salvation. Being saved from the sins of the past we are automatically saved from the wrath of the future, for the inevitable consequence of sin is judgment.

We must not forget the double aspect of the Christian's salvation. We are saved "from" something as well as "to" something. It is true that we are saved to serve—good works and noble living. But it is equally true that we are saved "from wrath;" that is, the penal consequences of sin.

A man is drowning and someone plunges into the

water and rescues him. The word goes out that a man has been saved. What do we mean when we say he is saved? Do we mean "from" or "to"? We do not mean in our ordinary idea that he was saved to eat, to work, to breathe, and to play. When we say that such a man is saved, we mean that he was saved from death and corruption. And in that sense, the "from" of his saving is greater than the "to" of his saving, for if he had not been saved "from" he could not have been saved "to." It is equally so in a Christian's salvation. He has been saved "from" great loss, great tragedy and great ruin. The measure of this saving is the measure of its great blessing.

(3) *Who are saved from falling.* Verses 10, 11.

"For if, when we were enemies, we were reconciled to God by the death of his Son, much more, being reconciled, we shall be saved by his life. And not only so, but we also joy in God through our Lord Jesus Christ, by whom we have now received the atonement."

This is the present of salvation. We have had, (as Bishop Moule has pointed out) the *Law* aspect of salvation in chapter four and the *Love* aspect of salvation in the previous verses. Now we see the *Life* aspect of salvation in the consequences of Christ's ministry as our High Priest in heaven.

The argument of Paul proceeds from the previous verses where he pointed out that Christ died for us while we were yet sinners. If that was so, then, how much more is He willing to keep us saved now that we are reconciled?

In the tenth verse it speaks of our past and present state. In the past, we were "enemies," but in the present we are "reconciled." When we were enemies, Christ died for us and effected our reconciliation. Now that we are reconciled, Christ lives for us to keep us against the day of our completed redemption which will include our bodies as it now includes our souls.

The assurance of salvation from sin is Christ dying while the assurance of salvation from falling is Christ living.

There are both the death aspect and the life aspect of Christ's salvation to be considered. That Christ died "to put away sin by the sacrifice of himself" is one side. But the other side is that Christ "is able also to save them to the uttermost that come unto God by him, seeing he ever liveth to make intercession for them." It is Christ dying who saves from all the past. It is Christ living who is the guarantee that the redemption commenced at our justification will be completed at our glorification. Salvation was begun at the Cross and will be completed at the Throne. We were saved by Christ, "the Lamb of God," dying. We are kept saved by Christ, "the High Priest of God," living. If the death of Christ was the means of our reconciliation, the life of Christ is the means of our preservation.

By the statement of verse 10, which says, "we shall be saved by his life," it literally means "kept saved by His life." The life of Christ that is mentioned here is not His earth-life before His death, but His heaven-life after His death. Following His death, Christ returned to heaven to continue His high priestly ministry. On Calvary, His priestly ministry was sacrificial but now it is intercessional. He is at this moment in the Father's presence conducting this ministry of intercession. He understands our infirmities and weaknesses. He is throwing in re-enforcements of grace at our weak points. He is sustaining us in our infirmities.

II. THE EFFECT TO THE RACE. Verses 12-21.

To read the passage of Scripture which follows might, for the most of us, confound confusion. But as we read it again and again, we see the pattern of the apostle's thought, and through that thought the purpose of God's revelation. Surely, whatever we encounter here, we must remember this truth, that while the Bible contains much that we cannot explain, there is nothing we cannot believe.

To begin with, we should remember that what we are to be shown here is the effect of justification to the race as previously it was the effect to the individual. Once it was dealing with sins, while now it is dealing with sin. Once it was the condition of man in sin; now it is the cause of man's sin. And this effect puts into both contrast and comparison two great Bible and world characters, namely, Adam and Christ. From one the issue is ruin, while from the other the issue is redemption. One results from disobedience, while the other results from obedience. In one we see the great mystery of the fall, while in the other we see the great glory of the redemption.

Let us consider these verses in the light of three things, remembering that we have before us the presence of evil in the race and the effects of justification through redemption.

1. The Origin of Evil. Verse 12.

The origin of evil is stated in the words, "sin entered into the world." Whatever the statement means, it does not mean what men say, that evil is a remnant of savagery. It is not merely something left over; it is something come in. It is something that entered at a time when there was nothing of its kind either in man or in the world.

Further than this, evil is something that came from the outside and now resides on the inside. It came from another source. The only evil in existence, before man became evil, was the Evil One. And the logic of the case is that the evil which "entered into the world" came from outside the world.

But this is not all that this verse says. Notice its statement that this sin entered by "one man." This places the origin of evil at a certain time and with a certain event. This event is almost as old as the race. It produced a cause which has followed the fortunes of humanity from its cradle in the Mesopotamian Valley to its present wide extent throughout the world. It has soaked our battlefields with blood; filled our jails with criminals; filled our hospitals with sufferers; filled our cemeteries with dead; filled our homes with discords and our hearts with unrest.

Of the origin of evil, the Bible gives the only adequate explanation. In its first three chapters, you will find the origin of everything except God. God cannot be explained. He must be believed. There then follows, after the presence of God, the existence of the universe; then man in the universe; and finally sin in man. And from the third chapter of Genesis, the Bible becomes a dual history. It is the history of evil resulting from one man's disobedience, on the one hand; and the history of redemption resting in one Man's obedience on the other hand.

Behind the existence of beauty and perfection in the world of nature, there is personality—the personality of God. "There is no conclusive scientific reason why the world should be beautiful; why the sky should be blue, the sunset golden, and the sunrise on our mountain snows rose-colored." We know how these things happen, such as the refraction of light, but we do not know why they should be. There is no why but God. Because He is beautiful, the world He made is beautiful.

By the same token we find, behind the existence of evil in the world of mankind, that there is a personality —the personality of Satan. There can be no conclusive scientific reason why the world should be full of suffering, disease, and death. There is not a single reason except the one given in the Bible, namely, that "sin entered the world" from an outside source through "one man."

Another thing that is revealed here is the consequence of this origin of evil. When "sin entered," something followed as a consequence. Death followed when sin entered. Because the consequence of sin was racial, the effect of death is racial.

The simple, but awful fact is that death came by sin. How can we explain the existence of death apart from the existence of evil? We cannot explain it at all. There is not a single scientific reason why man should die. To begin with, he was created a deathless being, as we know death. Without sin, there would have been change but not death.

We must reckon with death as a consequence of sin.

(1) *Death as a penalty.*

"For in the day thou eatest thereof, thou shalt surely die."

(2) *Death as a liability.*

This liability has been attached to life not since the creation but since the Fall.

2. The Extent of Evil.  Verses 12-14.

> "Wherefore, as by one man sin entered into the world, and death by sin; and so death passed upon all men, for that all have sinned: (For until the law sin was in the world: but sin is not imputed when there is no law. Nevertheless death reigned from Adam to Moses, even over them that had not sinned after the similitude of Adam's transgression, who is the figure of him that was to come."

The fact of death universal is proof of sin universal, for it says in verse 12, "so death passed upon all men, for that all have sinned."  This is inclusion and not exclusion.  How can this be?  Is there any valid explanation?  There is.  In the first place, the moral consequence of sin is just as real as the natural consequence of life.  God said that all life would exist "after its kind."  Man would exist after his moral kind or his sinful kind, depending on either the absence or presence of sin.  If he was without sin, his kind would be without sin.  But if he was sinful, his kind would be sinful.  This effect and extent of sin was inevitable in the nature of man and was not merely a penalty imposed by God.  Man sins because he is a sinner.

Thus, man's many sins are from man's one sin.  The late Chief Justice Thompson of Pennsylvania said, "If those who preach had been lawyers previously, they would know and say far more about the depravity of the human heart than they do. The old doctrine of total depravity is the only thing that can explain the falsehoods, the licentiousness, and the murders which are so rife in the world. Education, refinement, and even a high order of talent cannot overcome the inclination of evil which exists in the heart, and has taken possession of the very fibres of our nature." That opinion is from a jurist, observed through contact in court life. It conforms to this opinion that sin by one man became sin upon all men.

All of this does not necessarily mean that we are responsible for Adam's sin. That cannot be if right is to prevail. We are responsible for our own sins. But the fact still remains that we sinned because he sinned. The result of his sin is not our guilt, but rather our nature with which we inherited a tendency that results in sinful acts. Our guilt does not go back to Adam's sin but our nature goes back to Adam's nature; and therefore, the result is sin on our own account and guilt in our own name.

If Adam had not sinned, sin would have been possible anyway, because the right to sin is in the very construction of human nature. Let us not hide behind Adam nor blame God. If we think we would have done differently, we deceive ourselves. If we think God should have done differently we fail to notice divine providence over-ruling the effects of evil.

God did not plan evil but He permitted it. "If evil had never been permitted, the wisdom of God could not have appeared in over-ruling it; nor His justice in punishing it; nor His mercy in pardoning it; nor His power in subduing it."

To any who think that sin is merely the consequence of being a Mosaic lawbreaker, Paul states in
verse 13: "For until the law sin was in the world; but
sin is not imputed when there is no law." This says
that sin existed as a fact before it existed as a guilt.
It was a life-fact before it was a law-guilt. The law
did not make men sinners, although it did make them
transgressors. Sin did not come by the law, rather the
knowledge of it, for "by the law is the knowledge of
sin."

Men were life-sinners long before they were law-
breakers. This is proved by the fact stated in verse 14
that "death reigned from Adam to Moses, even over
them that had not sinned after the similitude of Adam's
transgression, who is the figure of him that was to
come." Because death is associated with birth, it is
proved that sin is associated with life.

Three things are declared in this verse.

(1) *Death is reigning.*

"Nevertheless death reigned from Adam to
Moses."

Four times in this chapter it speaks of reigning
sovereigns. In verse 14—death reigns. In verse 17—
righteousness reigns. In verse 21—sin reigns. In
verse 21—grace reigns. Death is king over the lives
of men during a long period of time from Adam to
Moses. This is pointed out to show that, since there
was death, there must have been sin.

(2) *Sin is personal.*

"Even over them that had not sinned after the
similitude of Adam's transgression."

We notice further that death came to those who had not sinned in the same identical manner that Adam had. Multitudes died who had not broken any formal command. The command Adam broke was that of the Creator. After Moses, it was the command of the Law-Giver. But here were those who had no such commands to break, yet they were sinners. They were sinners in their own right and their sinfulness was in their nature and their character. It means that wherever there is human nature, there is both the absence of righteousness and the presence of sin.

Let us get this point clear. Humanity may be sinners because of the Law of Heredity but they are sinful because of desire and choice. This makes it a personal matter with every human being. It is a fact that must be reckoned with in the conduct of life. It is not a deficiency of body cells but a deficiency of character. It cannot be corrected by chemicals, for since the cause is spiritual, the cure must be spiritual. And the cure is intimated in the very next phrase.

(3) *Christ is coming.*

"Who is the figure of him that was to come."

The cause was in Adam while the cure is in Christ. Adam is the first man of the old life while Christ is the first man of the new life. Adam stands as a type or prefigurement of Christ. It was so from the beginning and, being so, we discover that the recovery of humanity from its predicament was not left to chance. It was of divine origin. It comes to us as a revelation and not a discovery.

When we declare the salient facts of the Christian faith, we are not passing out platitudes invented last week. Here is a substantial arrangement of life that has been founded in divine revelation. Here is a cure for the world's ills that commends itself immediately to any fair-minded and honest person.

The world struggles with its increasing problem of war, but where do wars come from? We know the answers of statesmen, economists, and sociologists. The real answer goes as deep as human character. Said James, "From whence come wars and fightings among you? Come they not even of your lusts that war in your members?" If we are to have peace anywhere, be it individual or international, what we need is neither military disarmament or moral rearmament. We must have first of all a moral and spiritual disarmament. Disarm men's souls and not their bodies, and you have laid the groundwork for peace. When the Washington Disarmament Conference was in progress, Dr. Jowett said, "Washington will bury a lot of dreadnoughts, but not the old Adam."

What is true in respect to the problem of the nations is just as true of the individual. It is the problem of nature. When Melanchthon was first converted, he thought it was impossible for men to withstand the evidence of the truth in his preaching. But after preaching awhile, he said, "Old Adam is too hard for young Melanchthon." Old Adam is the personal problem of all of us. The historic remedy is the last Adam who is Jesus Christ. The experimental remedy is not reformation, but regeneration. In this, the cure is linked with the cause.

If the Bible reveals the cause, it also reveals the cure and presents a panacea capable of coping with our problem.

"For every sin God gave the Lamb.
For every sigh God has a psalm.
For every sore God brings a balm.
For every storm God sends a calm."

3. The Conquest of Evil. Verses 15-21.

If there is a similarity between Adam, the first man of the natural life, and Christ, the first Man of the spiritual life, there is also a dissimilarity. If Adam is like Christ in position, Christ is equally unlike Adam in conduct. Out of the first man came ruin, and out of the last Man redemption.

We find two contrasts between these two Adams in the following verses:

(1) *The first contrast.* Verses 15-18.

The contrast here is between Adam's "offense" and Christ's "free gift." The word, "offense," could be better stated as a false step so that we have a striking contrast between one man's false step and one Man's "free gift."

It is pointed out that Christ's free gift is not the same in its effects as Adam's false step. From both came certain effects to the human race, for both Adam and Christ stand as world figures. Through the one man's transgression there was resultant death upon the human race. It was so because of the hereditary qualities of life. There was no escape from these consequences any more than there is from a physical consequence. But if this was true of Adam's false step, its effect is as nothing to that which results from the free gift of Christ. In Him is to be found a new beginning of life in which all the consequences of former living and previous sinning are neutralized. In this new beginning there is the promise of the ultimate correction of all the ills that resulted from Adam's false step. For this reason we see the overshadowing and overwhelming significance of Christ's free gift as against Adam's false step.

The statements found in these immediate verses are most difficult to understand unless we break them up. They break up very beautifully in four parts, one part to a verse. We see the contrast between Christ and Adam carried out according to the following pattern:

a. The effect of death and life. Verse 15.

"But not as the offence, so also is the free gift. For if through the offence of one many be dead, much more the grace of God, and the gift by grace, which is by one man, Jesus Christ, hath abounded unto many."

The effect of Adam's false step was death. It was universal and individual. It was natural and spiritual. It was temporal and eternal. The effect of Christ's free gift was the opposite. It was life. It is distinctly stated that "not as the offence, so also is the free gift." If one produces death, then the opposite must be true of the other. In fact, we know this to be true because we know that Christ's mission was one of life. Christ was more than a life-giver; He was the Life. He was more than a way-shower; He was the Way. He was more than a truth-sayer; He was the Truth.

If Adam's act was a false step and if he set the gait of humanity then all of us, as we are found in natural Adam, are out of step with God. Only when such men as Enoch find a new life, is it possible to walk with God. We have to learn how to walk right if we are to have access to God and success in life. Get into Christ and you will get in step with God.

b. The effect of condemnation and justification. Verse 16.

"And not as it was by one that sinned, so is the gift: for the judgment was by one to condemnation, but the free gift is of many offences unto justification."

The point that is under scrutiny here is this thought: if one representative man's sinful act resulted in ruin would it not be much more true, that since God was employing the agency of another representative man, that this second man's righteous act would result in redemption? Indeed it would and did. For since Adam's false step brought condemnation, then we find that Christ's free gift brings justification.

We see here the emphasis and importance of "one man" both in respect to the world's ill and the world's good. It is not surprising that this should be. The construction of the universe is based upon the principle of the Law of Kind. All of God's creation reproduced itself "after its kind." Bird life produced bird life; plant life produced plant life; animal life produced animal life; and human life produced human life. Lift it a step higher and we find that spiritual life produces spiritual life. Since Adam was originally spiritually perfect, his subsequent false step made him spiritually imperfect, and from him proceeded a race of the spiritually imperfect. Thus, Adam's sin became our sinfulness.

And so we find the historic and spiritual significance

of this "one man." Here is the one man of the natural world—Adam, and the one Man of the spiritual world —Christ. Ultimately, we must come to see that whatever hope we shall ever have of resolving the world's ills must be through Christ. And that, mind you, not so much by taking His words and saying to the world, do as He says. But, instead, by becoming as He is. It is a matter of birth and life and not example and ethics. The world needs a re-birth, and this will come by what the little Indian boy called a "re-Bible."

We notice that after His resurrection, Jesus charged His disciples to go to Jerusalem, where He had been put to death, and tarry in this city of hostility and hatred until they found what His death had released, that is, His life through the Holy Spirit. But notice that those disciples were sent back to the very city that put their Master to death. Jesus did not try to change the city before He sent His disciples into it. He changed the disciples and they went out to change the city and the world. And how did He change them and they it? He put Himself in them—"I in you and ye in me." This is the formula of the new life. It is the new man to take care of the old man. It is Christ to conquer Adam. We are all born of Adam; we must all be born again of Christ. We receive an old life and its sin from the one, and a new life and its righteousness from the other.

c. The effect of death reigning and righteousness reigning. Verse 17.

"For if by one man's offence death reigned by one: much more they which receive abundance of grace and the gift of righteousness shall reign in life by one Jesus Christ."

Here are two of the four reigning sovereigns in life. One is "death reigning" and the other is "righteousness reigning." The sovereign death is the result of one man's false step, while the sovereign righteousness is the result of another Man's free gift.

Is this righteousness, this life eternal, this new order of life—produced in and by Christ—applied automatically and categorically to all men and women just because they happen to be alive? In other words, does the life of the new man automatically wipe out the death of the old man? If the one is by chance, is the other by chance? Not at all. One is by chance, but the other is by choice. One is because we are born and the other because we are born again. The one comes by the fall, while the other comes by faith. The provision of this new life is for sinners, while the possession of this new life is for believers. It is so stated in this verse—"much more they which receive abundance of grace and of the gift." It is something we receive as the result of a conscious act of faith. Thus, its effects are not automatically to all the race, but such part of it as consists of believers.

Those who receive this grace of Christ's free gift will reign in life and possess the means of a mighty conquest. This conquest will first be in themselves, for "before we are ready to deal with the sins of the world, we must deal with the world's sin in us." It gives the potential conquest of every sin, every habit, and every tendency which hitherto went uncontrolled and unchecked. After this the grace that reigns in us will extend its conquest to our surroundings and make for us better homes, better offices, better schools, better nations, and a better world. But all of these better things are predicated on the basis of the new life, "I in you and ye in me."

d. The effect of judgment and justification. Verse 18.

"Therefore as by the offence of one, judgment came upon all men to condemnation; even so by the righteousness of one the free gift came upon all men unto justification of life."

This says in substance that the effect of Adam's false step was our judgment, while the effect of Christ's free gift is our justification. The judgment spoken of does not in any manner mean that we are judged because Adam sinned, for it is only true that we are judged because we sin. But on the other hand, we sin because Adam sinned, for we are an integral part of the race of which he is the progenitor.

While the term, "all men" is used in both instances, it does not indicate, equally, the extent of judgment and justification. While it is true that judgment passes upon "all men," it is not equally true that justification becomes true of these same "all men" who are under judgment. Justification comes only as the previous verse declares, to those "which receive" the abundance of grace offered them in Christ. If judgment comes by being born then justification comes by being born again. In fact, that very thing is stated in this same verse, for it speaks, as you notice, of "the free gift." This fixes our individual responsibility very definitely. It shows the difference between being human and being Christian. This puts Christianity upon the plane of a great challenge to all the race. It makes life's secret the result of a great choice, for there must come a high moment and a solemn hour when we receive the Son of God as the Saviour and Master of our lives.

We have the contrast in this verse between separate acts of different men and their consequent effects upon us. Adam's act is described as an offence that resulted in judgment, while Christ's act is described as righteousness that results in justification.

Just what are we to understand Adam's act of offence and Christ's act of righteousness to be? Apparently they were individual acts. It was not Adam's whole life that brought judgment, nor is it Christ's whole life that brings justification. In Adam the act that ruined the world was the one deliberate moment of sin when he disobeyed God. In Christ, that act that redeemed the world was that one deliberate moment when, on the cross, he chose to die for us and said, "It is finished."

Thus, by one man's act of sin, we as a race were brought out of life into death while by one man's act of righteousness we, as believers, were brought out of death into life.

The thing that commends the gospel as a divine provision is its complete anticipation of the human need. Whatever is anticipated is also met with an adequate provision. The gospel never leaves us suspended over the thin air of human despair.

(2) *The second contrast.* Verses 19-21.

"For as by one man's disobedience many were made sinners, so by the obedience of one shall many be made righteous. Moreover the law entered, that the offence might abound. But where sin abounded, grace did much more abound: That

as sin hath reigned unto death, even so might
grace reign through righteousness unto eternal
life by Jesus Christ our Lord."

Here the contrast is principally between Adam's disobedience and Christ's obedience. Here are two acts
and two characters. Here are two sources of life and
two streams of destiny. The progeny of the one is sinners, while the progeny of the other is righteous.

What does it mean when it says that "by one man's
disobedience many were made sinners" and "by the
obedience of one shall many be made righteous?" It
means not the act but the effect. Adam's act did not
actually make me a sinner, for then I, who had nothing
to do with it, would be penalized by something of
which I was completely innocent and that would be
unjust and unfair. But the effect of Adam's act made
me a sinner because I partook the life which descended
from him. Therefore, the effect was in his act as a
matter of character as the same effect is in my acts as
a matter of conduct.

On the other hand, Christ's act does not make me
righteous by some automatic process with which I
have had no part or connection. It also is the effect
of an act. The time comes when I decide to participate
in that act of Christ's by an act of my own. My act
is an act of faith, and faith is a law of the spiritual
world that instantly links me, a sinner, with Christ,
the righteous One, and His righteousness becomes
mine.

It is easily seen in this array of events and effects
that Christ, "the Last Adam," corrected every mistake
and retrieved every loss of "the First Adam." And in
this connection, since this is so, we see sin out of

creation and salvation out of incarnation. We also see the hope of humanity resident in the person of Jesus Christ. But this is not all. The work of Christ does not merely neutralize the effects of Adam. It does not merely counter-balance the liabilities he created. It goes far beyond this to where the work of Christ transcends the effect of Adam to an infinite degree. And this is revealed in the statement of the twentieth verse, that "where sin abounded, grace did much more abound."

The gospel does not leave us negative saints; it makes us positive conquerors. It does not leave us with mere piety; it gives us power. It does not say go and sin less; but "go and sin no more."

When a person is in Adam, sin conquers him, but when a person is in Christ, grace conquers sin. And the measure of this grace is in inverse ratio to the sin which we had, for if sin was much, grace is much more. If sin abounded, then grace much more abounded; that is, grace superabounded.

Let us not hurry away from this good thought that Paul injects into his teaching on justification. Remember that he is speaking of the effect of justification in the life of the believer. It is, as you see, something much more than a pronouncement of acquittal upon a person's life and record. It includes with that a deposit of new life which is a commodity called grace. But it is grace in such measure as to meet the exigencies and emergencies of life at every point.

Grace is mentioned, as you notice, along with law. Grace and law stand at opposite poles of truth. Here it declares, "Moreover the law entered, that the offence might abound. But where sin abounded, grace did much more abound." Thus we find that the law entered to cause sin's offence to abound or to make the transgression of the law to appear more apparent. Then, while sin abounded, grace entered with a greater abundance that it might obliterate and put away the effects of the law's condemnation. In this way we see that the law was never intended to be a salvation from sin, but a standard of measurement and a means of moral magnification. Salvation came in and through grace. And when grace came, it came in such proportions as to completely cover every offence and wipe out every deficiency.

The law, therefore, was not intended to be a permanent institution, for the word, "entered," means "to come in sideways." It was a provisional measure which "educated the human conscience." It educated the conscience by putting restrictions upon man, thus creating a multiplicity of offenses. Without the law man would have gone on without a model to look at or a measurement to be measured by. But this was not to be his salvation. His salvation was to be by grace.

The effect of abounding sin is continual failure, while the effect of abounding grace is increasing victory. Here lies the secret of conspicuous success in Christian experience. It is found in God's super-abounding grace. It is a store of divine power and a treasury of divine wisdom upon which we may continually draw for the resources of life.

If our problem is temptation, there is more than enough grace available to meet it. We do not need to be continually beaten on the battlefield of life. Grace can take the measure of any foe and conquer it.

If our problem is a nasty tongue and an uncontrolled temper, there is more than enough grace available to meet it. No Christian need spoil his own life and the lives of others by his explosions and nasty displays of ugliness.

If our problem is suffering, there is more than enough grace available to meet it. In fact, grace is the Christian's antidote for misfortune. Strengthened by grace we may rise up out of the painful circumstances and live victoriously.

If our problem is obscurity, there is more than enough grace available to meet that also. No small corner need be obscure and hidden to one whose companion is God. Our place may be the junction between heaven and earth and in it we may transact the business of eternity.

If our problem is poverty, there is more than enough grace available to meet that problem too. This does not mean merely to make you content to be as you are, but grace to be better than you are. We ought not let the cults monopolize faith's philosophy of success. There is plenty of success found in the Bible. There is abundant reward awaiting the child of God. Link your life to the law of faith and you will succeed.

The chapter concludes by throwing into contrast the last two of the four reigning sovereigns we found in it. "That as sin hath reigned unto death, even so might grace reign through righteousness unto eternal life by Jesus Christ our Lord."

a. Sin reigns unto death.

Here is sin in the role of a moral monarch and a relentless dictator. Sin regiments all the powers of spirit, mind and body, and drives them in a despotic rule of conquest. Sin is the master. Sin is the monarch. But it leads to one inevitable end—death. It is the old story of the "way that seemeth right unto man, but the end thereof are the ways of death."

b. Grace reigns unto life.

How different is grace. It exercises the royal prerogatives of a perfect ruler and directs the life into pleasant places and fruitful fields. It brings life at last into the ever-expanding and increasing joys of eternity.

Although we have never verified this, we understand that on the beach at Redondo Beach, California, stands a home called "Flotsam," built entirely from lumber cast up on shore by the sea. It is the home of a man who, financially discouraged and ill, decided he must have a home on the beach. His dwelling, according to reports has cost him but 20 cents, the amount expended for a lock.

Build your house, not out of the driftwood left in the wake of life's wrecks, but build it out of God's new building material of grace. It lasts longest, wears the best, and looks most beautiful.

# 8

## THE SINNING MAN
### *Romans 6:1–23*

YOU are asked to look first at what place we have arrived in our progress through this book. The gospel was first presented to us as God's great remedy for man's great need. The extent of sin in human history and the depth of sin in the human heart were then pointed out in a great panorama of evil events. The entrance of Christ into the world at a point of history reveals His atonement for sin, and His entrance in the heart at a point of faith reveals His justification of the sinner. The effects of this justification were then portrayed in the individual in particular and in the world at large. And now we turn to another aspect. We see sin in relation to the actor instead of the act. We see it not now as an offence but as a master seeking to hold dominion over us. In chapters one through five is set forth the consequence of sins while from chapters six through eight there is set forth the dominion of sin.

The matter is now turned inward and we are made to consider the question of personal triumph. We are to determine now whether we shall live as negative saints or as positive conquerors. It is a question whether we shall live under the personal handicap and liability of a stumbling life, or whether we shall accept the conditions of personal sovereignty conveyed to us in the gospel and be masters of our life situations.

Do you ever have a great urge to be someone better than you are? Do you ever long to rise out of the narrow rut in which you may live and be free from the enslavements of small-minded desires and passions? Think of the vast company of human slaves that move like senseless animals from dawn to dusk without any plan, any purpose, or any goal in life! Christ will emancipate all such if they will let Him. He will not only emancipate them from something but enable them to be someone. For this purpose this scripture not only supplies the information but contributes the inspiration.

We live in the world's most enlightened age. Enlightened for what? We are masters of our machines. We are masters of our science. We are masters of our governments. But we are not masters of ourselves. All our progress and all our education has not taught us self-conquest. Until that comes, we have not gone anywhere. And we will never get anywhere until we find the secret of personal living in the Bible. The most important education one can get is that which teaches him who he is, what he needs and how to get it. That education he will find in Romans where a curriculum of life is offered. And remember, "An educated man is not a man who knows everything, but a man who can put what he knows to the best use, however limited that knowledge may be." Here is a chance for an education in how to live.

Before taking up in some detail the contents of the chapter, let us emphasize its truth by a comparison.

In chapter five we saw what we have through Christ, while in chapter six we see what we are in Christ. What we have potentially will never do us a particle of good until and unless we translate that into practical living. And so we now find ourselves moving from the truth of justification into the truth of sanctification. We find the past of our lives fully met in the redemption of Christ. But that is not all. The present is equally fully met for Christ steps in to manage our affairs and to lead us to conspicuous triumph.

It is no longer a question of sin as a guilt that concerns Paul, but rather sin as a power over the passions. It is no longer a question of our standing before God, for that is settled. Now it is a question of our state. What will we be like and how will we live in the arena of life? Not now what we will believe but how we will behave. It is no longer a question of our judicial position in relation to God's divine standards. It is instead a matter of our spiritual condition in view of the mighty power released to us in the Cross.

This chapter is dealing with the question of sin as it affects the believer's life. The chapter is divided into two parts by two questions. Both questions have an emphatic answer supported by a vigorous argument to the effect that sinning should have no favored place in a believer's life.

I. SHALL WE SIN IN ORDER TO OBTAIN GRACE? Verses 1-14.

In reply to both this question and the one in verse 15 we have identical answers. We have in both cases two things: first, a divine protest—"God forbid," second, a divine proof—"Know ye not?"

Before we consider this protest and proof, let us speak a moment about the question itself. It is this, "Shall we continue in sin that grace may abound?" It is not, as you notice, simply the question, "Shall we continue in sin?" but rather the question of continuing in sin in order that grace may abound. This continues from the thought expressed in the previous chapter that "where sin abounded, grace did much more abound." Therefore, would it not be sound practice, the question asks, to continue sinning in order to produce the manifestations of God's grace? In other words, if sin brings grace, then why not have more sin in order to have more grace?

Do not miss the point that this is a question of sin in the individual life, or sin as a practice. Back in the fifth chapter it was sin in general, or sin as a principle. Here, however, it is not the sinner's relation to sin, but the believer's relation to sins. It is in the life of one in whom grace has already appeared. Shall that person continue in sin because there is grace to counteract its effects? In other words, is the presence of grace the excuse for the presence of sin? Is liberty any just reason for license? Does a believer have the inherent right to do anything he pleases and live any way he likes?

There are two personal attitudes that we may take to sin as it relates to our practice.

In the attitude of sinful subjection one may say, fatalistically, that it must be. It is inevitable. It is justified because more sin means more grace. This, of course, is both unreasonable and unchristian.

The attitude of sinless perfection is the attitude that regeneration eliminates sin from the soul and it is equally untenable, for it is unscriptural. There is Christian perfection but not sinless perfection. Between these two there is a great difference.

In answer to the attitude of the sinless perfectionist, we have but to read I John 1:8. "If we say that we have no sin, we deceive ourselves, and the truth is not in us." We literally make ourselves liars. It is just as bad for a Christian to claim sinless perfection as it is for a non-Christian to claim moral perfection.

The sinless perfectionist makes himself a liar while the moral perfectionist makes God a liar. It says in I John 1:10, "If we say that we have not sinned, we make him (God) a liar, and his word is not in us." His Word has said, "All have sinned" (Rom. 3:23).

But on the other hand, we must not forget that Christian perfection is a definite obligation for all believers. We are repeatedly told to seek perfection. And the increase of perfection is found in the decrease of sin's dominion. It is the refusal to practice sin in the midst of the presence of sin.

Someone has put this matter into three splendid statements. "To say that I must sin is to deny the foundations of Christianity. To say that I cannot sin is to deceive myself. To say that I need not sin is to state a divine privilege."

Let us look at the answer that is to be found in the divine protest and the divine proof.

1. A Divine Protest. Verse 2.

"God forbid. How shall we, that are dead to sin, live any longer therein?"

God protests against it. Sin is abhorrent to Him. It must not exist willfully in those whom the Cross redeemed. Christ "died to put away sin." And it is inconceivable that we should live to practice sin. The protest is backed up by a fact. It is the fact of death. "How shall we, that are dead to sin, live any longer therein?" Death has two relationships to sin.

(1) *The relationship of a penalty.*

It is said, "the soul that sinneth, it shall die." Death came upon all men as a result of this penalty.

(2) *The relationship of a remedy.*

Death came upon Jesus Christ in a sacrificial sense to provide this remedy. Now, the effect upon us is that the act of our faith identifies us with the act of Christ's death and we are considered not only to have died in penalty of sin but to have died and partaken of the remedy for sin. For it says here, "How shall we, that are dead to sin, live any longer therein?"

Once as sinners we were dead *in* sin. Now as believers we are dead *to* sin. When we were dead in sin the goodness of God led to repentance. But now being dead to sin the grace of God leads to triumph.

You, of course, are careful to notice that it says, "we are dead to sin." It does not say that sin is dead to us. That puts the secret of our victory over sin and our successful behavior, not in our attitude to sins, but rather in our attitude to our own relation to the historic sin question. And our relation to sin is that of a dead man. When Christ died we died, not with Him but in Him. In that case the sin that made Him die brought the death that now makes us dead to sin. And so the question is, "How shall we, that are dead to sin, live any longer therein?" how can one upon whom the sun has risen go back and walk in the dark?

Christ died as much to keep me from sinning as He died to pardon my sins. He died for what I am as well as for what I did.

2. A Divine Proof. Verses 3-14.

In the third verse the apostle intimates ignorance, "Know ye not, that so many of us as were baptized into Jesus Christ were baptized into his death?" It certainly is not for lack of provision that Christians live defeated and ignominious lives. The provision is both actual and ample. Our defeat lies largely in our ignorance of the facts. There is available in Christ the power of a great life. That power is not the result of imitation. You can not avoid sinning by imitating Christ. There is no charm in repeating phrases. Even prayer itself is not enough. It is the appropriation of the divine provision and the application of this to the actual problem of sin in our lives.

The ensuing argument against a habitual life of sin and toward a life of conquest, as found in this section from verses three through fourteen, is grouped around three significant phrases. These words comprise a threefold secret of victorious living.

(1) *"Know ye."* Verses 3-10.

"Know ye not, that so many of us as were baptized into Jesus Christ were baptized into his death? Therefore we are buried with him by baptism into death: that like as Christ was raised up from the dead by the glory of the Father, even so we also should walk in newness of life. For if we have been planted together in the likeness of his death, we shall be also in the likeness of his resurrection:

Knowing this, that our old man is crucified with him, that the body of sin might be destroyed, that henceforth we should not serve sin. For he that is dead is freed from sin. Now if we be dead with Christ, we believe that we shall also live with him: Knowing that Christ being raised from the dead dieth no more; death hath no more dominion over him. For in that he died, he died unto sin once: but in that he liveth, he liveth unto God."

God blesses knowledge. We cannot remember any place where He either blesses or uses ignorance. We do not know that God even excuses ignorance. It is particularly so when it concerns success in life. And here, where it deals with the conquest of sin, it begins with knowledge. We must know certain things and then intelligently act upon those things. But remember, this is not a cold-blooded adventure in intellectuality. It is facts plus faith. It is a spiritual venture.

The reason that knowledge is required is because we are dealing with that phase of the Christian life which is its most practical demonstration. The Christian life is Christ's life in a Christian. As He came to "put away sin by the sacrifice of Himself," so we are to put down sin by the surrender of ourself to the laws of this new life.

Having declared that, "we are dead," Paul now proceeds to show what that death is and what it means. And he does so by explaining the significance of Christian baptism. Three things are called to your attention:

a. Baptism is a form of death. Verse 3.

It must be plain that baptism is a form. It is not in itself a means of salvation. It is a previous faith which saves. It is not our death that is set forth in the form of baptism, but Christ's death which alone is the means of our salvation. Baptism is a means of my identification with Christ's death through confession.

The water of baptism is an emblem of death and, of course, Christ's death. To be baptized means that we are united with the death of Christ. It means that when He died we died. Since He died for sin, we consequently died unto sin. Therefore, we are spiritually dead to any claims sin may have on us. We are spiritually dead to any necessity to sin.

Christ died not only to destroy the penalty of past sin but to cancel the power of present sin. Therefore, when we know this, we know at least one great reason why we should not and need not continue in sin.

b. Baptism is a form of burial. Verse 4.

Entombment always follows death because death produces corruption and corruption must be put away. Thus, the burial symbolized the entombment of the corruption and all the fruits of human sinfulness. Mind you, not Christ's corruption, for since He died our death it was our corruption which was thus symbolically buried and put away. Therefore, to be buried with Him signifies the putting away and the covering up of the fruits and consequences of sin. In that case, we have no valid reason to show those fruits of sin in our lives for our entombment with Christ has buried and locked sin up in a grave of death.

c. Baptism is a form of resurrection. Verses 4, 5.

In none of this is there anything said of a physical resurrection. It is dealing with the significance of baptism as regards the believer's spiritual life in relation to the matter of sin.

The connection here is very definite and explicit. It

is "like as Christ . . . so we also." As the resurrection of Christ brought release from the confinement of death and led into a new and wider experience of life, so our identification with Him should lead us to "walk in newness of life." This is revolutionary. It is not trying to humanly live a divine life but the exact opposite. It is to divinely live a human life. In our relation to Christ through His death and resurrection we partake of His divine life and walk in its newness and strength and power.

We cannot stress the idea of "newness of life" too much. It is not our old life that we live in a new man. It is Christ's life that is lived through us. It gives us a new view of life and a new purpose in life. It gives new ideas and new ideals. It gives us new joys and new experiences. It expands the whole horizon of living until it stretches its curtain to the bounds of infinity. It gives us a new understanding of God and a new appreciation of His handiwork.

Paul argues on the basis of an "if." "If" on the one hand "we were planted in the likeness of His death," then on the other hand, it is a guarantee that "we shall be also in the likeness of His resurrection." And this, remember, is a spiritual resurrection and not a physical one. It has to do with conquest over sin. It has to do with triumph in ordinary everyday life. It is a new era in human life. It is a new venture in living. It is a new plane of experience. We are not on the sin side but the salvation side. We are not on the corruption side but the conquest side.

All of this goes back to Christ's death. Because He died, we died with Him. Because His death was vicarious, our life is to be victorious.

Up to this point the apostle has been reviewing an event. With Christ it was an event of fact; the fact of His actual death, burial and resurrection. With us it was an event of faith, through baptism in which we saw portrayed our identification with this death, burial and resurrection. Now we are to see the effect of this event. Paul goes on to say in verse six, "Knowing this." If knowledge is to be the first phase of a victorious life, then we have it. The effect of knowledge should then be seen in our attitude to our sin problem. The effect is to be seen in at least one great consideration. It is found in verse six and it is this, "henceforth we should not serve sin."

Sin in its natural state is a master. It makes servants and slaves out of those whom it controls. Think for a moment of the many ways in which sin makes men its slaves. The liquor addict is a slave to appetite. The smoker is a slave to habit. The gambler is a slave to the lure of money. But this is not the whole story. The mastery of sin is not merely seen in the addicts for it is found not only in sins of the flesh but also of the disposition. It controls and shackles men's minds and desires in every phase of life. If we could release all men of all the world instantaneously from the enslaving power of sin, we would bring this world into an immediate state and condition of beauty and perfection.

There are several reasons why we should not serve sin.

*"Our old man is crucified"* (Verse 6). This means that the seat or place of sin's residence has been crucified. This is our old nature. It has had a crucifixion. Christ died not only for what we do but for

what we are. He died not only for our sins but our sinfulness. Thus, He removed all good cause why we should give expression to sin through ourselves. When we say that our old nature has been crucified, it does not mean obliterated, for then we would have neither feeling nor understanding. You could not destroy the old nature, without destroying the man. It means its legal crucifixion. It means that all the previous rights sin had for dominating and commanding us are cancelled and gone. We can now in our new nature stand up and denounce and defy our old nature. We can now in our new nature deny the expressions of sin in our old nature. We can now in our new nature command sin to be gone in our old nature. We can do this because the Master of our new nature is the Conqueror of the master of our old nature. And so we should remember that essentially it is not the question of mastery, but the Master. It is not the question of sanctification but the Sanctifier. It is not the question of victory but the Victor. It is not the question of our new experience, but a new existence.

It speaks here of two items of man's being that should be clarified. It speaks of "the old man" and "the body of sin." One refers to our old spiritual nature while the other to our physical body. One is the source of our sinfulness while the other is the place where sin operates. Sin originates in our Adamic nature and operates in our physical body. It is first psychic and then physical. It employs our intellect, our feelings and our physical members in its service. It controls and masters the physical. But since the old nature has been crucified, the use of the body as the servant of sin has been cancelled. If we know this and practice it we have the first secret of sin's conquest.

*We are "freed from sin"* (Verse 7). This means that sin has no claims upon a dead man. This is so in ordinary life, why should it not be so in personal life? The claims of money are invalid against a dead man. The moment a man dies, he is freed from all his financial obligations. He may owe millions but no debt-collector can reach him in the state of death. The claims of the law are invalid, against a dead man. Death puts him beyond the jurisdiction of the law. The law may guard its man with jealous care before the execution, but it has not a bit of interest in him after he is dead. The claims of war are invalid against a dead man. The summons to war may come to a dead man's house but it cannot affect him for he is beyond its reach.

It is exactly so in regard to the claims of sin. When we are dead to it, the claims of sin are invalid against us. We have been released from all previous obligations to it. We have been freed from all its claims. Because we are dead to it, there is no living reason why we should continue in it.

*"We shall also live"* (Verse 8). Just what difference does this make? It is the difference between knowledge and ignorance. Knowledge is power if acted upon.

In Christ's career, life was the consequence of death. It was not as it is usually that death is the consequence of life. What was true of Christ is to be true of the Christian. Life is to be the consequence of our death with Christ. This life holds new powers and new possibilities.

You will be careful to notice that it is death "with Christ" and life "with Him." Because of death, there can be life. This is the new order of Christian experience. The old order was—because there is life there was death. Now it is reversed. This indicates a new relationship. It is that of union with Christ. Physically our union was with Adam and all the handicapping consequences of such life. Spiritually, our union is with Christ and all the emancipating consequences of His life.

This union is an organic union. It is a union produced by birth. It is united by a new species of life. It does not rest on artificial relationships. It has nothing to do with racial priorities. It is not sponsored by ecclesiastical orders. It is as binding and as real as that between God and Christ. This means a magnificent flow of power and life into our soul from His. It is a new source of supply for living. We are no longer subject to Satan's blockades and embargoes. The straitness of the circumstance cannot cramp the breadth of our experience. Happiness is not bound up with happenings. Life is as expansive and as generous and as glorious as God because we are united with Him by the life-link of the new birth.

This is expanded further in verses nine and ten. "Knowing that Christ being raised from the dead dieth no more; death hath no more dominion over him. For in that he died, he died unto sin once; but in that he liveth, he liveth unto God."

The extent of the argument is this, because Christ died for one reason He now lives for another reason. The purpose of His dying is finished. It shall never occur again. But the purpose of His living goes on and on and on, lengthening forever into the never ceasing ages of eternity. Consequently, since we are united to Him, we have a new purpose in life. Because He died for sin, we should be dead to it. Because He lives for God we should live for Him.

What does it mean to "live unto God?" A lot of meanings are assigned to it. To some it means to perform certain religious exercises, to follow certain prescribed rules and to live in certain so-called holy precincts. But is this what it actually means? We cannot all leave the normal pursuits of life, forsake our families, and leave our occupations. Is it possible that we can "live unto God" under these profane circumstances? Indeed it is, for this is the very place where we are expected to live. The theatre of Christian living is to be at home and not in the temple. Jesus said to the man healed of demons, "Return to thine own house, and show how great things God hath done unto thee." We have gone off to church to find God and finding Him, left Him there. Let us take Him home with us.

When they were building the great Temple of Solomon and many men of Israel were away in the forests of Lebanon, a regulation was passed by the King in which it was declared that "a month they were in Lebanon, and two months at home" (I Kings 5:14). In the duties that men were to perform in the matter of labor, God took care to see that the home should not be neglected.

In thinking of what it means to "live unto God," let us not get the idea that such living and such service are what we term strictly religious service. By that we mean professional religious service. It is service in keeping the house, caring for the children or running the store. Sir Wilfred Grenfell said: "You can grow potatoes for the love of God just as well as you can preach a sermon." Let us put that idea to work each day. Take some duty you have and make it sacred by doing it for God.

Now we pass on to the second phase of the principles of success in victorious Christian living.

(2) *"Reckon ye."* Verse 11.

"Likewise reckon ye also yourselves to be dead indeed unto sin, but alive unto God through Jesus Christ our Lord."

The first part is information. This second part is calculation. The knowledge we possess is now to become the basis of definite and decisive action. That action is first to be an attitude of mind and heart to the position we occupy as Christians.

The word "reckon," as used in the eleventh verse means "to take account." It is to be done in the same manner that an accountant will take account of the figures from which he gets his balance. By that balance he determines the exact status of his accounts and from those accounts, the condition of his business. In the greatest business of all—the business of life— we, too, need "to take account." Add up the figures found in the ledger of life, strike a balance and if the figures and the sums are right, then life will be "dead indeed unto sin."

In this case the figures are the things that have been said about the Christian's union with Christ. In that union he is "dead to sin." He has been buried and raised up to "walk in newness of life." He "should not serve sin." He is "freed from sin." He should "live unto God." Add these up, and the sum of their truth will give conviction and occasion for a victorious life. Let him "reckon" this to be so and he has all the rights of spiritual mathematics to live a new and better life.

Let us examine this reckoning in some detail. It tells us here that we are to reckon or "take account" of two things.

　　a. That we are dead to sin.

We are to conclude to be true in us what God has declared to be true about us. His declaration is very plain. It goes back to Christ's atonement for our sin. In that atonement Christ died and we were seen to have died with Him. We died unto the sin for which He died. Therefore, the necessity of submitting to it is gone.

Be sure to notice that God does not ask us to reckon with sin. He does not ask us to conquer sin. He has already reckoned with sin. He did that in His Son on Calvary. He has already conquered sin. The thing God is asking us to do is to reckon with ourselves as regards our relation and attitude to sin. We are to consider ourselves "dead." We are to consider it so because it is so. It is a fact with God; it must now become a fact with us.

Reckoning is not acting as if it were so. It is acting because it is so. You see what a great difference there is between reckoning as if and reckoning because. One is a false optimism. The other is considering and acting on the facts. Let us act on the facts; and the facts are these that we are "dead indeed unto sin."

　　b. That we are alive unto God.

Being dead is only half the story. If this were all; it would only be half enough. The other fact is that we are living in a new and triumphant sphere of life, for God has seen to our spiritual resurrection in which we are "to walk in newness of life."

Our victory is not alone in our deadness to sin but in our aliveness to God. The death to sin is negative while the life in God is positive. The one removes penalty, while the other gives power. And when we consider this to be true, we will have all the necessary enablement for this new and better life.

Remember that strength and power always lie in the realm of life. Flowers open toward the sun, but only one follows the sun continually. That flower is the sunflower. Be like it by keeping the Source of life in constant view. Follow with faith the Son of righteousness and the shining blessings of His heart will be constantly yours.

Did it ever occur to you how this double reckoning of death and life would affect your life? When temptation comes, you say "I am dead" because a dead man is insensible to enticement and allurement. Temptation then cannot touch you. When injury comes, you say "I am dead" because you cannot injure a dead man. He is beyond feeling and injury and abuse and suffering. When insult is hurled at you, you say "I am dead." Look at your own death certificate. These things cannot reach you nor hurt you. A dead man, does not exhibit a bad temper that runs amuck over others' feelings. He does not have vindictive or recriminating motives. He does not quarrel or fuss. He does not respond to the desires of an evil solicitor.

To one who asked him the secret of his distinguished service for Christ, George Muller, replied: "There was a day when I died, utterly died." And as he spoke he bent lower, until he almost touched the floor. "Died to George Muller, his opinions, preferences, tastes, and will; died to the world, its approval and censure; died to the approval or blame even of my brethren and friends; and since then I have studied only to show myself approved unto God."

But considering all this to be true, so undeniably true, it is still a fact that dead men are negative. They do not respond to temptation or pride, nor employ vindictive motives. But that is not enough. Dead men do not bless the world. Dead men do not fill the world with cheer and song and love. Dead men do not become our missionaries and agents of mercy. They are not the heroes of faith. It is only when we realize our heritage of life and power, and say, we are "alive unto God through Jesus Christ our Lord," that we become conspicuous in the qualities of character and service.

When duty lays some task in your hands, say "I am alive." When opportunity affords you the privilege of doing some good, say "I am alive." When faith presents a great challenge, say "I am alive." When God seeks your life for a channel of blessing to a sore smitten world, say "I am alive." When God desires to use your time or your talents or your money as instruments of grace, say "I am alive." You will become a world-winner if you step out on the strength of His life in your life.

We look now at the third phase of these principles of victorious living.

(3) *"Yield ye."* Verses 12-14.

"Let not sin therefore reign in your mortal body, that ye should obey it in the lusts thereof. Neither yield ye your members as instruments of unrighteousness unto sin: but yield yourselves unto God, as those that are alive from the dead, and your members as instruments of righteousness unto God. For sin shall not have dominion over you: for ye are not under the law, but under grace."

The first phase was *information,* "Know ye." The second phase was *calculation,* "Reckon you." The third phase is *regimentation,* "Yield ye." We are now to assemble and arrange all the faculties of soul, mind, and body for a holy use. We are not only to partake of Christ's life but also to participate in the Christian life.

There are two things that enter specifically into this phase of life. In verse 12 it speaks of "your body," and in verse 13 it speaks of "your members." We are to determine now what place our bodies are to play in the great drama of life. What use will we make of our bodies? Will they be temples or toys? Toys serve but a childish and transient purpose. They are later laid aside, battered and worn and unattractive. Is that what your body is to you? How empty and vain such a life! Temples are for the presence of God. They are made to hold communion with him; to be filled with music and to be dignified by worship. They are to be stately objects of beauty and the reminder among men of both the presence and power of God.

Every believer's body is to be used as a temple. So said Paul in I Corinthians 6:19, 20: "What? know ye not that your body is the temple of the Holy Ghost

which is in you, which ye have of God, and ye are not
your own? For ye are bought with a price: therefore
glorify God in your body, and in your spirit, which are
God's."

With this new view of our body we should take a
very positive attitude toward sin. If we knew it to be
an issue met by Christ, we must now deliberately
deny its supremacy in the realm of our body.

Sin is first spiritual, then mental and finally physical.
We see it in its most corrupting effect as a physical
indulgence. Its conquest is spiritual and its recognition is mental; now its denial must be physical. It
must not have the mastery in the lowest realm of life.

Let us say very vigorously at this point that we must
not temporize or tolerate that type of teaching that
says, "let God do it all." God, indeed, has done all
that is necessary but here is a very clear and definite
responsibility for man. It is specifically charged. "Let
not sin therefore reign in your mortal body." Who is
to deny it this rule? We are. It is our personal responsibility. Having been justified by the Lord's death
and united to the Lord's life, we should now use the
divine resources of grace for our personal lives. It is,
in simple terms, something we must do, because of
what God has done.

In facing this personal responsibility, let us remember that the denial of sin's rule is something more
than an act of will. It is, indeed an act of will based
upon a fact of faith. It is based upon Christ's conquest
of sin and our union with Christ. Recognizing this
fact, we should then rise to the high place of grace
in which we reside and deny sin's rule through our
physical desires.

But if this is to be done, how can it be accomplished? Notice verse 13, "Neither yield ye your members as instruments of unrighteousness unto sin: but yield yourselves unto God, as those that are alive from the dead, and your members as instruments of righteousness unto God."

*It is to be first, negative*—"Neither yield ye your members as instruments of unrighteousness unto sin." This is what we are not to do. It is to be a definite policy of our lives. It is to be done by our own will.

These "members" are our faculties. They are mental, emotional, and physical faculties. They are those qualities of body and mind with which we exercise and express life. They are the head to plan, the eyes to see, the ears to hear, the tongue to speak, the hands to act and the feet to carry. Since all of these have been both redeemed and regenerated, it is unfitting that they should be devoted to unrighteousness. They rightfully belong to God and therefore have no right to be employed in sin. Their use must now be as high and as holy as their redemption.

*It is to be second, positive*—"but yield yourselves unto God, as those that are alive from the dead, and your members as instruments of righteousness unto God."

If a Christian must have a righteous "no" in his vocabulary, he must also have a disposition to say "yes." He is not to passively "yield" his faculties to God. They are rather to be gladly "presented" to Him and placed at His disposal.

Man is so made that he must be mastered. He was not created to be his own master as an independent moral monarch. He was created to be mastered by God. But with sin's coming, he came under another master, sin. It is to be one or the other. This explains our hero worship, our ideologies, our dictators. Men will have their heroes and their masters. Let us recognize our need of mastery by God and "present ourselves to God."

This yielding or presenting must be done in one act that becomes a continuous act. It is not done once for all, but many times. In fact it must become a formula of life. It must be habitual and continual. It is the placing of one's life in the hands of a competent master and keeping it there. In such hands, the best interest of our lives will be fostered and developed and enlarged in keeping with His great power.

There comes now, in the order of these remarkable verses, a very positive and convincing statement. It is in verse 14, "For sin shall not have dominion over you: for ye are not under law, but under grace." Here is a consummate answer to the question we began with, "Shall we continue in sin that grace may abound?" It does not say that we will not, but it does imply that we need not. If you want it so, "sin shall not have dominion over you." If we say it will not, then it shall not. Why? Because of the strength of our will? No. Because it is God's will, "for ye are not under the law, but under grace."

The law prohibits sin but grace conquers sin. Therefore, because we are under grace, we may claim all the benefits of Christ's conquest and employ all the regenerated instruments of righteousness for a complete and glorious victory over sin.

There is a very splendid leaflet in print entitled, "Must Christians Sin?" It was written by the late Dr.

W. H. Griffith Thomas. In it he discusses three views about the relation of sin to a believer, and the believer to sin.

First, there is *Eradication*. It means that eradication or complete removal of the sinful principle within. This goes too far because it goes beyond Scripture. Sin is in no sense eradicated, for "if we say we have no sin, we deceive ourselves." The effect of Christ's death was to remove sin's penalty and to destroy sin's power in the sinner, but never to destroy sin. Sin is not dead, but the sinner is to be dead to sin.

The second view is *Suppression*. This means the inward suppression of desire and the constant inner struggle against sin's solicitation. This does not go far enough. Suppression is dangerous because it leads to serious and sometimes tragic complexes. Suppress steam and you have an explosion. It is so emotionally. The Scriptures do say, "neither yield ye," but they do not stop there, for they go on to say "but yield yourselves." It is not suppression against unrighteousness, but expression in righteousness that is the real secret of getting on in life. It is not our faculties which are wrong, but the use of them in the wrong way. We must, therefore, learn the right use of them.

The third view is *Counteraction*. This goes far enough and is the true view because it expresses the scriptural truth that "the law of the Spirit of life in Christ Jesus hath made me free from the law of sin and death" (Rom. 8:2). Here are two laws—one of life and one of death. The law of life counteracts the law of death.

The same thing is expressed in the sixth verse, "knowing this, that our old man is crucified with him, that the body of sin might be destroyed, that henceforth we should not serve sin." Here, destroyed means "to render inoperative." Sin is put out of operation. It has been robbed of its power. To recognize this, and to act on it is to bring into operation and action all the powerful forces of righteousness of this new law of "the spirit of life." And the success of it is not in the force of will, nor in the strength of mind, but in the new mastery of life through Jesus Christ. It is, therefore, not natural law, not legal law, but spiritual law. It is neither man nor Moses, but Christ. It is not law, but life. There is no more important truth to grasp that will so practically affect our lives and assist us in living life at its best than to thoroughly understand these principles of Christian victory.

A young man had set out to become a missionary. Someone called his attention to the dangers of the land to which he was going. It was suggested that he might die in the midst of such grave dangers. And to that suggestion, the young man bravely replied, "I died when I decided to go." To live demands death.

II. SHALL WE SIN BECAUSE WE ARE IN GRACE? Verses 15-23.

In verse 15 the question is asked, "What then? shall we sin, because we are not under the law, but under grace? God forbid." In answer we have the same two replies that we had to the previous question which was "shall we sin in order to obtain grace?" (Verse 1).

1. A Divine Protest. Verse 15.

"God forbid."

God protests again against sin. He abhors it and we should abhor it to the point that it should be absent from our conduct. We should abhor it, for "he that hath slight thoughts of sin never has great thoughts of God" (Owen).

Abhor what? Abhor murder, lying, thievery? It does not say that. It says that God forbids "sin." What is sin? What constitutes a sinful thought or act? What marks the line between right and wrong? Where in the Bible does it give a list of sins that we might avoid them? It would be quite convenient to have such a list, but God does not itemize sin. The only time God issued a list of sins was in the laws of Moses. Outside of a few references in the New Testament, including the Beatitudes and in Colossians, sins are not listed. The reason for this is because we are living under a higher law than the commandments. We are under the rule of grace. The law prohibits sin with "thou shalt not." Grace promotes righteousness with "thou shalt."

Susanna Wesley said this, "Whatever weakens your reason, impairs the tenderness of your conscience, obscures your sense of God, or takes off the relish of spiritual things, that is sin to you."

The Scripture says, "Whatsoever is not of faith is sin" (Rom. 14:23); "Therefore to him that knoweth to do good, and doeth it not, to him it is sin" (Jas. 4:17); "All unrighteousness is sin: and there is a sin not unto death" (I John 5:17); "And when he is come, he will reprove the world of sin, and of righteousness, and of judgment; Of sin because they believe not on me" (John 16:8, 9).

The judge of sin is the Holy Spirit who judges according to the principles of this book of standards, the Bible. Jesus said this about the Holy Spirit. "Nevertheless I tell you the truth; It is expedient for you that I go away: for if I go not away, the Comforter will not come unto you; but if I depart, I will send him unto you. And when he is come, he will reprove the world of sin, and of righteousness, and of judgment: Of sin, because they believe not on me; Of righteousness, because I go to my Father, and ye see me no more; Of judgment, because the prince of this world is judged" (John 16:7-11).

2. A Divine Proof. Verses 16-23.

Paul counters here as he does also in the first question asked in the first verse with a "Know ye not?" Sinning is, in the last reduction, a result of ignorance while victorious living is a matter of enlightenment. The proof of this is unfolded in what follows.

There is no reason why we should succumb to the inevitable dominion of sin. We should not assume that because we are under grace and not law that we have such an adequate provision for sinning that we can deliberately do what we will because of that grace. There are people, sad to say, who take such a position as this. Because they are not under law, they presume that grace gives them such broad powers of conduct that they can live as they like and do as they please, because grace will cover and meet anything they do. This is a form of what is technically known as antinomianism. It is unworthy of a true Christian. It is entirely unethical and extremely unchristian.

We are not commanded to blindly follow some precept. Paul substantiates every condition of the new life with a claim and a reason and he follows with five of them.

(1) *A new obedience.* Verse 16.

"Know ye not, that to whom ye yield yourselves servants to obey, his servants ye are to whom ye obey; whether of sin unto death, or of obedience unto righteousness?"

If any think that they can sin with impunity, let them remember that sin never leads to benevolent results. If we sin, we become sin's servants and sin becomes our master. The effect of sin is slavery. We become the moral subjects of our deeds and thoughts. We cannot live in a world of righteousness and a world of unrighteousness at the same time. For this reason, everyone should immediately renounce sin as a policy of life. Not only that, but remember that it can be overcome and completely met in the divine provisions of Christ.

Most people deal with the problem of sin outside, at the place of its commission; whereas we ought to deal with it inside, at the place of its temptation. We should also remember that the most complete enslavements of sin begin with small and little matters.

Here is a good thing to remember, "If Christ is on the throne, self is on the cross. If self is on the throne, Christ is on the cross." The dominion of life cannot be held by things inimical to each other. Holiness is as much the proper atmosphere of Christianity as clean air is of the body.

In the midst of our struggle to win earth's prizes and places, let us remember that we dare not temporize with sin. We dare not stoop to questionable tricks. It is better to lose fairly than to win unfairly. Perhaps you think that it does not matter because you are in such an obscure place that no one is observing you. If man does not, remember, God does. But, observed or unobserved, you have your own conscience and your own responsibility before God.

Someone was once asked this question, "What argument convinced you of the value of character?" The answer was this, "The life of one who never knew that I was watching him." And although we may not be under law and regulation, our greatest incentive to live clean and straight is grace.

(2) *A new influence.* Verse 17.

"But God be thanked, that ye were the servants of sin, but ye have obeyed from the heart that form of doctrine which was delivered you."

Here were people whose lives were marked by a great sincerity. They had been people in sin. But what they once were they were no longer. They "obeyed from the heart." Their conduct originated from within. It did not depend upon their circumstances but rather on their character.

But this was not all that was true of these people. There was a new pattern for their lives. It was a form or rather mould of truth. The truth of the gospel not only saves but it also shapes. It shapes and moulds character. The doctrine of the Bible, which is the thing most certainly meant here, is, as declared, a "form." It is like a mould into which moulten metal is poured so as to take the shape of the mould. If that is so, then the truth of the gospel has definitely determined proportions. It is not something which changes with the latest theory of psychology or the latest discovery of science. It is, instead, a body of truth which is unchangeable. It is of a definite form and cast. It influences life; life does not influence it. It changes men; men do not change it. It determines destiny; destiny does not determine it.

What a beneficent effect it would have upon our badly battered twentieth century civilization if we brought out this mighty mould of character and allowed ourselves to be melted and poured into its conforming shape.

(3) *A new freedom.* Verse 18.

"Being then made free from sin, ye became the servants of righteousness."

We are carried back to our soul's liberation from sin's legal claims upon us. We have been emancipated. It is our heritage as well as our privilege to live free of its bondage.

(4) *A new service.* Verses 19, 20.

"I speak after the manner of men because of the infirmity of your flesh: for as ye have yielded your members servants to uncleanness and to inquity unto iniquity; even so now yield your members servants to righteousness unto holiness. For when ye were the servants of sin, ye were free from righteousness."

Once service and obedience was to the old master. It controlled life from thought to deed with an inexorable and unbending dominion. Once it was a life from one iniquity to another. Sin always leads to consequences. The consequences of one sin is another sin.

But now a new service employs our faculties. It is to lead from righteousness to holiness. The new Master leads to a new employment. And what a change of employment it is! No longer using the mind as the planning place of evil. No longer using the emotions for response to the unlovely. No longer using the will as the executive of sin. But all of these things used now to plan and execute righteousness. What a new service this is indeed!

(5) *A new incentive.* Verses 21-23.

"What fruit had ye then in those things whereof ye are now ashamed? for the end of those things is death. But now being made free from sin, and become servants to God, ye have your fruit unto holiness, and the end everlasting life. For the wages of sin is death; but the gift of God is eternal life through Jesus Christ our Lord."

The test of a tree is in the fruit. It is not only the kind of fruit, as far as the species is concerned, but it is the quality of the fruit. Lives, too, have their fruit. Once in sin, it was fruit that resulted in death. It was corrupting and revolting. Now it is fruit of the essence of the new life. It yields holy and beautiful effects. It nourishes and inspires. It contributes to the blessing of the world.

If there is any incentive that we need, other than the considerations presented, it is found in the contrast of the last verse. "For the wages of sin is death; but the gift of God is eternal life through Jesus Christ our Lord." This is an appeal primarily to Christians. It is an effort to lay before us the contrasting effects of sin in the life and God in the life. Sin pays a "wage." Here it is a military term indicating the wage paid a soldier and in keeping with the previous description of the militarizing effect of sin's dominion. But, on the other hand, God has a "gift." It is the gift of eternal life. This gift results from our union with Christ.

Here is our answer completed. It answers the inquiry about sin. And the summary of what has been said is this. A Christian not only should not sin, but he need not sin if he places himself under the control and under the influence of divine grace.

# 9

## THE DEFEATED MAN
### *Romans 7:1–25*

WE HAVE before us, in this chapter, a self-painted portrait of Paul in which all may behold a similar likeness to themselves. This is an autobiographical account of Paul's personal experiences and relates in unmistakable language the story of his own personal struggle.

Paul's struggle was not a contest with his environment but with himself. At the conclusion he records this verdict. "O wretched man that I am! who shall deliver me from the body of this death?"

Paul's contest reminds us that men and women may be materially prosperous and spiritually poor. They may be physically strong and spiritually weak. They may be material successes and moral failures. They may win in every battle except the most important one. How often history has recorded the story of great monarchs who have been sovereigns and despots over large empires who have been unable to rule themselves! It was Paul's story and it may be ours.

These two chapters, namely seven and eight, answer a great question. That question has passed the minds of most of us sometime in life. It is this, "Is life worth living?" In chapter seven there is to be seen life's futility. It is defeated and beaten and battered and inglorious and as such not much worth the living. But in chapter eight it is different. Here life's secret has been found and with it the worthwhileness of life.

Is life worth living? Of course it is when one has health, wealth, friends, pleasure, and useful occupations. Then every prospect is bright and life is very attractive. But you may say that it is not worth living when one is sick, poor, handicapped, unemployed, and alone. It is not worth living when the next day is an uncertainty. It is not worth living when your friends are gone, when your family is gone, when you have been treacherously treated and when people have been unfair and made you the victim of their dishonest schemes.

But, even under these unhappy circumstances, there is a life that is worth living. When life holds no better prospect than can be told by material and physical accounts, then it is not much worthwhile. If we must depend upon fate, then it is not worth the next breath. But there is a life, beyond the dire descriptions of our sadness, that is worth living. That life is the one Paul describes in the eighth chapter. But in order to lead into its precincts, you must be stripped of every false pretense and confidence. It is not necessary to live as life is described in chapter seven, but if any disregard life's laws of victory, he has but to see this portrait of the defeated man to see the consequences of such a life.

Life is *worth living* if you will find that life which is *worthwhile*. This worthwhile life is the life of Christ and is available to all on the simple, yet sufficient, terms of faith.

At the conclusion of a nation-wide broadcast, the narrator spoke of his sponsor's great scientific achievements. He told of the scientist's ceaseless efforts to improve the old and create the new. He concluded with a statement something like this: "It may be that the scientist's way of discovery is to be the way of life for all. His way is the calm and reasoning way and it may lead all men into a better life." Is the scientist's way, after all, to be the way to worthwhile living? We are indebted to the scientist for many wonders of invention. He can do miracles for our circumstances, but not until he can do something for our characters can he do anything for life. Conveniences never improve conscience.

Indeed, it is not the scientist's way of life, nor the philosopher's way, nor the historian's way, nor the educator's way. The best way of life is the Christian's way. Jesus said, "I am come that ye might have life and that ye might have it more abundantly." Here is life worth living.

But now, for the moment, we look into the face of a wretched, unhappy defeated man. Why is he like that? Unhappiness is of the essence of sin. The kind of unhappiness that is confessed here by Paul is not merely that which is emotional, or social or economic. It is the essence of all unhappiness because it is spiritual unhappiness. Here is a man who cries out against the heinousness of sin, and the helplessness of self to deal with that sin.

The two great enemies of human welfare are the direct fruits of sin. One is death and the other is unhappiness. Death is the penalty for sin while unhappiness is the product of sin.

What would be the state of life if man had not sinned? Its fruits would not be borne. That means that neither death nor unhappiness would exist. On the Mount of Transfiguration, Jesus was transformed before his three disciples. In that moment He was the pattern of the consummation of every life, had man not sinned. We would never know an open grave. Death would be a process of transformation instead of corruption. It would be an instantaneous metamorphosis from the earthly to the heavenly. Instead of the cruel and painful bludgeonings of disease until death seized a pain-wracked body, it would be like an evening guest. When life was complete and our cup of earthly experience was full, and the last lesson learned, we would see the beckoning hand of God and in the gathering twilight the clouds would open and we would walk up to God on the star-lit stairs of the air. Our metamorphosis would drop the drapery of flesh and the spirit would be clothed in a vesture like unto His glorious body. That is what death would be like without sin.

Like death, unhappiness would not be here except for sinfulness. The happiness of the original man was not in his perfect circumstances. He was perfectly happy because he was perfectly sinless. His happiness distilled out of his heart and came from his fellowship with God.

The admitted and coveted goals of modern science are toward the betterment of life. We hope not only to postpone death, but to prohibit it. We have in existence a National Life Extension Institute. It publishes a book entitled, "How to Live and Add Ten Years to Your Life." But even so, life extension faces life extinction and it will ever be so as long as there is sin.

How can we become a happy people? There are first to be considered in this seventh chapter the facts of futility. Here is a man who tried and exhausted all other means of becoming happy. They led him to a cry of despair, "O wretched man that I am! who shall deliver me from the body of this death?"

Out in the forest and the field you will discover that whatever handicap there may come to its denizens, the Creator has given compensatory assistance to overcome it. Here, for example, is the snow-white deer, very rare, of course. It is an object of exquisite beauty. Yet its beauty makes it an object of pursuit. But this beautiful animal, feeling itself conspicuous by its color and beauty, develops amazing ability to take care of itself, and, as a consequence, is rarely seen and scarcely ever taken by a hunter. Then we know the more familiar cases of birds and beasts which are protected by coats of fur and feather which conform to their natural surroundings so perfectly that they can scarcely be seen. The natural world has compensations for its handicaps. But there is no compensation in the spiritual world adequate for the handicap of sin. There is no natural conquest of it. It comes only by a supernatural provision for it. And so, there is set before us the contrasts of life in these two chapters. In chapter seven it is law, while in chapter eight it is Christ. And, in consequence, in the one chapter it is defeat, while in the other it is victory.

If you will earnestly determine to know the simple truth and the truthful facts of these chapters, you will enjoy the priceless experience of living life at its best. It will become eminently worthwhile.

Here is a good rule for solving problems. First, find the facts. Second, face the facts. Third, follow the facts. The facts of life are here. Let us find them, face them, and then follow them.

I. FACING THE LAW. Verses 1-13.

Paul recounts his efforts to find a means of conquest in life. He searches everywhere and tries everything. Because he was a learned Jew, he knew the law. He writes now of the law in relation to three things:

1. The Law and Death. Verses 1-3.

"Know ye not, brethren, (for I speak to them that know the law,) how that the law hath dominion over a man as long as he liveth? For the woman which hath a husband is bound by the law to her husband so long as he liveth; but if the husband be dead, she is loosed from the law of her husband. So then if, while her husband liveth, she be married to another man, she shall be called an adulteress: but if her husband be dead, she is free from that law; so that she is no adulteress, though she be married to another man."

He uses an illustration to expound his point. The point is that in Christ the believer is free from the law. But while he is free from the law, he is not free to commit lawlessness.

He cites a case of marriage. So long as a woman is married and her husband lives, she is bound by her own vows and the laws of the state to that husband. There is a singleness of union here that is subject to but one sundering, that of death. When death comes and the husband is removed, then the wife is free. In like manner, all who were under the old order before the Cross were bound to the law. But now in Christ we are considered as having died and therefore are dead to the law and in consequence freed from its sphere of dominion.

This passage is not dealing primarily with the subject of divorce. This is merely an illustration and is not therefore the Scriptures' chief pronouncement on the subject of marriage and divorce. It does not principally teach the union of marriage, but the believer's new union of life with Christ. The burden of the passage is to point out that so far as the believer is concerned, the law has now no dominion over him. He is, in fact, "not under law but under grace."

Paul experienced the law's inability to aid him. In the midst of his great struggle for personal purity and personal victory, he found the law helpless. It could condemn but not convert. It could pronounce but not rescue. And so he assures himself, and all other believers with him, that so far as the legal aspects of the law are concerned, he has no obligations to it. But when we say that, pause for a solemn consideration. The person who glories because he is not under law cannot glory in a life of lawlessness. Not to be under law is not to be without law, for we are under a higher law.

It is forever true that liberty lives by law. Liberty would cease in America if the law were suspended. The suspension of statutory law in Russia and Germany robbed their peoples of liberty. And so to preserve liberty, we must act within the sphere of law. But what law is the sphere of the Christian life? It is definitely stated that the Christian sphere is "not

under the law but under grace." And if we are to
attain to a rich place of both experience and expression
in Christian life, we must act within the sphere of the
law of our new life which is grace.

2. The Law and Christ. Verses 4-6.

> "Wherefore, my brethren, ye also are become
> dead to the law by the body of Christ; that ye
> should be married to another, even to him who is
> raised from the dead, that we should bring forth
> fruit unto God. For when we were in the flesh,
> the motions of sins, which were by the law, did
> work in our members to bring forth fruit unto
> death. But now we are delivered from the law,
> that being dead wherein we were held; that we
> should serve in newness of spirit, and not in the
> oldness of the letter."

The Christian is not relieved of moral restraint and
responsibility because he is not under the law. Instead, there is released unto him the power and
dominion of a new life. That life is in Christ and
through Him it is in us. Christ's death releases us
from the law, in order that we might join and enjoy
a higher and a loftier union of life.

If death released us from one union, it also unites us
in another. This new union is with Christ and it
has a twofold characteristic according to this fourth
verse.

(1) _It is a union of life_—"even to Him who is raised
from the dead."

Here is the secret of the strength of the Christian
life. It is a union with life. This union is not artificial
but like any life-union it must be organic. The most
skillful occulist in the world could not unite an eye to

my body. Eyes must be born. And a life-union to Christ is a birth union.

(2) *It is a union of fruit*—"that we should bring forth fruit unto God."

If the chief function of the law was to pronounce, we see that the chief function of life is to produce. It is to produce fruit and the fruit is of the nature of the life. Since it is God's life in us, it is godly fruit through us. What a new dignity this lends to life! Pause here a moment. It says "fruit unto God." It is a harvest of high and holy fruits. It is a practical and productive life. It is not consumption but contribution. God help us to see that in true Christianity the flow of life into us from God becomes a flow of life from us for God. Here is something to challenge complacent Christians. Christianity is not a sop to keep people quiet. It is dynamite to blast them loose from their prejudices, their weaknesses, their besetting sins, their unclean and unchristian habits, their petty selfishness and all the rest of the things that enchain their lives to mediocrity and meanness.

The continuing condition of life under grace is that of both sanctity and service. If the law demanded sanctity, it is much more true in grace. It is not now the question of restraint from doing the wrong thing, but freedom and desire to do the right thing. There are some things one will not do as a Christian. It is not because there is a law against them, but because the spirit of a new life calls us to better things. There is a sense in which one has a perfect right to do anything he pleases, except, of course, the specified items of the Commandments. But there are some things he no longer wishes to do or desires to do or cares to do.

While "all things are lawful for me, all things are not expedient." The judge of lawfulness and expediency is not "the oldness of the letter," but rather "the newness of the spirit." He now has a new arbiter over his actions. It is the Holy Spirit who, it was promised, would guide into all truth and, in consequence of that truth, into fitting conduct.

But it is not only sanctity that grace demands. It is service as well. Service means consecration. If God has your heart, He will have everything else and the secret of the power of a great Christian life is its yielded heart. If the heart is yielded, so also will be the hands, feet, mouth, eyes, mind, emotions, and will. If it is anything, it must be everything.

3. The Law and Sin. Verses 7-13.

The question of verse 7—"What shall we say then? Is the law sin?" is drawn from a condition previously described as Paul's personal experience with the law in which he says, "For when we were in the flesh, the motions of sins, which were by the law, did work in our members to bring forth fruit unto death" (verse 5). This might lead some to conclude that sin was the effect of the law and, therefore, the law being the author of sin was itself sinful.

But the general answer found in the ensuing verses is to the effect that the law is not the author of sin; it acted only as the arbiter, the umpire, for the sinner.

Dr. W. Griffith Thomas points out six things here.

(1) *The law reveals the fact of sin.* Verse 7.

"What shall we say then? Is the law sin? God forbid. Nay, I had not known sin, but by the law: for I had not known lust, except the law had said, Thou shalt not covet."

The purpose of the law was not to make things sinful, but when in the course of desire and deed, someone under the law committed an act of sin, the law made that act of sin apparent and abhorrent. It did not make it sinful, but it did make it understood as sinful. Sin was sinful before the law as it is since the law. But with it (the law) in force, it accentuated its sinfulness.

(2) *The law reveals the occasion of sin.* Verse 8.

"But sin, taking occasion by the commandment, wrought in me all manner of concupiscence. For without the law sin was dead."

This does not mean that the law brought sin or created sin. Its function and province was to make up the sense of its sinfulness in the conscience of the sinner. In this way the law's primary office was toward the sinner. It served the sinner by increasing in him his sense of sin.

(3) *The law reveals the power of sin.* Verse 9.

"For I was alive without the law once: but when the commandment came, sin revived, and I died."

There was a time in Paul's life when the full force of the commandment became apparent to Paul. In that moment it revealed to him the power of the evil which was inherent in him. But while this law had legal-power to convict of sin, it had no life-power to deliver from sin. And in that state of despair, Paul found himself as a man already dead. He was doomed by the law's verdict, totally bereft of power to help himself and certainly without peace of heart and mind.

(4) *The law reveals the effect of sin.* Verse 10.

"And the commandment, which was ordained to life, I found to be unto death."

The effect of sin was death. This was not necessarily the effect of law, for death was in the world before the law was given. What the law did was to legalize a natural consequence.

(5) *The law reveals the deception of sin.* Verse 11.

"For sin, taking occasion by the commandment, deceived me, and by it slew me."

Sin is life's most beguiling deceit. It deceives us into thinking wrongly about God. We assume that He will condone sin. It deceives us into thinking wrongly about ourselves. We assume that we can sin with impunity. It deceives us into thinking wrongly about itself. We assume that sin is enjoyable and pleasurable and that its indulgence holds the promise of satisfaction and delight. But that is not so.

(6) *The law reveals the sinfulness of sin.* Verses 12, 13.

"Wherefore the law is holy, and the commandment holy, and just, and good. Was then that which is good made death unto me? God forbid. But sin, that it might appear sin, working death in me by that which is good; that sin by the commandment might become exceeding sinful."

Here is the ultimate end and, in a proper sense, the purpose of the law. It is the exposure of sin. By the exposure of sin in the conduct of the sinner it, of course, must necessarily impose a penalty upon the sinner. But the imposition of that penalty is not the chief purpose of the law. It is to protect the person who conscientiously abides under the jurisdiction of the law. The exposure of the law-breaker is the protection of the law-abiding citizen. When the law did this, it proved the sinfulness of human nature as well as the heinousness of sin. And so in any case the law and the commandment served a good and holy purpose. That purpose being to prove the spiritual deadness of the sinner and to reveal his need of salvation and assistance.

None of us are in Paul's particular case. We are not as he was, living under the jurisdiction of the law. What is there that will awaken in us a sense of sin and an appreciation of need? We go back to a previous statement to say that while the law is not now the active arbiter over our conscience, there is one nevertheless. It is the person of the Holy Spirit. To the believer, He is the *Comforter* while to the sinner, He is the *Convictor*. Of Him, Jesus said, "And when he is come, he will reprove (convince) the world of sin" (John 16:8). His mission is one of conviction in respect to sin. It is one of the sad facts of life that we are so busy pursuing our physical objectives that we pay scant heed to the Holy Spirit. Fame and ease and personal preference cause us to be insensible to our perils and dangers.

II. FACING ONE'S SELF. Verses 14-25.

We are about to see a man in the midst of a titanic struggle to become what he ought to be. We are to see his desperate and sincere efforts extended to the very limits of human endurance. We are to see a man straining every nerve and fibre of his body and every capacity of his soul in this supreme struggle. But at the end we will hear this same man crying out, "O wretched man that I am! who shall deliver me?" He is bowed in defeat, but it was in that very defeat that he found his greatest hope, for in that defeat he found the one who holds the secret of conquest and victory for each of us, the Lord Jesus Christ.

As we read these verses, we observe a man's despairing efforts for self-conquest and self-control. We see a man struggling, not with his environment, but with himself. It is not the exterior that is his problem, but the interior. As we watch the struggle, we will probably ask ourself a question. Whose experience is being portrayed here? Is it the experience of an unregenerate man or is it the experience of a regenerate man? Obviously, it is Paul's experience, for we have an autobiographical sketch of the author. In that case, it cannot be the experience of an unregenerate man, even the man, Saul of Tarsus; for no unregenerate person would "delight in the law of God after the inward man" as is expressed in the twenty-second verse. If it is not the experience of an unregenerate person, neither is it the normal experience of a regenerate person. These struggles surely cannot express an ideal Christian experience, else where would be the benefits of Christianity?

If they are neither the normal experience of the unregenerate or the regenerate, then what are they? We have here the experience of a regenerate person not the normal or the ideal experience, mind you, but the experience of a believer who has forgotten both his own position and his Lord's power. In other words, it is the experience of a Christian out of character.

The secret of any normal Christian conquest is the indwelling, reigning, dominating, motivating, life of Christ through the resident Holy Spirit. In that case, the Christian does not act himself but Christ. We say, "be yourself." That is exactly what we must not be. Human philosophy and every current scheme of life-success urge us to be ourselves. But the Bible contrarily urges us to "be Christ." With the portrait of Romans three before us, who would want to be what we are? This is precisely what is wrong with the world. It is because men are being what they are that we have crime, war, greed, unhappiness, and unrest. Restraints of law, compromises by treaty, and all these artificial efforts will never do what the simple formula of the gospel will do. And yet witness the tragedy of lost opportunity in our churches. We are talking about church programs when what we need to exploit is a passion for life. It is not a program that the church needs at all; it is a passion.

But here is the case of a man who "acts out of character as a regenerate man." (Moule.) He has reverted to his former life and efforts. He is acting as if he did not know Christ. He is struggling as if he were a spiritual orphan. He has tried to meet the law on the basis of his own character. He is trying to meet temptation and desire and ambition in his own strength. He has stepped down from the spirit into the flesh. He has reverted from the spiritual to the natural. He has retreated from Christ to himself. And from this point on the dominant word is the personal pronoun, "I." You count it exactly twenty-six times from verse fourteen to twenty-five. Paul reverses what he later expresses in Galatians 2:20. There it is not I, but Christ, while here it is not Christ, but I. Such a life-policy can only end in ignominious and inglorious defeat, and the self-appointed title of "O wretched man that I am!"

The significance of Christianity is that it creates a new character by a new birth. The principles of victorious living teach us that a victorious person is one who lives in this new character. And in this new character we have two things: First—a spiritual position—we are now found "in Christ." Second—a spiritual power—Christ is now found in us.

If and when we reckon ourselves dead unto sin and alive unto Christ, and take knowledge of this position and power, and live in character, the conquest of life is but a routine matter. It is as normal to live in peace as it is normal to live in health, if we observe and obey the laws of hygiene.

But Paul tells us what happens when we step out of character and act, not as a spiritual Christian, but like a carnal Christian. He tells us what happens when we live down to our circumstances and not up to our character. He tells us what happens when we act ourselves instead of acting Christ. He tells us what happens when we try to be good without God. Here are the earnest, sincere, well-meaning, zealous, conscientious efforts of a believing man trying to be good by his own inherent efforts, but who is beaten back by indwelling sin. Never until we meet sin on the basis of Christ's conquest of it, will we ever defeat it. Never until we meet temptation on the basis of our spiritual position, as dead to sin and alive to God, will we ever conquer it. A Christian life has a new level, new weapons, new rules, new laws, new powers, and above everything else, a new Master. *Live what you are and you can become what you dare.* There is illimitable power and peace in a truly lived Christian life. There is not a single undefeated foe to face, be it death or sin. It is yours to command your way to power, peace, and personal supremacy.

Look now at this man living and acting out of character. He had faced the law and found it totally inadequate to assist him. In fact, he found that the law increased his guilt instead of lessening it. This was not the law's fault because it was not the law's purpose. The purpose of the law was to denounce sin and not to deliver from sin. Hence, it offered no way out but instead a deeper way into despair and defeat, for its standard showed him what he ought to be but could not help him become.

This, remember, does not lessen the prestige of the law nor cause us to assume that we can be lawless. To the contrary, the Christian has obligations of life far more binding and far superior to those of the law. But it does declare the fact that legalism, as such, is not the way out of personal defeat.

Paul says to himself, in substance, if the law cannot help me, then I can help myself. If I cannot be religiously perfect, then power and idealism and ambition and pride in myself will win the battle. And in a courageous spirit of self-confidence, which, to a great degree, one admires, for at least he was not a quitter, he faced sin arrayed in many forms of habits, propensities, desires, weaknesses, and ambitions. But he had not properly reckoned with his foe. He struck swords with the enemy without measuring him. And, what was more, he had not properly reckoned with or measured himself. He went to the battle with a false optimism. It was "I"—"I"—"I." And, at last, after blow upon blow and failure upon failure, he sees the hopelessness of his situation. He has the courage in the hour of defeat to face the issue. The issue is himself. He faces himself. What did he see?

1. He Saw a Man "Carnal." Verse 14.

> "For we know that the law is spiritual: but I am carnal. . ."

What does it mean to be carnal? This was Paul's experience and he was talking in the present tense, for he said, "I am." It was what he was as a Christian out of character.

There are two original words translated "carnal." One means "material," and the other "ethical." A carnal Christian is one descended from his high place of privilege to fight and live by material means—means which are perfectly ethical according to popular standards. They conform to the latest theories of psychology and religious education. And being this, they are good but not good enough. They are fine but not final.

To be carnal means to mind the flesh or in other words to give oneself to natural propensities. It means to think, feel, act, and desire what a soulish man desires, but not what a spiritual man cares for. There are soulish Christians and there are spiritual Christians. A soulish Christian may move in the realm of responsibility. He may not be vulgar or evil, but he is nevertheless prompted by such desires as bring him into a very limited place of experience. And further than this it is a place and sphere where he is openly vulnerable to attack and defeat. You cannot defeat Satan by culture. You cannot conquer sin by psychology. You cannot meet temptation with platitudes of philosophy. This is a realm where higher forces and powers must be brought into the battle and only a spiritual person has them at his command.

2. He Saw a Man "Sold." Verse 14.

". . . sold under sin."

How could this expression describe a Christian? In this way. As a carnal person, one is automatically released from the protections and powers of the victorious spiritual life and comes into instant bondage to sin and all its sinful consequences. He is like a slave and captive. As someone has put it, "In Adam we are sold in gross; in ourselves we are sold in retail."

Now while this is true, it is not to be considered as the normal Christian experience. That a Christian is delivered from the penalty of sin and need not live under the power of sin is normal Christianity. But reverting to a carnal and soulish life one may fall into sin's clutches and live far below his character level. In this state of life "sin is in the saint; that is his lamentation. But his soul is not in sin; this is his consolation."

Being both carnal and captive is to be in a place where one's best efforts are only self efforts. We are powerless to help ourselves and Christ is powerless to help us. It is because carnality is out of the sphere where the law of the spiritual life operates. It is not because Christianity has failed, but because we have failed. Peter walked on the water just as long as he looked at the Lord, but when he looked at the water he was out of the sphere of faith, and consequently in the sphere of failure.

3. He Saw a Man "Defeated." Verses 15-23.

We naturally should inquire why he was defeated. There is no reason to inquire at all unless we know reasons and causes so that we may be helped in our own lives. After all, the very purpose of our inquiry and the object of this book is information for better lives. Apart from this it is both a waste of effort and time.

Why was Paul a defeated man in spite of the expenditure of so much zeal and energy to win?

His defeat resulted from two things:

(1) *Indwelling sin.* Verses 15-20.

"For that which I do I allow not: for what I would, that do I not; but what I hate, that I do. If then I do that which I would not, I consent unto the law that it is good. Now then it is no more I that do it, but sin that dwelleth in me. For I know that in me (that is, in my flesh,) dwelleth no good thing: for to will is present with me; but how to perform that which is good I find not. For the good that I would I do not: but the evil which I would not, that I do. Now if I do that I would not, it is no more I that do it, but sin that dwelleth in me."

Twice it states in this section that evil is not the consequence of either the man's desire or intention, but rather "sin that dwelleth in me." (Verses 17, 20). Man was not the master of sin but sin was the master of man. It drove him with a relentless servitude. And remember that when we speak of sin in Paul it was not criminal sin but cultural sin. It was not a reprobate's sin but religious sin. Here was a great scholar and leader. But in spite of his training and position, he was a personal failure.

His confession includes a statement like this, "For that which I do I allow not: for what I would, that do I not; but what I hate, that do I. If then I do that which I would not, I consent unto the law that it is good" (Verses 15, 16). He is driven blindly and unknowingly to do the thing he does not wish to do and what he hates to do. And so he comes to the conclusion found in verse 17. "Now then it is no more I that do it, but sin that dwelleth in me." It was not only sin dwelling in him but sin ruling over him. Indwelling sin means outlived sinfulness.

This produces the discovery of the eighteenth verse, "For I know that in me (that is, in my flesh,) dwelleth no good thing: for to will is present with me; but how to perform that which is good I find not." Here "flesh" does not mean the physical nature but human nature. It is a reference to the natural condition of man's moral nature. While it does not mean that there are no good thoughts or good desires, it does mean that the power of accomplishing good is absent. There is the desire for good, but no strength to execute the deed, for he goes on to say, "For the good that I would I do not; but the evil which I would not, that I do."

We can best illustrate this predicament of the defeated man by pointing out the physiology of our nervous system. Here are found the sensory and motor nerves. The sensory nerves convey nerve impulses of desire and action from the sense organs to the nerve centers where these are transmitted to the motor nerves which pass on to the muscle and by the impulse, which they transmit to that muscle, cause movement and action. There are pathological conditions in the nervous system where the sensory nerves function but where the motor nerves cannot carry out the desire. It was spiritually so with Paul. He desired good, but could not execute it. The impulse of desire transmitted was not strong enough to be carried out in his life. Sin was the dominant force. It brought him once more to the conclusion found in verse 20, "Now if I do that I would not, it is no more I that do it, but sin that dwelleth in me."

(2) *Inherent law.* Verses 21-25.

"I find then a law, that, when I would do good, evil is present with me. For I delight in the law of God after the inward man: But I see another law in my members, warring against the law of my mind, and bringing me into captivity to the law of sin which is in my members."

Paul found his actions controlled by law; not the Law of Moses but the law of human nature.

Four laws are spoken of here: The law of God, the law of the members, the law of mind, the law of sin. The first and the last and the two middle laws are contrary to each other. They are opponents for the control of man. The law of God operates against the law of sin. In endeavoring to execute the law of God, Paul found the law of his members warring against the law of his mind. In other words, as much as he desired to do right and follow God, the law of his mind was insufficient to control the law of his members.

At the conclusion of Paul's resumé of his experience, he cries out, "O wretched man that I am! who shall deliver me from the body of this death?" It is the complete prostration of human effort and human ability. He does not know what else to do for he has done all that he can and it is not enough. He cries out for deliverance from "the body of this death." What is this body of death that he asks deliverance from? It is his own nature. It is the sum of his habits, passions, desires, and temper. It was a nauseating reality to Paul and constituted such a liability to his life that it brought perpetual defeat.

Paul knew what a body of death was, for in his day Roman tyrants would chain dead bodies upon captives that fell into their hands or, in some instances, criminals were made to carry upon their back, the putrefying bodies of their victims. During the reign of Richard I of England, it was enacted that "he who kills a man on shipboard shall be bound to the dead body and thrown into the sea. If a man is killed on shore, the slayer shall be bound to the dead body and buried with it." And Paul's defeat was to him the loathsome bearing of a body of death. He was a captive of his loathsome contemplation, he cries out for deliverance, "Who shall deliver me?" There is an immediate answer, for Paul had found the secret of life, and from despair he goes to praise, "I thank God through Jesus Christ our Lord."

To any despairing and defeated person the Bible holds out no goal and no anticipation that you cannot reach. This is so because what it says is not a collection of antiquated religious phrases. It is not filled with a lot of wishful thinking. It deals with the facts of the moral and spiritual life in a superb and consummate fashion. It finds a man at variance with life because he is in the grip of a law of evil. He struggles, as Paul did, to serve the law of God with his mind, yet he finds himself serving the law of sin with his flesh. His flesh is superior to his faith. His members are superior to his mind. He goes from defeat to despair. But into this despairing arena of defeat, God introduces a new law of life. This new law of life is the law of the spiritual life through the Holy Spirit, and has its complete and triumphant enunciation in chapter eight.

It becomes triumphant and victorious because it deals with the fundamental failures that had been besetting Paul and likewise us. Paul cried out for a deliverance from "the body of this death." There is an adequate answer and deliverance in the gospel and it is achieved in this way. For "the body of this death," there is the body of His death. And the effect of the fact of His death is to deliver us from our death.

Do you cry out, "Who shall deliver me?" You may join in a paean of praise and say with Paul, "I thank God through Jesus Christ our Lord." He will deliver you. Do you say, "O wretched man!" You may say, "O happy man," for in Christ you may exchange your wretchedness for His happiness; your defeat for His victory.

# 10

## THE VICTORIOUS MAN
### *Romans 8:1–15*

W E HAVE arrived at one of the greatest chapters in all the Bible. Certainly, for practical, daily living nothing exceeds it in all the Book.

It is with mingled feelings that we come to the threshold of this great chapter. They are feelings of joy and fear. Joy, because of its wealth and beauty. Fear, lest one fail in doing justice to its depth and breadth of truth.

First of all we should see the chapter in relation to the whole Epistle and particularly in relation to its preceding chapter. This eighth chapter is the story of victory, triumph, assurance and security. But these things have sure footings. They do not float in from the nebulous thinking of godless men. They have been built up step by step and fact by fact and law by law through the previous chapters of the Romans.

The book of Romans began with an account of universal condemnation. This was followed by divine redemption, then faith's justification, the believer's sanctification, and finally a believer's tragic defeat as he steps out of character and tries to live a regenerated life without the Regenerator. With his cry comes God's reply and the new secret and the new law of life.

Chapter eight unfolds, not the experimental strivings of a religious novice, but the triumphant conquests of a victorious Christian who lives life upon this new level of "the Law of the Spirit of life in Christ Jesus."

The man in chapter seven was a saved man, but he was living out of character. He was a slave, "sold under sin" but in the eighth chapter he is the victor over sin. In the seventh chapter we see a man "in sin," in the eighth chapter we see a man "in Christ." In the seventh chapter he is a "wretched man" seeking deliverance, in the eighth chapter he is a "victorious man" happy in his security. In the seventh chapter it was Christ's work for us, in the eighth chapter it is Christ's work in us. In the seventh chapter he is a victim crying out, "who shall deliver me?" in the eighth chapter he is a victor who says, "in all these things we are more than conquerors." In chapter seven it is the efforts of the human personality, in chapter eight it is the effect of the divine personality of Christ in us through the Holy Spirit. In the seventh chapter the personal pronoun "I" is mentioned thirty times, in the eighth chapter only two times.

On the other hand, in the eighth chapter the Holy Spirit is mentioned twenty times while in the seventh chapter only once. In chapter seven we see a man with a despairing cry, in chapter eight we see a man with a conquering Christ. In chapter seven there is the record of a conflict while in chapter eight there is the record of a conquest. Sooner or later the universal problem of sin resolves itself to the personal equation. It reduces itself to the terms of the individual. It grips us all in the throes of a mighty and mortal conflict. Our refuge is to step over into chapter eight with its law of the new life. Chapter eight begins with "no condemnation" and ends with "no separation," while in between is "no defeat."

Between these two chapters there are differences of experience and yet they are closely bound together by one's closing verse and the other's opening verse. In the last verse of chapter seven it is "through Jesus Christ," while in the first verse of chapter eight it is "in Christ Jesus."

It was because the defeated man in chapter seven stepped out of the character of the life "through Jesus Christ," that he went down to defeat. And it is because the victorious man in chapter eight recognizes his union with Christ and lives in the sphere of the new law of a life "in Christ Jesus," that he goes on to victory.

"I defy any man to get out of the seventh chapter of Romans into the eighth except by that one word, 'Christ'" (H. W. Beecher).

From chapter eight there is a decided change in the attitude and content of the book. Its characters, from this point on, are people who are walking "in Christ" except in certain parenthetical passages. When the writer concludes his message with a list of names prominent in the Christian community in Rome, he invariably adds to their names the words, "in Christ" or its equivalent. This sets the tempo and rhythm of victorious and significant living. It puts life in the pre-eminent category of a life credited with all the resources of God. They may have resided in Rome, but they lived "in Christ." They may have had citizenship under Caesar but they had conquest under Christ.

While it was true that the victorious man was a man "in Christ," it was not by that same token true that all the men "in Christ" are victorious Christians. This is so because we must not only be "in Christ," but we must live there. We must not only stand "in Christ," but we must walk there. In Christ there is a law of life by which we may live above the level and average of ordinary life. If we find and follow this spiritual law, life is the victorious effect of a triumphant cause.

It is not only the application of a new law but the identification of a new walk, for "there is therefore now no condemnation to them which are in Christ Jesus who walk not after the flesh, but after the Spirit." Here it is "walking not," after one manner of life. And again it is "walking" after another manner of life. This means discrimination and decision. It means a choice between one way and another. It is a choice between the flesh and the Spirit. It is between a Christian out of character, and a Christian in character. A Christian is out of character when he is in the flesh. He is in character when he is in the Spirit. The one results in condemnation and the other in conquest.

There are many who give no attentive thought to the character of their Christian walk. With them Christianity is a phrase to be repeated by the lips and forgotten the next day. It is a set of religious genuflections without a single application to daily life. There are those who are satisfied with justification and stop there. It must be said that it is a lot to be satisfied with, but stopping there will be fatal to the fullest development of Christian experience and consequently life success, for a justified man may be the case of a wretched man as it was with Paul.

In the legitimate Christian vocabulary there is a companion word to justification. It is sanctification. It means "to make holy," and by its process we achieve that perfection of life which is the legitimate and expected goal of a Christian faith. Justification brings sanctification as a position. For in Christ we are brought immediately into a positional and legal state of holiness and made fit for the fellowship of God. But "it is only when this position is realized in experience that there comes a difference in regard to progress" in a Christian's life.

A positional sanctification may permit you to "walk after the flesh." But an experimental sanctification requires that you "walk after the Spirit."

Sanctification is not a struggle. It is not excruciating religious exercises out of which one evolves a gradual goodness. It is rather a surrender. It is a surrender to the powers of a new law, "the law of the Spirit of life in Christ Jesus." In fulfilling the principles of this law, one is not walking in the flesh but in the Spirit.

The pre-natal conflict of the Christian, and by that we mean the conflict before one becomes a Christian, was a conflict between right and wrong with conscience as arbiter. But after the new birth, the conflict of the Christian is no longer between right and wrong. It is now between flesh and Spirit. It is whether the flesh will dominate and predominate and lead into the wrong; or, whether the Spirit shall control and lead into the right.

There are, in substance, two moulds of life. One is the mould of the flesh from which the product is turned out with an external culture that death strips from us. The other is the mould of the Spirit from which the product is turned out with a character that is both God-like and fruitful, possessing eternal values that never depreciate.

For a Christian to climb and grow to a better life is natural to his very spiritual constitution. Time after time, the highest of the Himalaya peaks, Mt. Everest, has defied conquest. Party after party have courageously assaulted its windswept summit. These climbers have devoted their money, their time, their energies and, some, their lives. Their single occupation is climbing in order to conquer the only part of the earth's surface untrodden by human feet. What are Christians for? To sing hymns and talk religion? Not in the highest sense. We too are climbers. A life of conquest lies ahead. It is the realm of practical Christianity. It is the life of supremacy and service.

If you were to go into most any Swiss village near the Alps during the climbing season, you would see along the streets, in the public squares, and around the hotels, groups of strong and sturdy men. They are dressed in dark blue uniforms and wear silver badges on their coat lapels. These men are mountain guides. They were born into it. They went through careful training. They have passed rigid tests. They have but one business in life; it is climbing. That is the business of the Christian. His is the challenge of higher altitudes. His is the life that goes on from one degree of glory to another. Let us then live to the highest. Let us reach for the most instead of being content with the least. Let us strike out for the heights. God will attend us.

The secret of conquering Christianity and personal victory is disclosed in this eighth chapter. We speak of it with great emphasis because it is of the greatest importance to every Christian. There are many who are living far below their position and privileges. There are many who are victims instead of victors.

All life is basically founded on law and the intelligent person will look for it in the highest form of life as well as the lowest. We find the highest form of life in the spiritual world. And in this spiritual world, into which the Christian has come by birth, there is the dominant principle of a spiritual law. This law concerns spiritual hygiene, dietetics, strength and all the elements of a healthful spiritual experience. That law is "the law of the Spirit of life in Christ Jesus." So, now, it is not a question of artificial religion. It is not a matter of creed saying and hymn singing. It is the vitality of a new life.

This chapter of our book, as well as the next two, has a division which runs consecutively through it. The key is in the phrase "in Christ Jesus" found in the first verse of Romans eight.

I. UNION WITH HIM. Verses 1-9.

This union reveals seven intimate things about this new life which it is important to itemize (W. Griffith Thomas).

1. The Pronouncement of the New Life. Verse 1.

"There is therefore now no condemnation. . ."

This is a legal pronouncement of complete freedom from legal guiltiness. Whatever condemnation was justly due for historical and personal guilt was completely met in Christ, a fact which is definitely included here because of the believer's union with Christ.

The great difference between a believer and a non-believer lies in the fact that in the unbeliever his judgment day is before him. But in the believer his judgment day is behind him.

But this pronouncement has something more than a legal significance to it, for the words "no condemnation" literally mean "no handicap." This is evidently so and logically so, for as we stepped into this chapter out of the previous one, we heard a man crying out for deliverance from a loathsome and hindering handicap. It was the handicap of "the body of this death." Paul had to figuratively carry it everywhere he went. He slept with it, ate with it, walked with it, transacted business with it, carried on social intercourse with it; and all the while it was a source of constricting and condemning hindrance. Now that is all gone. Its nauseating presence is gone. Its binding burden is gone. It is all gone because Christ has come. So, "there is therefore now no handicap."

But notice what this handicap was. It was not a physical disability, nor a mental disqualification, nor economic restriction. It was something spiritual and personal. It was Paul himself. After all, you are your greatest handicap. When you get straightened out, your life will be a race course of triumph. The body of death that handicapped Paul was the sum total of all his personal disabilities such as his disposition, habits, temperament, etc. But he turned all that over to Christ and it was buried and put out of the way, and from henceforth Paul lived an unhandicapped life.

We should be careful to notice what it says in the opening statement of the chapter. It does not say that there are no mistakes and no inconsistencies. That does not mean that if such come that the Christian has no responsibility for them. Indeed, he has. But their occurrence does not affect his status before God. They may affect his personal feelings but not his relationship with God. There are no degrees of relationship in our union with Christ. We are either vitally and wholly in union or else not at all. And that union is complete at all times. While there may be an experimental and an emotional condemnation, there is no judicial or spiritual condemnation. It is an association that is not to be hindered by the lesions and wounds of the daily life. God has made it both divinely sufficient and fool-proof.

2. The Position of the New Life. Verse 1.

". . . to them which are in Christ Jesus."

This position is the result of the believer's union with the Saviour. That union is not the result of an artificial graft which preserves the separate identity of both the graft and the parent plant. It is the union of a spiritual birth out of which the born-one comes with the likeness of its parent. Thus, all similarity to the former likeness is gone. Contamination has gone. Condemnation has ceased. And the prevailing pattern of life is the life of the parent.

This position has organically placed the individual in touch with all the resources and reserves of life resident in Christ. It is, therefore, not merely the negative status of "no condemnation," but the positive power of a new conquest, for in Christ, he is in the sphere of all the power of Christ's life. It is not merely a deliverance but a discovery. It is not merely that you are not now what you once were, but what you are going to become. Christians roll their thumbs in satisfied piety while they ought to be climbing and growing.

There comes a time when a decision follows a decision. The first decision was that of conversion. The second is that of consecration. At conversion you decided to cease being what you were. At consecration your decision is to be what your new birth meant you to be. The sinner has been brought to Christ; now the Christian needs Christ brought to him in the new life of triumph. This may sound a little strange and yet the fact is that many Christians need a new conception of Christ. To them He is a picture painted on a canvas or a name to be repeated. He is instead a life to live through your life. He is a Master to master you. Think of yourself, henceforth, as being "in Christ Jesus," and you will think of yourself in the terms of new power and blessing.

3. The Power of the New Life. Verse 2.

"The law of the Spirit of life in Christ Jesus. . ."

There are many religions in the world but none of these offer the semblance of reality that we have in the gospel. There are platitudes to be repeated and rituals to be followed, but here is a new life governed by a new law. Follow the law and you will find the life. The law of this new life is not a regulation or a principle. It is not an impersonal thing at all, for it is described as "the law of the Spirit of life in Christ." It is the law which is the Holy Spirit Himself. This law is life and this life is Christ transferred to our lives and experienced in our experiences.

The difference in life is the difference, not of life's circumstance, but of life's character. It is the difference of birth and nature. The Christian is the result of a new birth and the partaker of the divine nature. From this point on life follows the pattern of the law that governs it and that law is the spiritual counterpart of the natural law, known as The Law of Conformity to Type. "According to this, every living thing that comes into the world is compelled to stamp upon its offspring, the image of itself." Even as bird-life builds up a bird which is the image of itself, and human-life builds up a human which is the image of itself, so Christ within who is described here under "the law of the Spirit of life in Christ Jesus," builds up a Christian, the image of Himself in man's inner nature. This is the normal consequence of every Christian experience when it is surrendered to this "law of the Spirit of life."

You notice that Christianity is the spiritual duplication of creation. One creates a natural life while the other creates a spiritual life to take the place of that original spiritual life destroyed by sin. And for this same reason real Christian theology is nothing more than spiritual biology.

In the terms of spiritual biology the Christian life must begin with a life substance. In physical life we call it protoplasm, but in the spiritual realm it is Christ's life. As in physical life there must be a creation of protoplasm that has the power of reproduction, so in spiritual life. Every human being is not naturally Christian nor spiritual. He is naturally sinful and must have a new creation. Every natural birth gives us the capacity for God, but only the new birth can fill that capacity with the presence of God.

In this manner the Christ-life is resident in the new nature. This life is not an improvement nor a cultivation of the natural life. It is a new life born of God. Now the question is how is the newborn Christian to be conformed to Christ, the great type? Certainly, not merely by imitating Him or admiring Him, for the Christian life is not artificial. It is biological. It is not by toiling and struggling and agonizing that the Christian conforms to Christ. He does not fashion himself. In the natural world, matter does not form the life but the life forms the matter. And in the spiritual world the man does not form the Christian, but Christ's life within forms the man. In other words, it is Christ who makes the Christian. And so, there is an ideal for every Christian. It is this, "until Christ be formed in you." Therefore, the goal of the Christian life is not merely to be finally saved; not just to gain heaven; not to be artificially religious. It is to be conformed to the image of the Son. No wonder Paul cries out with this assurance. "Being confident of this very thing, that he which hath begun a good work in you will perform it until the day of Jesus Christ" (Phil. 1:6). No wonder John reveals the ultimate completion of the Christian, "Beloved, now are we the sons of God, and it doth not yet appear what we shall be: but we know that, when he shall appear, we shall be like him; for he shall see him as he is" (I John 3:2).

The Christian is a person beginning naturally as God's creature and ending supernaturally as God's child. And all of this is within the sphere of "the law of the Spirit of life in Christ Jesus."

4. The Protection of the New Life. Verse 2.

". . . hath made me free from the law of sin and death."

Deliverance now becomes an experience. This experience is the power of a new freedom. We are free from something and for something. It means not only acquittal from sins but power over sin.

Sin is not a question of circumstance but character. It is not a force outside but inside. When a person becomes a Christian, a new nature is implanted, with the old nature remaining. But while in the very structure of life the old nature of sinfulness remains, it is under condemnation. Its power has been cancelled. Its authority has been removed. It is under death. In the new nature resides the power of the new life in this "law of the Spirit of life."

In his own nature and strength, no believer could rise to conspicuous holiness and godliness. He could no more do it than a man could, of his own power, rise bodily off the ground into the skies. The reason for this inability is not because he has a body, but because the law of gravitation decrees that bodies must be earth-bound. But if that person gets into an airplane, the law of motion counteracts the law of gravitation, and he ascends bodily wherever he wills to go. In the same manner the higher law of "the Spirit of life in Christ Jesus" delivers and makes free from "the law of sin and death," and causes us to live beyond the limits and ability of ordinary human life. Thus, the dominating force of the new life is not the law of legalism but the law of life in Christ Jesus. It is not struggle but surrender. It is not an effort but an effect. It is not psychology but spiritual biology. It is not I, but Christ.

5. The Provision of the New Life. Verse 3.

"For what the law could not do, in that it was weak through the flesh, God sending his own Son in the likeness of sinful flesh, and for sin, condemned sin in the flesh."

Christians are not spiritual orphans nor a species of spiritual paupers to be pitied for the paucity of their resources. We have at heart, and ready for instant use, a great store of spiritual wealth. Everything needful for a full and abundant life has been provided. This provision is in Christ.

This provision is the outgrowth of the great deliverance of verse two. We are delivered from the law. The law was a divine institution and it served a divine purpose. It was both righteous and efficient. But despite these considerations, we must remember that while the law had authority to condemn sin, it had no power to conquer sin. And so it is stated here that "what the law could not do in that it was weak," (because it was no stronger than the flesh in which it operated) God has now accomplished by "sending His own Son in the likeness of sinful flesh." In the very sphere where the law failed, Christ lived and died and wrought a redemption sufficient to adequately deal with sin. He did it by a sacrifice for sin and "condemned sin in the flesh." Because He condemned it "in the flesh," that is exactly where we can conquer it. Because He condemned it in this life we can conquer it in this life. Because He condemned it in the sphere of its expressions, its habits, its disposition, we can conquer it there. Because he condemned it in the ordinary circumstances of life, we can conquer it there. We do not have to retire to some retreat or to a monastery or to a mountain top. The place of our conquest is the city street or the country lane; the kitchen sink or the office desk; the hospital bed or the playing field. It is here and everywhere that sin is to be met and mastered because Christ condemned it in the flesh which is the field of its operation.

There are three great facts of the Christian faith found in verse three.

(1) *Deity*—"his own Son."

If Christ is no more than a man except in degree of achievement and depth of character, the Bible is an unworthy record because it declares Him to be what He is not, if He is not the divine Son of God. We dare not reduce the character of Jesus by putting Him into a human category.

(2) *Incarnation*—"in the likeness of sinful flesh."

This is God coming down to man which results in man going up to God. Without the incarnation, there could never be regeneration. We are utterly dependent, for what we are to become, upon what Christ was and did.

(3) *Atonement*—"for sin."

We are not only dependent upon what Christ was, but what He did. We can live without the condemnation of verse one because of this condemnation in verse three. Sin was condemned through His death that it might be condemned in our life. It was not only the sin-principle but the sin-practice. And what God condemned, we should execute through the power of the law of our new life.

The secret of victory over sin is in the source of sin's conquest. It was in Christ's death. Count Zinzendorf who so nobly led the Moravians to such conspicuous Christian service, was the spiritual father of a great company of people. The Moravians were devoted Christian leaders. They made a profound impression on John Wesley. In fact, Methodism was cradled by the Moravians. Wesley, being troubled because of manifold temptations, asked a Moravian brother what to do. He replied: "You must not fight with them as you did before, but flee from them the moment they appear, and take shelter in the wounds of Jesus."

6. The Possibility of the New Life. Verse 4.

"That the righteousness of the law might be fulfilled in us, who walk not after the flesh, but after the Spirit."

This sounds almost incredible and it would be altogether unbelievable if it was not for the fact that it is God's promise. Not only that, but it is His actual provision.

Our redemption and regeneration is not something negative. It blots out a past but offers a glorious present. It disengages hands and feet, heart and mind, from unworthy occupations, and gives them the dignity of a new service.

This indicates the practical purpose and natural effect of our salvation. It is the achievement of righteousness. It is not an abstract or theoretical thing but something as definite and tangible as washing the dishes or auditing a set of books. Remember that we are dealing with life. It is not for the temple alone. This new life is to be achieved, in what is here described, as "a walk" for it becomes a part of those who "walk not after the flesh but after the spirit."

Why did the Holy Spirit choose this word out of the human vocabulary to describe the Christian life? Could it be because walking expresses one of the most perfect forms of movement? Next to swimming, walking is the most perfect form of exercise and body movement there is. And swimming is walking's equivalent in water. And so, we find that our Christian walk gives us the most perfect display of the provisions of the work of Christ. In other words, our walk is by His work.

This possibility marks a new era in living. We can do now what could not be done before. In the previous verse the law's deficiency is stated thus: "What the law could not do, in that it was weak . . ." Now it is possible for us to do what the law could not do, for this verse states "That the righteousness of the law might be fulfilled in us."

The reason the law could not do this was because it must operate in the sphere of sinful flesh. The reason that it can now be fulfilled in us is because we live in the sphere of redemption and the new spiritual law, the law of the Spirit of life in Christ Jesus. Therefore, the righteousness of the law can be fulfilled in us because we are living and walking in the redemptive and regenerating power of the work of Christ. It is not a case of our trying to conform to a legal law but the case of a new law operating in us and bringing into play all the powers, resources, and graces of Jesus Christ. What a different thing this makes the Christian life!

You will also notice that it says here that "the law might be fulfilled in us." The law was fulfilled *for us* in Christ's career and death. That is what verse three means, "for what the law could not do, God sending His Son." In life, Christ was the perfect man and in death He was the perfect lamb, and in both life and death He fulfilled the law for us. But now it is to be fulfilled *in us.* Just how is this to be done? Is it to be fulfilled in us by ourself or by a third party? It is to be both. Certainly it is to be fulfilled in us. It is to be fulfilled in the sphere of our actions and thoughts and desires. And it is also to be fulfilled *by us;* but only by us when "we walk not after the flesh, but after the Spirit." In other words, we can only reach the high point of Christian idealism and excellence when we live in the sphere of the law of our new life. That sphere is not the sphere of the flesh but of the Spirit; not the sphere of the natural but the supernatural.

This proviso is a stipulation of essential importance because it is a recognition of the fact that the highest Christian life is not an effort but an effect. It is not by chance, but choice. It is the choice of a level of life. It is a level we must choose not only once but continuously. We must choose it and keep on choosing it.

What is it that makes the difference between Christians? It is not in their faith but their walk. Some are selfish and others sacrificial. Some are sour and others sweet. Some are temperamental and others temperate. Some are grouchy and others gracious. The difference is in their walk because some "walk after the flesh" while others "walk after the Spirit."

7. The Principle of the New Life. Verses 5-9.

The principle of the new life is as natural as it is spiritual. If in the natural world we find that life is a correspondence with its environment of air, food, and water, so in the spiritual world the new life is a correspondence with its environment. The environment of the natural man was the flesh. Now the environment of the Christian is the Spirit. It is not as some think it to be, justification by faith and sanctification by struggle. It is not self-perpetuating power. God does not wind up our moral and spiritual springs at conversion and go off and leave us. The power of the new life is the power of the indwelling God and the believer's constant contact with the new spiritual environment in which he has been placed.

Let us notice the naturalness of the spiritual life. So far in Romans we have seen life at its worst, steeped in the blackest sins. The redemption of Christ then provides a justification which lifts life to a new plane. Now its practical aspect presents itself and we are faced as Christians with daily duties. All the resources of Christ are at our disposal. How shall we utilize them? In other words, how shall we live? By some artificial religious rules that will all end in despair? Or, will it be by "the law of the Spirit of life in Christ Jesus"? Let us point out to you how simple and natural the spiritual is.

In the natural world there are two universal factors that govern all life. One is heredity and the other is environment. One means birth and the other means growth. One begins and the other sustains. The great function of environment is to sustain, develop, and enlarge. Our physical environment is that in which we live and move and have our being. It is the air we breathe, the water we drink, the food we eat. Heredity gave us life but environment must sustain that life. It is identically so in the spiritual world. We are born a new spiritual creature in Christ. We are from that moment a spiritual organism. But that organism is not self-existent. It requires a spiritual environment. That environment is to be "in Christ." The faith which gave us spiritual birth now is faith that sustains our spiritual life. But faith is only an attitude. It is an empty hand reaching out for the sources of spiritual supply. We do not live *on* faith but *through* faith. It is faith that helps us appropriate the powers of Christ in whom we live and through those powers come our abundant life.

Herbert Spencer tells us that it is a primary law of nature "that whatever amount of power an organism expends in any shape is the equivalent of a power that was taken in from without." This is the problem of dynamics. It reminds us that in the Christian life communion with God and union with Christ are a scientific necessity. But remember that communion is not to be occasional but continual when we are Christians. It is not satisfied with a Sunday look at God. It is to be as continual as breathing and eating. The arrangements for the spiritual life are the same as for the natural life. Nature is not more natural to our body than God is to our soul when we are Christians. All the means of living above the level of sinning and in the joy of triumphant grace come through our organic union with Christ. To maintain that union is to fulfill the conditions of victory. We do not have to fight or struggle, but just be what we are in Christ.

The Psalmist cried out, "As the hart panteth after the water brooks, so panteth my soul after Thee, O God." The water brooks are the environment of the hart and God is the environment of the soul. As the water brooks are designed by the Creator to the natural wants, so God implements the spiritual need of man. This is not by repeating phrases or saying artificial prayers, but by organic life union through a new birth and a new environment. There is a Bible anthropology and when we find its simple secrets, we find the ways of the abundant life.

Where Christians make such a fatal mistake is at this point. They are content with justification. They receive and confess Christ and content themselves with conversion. But birth must be followed by growth and in a normal and natural spiritual growth there are the normal and natural results of an abundant life.

Now the question arises, how is this possible? It goes back to Jesus' observation: "Consider the lilies, how they grow." How does a Christian grow? After all, it is the simple fact that normal growth means normal life. If a Christian will grow in the conditions of the Christian life, he will live in the privileges and powers of the Christian life. He will not need to seek an experience or a blessing; he will not need to struggle and strain.

But how do the lilies grow? Where does organism on the one hand, and environment on the other hand, meet? After all, the meeting of life by birth and the sustaining of life by growth is the secret of the abundance of life. They meet at the place of receptivity. The organism receives the environment and the environment receives the organism. And in the spiritual life it is the same. It is to "abide in me." And if we will "walk in the Spirit," thus fulfilling the law of the spiritual world, we, too, will live in the abundance of grace and power. There is no other formula to follow, no other rule to obey. Simply "walk in the Spirit." Abundance is ours, not for the asking, but for the walking.

Notice the significance and meaning of this walk in the Spirit as unfolded in these five verses from verse five to verse nine. Here we find three things: And remember all of these are to be found under the seventh of the intimate things in our union with Christ, namely, The Principle of the New Life.

(1) *Two classes.* Verse 5.

"For they that are after the flesh do mind the things of the flesh; but they that are after the Spirit the things of the Spirit."

The two classes are they who on the one hand are "after the flesh," and they who on the other hand are "after the Spirit." To be after the flesh means to serve the principles of our earthly nature which is the source of our natural affections, inclinations, and desires. The flesh stands for human nature which is the dominant element in the unregenerate man. To be after the Spirit means of course the Holy Spirit. It means to serve the principles of our new life. The Holy Spirit is the resident power of our new nature.

And we are now to walk under the operating power of the Spirit of God. Thus, we fulfill the law of the new life.

(2) *Two issues.* Verses 6-8.

"For to be carnally minded is death; but to be spiritually minded is life and peace. Because the carnal mind is enmity against God: for it is not subject to the law of God, neither indeed can be. So then they that are in the flesh cannot please God."

One is the issue of carnality, and the other is the issue of spirituality. Observe carefully that it is all in the sphere of regenerate Christian experience. One is normal and the other is subnormal. One is conducive to power and life and blessing, and the other brings confusion and the displeasure of God.

It speaks of being "carnally minded" and "spiritually minded." This literally means to be "flesh-wise" and to be "spirit-wise." One is to be dominated by a mind that is of the self-life while the other is to be dominated by a mind that is of the Christ-life. The old law, "As a man thinketh in his heart, so is he," operates according to its affinities. If the affinity of our mind is self, then the consequence is death and disorder. But if the affinity of our mind is Christ, the consequence is life and peace.

The Bible divides men into three categories.

There is the *natural man.* He is unregenerate and Adamic. His nature is untouched and unchanged by the grace of God. This man is incapable, as such a man, of both appreciating and appropriating the blessings of the Christian life until he has experienced the new birth. Paul says of this man, "But the natural man receiveth not the things of the Spirit of God: for they are foolishness unto him; neither can he know them, because they are spiritually discerned" (I Cor. 2:14).

There is the *carnal man.* While regenerate and with all the resources of the spiritual life at his command, he is the man who is minding the things of the lower nature. He is not dominated by the spiritual mind but the carnal mind.

"The carnal Christian has a Saviour but not a Lord; but the spiritual Christian has both a Saviour and a Lord. The carnal Christian remains between Passover and Pentecost; he is on the right side of the Cross, but on the wrong side of the throne. He has life, but not liberty. He is out of Egypt, but not in Canaan."

Then there is the *spiritual man.* He is not only regenerated by Christ but surrendered to the control and dominion of the Spirit of Christ. He not only has life from Christ but lives in the law of the life of Christ. He refuses the desires and dictates of the nature of his flesh and walks in the sphere of the life of the Spirit. As he walks after the Spirit the image of Christ breaks forth upon the background of his regenerated personality.

Michelangelo used to say while at work on some piece of sculpture, as the chips fell thick on the floor, "While the marble wastes, the image grows." In all true spiritual living the marble wastes and the image grows. We are marble and Christ is the image . . . "He must increase and I must decrease."

A Christian man is no longer a natural man, although he may continue to be a carnal man. The issue

in this is one between carnality and spirituality. To
be carnally minded, in scientific language, is to be
limited to the environment of the natural man. It is
to mind the flesh, and the flesh by its very nature
is death. In the case of the carnal man, this death is
not the death of his soul, but that spiritual death
which limits him to the sphere of the natural world.
As Paul expresses it elsewhere, "She is dead while
she liveth."

It is ours to determine the sphere of our life, whether
it will be carnality or spirituality. We are the creatures of two natures, one of which will dominate
and predominate.

Let us look at these verses analytically. There are
three things said about the carnal mind which in their
very nature are untrue of the spiritual mind.

a. The effect of the carnal mind. Verse 6.

It is death, for "to be carnally minded is death." To
live in the sphere of carnality is to live in the atmosphere of death. This, of course, is moral and spiritual
death. If I live in the spiritual environment, it is life
and peace. But if I live in the carnal environment it
is death. And remember that it is the choice of a
believer to live in either environment. If you live in
the flesh, the effect will be fleshly. If you live in the
Spirit, the effect will be spiritual. If you live after
the world, the effect will be worldly. If you live after
God, the effect will be heavenly. It is just as possible
to dwarf a soul as it is to dwarf a plant or a tree.
The way the Japanese have been able to make such
remarkable dwarfs is by depriving a normal tree of its
normal environment of food and nutrition. Do that
with your soul and you will dwarf it and stunt it. A

dwarfed tree may be a curiosity but it has lost its productive value. Will you be content to be a religious curiosity? A dwarf or a giant, which will you be? Your spiritual stature is in your own hands.

　　b. The nature of the carnal mind. Verse 7.

Its nature is "enmity against God." There is a natural animosity between man and God. It is not natural to love God or submit to God. It may be natural to worship some kind of deity and it is something we do intuitively. But a rational, intelligent love of God is foreign until we have the life of God. The new birth gives a family relationship and then we love God because we are a spiritual part of Him. We were once physically and spiritually a part of Him at creation. The physical remains and the spiritual is gone, and in our natural state there is an antipathy instead of an affinity. And so, when we revert to carnality, we live in this state of antipathy and there is no affinity between our spirit and God's Spirit.

　　c. The futility of the carnal mind. Verse 8.

The futility is the impossibility to "please God." A man may be carnal and yet religious. He may fill all the prescriptions of a religious life. He may be cultured and correct, but even in such a state it is impossible to please God. Are you anxious to meet all the social standards of men, yet heedless of the fact that you are missing the highest standard of all which is the divine? Dare you think that you are failing to please God, and do not fly to the very arms of God in humble contrition? To "please God" ought to be the first and the noblest ambition of our lives. And when we please Him, we will enjoy the pleasure of a great life.

(3) *Two spheres.* Verse 9.

"But ye are not in the flesh, but in the Spirit,
if so be that the Spirit of God dwell in you. Now
if any man have not the Spirit of Christ, he is
none of his."

In verse four it was walking "after the Spirit" or
"after the flesh," while here it is living "in the Spirit"
or "in the flesh." These are the two spheres of life in
which we may move.

In verse four "after the Spirit" was a matter of
practice, while here in verse nine "in the Spirit" is a
matter of position. And this means that we are not
only in a spiritual position but being in that position
it means that the Holy Spirit is in us. We are in the
Spirit as a sphere of life while the Spirit is in us as the
secret and power of life.

When Paul says, "ye are not in the flesh but in the
Spirit, if so be the Spirit of God dwell in you," he
obviously does not mean that we are out of our body
and in some immaterial form. But what he does mean
is this: if we have the Holy Spirit as the resident
portion of the Godhead in our lives, then we are no
longer mere unregenerate flesh, but instead are in
the new state and the new sphere of the spiritual. We
might correctly read this verse as Way translates it,
"You, however are not controlled by your animal
nature, but by the Spirit of God, if God's Spirit really
has His home in you." But the control of our lives
by our lower or higher nature is entirely up to us.

All Christians have the Spirit but not all Christians
are controlled by the Spirit. It is utterly impossible
to be a Christian and not have the Holy Spirit. This

is exactly what the latter half of this verse states. "Now if any man have not the Spirit of Christ, he is none of his." This is fundamental to Christian existence as being controlled by the Holy Spirit is fundamental to Christian experience. We cannot be Christians until and unless we have had a birth by the Holy Spirit into the Christian life. Nor can we live a normal successful Christian life until and unless we are controlled by the Holy Spirit. In other words, our outer life must correspond to our inner life.

If the beginning of the Christian life demanded a choice of faith, the continuance of that life in victory and power demands a surrender of faith to the Holy Spirit's control. In one case the choice was of Christ. In the other case the surrender is to the Holy Spirit. But in no case do we have to seek a special coming of the Spirit. We may have to have a crucial hour of surrender to Him and a continuous surrender from that time on. But it is not a case of breast-beating and praying and agonizing for the Spirit to come as our guest. There cannot be any spiritual life in us unless the Spirit is in us. But the outworking of that inner life demands our surrender to the Holy Spirit's dominion and control.

Let us be sure we do not mistake this statement. When it states that "if any have not the Spirit of Christ, he is none of His," it most assuredly does not mean spirit as an influence but as a person. It is not the things of Jesus' life like love and truthfulness and tolerance. But, rather, the Holy Spirit who is named the Spirit of Christ, as in the forepart of the verse He is named the Spirit of God. We must insist on the Bible's biology, for the Holy Spirit is the agent and author of life in the new creation. Christianity is a life and not merely a formula. It is something coming from above which is felt within and then affects everything around us.

II. Living for Him. Verses 10-13.

Philosophical and ecclesiastical Christianity have led us into two grave and contrary errors. One is that God is an influence of goodness dwelling in the human mind. The other is that God is an unapproachable deity dwelling in the heavens. God is more than an influence. He is a personality with all the attributes and attractions of practical holiness. And while it is true that He does have a heavenly locality, He also has an earthly one. He is not localized in heaven to the exclusion of earth. Nor is He localized on earth in buildings called churches, to the exclusion of our homes and hearts. Isaiah tells us of the two places where God is localized, "For thus saith the high and lofty One that inhabiteth eternity, whose name is Holy; I dwell in the high and holy place, with him also that is of a contrite and humble spirit, to revive the spirit of the humble, and to revive the heart of the contrite ones." The New Testament tells us of the secret of God in the heart, which is by the biology of spiritual birth. It is the significance of this immediate verse—"If Christ be in you."

This is a revolutionary conception of God entirely unlike that artificial conception of theoretical and ecclesiastical Christianity as well as the abortive conceptions of civilized culture which push God off into a corner of His universe. He is not only on earth but

He is in us. This carries with it all the practical effects of both an imminent and an intimate God.

This section deals with our life in God and God's life in us.

1. The Resident Life of Christ. Verse 10.

> "And if Christ be in you, the body is dead because of sin; but the Spirit is life because of righteousness."

Notice the contrast we find between verse one and verse ten. In verse one it says *in Christ* while in verse ten it says *Christ in you.* In verse one it is position. In verse ten it is possession. There is a great practical difference between our positional relation to Christ and our possessive experience of Him.

Christ's presence in us does not now change the chemistry of our body. It does not cancel the primeval sentence of death. The penalty of sin may remain physically but the power of sin is gone because we have an indwelling Christ who has brought life to our spirit. We, therefore, have, as Christians, the new and higher incentive of life on the new and higher plane of the spiritual as compared to the physical.

2. The New Energy of Life. Verse 11.

> "But if the Spirit of him that raised up Jesus from the dead dwell in you, he that raised up Christ from the dead shall also quicken your mortal bodies by his Spirit that dwelleth in you."

Instead of a mere physical existence, the Christian has a new spiritual existence. And, likewise, instead of a physical energy he has a spiritual energy. This new energy is from the indwelling Spirit. It results in the quickening of these mortal bodies.

Of what does this "quickening" consist? This does not have any reference to our future physical resurrection, for the context has nothing to say about a physical resurrection. It is dealing with the present problems of life.

While this verse does not mean some mystical reinvigoration or rejuvenation of our physical bodies, it nevertheless refers to a specific effect on our present body life. The extent to which we can carry this thought requires caution lest we be involved in false conceptions. It does not exempt the body from illness or retard decay or eliminate handicaps. But certainly we can all see how spiritual blessings react upon the physical body. The body is to receive the beneficent effect of the joy and peace and forgiveness enjoyed by the spirit. A normal Christian experience should increase both the efficiency and the enjoyment of our bodies. Surely when the load of sin has gone and the indwelling Christ has come, we have a new source of spiritual energy which will "quicken" our very physical existence. The word quicken means "to preserve life." And in a Christian, clean habits, temperate indulgences, worry-free minds, will certainly aid and assist in the preservation of life. We believe in definite and tangible dividends for Christians right now. Christianity was intended for this world as well as the next. Eternal life has a present value as well as a future value. The indirect effects of a clean life, as well as the direct effects of an indwelling Spirit, must certainly react to our physical welfare or else there is nothing practical whatever in being a Christian now. And all of this is in perfect keeping with the biology of the Bible. The spiritual life has fruits that are normal and natural to our present daily life.

3. The Cancelled Debt. Verse 12.

"Therefore, brethren, we are debtors, not to the flesh, to live after the flesh."

We are debtors but not to live down to the demands of our lower, Adamic nature. We have no obligation to it. The Christian's debt to sin being cancelled, he arises to meet the challenge of a new obligation. If it is not to live after the flesh, there is but one other alternative, to live after the Spirit. Thus, our debt is not merely a negative one. It is not merely that "we are debtors not to the flesh." We are also by that token debtors *to* something. The excellence of Christian virtue is not merely to refrain from stealing or lying. That is but one side of our obligation. The other is the side of creative righteousness. It is the side of positive holiness. It is the new obligation to let our body and mind be the implement of the indwelling Spirit, for the creation of such deeds and acts of life as will indelibly mark us with the possession of a new life. Saints are not spirits retired to the seclusion of death. They are Christians thrilled and throbbing with a new life who walk our highways and live in our homes. This is the sphere of holiness.

4. The New Secret of Life. Verse 13.

"For if ye live after the flesh, ye shall die: but if ye through the Spirit do mortify the deeds of the body, ye shall live."

The new secret of life is to "mortify the deeds of the body." This is the human aspect. The divine aspect is that the Holy Spirit indwells the body. But that does not mean automatic holiness. It does mean a positional holiness but there is to be considered also a practical holiness. It will not be demonstrated until and unless we "mortify the deeds of the body." "Mortify" means "to make to die." It is not a sudden process but a gradual one. When it comes to sins of the flesh like drunkenness, there is but one course. It must cease summarily. But there are sins of the disposition which are not given the same stigma. These we must mortify. We must put them to death. We must deny them expression. It is our initiative but the Spirit's enabling. But unless it is done by us it will never be done in us.

This mortification of the body's sinful deeds is accomplished through a law of degeneration found also in the natural world. By this law the undesirable member is relieved as much as possible of all use until at last it decays and atrophies. Thus, death is accomplished through denial.

In this way the more death we bring to our sinning members and execute in our sinful desires, the more life there will be in our useful members. For here the reward of death is life, for "if ye through the Spirit do mortify the deeds of the flesh, ye shall live."

Notice the evident emphasis the thirteenth verse puts on the matter of the righteousness of life. It is something which is to be accomplished in the body. Instead of the body being a clod and weight handicapping us with a hopelessness, that it seems impossible to overcome; instead of its being some dismal prison of the soul; it is to become the implement of God for a conspicuous life of beauty and power.

But this means bodily holiness if it means anything. It means practical righteousness. It is not something reserved for the sanctuary of the church. It may begin there but does not end there. In fact, what is proclaimed in the church must be practiced in the world. We do not have a complete view of the gospel until we recognize its personal application to the problems at large. It is our great privilege and obligation, to give such a practical proof of our faith that the world will have an irresistible evidence of the reality of Christ. But if this is ever to be so, it will only come through self-surrender and God-possession.

The Spirit's antagonist in the realm of actual everyday life is the flesh. The Christian is not in the flesh but in the Spirit. Nevertheless, the flesh is in him. And the problem of his new life is "not how to change the flesh into something good, but how to live with the flesh every day without being overcome by it." Given the problem by one birth, as a natural man, the Christian is given the answer by another birth, as a spiritual man. It is by the indwelling Holy Spirit. It is "through the Spirit" that we "mortify the deeds of the flesh."

Notice the effect of this self-mortification. It is described in these words, "Ye shall live." You will live in a new freedom from fleshly handicaps. You will live in a new purity from fleshly corruptions. You will live in a new enjoyment, being freed from fleshly limitations.

What thrilling words are these, "Ye shall live!" Are you living or just existing? Are you Christian enough to be "saved yet so as by fire," or are you Christian enough to be "more than conquerors through Him

that loved us?" Is it a minus Christianity you have
or a plus Christianity? Are you enduring your religion or enjoying it? Is it a load or a lift? Dare
to measure yourself by this Epistle and then implement yourself with its provisions for the abundant
life. It holds out a thrilling prospect for "ye shall
live."

III. ADOPTED BY HIM. Verses 14, 15.

"For as many as are led by the Spirit of God,
they are the sons of God. For ye have not received the spirit of bondage again to fear; but ye
have received the Spirit of adoption, whereby we
cry, Abba, Father."

In our view of Christian life and experience, we
must not lose sight of the fact that it is not something we originate by our own private and independent
religious activities. It is not manufactured out of our
personal moralities. Instead it is created by birth.
It is a life which comes from antecedent life. But
like all other life, birth means parents and parents
mean families. So it is here, and we are about to be
introduced to the legal family status and the intimate
family life of the Christian. Before it was the Christian as a new creature. Now it is to be the Christian
as a child.

Up to this point, we have not heard a word about
sons or children. That appears for the first time in
verse fourteen, "For as many as are led by the Spirit
of God, they are the sons of God." And this presents
us with the family relationship of the believer.

The test of Christian sonship is the Holy Spirit's
leadership. It is "as many as are led by the Spirit

of God." This is a sure test of genuine Christian experience because it indicates our affinity to God. It means that leadership is followed by obedience. It means a link of life between God and ourself. It is not a set of rules or a lot of restrictions and regulations. It is just the persuasion of an inner conviction. This is enough and it is sufficient to reveal our close relationship to God.

The significance of this new relationship is twofold and is found in verse fifteen.

1. "Ye Have Not Received the Spirit of Bondage."

This new relationship is free from any kind of slavery. Sons are never slaves and God will never put His sons in any bondage. It is neither bondage to legalism, nor bondage to any other form of restriction. But if it is freedom from such bondage, neither is it the extreme of license. The one-time subjects of law are now the sons of God. The erstwhile slaves to personal habits and passions are now sons. In any well-regulated family, there is an implied law. It is the law of life, the father's life in his child. The child will obey because of the affinity between them. It is also the law of love, the father's love for his child and the child's love for his father. One will require and the other will render obedience because of the affection between them. This is the relationship that now maintains between the believer and the Father. Not law but life and love.

2. "Ye Have Received the Spirit of Adoption."

The Spirit of adoption is, of course, the Holy Spirit. And the effect of His reception is our adoption. Notice that it says, "Ye have received" implying a fact completed. This is in keeping with the proper order of every experience of regeneration. It is impossible, as the previous ninth verse states, to be a Christian without the Holy Spirit.

Adoption indicates a family relationship. It implies our being brought into the family of God. In our modern language, adoption signifies the selection of a child and heir who was not born of us. It is bringing someone legally into the family who was not brought in by the process of birth. But that does not fit this picture of adoption for all God's children are such by a new birth. Here, however, it has to do with a born child of God coming to age, and the procedure of recognizing him as an adult son. And so we receive the Holy Spirit with all the rights and privileges and honors of the adult sons of God. The newest born child of God may share, to the widest extent in the Father's blessings, with the oldest child of God.

What happens when this occurs? It is a cry, "Abba Father." "Abba Father" literally means "My Father, my own dear Father." It is a term of endearment and of intimacy. It is not the Jewish cry of Jehovah. It is not the Gentile cry of Creator. It is not the distant, far away, formal name that an outsider ascribes to deity. It is something new and intimate. It is a family name. It is a personal name.

# 11

## THE GLORIOUS MAN
### *Romans 8:16–25*

THERE is a progressive character in the revelation of the portraits of the men so far reviewed in our study of Romans. They lead us from the dire darkness of deep and universal sin into the blood-marked pathway of individual redemption. And now we stand at the threshold of a great universal redemption that touches, not only the soil beneath our feet but the sky above us.

The salvation offered in the Christian gospel is not merely a brief and momentary flash of grace. It has its beginning in the crisis of a moment of faith. It has its continuing in the process of a life of grace. It has its consummation in the redemption of both our physical body and our earthly environment.

The so-called literati scorn our faith because they say it is so impractical and other-worldly. They ask for a more practical faith but they do so in ignorance; not knowing the great scope of our gospel. The purposes of redemption include two worlds. They include man's spiritual nature and his physical nature. They deal with the chemical construction of the universe as well as the character of the race.

If you belong to the succession of faith in the Nazarene carpenter, you possess the beginnings of an eternal romance that will never cease. You are now in the beginning of the great procession of events that will bring you at last into an expansive universe of new life and into the very presence of God. No wonder Paul could say, "Eye hath not seen nor ear heard, neither have entered into the heart of man, the things which God hath prepared for them that love him."

Let us look at this "glorious man" and see what features he bears and what surroundings he is found in. The key is in the phrase "in Christ Jesus" found in the first verse of this eighth chapter.

I. HEIRS WITH HIM. Verses 16, 17.

Preceding this we have had in view our union with Christ, our living in Christ, our adoption by Christ, and now we have heirship with Christ. It is natural to move from the thought of adoption into the thought of inheritance, for the very purpose of adoption is to provide an heir.

It is natural, too, to move from the thought of sonship and the family relationship into the thought of family problems such as home and suffering. God has made us heirs to provide us a home. The home of God's heirs is the universe. God made the world to begin with that it might be the home of a race created in His image. But that world went into a state of vast corruption and disorder. Now with the redemption of man, comes also the redemption of the world he lives in.

This is the next great event in the schedule of redemption as set forth in Romans.

1. The Christian's Inner Witness. Verse 16.

"The Spirit itself beareth witness with our spirit, that we are the children of God."

The Christian's inner witness is not so much an emotion as it is a possession. That possession leads to a conviction. In saying this, we would not intentionally divest Christian experience from any experience of the emotions. Christian experience is an experience of love and love is the most exalted emotion we have. What we wish to emphasize is the peril of the prostitution of our emotions with false experiences. And the gravest danger of that peril lies here.

The Holy Spirit has come to be a witness. His supreme purpose is not for an emotional exercise that might lead us into highly spectacular experiences. His supreme ministry is twofold. It is first that we might know the Lord, and second that we might know the Word.

It is a mistake to assume that we cannot have here and now a present assurance of our salvation. The Spirit of adoption in us cries out, "Abba Father." This is assurance.

There are three witnesses by which everyone may determine his relationship to God.

(1) *The witness of the Spirit.*

"Hereby know we that we dwell in him, and he in us, because he hath given us of his Spirit" (I John 4:13).

(2) *The witness of the Word.*

"These things have I written unto you that believe on the name of the Son of God; that ye may know that ye have eternal life, and that ye may believe on the name of the Son of God" (I John 5:13).

(3) *The witness of the life.*

"Then said Jesus to those Jews which believed on him, If ye continue in my word, then are ye my disciples indeed" (John 8:31).

All three of these witnesses combine to make one authentic witness which will give both testimony and proof of the reality of our Christian profession. It is this, "He that believeth on the Son of God hath the witness in himself: he that believeth not God hath made him a liar; because he believeth not the record that God gave of his Son" (I John 5:10).

Men are no better than their convictions. What are ours? Men are no happier than their assurances. What are ours? Men are no more secure than their anchorings. What are ours? When one is a Christian, possessed of the new life, he will not need to hunt frantically for reasons to substantiate his faith. Supply the faith and God will supply the reasons to verify that faith. It is "the Spirit that beareth witness with our spirit"; it is not our reasoning nor our emotions.

The authentication of our Christian experience is not left to chance nor to conjecture. It is as certain as life itself. We know we are alive because of the manifestation of life. And we may likewise know the certainty of our new life. But this certainty does not emanate from us but from the One within us. It is not given by the preacher nor does it come from the authority of the church. Mrs. Catherine Booth, the mother of the Salvation Army, instructed its early workers very wisely when she said to them, "Do not tell anybody they are saved. I never do. I leave that for the Holy Spirit to do. I tell them how to get saved." It is well that we should remember this, for assurance is a divine prerogative which we dare not preëmpt.

Another thing to notice is that this inner witness by the Holy Spirit is not merely an abstract testimony to our feelings. It is rather an affinity with our own spiritual nature. It does not say "to" but "with." He comes in to affiliate Himself with our new nature. And it can be so because with our regeneration came a new affinity with God. Before, it was an enmity; now, it is an affinity. Before, it was away from God; now, it is with Him. Before, it was alienated; now, it is domesticated. What was once true in the beginning has become true again in this new beginning, for the image lost has now been restored and we find ourselves partakers of the divine nature.

2. The Christian's Inheritance. Verse 17.

"And if children, then heirs; heirs of God, and joint-heirs with Christ; if so be that we suffer with him, that we may be also glorified together."

The Spirit's inner witness confirms our experience and reveals our affinity. It is the affinity of child and parent. It is the affinity of a new nature. It is also the affinity of a new relationship. We are assured of our membership in God's family, for we are now "the children of God"; not the creatures of God. We were such by creation. But we are now the children of God, and we are such by the new creation.

In this new family relationship, there is, of course, the standing of heirs. We have automatically become the heirs of God. Heirship means an inheritance. In this case, it is the inheritance of God.

The protection of inheritances is one of the most precious prerogatives of our courts. Year after year, court battles are waged against false claimants to estates. And in this portion of the Bible are found the rules and regulations of a great spiritual inheritance. God's great estate of life and the future are not to be falsely appropriated by any but the legal heirs. The legal heirs of God's estate of life are those who "have received the Spirit of adoption, whereby they cry 'Abba Father.'" It is regulated by birth and blood ties. The birth is the new birth and the blood tie is the blood of the Lamb. It is by redemption that we share in the abundance of our Father's possessions.

We become possessors in prospect of a vast spiritual estate. But just what does this estate consist of? Is it something tangible? Is it in such form that we may appraise it? Indeed so, but only a small portion is apparent now, for Paul says, "Eye hath not seen, nor ear heard, neither have entered into the heart of man, the things which God hath prepared for them that love him" (I Cor. 2:9).

It is a vast inheritance kept in trust against the day of our completed redemption. But even so, the present moment and the present years are not wanting in the abundance of our Father's riches. They are "riches of grace." They are the riches of joy and peace. They are the riches of His fellowship. "For ye know the grace of our Lord Jesus Christ, that, though he was rich, yet for your sakes he became poor, that ye through his poverty might be rich" (II Cor. 8:9).

There is the old story of a man who had a piece of property, and who wanted to sell it very badly. He tried to sell it himself but being unsuccessful, he listed it with a real estate man and told him to write an "ad" for the next day's press. When the "ad" was submitted to him and he read the glowing description of the property, he said, "I don't think I'll sell that property. I've wanted a piece of property like that all my life." None of us "can ever long for as much as we have." We cannot possibly desire more than God has given to us.

Notice that it mentions "heirs" and "joint-heirs." The significance of this lies in the significance of Christ. It is His work that is in view here—not only His work of redemption but, equally as much, His work of creation. He is both Creator and Redeemer. "All things were created by him and for him . . . and by him all things consist" (Col. 1:16, 17). The creation, continuation, and consummation of the physical order was, is, and will be under the authority of the Saviour. Therefore, whatever heirship we have, we have by virtue of Him. It is not only "with Him," but it is as much "through Him." It is redemption that completes creation and if we wish to share in the completed creation, we must share in His finished redemption.

The new order lies in Jesus Christ. What holds the universe together so that it works as one perfect whole? What holds the stars in order and harmony so as to keep them in their orbits? What holds the atoms in order and the electron in its orbit around the proton and neutron in that infinitesimal solar system we find in the atom? You say law. But who is the authority for and guarantee of law? The only answer is God in the Second Person of the Trinity who is Jesus Christ. He it is who will perfect the world through the process begun in redemption. The present disorder will be corrected. A new world and universe system will arise. A new race will populate it. A new order will come. It will come by the Son of God. It will come through a completed redemption. A new cosmos will come out of the old chaos. A new life will come out of His death. And our place and participation in it lies in these words, "joint-heirs with Christ." We are an "heir of God" only because we are a "joint-heir with Christ."

Two words in the latter half of verse seventeen introduce us to this new order. One is the word "suffer" and the other is the word "glorified." They, of course, are at the antipodes of experience. One speaks of our present order. The other speaks of the order to come. One dates from sin. The other dates from completed redemption. The interim may include suffering but the end is glorification.

How can suffering be reconciled to the goodness of God? It cannot because it was never intended to be. This is not the order of life which God created. It is the one which man has created with his sin, his greed and his passion. God's order is coming. It may seem a long way off, but it is on its way. Be sure you are in the way of its glorious procession.

God will build the new world with a new people. He will not use the materials of our morals nor use the ruins of our failures. It will be built by Christ with blueprints scaled to infinity and eternity. It is good to live with this far-view of life before us. If we see life through the sweat that drops from our brows or through the care that furrows our faces, we may be constantly discouraged. Unless there is a purpose to divinely execute and a certainty of fulfillment behind all the tragedy of the present moment, there is not much point in living. God means us to be more than beasts who scurry for a living. He means us to be sharers with Him in a great program of reconstruction and redemption.

The present moment is the matter of largest consequence to so many people. Their perspective is wrong, therefore, their life is warped. If suffering comes, there is no explanation for it. It is just so much pain that must be endured. But there is a new management of our lives to be found in the Bible. In God's new order, "suffering" has its counter balance in "glory."

II. SUFFERING WITH HIM. Verses 18-25.

We call attention to five things:
1. The Sufferings of the Present. Verse 18.

"For I reckon that the sufferings of this present time are not worthy to be compared with the glory which shall be revealed in us."

The sufferings of the present are not the prospect of the future. Notice that Paul "reckons." It is not a speculation. It is calculation with a considered judgment. Notice what Paul reckons. He reckons "that the sufferings of this present time are not worthy to be compared with the glory which shall be revealed in us." Two things are thrown against each other by comparison. The word "compare" was used originally in connection with weights. And so Paul suggests that when present suffering is put in the scales, with future glory, they scarcely show any effect. They are not even worthy to be compared to the coming glory.

The tragedy is that so many of us have such a cheap and shallow conception of the Christian life. It is what we can get out of it now that concerns us most. And we do not minimize what we can get out of it now. But we must also consider what we can put into it. What we put into it will be the measure of what we get out of it. We are thinking of seventy years but God is thinking of an endless eternity. We are thinking of today, but God is planning for tomorrow. We are thinking of an easy time, but God is thinking of a better man and woman. And in that case, our trial of bitter things may be God's furnace of better things.

Suffering today is natural, but it certainly is not normal. This is so because the natural is not normal to God's original order. It is subnormal and has brought this subnormality into every phase of life. A good rule of life, in view of this fact, is to always keep the big objectives in view. Give as little permanent attention to the disturbances that arise today. Hold the goal in view. Do not allow the sufferings and disappointments of the present to disengage your thought from the goal or you will lose sight of the primary importance of life. The unkind word, the unfaithfulness of a friend, the evil deed of the hypocrite, the temporary triumph of wickedness, the pain of the present suffering, may so disaffect you as to completely unfit you for any good God would have for you to do.

In other words, keep your eye on "the glory" and not on "the sufferings." Of course, this is easier said than done. But it is not impossible, for if we walk in the Spirit we have His aid and power. Nor is this some visionary scheme of ignoring the facts. We cannot ignore reality but we do not need to be handicapped by it.

Man has but three days in his span of life. He has a yesterday, a today, and a tomorrow. His yesterday is gone, gone forever. He cannot retrieve a single mistake nor erase a single deed. His only hope for yesterday is God's forgiveness through justification. His today is here. He is accountable for it. He must live in it. It will be gone very quickly. In the face of its exacting demands, there is but one hope. It is God's grace in sanctification. His tomorrow is on the way. No human effort rendered apart from God will be sufficient for it, but if he will add the God of his yesterday to the grace of his today, he will have glory for his tomorrow. Thus, his three days are met and matched by the gospel's justification, sanctification, and glorification.

2. The Manifestation of the Sons of God. Verse 19.

"For the earnest expectation of the creation waiteth for the manifestation of the sons of God."

The link between creation and creature, between matter and man, is in the fact that man is made of the soil beneath his feet. Yet he is more than soil; he is soul as well. Although by his mind he is master over matter, this does not reveal the ultimate greatness of man. Both man and the creation partake of a common corruption. Both have a destiny of death.

But the Bible tells us of a day when God is going to link the creation with the unveiled glory of His redeemed and glorified children. In this manner glorification will swallow up corruption. In this same manner God has identified the destiny of the soil to the soul of man and the destiny of all the physical creation to the coming glory of the Christian. What a prospect this is!

It is apparent that whatever this "manifestation of the sons of God" means, it is not now in force. It is something yet to be. But it is of a certain and definite nature. It is to be a manifestation, or an unveiling, which means to bring out to view. Someday the sons of God will come into their own. They may be the minority group now. They are "wrapped up in the common brown paper of flesh looking outwardly like other folks." Another day is coming when the new nature, which now is spiritual, will be physical as well. The salvation which now concerns the soul will extend to the body. The powers of mind and spirit, which are now limited by reason of creation's curse, will be expanded into every realm and the redeemed man will be complete master of every law and every force in the universe. This will all come with the unveiling of the Christian.

Since in the beginning we find that the creation partook of the curse which came upon the sinning creature, so also in the new beginning we find that the creation will partake of the glorification of the redeemed creature. Toward this day it seems to instinctively look. In fact, it is its "earnest expectation." It is longing and yearning for the great unveiling day.

Do we catch the force of this? The whole prospect

of a better world lies in the Cross of Christ. The new era is linked to redemption. The whole world of matter and man, earth and sky, land and water, flower and tree, plant and animal, will partake of the benefits of sin's conquest. But it will do so only at the manifestation of the sons of God.

Just when will this unveiling occur? Is it the gradual process of a slow conquest or is it sudden and revolutionary? I John 3:2 reads like this, "Beloved, now are we the sons of God, and it doth not yet appear what we shall be: but we know that, when he shall appear, we shall be like him; for we shall see him as he is." Our unveiling and Christ's appearing will be simultaneous. His appearing is, of course, His second coming, at which time the unveiling of the Christian will take place and which will witness the gigantic transformation and liberation of the earth from the thraldom of decay and death.

3. The Subjected Hope. Verse 20.

"For the creature was made subject to vanity, not willingly, but by reason of him who hath subjected the same in hope."

The ultimate conquest of the earth and its subjugation to man is not to be by our mentality. It is, instead, associated with morality. Its subjection was associated with man's sin and consequent immorality. Even so, its conquest will come when man has been restored to his place of moral and spiritual perfection.

Sin has affected the constitution of every created thing. It is as it declares here, "subject to vanity." Weymouth says, ". . . made subject to futility." And Arthur S. Way says, "All created things have had to submit to a seeming purposeless existence." That is precisely what appears as we view our world apart from redemption. What is its purpose? It seems to have none. It is a perpetual futility. Life is accompanied by disease and succeeded by death. Catastrophies and cataclysms come with crushing consequences. Humanity passes through constant cycles of rise, decline, and decay. What does it all mean? What answer does the microscope give us? What answer does the telescope give us? There is no answer but in the Cross.

Here is a vast creation, throbbing with atomic power and literally bursting with prospect. But it is under subjection. This is not by accident, for God subjected it to the evil now resident in man against the day when evil shall be taken out of man. In other words, the creation is handicapped by the creature and made to share in his condemnation.

The Christian's hope embraces all of God's projected plans of redemption. It includes new men, new nations, and a new world. This future for the world is contingent upon the future of the children of God. They are those who are more than creatures. They are now children. They are not only born but twice born. They are not only created but regenerated. And, because of this, they are the first contingent of the new world and the new order that is coming. Because of their new nature, they fit into God's plan for a new world. What has happened to the Christian spiritually will happen to the world physically. And out of that great coming regeneration will arise the new world which is this great "hope" to which the whole creation has been subjected.

4. The Delivered Creation. Verses 21-23.

"Because the creature itself also shall be delivered from the bondage of corruption into the glorious liberty of the children of God. For we know that the whole creation groaneth and travaileth in pain together until now. And not only they, but ourselves also, which have the firstfruits of the Spirit, even we ourselves groan within ourselves, waiting for the adoption, to wit, the redemption of our body."

Herein lies one of the most thrilling prospects in all the declarations of the Bible. It is the· prospect of a great universal regeneration. It is the promise of the coming reconstruction of our vast system of nature. It is of such magnitude as to stagger the imagination and we stand in awe before the prospect of so gigantic a change as will come both to ourselves and the physical environment in which we live.

The small-minded critic of the Bible is sent scurrying to cover before such a fact as this, and deserves to hide his face in shame for his pitifully ignorant aspersions upon the Word of God. The Bible has taught us not only the fact of the unity of the race of man as a whole, but the connection of the destiny of the physical world with man. Man was created out of its chemical dust. He was given dominion over its destiny. He lost this through sin and was subjected to the disability of a curse, as the result of that sin. The physical creation suffered from the curse, for it is written, "Cursed is the ground for thy sake, in sorrow shalt thou eat of it all the days of thy life. Thorns also and thistles shall it bring forth to thee."

Not only matter itself but force partook of this

curse, for cyclones and similar natural disturbances were born out of a disordered world system. This connection between nature and man has caused the earth to suffer under man's sins and has procured what is described here as a groaning creation. But there is to come a renaissance in nature, for "The wilderness and the solitary place shall be glad for them; and the desert shall rejoice and blossom as a rose. It shall blossom abundantly and rejoice even with joy and singing" (Isa. 35:1, 2). Again it says, "Instead of the thorn shall come up the fir tree, and instead of the brier shall come up the myrtle tree" (Isa. 55:13). Not only vegetation but animal life shall be changed, for "The wolf also shall dwell with the lamb, and the leopard shall lie down with the kid; and the calf and the young lion and the fatling together; and a little child shall lead them. And the cow and the bear shall feed; their young ones shall lie down together; and the lion shall eat straw like the ox" (Isa. 11:6, 7). This is not all, for man himself will be different. "They shall beat their swords into plowshares, and their spears into pruning hooks: nation shall not lift up a sword against nation, neither shall they learn war anymore. But they shall sit every man under his vine and under his fig tree; and none shall make them afraid" (Micah 5:3, 4).

Here are grand descriptions of a renovated physical nature and a regenerated human nature. What a change from our modern world as a whole! This is what is in store for the world. The prospect of it is neither scientific nor political. It is spiritual. It is linked with the coming liberty of the children of God.

Here are three related facts:

(1) *The future liberty of nature.* Verse 21.

The liberty of nature is linked with the liberty of the believer. Here it is "the creature" and "the children." The creature means the creation; the whole world cosmos of land, sea, air; and their populated multitudes of man, beast, reptile, fish, and bird. The liberty of regeneration that is coming to the children of God is likewise coming to the creatures of God. Thus will be offset the vicious effects of sin. The destructions and disease and death of this present world are not the remnant of an unfinished creation. Nor are they the unfinished parts of a progressive evolution. They are the result of a spiritual deficiency which came to man through sin.

There is no adequate explanation of origin or destiny apart from the Bible. The materialist cannot tell how we came, for the explanation is not an intellectual one but a spiritual one. Let the naturalist explain the presence of disease and death. He has none because death is not natural. It is unnatural. Fear of death is everywhere found in nature. "If death was merely the resolution of the body into its component chemical parts, what would it matter to my atoms if they are to form new combinations? Why should chemical substances have such a horror of forming other substances? The reason is that death is more than a chemical change. It is a spiritual penalty."

Flammarion said at the grave of his friend Morpon: "If this grave is the end of existence, and its closing world, creation is senseless, and the infinite universe with all its suns and moons, with all its creatures, with all its light and hopes, less to the purpose than the most trifling action of the dog or the ant."

The present disorder of disease and death in the world is no proof that there is no purpose in the order of nature. It is no proof if the skeptic says that there is no God in intimate touch with our world and us. In spite of its disease and disorder, the continued existence of the world and the race without the natural destruction of the one and the self-destruction of the other proves that the course of both are systematically and providentially ordered. If this were not so, the whole creation would have collapsed in its first moments of existence. It is so because "the most trifling alteration would endanger the existence of us all. The slightest increase of carbonic acid gas in the air, or sea water in the place of fresh water, or one hundred degrees difference in the temperature, and we should be no more . . . A letter omitted from the chemical formula, one figure taken from the infinite series, and the world-equation would no longer be correct" (Bettex).

Although things are not as they should be, it is not the Creator's fault but the creature's. But God has a plan for a new world. And God's plan is linked with the completion of redemption. Until that time, the creature's hopes are inseparably linked to the Christian's destiny.

We notice such recurring expressions as "the glory that shall be revealed in us," and "the manifestation of the sons of God," and "the glorious liberty of the children of God," and "the redemption of our body." What do these mean? In brief, they refer to both an event and a time which will produce a grand-scale in redeemed man and nature. The event is the coming again of Jesus Christ. The time is the establishment of His earthly kingdom. But it does not say that here and for that reason it is not of any private or independent interpretation, for it is linked with the rest of the Scripture. And in the rest of the Scripture, we find God's plan to restore physical nature to its orginal perfection by a universal physical regeneration; just as He is now restoring human nature to its original righteousness by individual regeneration. The individual regeneration began as a result of Christ's first coming. The universal regeneration will result from Christ's second coming.

The present order of nature is described as "a bondage of corruption." How extensive does this penetrate into nature? Look into the throat of a lily and it takes a stretch of imagination to consider that as being corrupt. Yet leave that lily in water for a few hours and it will give off an offensive odor. It is because the process of decay is in every sphere of nature. Everything ends sooner or later in corruption. It is an order that should not be, but it is. It is a vast and penetrating corruption that is seen in its most devastating effects when it touches man's moral nature. Here is the corruption of purity, truth, honor and life in all its parts because man's moral nature has fallen under the dominion of sin's decay.

(2) *The present travail of creation.* Verse 22.

This verse begins with a possessive statement, "for we know." Who knows? The newspaper man? The scientist? The philosopher? The social planner? The economist? The poet? They apparently do not. But the Christian knows if he knows the Lord and the Word as he ought. He knows of a great universal disorder in nature and a coming new order. He knows that something is wrong and all is not as right as the poet suggests when he says, "all's well with the world." It cannot be a well world when it is sick in every atom of its creation. But because the Christian knows the Lord, he also knows of a time coming when the chemical disturbances will be readjusted and the inherent corruptions will be cleansed. And because he knows this, he knows more than the scientist knows. He knows thrilling headline news. He may not know everything, but he knows enough to give him an edge on optimism. In fact, he has the only right there is to be an optimist. He knows that what is wrong is wrong with "the whole creation." This does not merely mean the created order of our little planet but the entire universal creation.

This "whole creation groans and travails in pain." What a change has come to God's grand creation to which, when He had finished, He gave His own approval by saying, "and God saw everything that He had made, and, behold, it was very good." It was upon this occasion that there occurred that great symphony of nature when the cymbals and the flutes and the drums and the harps and the viols and the trumpets of the whole creation joined in music. It was then that "the morning stars sang together" in their first concert. The stars and the hills, the sea and the mountains are full of music and they will some day become articulate in song, for Isaiah speaks of the mountains breaking forth in choral singing.

But until that day of the coming song, we have this day of the sigh. There is a sigh in nature rather than a song. Pick up an ocean shell and you find its roar is tuned to the minor key. Listen to the wind blow its zephyr or howl its cyclone, and it is also tuned to the minor key. Listen to the birds sing and the beasts growl, and they too are tuned to the minor key. In fact, all nature has its pitch of life and expression in the minor key. That is why it is a sigh instead of a song. That is why it is a groan instead of a shout. That is why it is travail instead of triumph. All of the voices of nature are in the minor key and they will continue until the present bondage of corruption is succeeded by the coming liberty of the "children of God."

Notice the kind of pain in which the creation groans and travails. It is the travailing pain of child-birth. Nature is laboring to bring forth a new day. It groans "until now" to bring forth a new era. But the natal day of this new condition of creation is synchronized to the day of the Christian's unveiling. On that day he will be like His Lord. He will have a new body and also a new environment to fit that body. It will affect the soil which will be given a new fecundity and fertility. It will affect the seasons which will undoubtedly undergo some modification and adjustment. This will especially be true over desert and arctic areas where the extremities of heat and cold prevent normal life. It will affect the atmospheric circuits to produce a new cycle of moisture in new areas and in a more equable distribution. It will affect the flora, giving them more profusion and wider distribution. It will affect the fauna by changing the fierce destructive nature and habits of wild beasts into a mild and gentle disposition to harmonize with the pacific character of the peaceful earth.

And into this setting comes a new race. The children of God furnished with corruption-free bodies preside over the destinies of nations that war no more. The world is restored to an economic parity that has wiped out totalitarian aggression and has destroyed the fanciful theories of Socialism and other isms. We are relieved of regimentation and restored to a new freedom of individual security guaranteed by the righteousness of a new government under the King of Kings and Lord of Lords. Then "they shall sit every man under his vine and under his fig tree and none shall make them afraid" (Micah 4:4). This is economic security, indeed, but we hasten to remind you it comes by spiritual security.

In connection with our present world and its present evil there are three ways by which God deals with evil.

a. Restriction.

The natural tendency of nature is not, as we have been told, to evolve into better forms of life. This betterment only comes through mechanical selection. It is, instead, to revert to earlier forms of inferiority. This tendency would ultimately cause our self-destruction were it not for a divinely injected law of restriction. It is found in Deuteronomy 5:9, "Thou shalt not bow down thyself unto them, nor serve them: for I the Lord thy God am a jealous God, visiting the iniquity of the fathers upon the children unto the third and fourth generation of them that hate me." God thus set a limit to the heredity of evil. If this had not been so, the race would have long since become extinct. By its divine decree the effects of a parent's sins cannot be propagated beyond the great-grandchildren or the great-great-grandchildren. Thus creation's cumulative corruption is prevented by God's method of restriction through natural law.

    b. Regeneration.

This is God's intervention through incarnation and atonement by the Cross. It is not a natural law as in the former case, but a spiritual change. It puts God's Spirit into the human spirit. It brings divine life into human life. It puts a new nature into an old nature. It gives a law of life for a law of death. It is thus that God deals with evil in the individual.

    c. Glorification.

This is the final means. It has not yet been put in force. Do not think that we are being gradually glorified any more than we are being gradually regenerated. Regeneration is a crisis that leads to a process of sanctification. Glorification is likewise a crisis that leads to a process of perfection. The crisis has not yet come. It will come at a time when physical man and physical nature will be released from the limitation and corruption of sin's curse and be brought into a unison of blessing.

    (3) *The inner assurance of believers.* Verse 23.

Two groanings are found in two adjacent verses. The *creature's groan* is found in verse 22. The *children's groan* is found in verse 23. But how different these groans! The creature's groan is without knowledge. It groans under the liabilities that sin puts upon it. It groans in the blindness of an unknown end. The promise of an ultimate redemption and release is found nowhere in nature. It is not to be found in tree or rock, bird or beast. It may stray into a poem or a song but when it does, it is born out of a Christian faith, for the prospect of nature's redemption is only in the children of God. The children's groan is very different. It is not the hopeless groan of a helpless sufferer. It is not the groping grasp of a blind thinker. It is something intimate and personal. The promise of ultimate deliverance is within their very selves. It is the Holy Spirit resident in the Christian and is here called, "the firstfruits of the Spirit."

The "firstfruits of the Spirit" are not the imagined and conjured ideas of the mind. They are the revelations of the Holy Spirit. They are the Christian's joy, peace, power, and such things as relate to Christian experience. These firstfruits are the divine pledge that we will personally come to the time of the adoption or maturity which is here called "the redemption of the body."

In verse fifteen adoption affected our spiritual position and privileges, bringing us into the immediate rights of our heirship. But here it has to do with our physical body. It is the physical liberation from the present condition of weakness, decay, disease, and death.

If the children groan, are we to "groan within ourselves" while we wait for this day of completed redemption? Not, of course, as the creature groans. It is not the groan of a sigh but a song, for we are to wait with joy. The "firstfruits of the Spirit" give us the qualities of happiness that could not otherwise come. If we must wait that day in a wheelchair for a new body, or in blindness for new eyes, or in sickness for new health, or in poverty for new wealth, do it with the convictions of joy and faith. And, even then, remember that we may rise above our disabilities and make our life a blessing in the midst of adversity.

Before going on to complete this portrait of "the Glorious Man," let us go back to pick up a phrase from the present verse which indicates the high order of life possessed by the Christian. That phrase is "the firstfruits of the Spirit" in verse twenty-three. Here is indicated the difference between the natural man and the spiritual man. The natural man is purely natural. He may talk about spiritual values, but he does not have any basis for his calculation. The spiritual man has a new and higher form of life. It is not only akin to divine life, but it actually is. He has received with that life these "firstfruits of the Spirit." These firstfruits are from the Holy Spirit. They are not a lot of extravagant emotional ecstasies. They contain plenty of emotional experiences. Ours is a faith that feels. But it is more. It includes a restoration of the spiritual intelligence that man originally had as a spiritual being before he fell and became only a natural being. As originally created man was a spiritual person. For him, all God's creation and each of God's laws had a spiritual value and significance. In Eden there were no expressed laws except a negative one, "Thou shalt not." How did Adam know God's will and God's mind? We believe not only through the spiritual nature within him, which was in direct communion and fellowship with God, but also through the natural world about him.

As long as he remained sinless, the laws of nature were intelligible for him. In the life of the Garden he saw the law of birth. In the plants of the Garden he saw the law of growth. But when he fell, creation came to be a blank, material phenomenon. It was filled with dumb animals and insentient plants and inanimate minerals. To him, now, even with his science, it is a meaningless thing. The best that he can see behind creation is intelligence. He does not see personality; only some mysterious power.

But when he becomes a spiritual man, he has a new appreciation and a new understanding. He has "the firstfruits of the Spirit." He sees a new meaning. Instead of an endless chaos in the cosmos or instead of a blind evolution, he sees a God with a plan. That plan is tied up to both history and prophecy. The historical aspect is the Cross. The prophetical aspect is the great redemption day of nature in Romans. His indeed is the only rational and intelligent and sensible outlook for both himself and the world he lives in. The Christian possesses now what he will participate in later. Have the assurance and God will take care of the performance.

5. The Patient Waiting. Verses 24, 25.

"For we are saved by hope: but hope that is seen is not hope: for what a man seeth, why doth he yet hope for? But if we hope for that we see not, then do we with patience wait for it."

At this moment our faith is the assurance and anticipation of a great hope. It is so because, as yet, the great events of triumph which our faith expects have not occurred. But they will occur, and until they do, we are nourished and inspired and buoyed up by hope.

The first phrase of verse 24 is better read: "We are saved in hope," because we know we are not saved by hope. But being saved by faith we now are kept in strength and courage by this hope.

The Christian's salvation is a fact. It is not something he hopes will be true for he already has the firstfruits of it as the pledge of its completion. And we could properly say that he is saved unto a great hope. That hope being the expectation of the ultimate redemption of the body as well as the regeneration of the world.

There remain but two alternatives as we wait for the future. They are either hope or fear. A hope is the anticipation of something better. A fear is the frightful waiting for something worse.

What assurance has the natural man of any change and any betterment in the order of things as he finds them today? Surely it is not in history. Certainly it cannot be in experience. And if he thinks that a materialistic science is going to build a new order, he is doomed to disillusionment. The whole hope of the future is spiritual. It goes back ultimately to God. It is Bible-born. It is linked to a new birth. And, apart from these things, he has nothing but presumption upon which to rest his claims for a better world. The Christian is the only one who has a valid hope. It is authentic by reason of the Bible's declarations. It is authenticated in his own personal experience, for his hope is the expectation of the complete redemption of both his body and his environment. It is a fact already commenced in the redemption of his spiritual nature. Thus, what has gone on inside is the prophecy of what will take place outside. The regeneration of the inner world is proof of the regeneration of the outer world. The God of his soul will some day be the God of the world about him. As he knows Him in his emotions, so he will know Him in agriculture, commerce, and a thousand other ways.

But what the Christian hopes for he has not yet seen, "for what a man seeth, why doth he yet hope for?" Until he sees it, it will be a hope. But when he sees it, it will be a fact. And until it becomes a fact, it will constitute a great spiritual force in his life. For it says here, "But if we hope for that we see not, then do we with patience wait for it." Here is the secret of contented contemplation. It is in patient waiting. Our lives span threescore years and ten. But our existence is far greater. As possessors of eternal life, we have the prospect of illimitable existence. What then do a few years more or less here matter? Nothing we can do will hasten God's schedule to completion. We cannot worry it on. We cannot complain it into completion. We cannot work for its finishing. We must wait, but in waiting do it patiently. It is "with patience" that we are to "wait for it."

This suggests a timely thought that will be profitable to pursue. If we must wait for the realization of our great hope, then there are conditions of waiting we must fulfill. The first one is the one mentioned here—

    (a)   In patience—Verse 25.
    (b)   In purity—I John 3:3.
    (c)   In steadfastness—II Peter 3:17.
    (d)   In activity—Luke 12:37.

Happy indeed are the people of this hope. They are not only happy but they are furnished with the only implements of faith with which they can put their lives to the best use. Without these things, they are no better than the animals at their feet, except that instinct is intelligence. But intelligence without God is the most pitiful ignorance and darkness to be found.

Do we have such a hope as this? Does it lighten our load, comfort our sorrows, buoy us up in the midst of our despairs? Better still, does it implement us for a life of real service to God and man? Does it equip us for service and fill our days with deeds done for God?

# 12

## THE INSEPARABLE MAN
### *Romans 8:26–39*

WE LOOK now at the twelfth and final portrait to be seen in this art gallery of life and experience as found in the first eight chapters of Romans.

The twelfth man is the Inseparable man, and he is the climax of a series of men in which we see manhood in crescendo. We commenced in the first chapter, after being introduced to the series with the apostle's portrait, with the Inexcusable Man. We started with man in the vilest associations of sin, and end with him in the highest associations of holiness. We commenced with the writer saying of the principles of the gospel, "I am not ashamed." We end with that same writer saying of the effects of that same gospel, "I am persuaded."

Out of the gathering certainties that accumulated with each new picture has come an unshakable certainty of life that leaves us in the gospel's best mood. The child of God is not left to chance and uncertainty. He is not left even to the folly of his own mistakes. His destiny is not a pious probability. And when the apostle's pen describes the final characteristics of the Christian, it puts the Christian in a union of love and life with Christ which is inseparable. We can call it what we choose or deny it as we please, but it is here written,—"For I am persuaded, that neither death, nor life, nor angels, nor principalities, nor powers, nor things present, nor things to come, nor height, nor depth, nor any other creature, shall be able to separate us from the love of God, which is in Christ Jesus our Lord."

We find as we explore the truths of this section, that they deal with the Christian's personal security. There is a link between the redemption that is coming and the redeemed one who is waiting for that great day. In verse twenty-five it speaks of waiting "with patience" and in verse twenty-six it immediately strikes out with the words, "Likewise the Spirit also helpeth our infirmities." In other words, while we are waiting we have an inward sustaining.

I. SUSTAINED BY HIM. Verses 26-28.

The Christian does not only have a great hope for the future, but he also has sufficient help for the present. It is stated that "the Spirit also helpeth our infirmities." This help is the present portion and experience of our hope. It is that which makes Christian experience so practical and so necessary. Think then what it must mean to go through life without either this hope or this help. What a barren existence it must be! And yet it is the plight of the world outside of Christ.

As we come now to this place in the book and survey its truth and then consider what it has revealed, we must be impressed with the perfection of God's revelation. Step by step, truth by truth, conclusion by conclusion, we are brought to both the redemption of the individual and the redemption of the world. The Christian is redeemed now and waits the coming day of the world's redemption. But how does he wait? Is he left to his own devices and to depend on his own resources? Never! He is secured against that day by the operation of the two great spiritual laws. He is sustained in this interim of grace by two divine operations, the Law of Divine Intercession and the Law of Divine Intervention.

By the Law of Divine Intercession he is kept in spiritual strength and vigor. By the Law of Divine Intervention the events of his present earthly life are resolved into a marvelous unity of purpose so that all things resolve themselves into good things. In the midst of his infirmities is God's ever-present all-mightiness. And in the midst of his kaleidoscopic happenings is a supervising providence that makes good out of bad and triumph out of tragedy.

The first of these two laws operates in the inner world of our emotions. The other one operates in the outer world of events. The first one has to do with divine intercession, for "the Spirit itself maketh intercession for us." The second has to do with divine intervention, for all things are made to "work together for good to them that love God" and are the called according to His purpose.

Without either or both of these present divine operations in the believer's behalf, he could neither be sustained nor secured against his day of unveiling. There would be no semblance of an intelligent meaning to his life. He would be fate's victim, but now he is a victor through faith. As a bit of human flesh, he would be caught in the whirling vortex of life's maelstrom. But now he has a spiritual life destinated and secured by the operations of divine law to the completion of God's great purpose.

Mark well these two truths. Understand them clearly, for in them lie both your security and your serenity. We are sustained:

1. By the Law of Divine Intercession. Verses 26, 27.

"Likewise the Spirit also helpeth our infirmities: for we know not what we should pray for as we ought: but the Spirit itself maketh intercession for us with groanings which cannot be uttered. And he that searcheth the hearts knoweth what is the mind of the Spirit, because he maketh intercession for the saints according to the will of God."

In the first place, notice that it begins by stating a general fact: "Likewise the Spirit also helpeth our infirmities." The Spirit is the Holy Spirit. His ministry is to "help." It tells us how intimate God is to the Christian. He is not a far-off being beyond the hearing of our cry. Nor is He in some position where we have to beg and implore Him to help. He has already taken the initiative. He is already helping us.

The character of His ministry for us is in us and it is to help. It is God sharing our burdens. It is God taking hold of our problems. It is God strengthening us in our weakness. Yes, it is God helping.

But notice the specific character of His help. It is "intercession." Just what does it mean by intercession? We understand it as prayer. And it is. But it is more, for it primarily means "to go to a person for the purpose of consultation." In that capacity the Holy Spirit presides over the daily destinies of our lives as the divine consultant. You do not need the services of a phrenologist or an astrologer or a psychiatrist. Here is One instantly at hand.

The believer has two divine helpers. One is the Lord Jesus and the other is the Holy Spirit. The Lord Jesus is our helper in heaven. The Holy Spirit is our helper on earth. Christ is the advocate with God. The Holy Spirit is the advocate with man. Christ is in heaven preparing a place for us. The Holy Spirit is on earth preparing us for that place. Christ intercedes for us at the throne of Grace. The Holy Spirit intercedes within us in the heart.

Notice here a change in the Holy Spirit's ministry. It was formerly the ministry of inspiration by which the Old and New Testament writers were enabled to write the Scriptures. That ministry has ceased and the work of inspiration has now become the work of intercession. He now operates in the lives of all believers, for the specific purposes of sustaining and securing them against the day of their completed redemption.

Never allow yourself to sink so deep in the oblivion of your difficulties that you forget this phrase, "the Spirit also helpeth." There may not seem to be any way out, but there is a way up. Every other avenue may appear blocked, but there is a path in the sky. There may be a place where understanding breaks down, but there is still this path in the sky.

Having reached the twenty-sixth verse, we reach a place of high privilege. It not only speaks of the divine law of intercession but it gives us a new conception of prayer. The conception of prayer found here is prayer inspired by the Holy Spirit. With His presence, prayer is more than the recital of words. It is more than flattery to God. It is, in fact, a contact with God. For many, prayer reaches no further than the lips, but real prayer affects the whole life. It is a divine ministry within us that brings us into touch with the divine provision of God for us. We were taught subsequent to this of that great provision of Christ for us. Now we see the ministry of God in us, bringing into play all the forces of God for our good.

In such a conception of prayer, as we have here, we find its importance in relation to the indwelling Holy Spirit. We do not pray by ourselves or for ourselves. Ecclesiasticism needs to recover its perspective of prayer. It has been lost in our ceremonials. It is no longer a divine law which contacts God, but a parade of phrases that is somehow calculated to impress God with what we think of Him.

A few weeks before the last war crisis in England, the Archbishop of Canterbury declined to set aside a special day of prayer on the grounds that it would be "misunderstood or rather misrepresented by the enemy." Who cares what the enemy thinks as long as we know what God thinks? Let us not pray for human ears but for God's hearing.

Now, if the Spirit helpeth our infirmities, just what kind of infirmities does He help? There must be something specific meant here, and there must be something definite to which the help of the Spirit is directed.

(1) *He helpeth the infirmity of ignorance.*

It says that "we know not what to pray for as we ought." This is the lack of proper understanding.

Weymouth's rendering says, "We do not know what prayers to offer nor in what way to offer them, but the Spirit pleads for us." When we do not know how to express ourselves so that our prayers shall fit our needs, then the Spirit makes intercession. When we are ignorant of what is best for us, and when our weak judgments are incapable of choosing that which would result in lasting good for us, the Holy Spirit makes intercession with the right prayer. And right here is the reconciling place of such scriptures which say, "He shall give thee the desires of thine heart." Such desires as are not conformable to God's will are never transmitted to God. Here in the clearinghouse of the heart, the Holy Spirit compensates for our ignorance and foolishness and makes intercession for us only in accordance with the best interests of our lives.

When we are ignorant of what the will of God is, that is compensated by the Holy Spirit's intercession who "maketh intercession for the saints according to the will of God." And it is possible that any other prayer never reaches God.

(2) *He helpeth the infirmity of utterance.*

"But the Spirit itself maketh intercession for us with groanings which cannot be uttered."

Just what does this help mean? It appears that this is one of the most beautiful and needful provisions of the Christian's life. It means that when we are too tired to pray, the Holy Spirit prays for us. When we are too perplexed to pray, the Holy Spirit prays for us. When we do not know what words to use in prayer, the Holy Spirit prays for us. When we are too helpless to pray; and when we are unconscious and cannot pray, then the Holy Spirit prays for us. Name any situation that means infirmity, weakness, helplessness or weariness and in that situation the Holy Spirit makes common cause for us against every foe.

Notice what kind of intercession the Holy Spirit makes for us and in us. It is "intercession for us with groanings which cannot be uttered." Here is the praying of an unutterable groaning. It is with depth of feeling and conviction, yet not a word has been spoken. Wordy prayers are not necessarily the most worthy prayers. The most moving feelings are sometimes unexpressed. And prayers do not always have to be spoken. Nor is it diction and grammar that count. Bunyan said once, "In prayer it is better to have a heart without words than words without a heart.

Your attention is called to the groaning mentioned here. This is the third one. In verse 22 it was the Creation's groan. In verse 23 it was the Christian's groan. Here it is the Spirit's groan. How significant is this groaning of the Holy Spirit in us! He takes us in our bewilderment when troubles press from without and fears oppress from within. He breathes Himself into our thoughts and yearnings and causes the essence of our prayer to be right because it is He who prays both in us and for us. What a miracle of the spiritual life this is!

It is not a prayer book that we need so much as a prayer Spirit. It is He who will help the infirmities of our ignorance and our utterance and bring intelligence and power and spirituality into our praying.

Without Him, prayer is just a pious exercise that has no better effect than a mental stimulation. We may know it instead as a divine operation.

In verse twenty-seven we behold God searching the heart. It may be filled with all sorts of contradictory and contrary wishes, desires, ambitions, and motives. But presiding over all of these is the helping Holy Spirit, and through His intercession our prayers become intelligent and effective. Thus, in the temple of our bodies, God conscripts all our emotions and powers of mind and makes them fit the mould of His will. In this central traffic bureau our prayers get either the green light or the red light. They are either lost in the glamour of pious words or turned into divine power. For this reason, the Christian's prayer life is made both intelligent and important. It is a link to God. It is the fulfillment of a great divine law—the law of intercession by which God sustains us to the day of our completed redemption.

We consider the second of the two great laws that sustain and secure the Christian to the day of his completed redemption. We are secured:

2. By the Law of Divine Intervention. Verse 28.

"And we know that all things work together for good to them that love God, to them who are the called according to his purpose."

Here is God's providential supervision of the events of our lives. This is declared in what is undoubtedly one of the most beloved verses of all the Bible. Who has not quoted this great verse? And who has not sometimes wondered how it could be that all things work good things? Misery seems wrapped in mystery and the meaning seems always beyond us. Here we have not so much an explanation as the opportunity of an experience. For this is a case where faith operates in the sphere of human experience, and we see the providential operation of a great working purpose in our lives.

Here is a place where all life's events pass a point of providence. Here they are resolved to fit a pre-arranged and predetermined goal. That goal is "for good." Here is a conviction which will give a new complexion to life. It will give equilibrium in the midst of storm; poise in the midst of distress; faith in the midst of doubt; courage in the midst of danger; and hope in the midst of despair. Here life is removed from the fateful fruits of accidents and has a fixed purpose. The ultimate end of that purpose is good, although its immediate means may appear calamitous.

If there are those who will dispute this resolution of bad to good and tragedy to triumph, they are only such as are not in God's purpose, or such as have temporarily lost their view of their position in Christ. We must not forget what two laws are sustaining us and securing us against the day of our completed redemption.

If life seems to have dealt harshly with us and we are perplexed and bewildered by the crashing of events, here is a confident knowledge that can meet any emergency. If you are God's child you are in God's purpose, and in that purpose "all things work together for good." Duplicate the witness of Romans 8:16 and you will see the working of Romans 8:28. The witness of Romans 8:16 is the witness of the Holy Spirit "that we are the children of God." The working of Romans 8:28 is "that all things work together for good."

Your attention is now called to six things found in this Law of Divine Intervention.

(1) *The certainty of this providence—"we know."*

Here faith is removed beyond the place of speculation or conjecture and life is consequently removed from the realm of fate. Here is the cognition of faith and the recognition of facts. Faith says "we know." That kind of faith is not an impractical piety that puts a negative mark upon reality. It is a recognition of the facts but a further recognition that God is behind the facts.

It is reported of John Wesley that one day he was walking with a troubled man who expressed his doubt as to the goodness of God. He said, I do not know what I shall do with all this worry and trouble. At that moment Wesley saw a cow looking over a stone wall. Do you know, asked Wesley, why that cow is looking over the wall? No, said the man who was worried. Wesley said: The cow is looking over the wall because she cannot see through it. That is what we must do with our wall of trouble—look over it and above it and beyond it. But looking over your troubles does not mean overlooking their reality. When we have arrived at the place where we can look over our troubles, we have arrived at the place where we can live above them.

(2) *The scope of this providence—"all things."*

Here is faith for the whole pattern of life. It does not include only the good and fortuitous things, but "all things" of whatever color or character they may be.

This does not mean that all things are good things, for there are many things that occur to us, which in themselves are not good. They are painful and bitter and cruel. Nevertheless, their place in the whole pattern of the divine purpose will cause them to be resolved into good.

And so we have a faith to cover every event. What a faith and what a blessedness! Whatever may come and however it may come, it will be resolved for our good.

(3) *The continuity of this providence—"work."*

God's operations in the lives of His people are not spasmodic or conditional; they are continuous. This operation is like the law of gravity. There is no intermittent suspension and no lapse in its operation. It is constantly in force. It does not work today and languish tomorrow. It does not work in some things and fail in other things.

(4) *The unity of this providence—"together."*

This means that there is co-operation and agreement in events. One event, isolated and separated from all other events in your life may seem evil, but, as a result of this agreement, all the events result in a common purpose of good. Just as it is in the seasons, cold and heat, snow and rain, frost and sunshine work together out of seemingly opposite spheres to produce a harvest of good fruits.

This harmony of events is not unreasonable. Did not God give a harmony to His first creation in which everything fits a purpose? Should we think that God would fail in doing the same in the new creation? No! And because we are in His purpose, shade and shine, joy and sorrow, good and bad lose their apparent identity to become ultimately blended into the harmonious purpose for good.

(5) *The result of this providence—"for good."*

The word "good" does not necessarily mean that the event in itself is intrinsically good, but that its effect is both useful and helpful. Therefore, troubles do not hinder or deter Christians, but rather hasten their final purpose.

A story is told of the poet Cowper who was subject to fits of great depression. One day he ordered a cab and had himself driven to London Bridge. Soon a dense fog settled down upon the city. The cabby wandered about for two hours and then admitted that he was lost, though he had been in the business for many years. Cowper asked him if he thought he could find the way home. He said that he did and in an hour landed him at his door. When asked what the fare would be, he mentioned a sum, but said that he felt that he ought not to take anything as he had not filled his order. Never mind, said Cowper, you have saved my life. I was on my way to throw myself off from London Bridge, and he gave him double the usual fare. He then went into the house and wrote the hymn which bears the lines: "God moves in mysterious ways His wonders to perform, He plants His footsteps on the sea, and rides upon the storm."

(6) *The principle of this providence—"to them that love God, to them who are the called according to his purpose."*

The principle upon which this providence will operate in our individual experiences is twofold:

a. "To them that love God."

This is *the human side of the principle.* It has to do with our attitude and our relation to God. It specially mentions love but in a way hitherto unmentioned in this Epistle. Everywhere else it speaks of God's love for us. Now it is reversed to speak of our love for God. It is "to them that love God." And it is not simply a perfunctory religious love but a deep-founded affection that springs out of the affinity of a family tie. In this chapter we were introduced to the believer's family relationship. It is bound together not only by the new life but by a love of affection and esteem that indicates a close relationship to God.

It is commonly supposed by mankind that so long as God loves us, all will be well. Many glibly assume that God's attitude to us determines His blessing upon us. But here the fact stated is different. It is not a question of God's love but our love for God. It is not a question of God's attitude to us but our attitude to God. Therefore, it is only when our attitude to God is what it should be that we can rightfully and legitimately expect this providence to work all things for good. After all, we are dealing with the facts and laws of a new life and they are no more the result of fancy and imagination and wishful thinking than the laws of the natural world around us. We have an ordered and harmonious and logical plan of life in the Christian life.

     b. "To them that are the called according to His purpose."

This is *the divine side of the principle.* You notice that the human side and the divine side are as cause and effect. Our love for God is the result of His call of us. Our response to that call brought us into His family and produced this love. The calling of God is according to the purpose of God, for it is "to them that are the called according to His purpose." The Christian gospel is the revelation of that purpose and the Christian life is the experience of that purpose.

How substantial it makes one feel when he considers that he is a part of a great divine purpose. He is not a detached speck of life, or a nonentity in a mass of humanity. He is not lost in the bigness of things. He is someone that is the subject of a divine call because he is the object of a divine purpose. And, in consequence, he is not left adrift on the sea of life's events to suffer the fate of whatever wind and wave may come. He is in life as the object of a great divine plan and purpose. And the working of that purpose is going on now. It is going on day by day, week by week, event by event, deed by deed, and thought by thought. Everything that happens, without a single exception, is harmoniously worked in a co-operative agreement to one God-chosen end. It is "for good." But it is all within the two principles of our love and His purpose.

Any purpose that God has is not an afterthought. It is a forethought. That is exactly what this word "purpose" means. It refers to the eternal councils of God and has to do with a predetermination as broad as the intelligence of God and as eternal as the character of God.

What is this purpose? It is twofold. It was first creative and second redemptive. It conceived creation and spoke it into existence. Both creation and redemption came by God's Word. In creation the agency was God's spoken word—"And God said." In redemption the spoken word became the living word, for "The Word became flesh and dwelt among us."

In creation the pattern was the image of God. When He made man, the man He made was not a composite of the beasts at his feet. He was more than a plastic creature of chemicals. For "God said, Let us make man in our image and likeness." This pattern was more than physical, for it was both moral and spiritual In the subsequent events following creation came the damning and destroying effects of sin. Man lost his image of God in-so-far as his spiritual and moral character were concerned. But the purpose of God which both foresaw and foreknew, as was necessarily true of divine prescience, included another phase. It was redemption. If the pattern of creation was the image of God, then the pattern of redemption is the image of God's Son. All who are in the purpose of God are to be "conformed to the image of His Son" according to verse 29. That image is for the present, spiritual, but in the future it will be physical. In Ephesians 4:13 it says, "Till we all come in the unity of the faith, and of the knowledge of the Son of God, unto a perfect man, unto the measure of the stature of the fulness of Christ." In Philippians 3:21 it says, "Who shall change our vile body, that it may be fashioned like unto his glorious body, according to the working whereby he is able even to subdue all things unto himself."

The present is not forgotten in the ultimate. God does not merely intend to do something for us. He is now doing something in us. He is doing it by the Law of Divine Intercession and the Law of Divine Intervention. By the operation of this latter law, all the present events of our lives are conspiring to fit the ultimate purpose of God. For this reason, the least is not lost in the greatest. Today is not forgotten for tomorrow. What we are is not neglected for what we will be. The glory does not overshadow the sufferings. In other words, God has not forgotten what we need today. He has made wise provision for it all. And while we may not fully understand or comprehend the mystery of Divine Providence, we may rest by faith in the integrity of God. We may know assuredly that our daily life will fit into His purpose that we will be conformed to the image of His Son.

Having been shown that the Christian is the child of a great divine purpose and that that purpose governs the events of life, we are now introduced to the scope of that purpose. It reaches backward into the eternity of the past and forward into the eternity of the future, and it make us the subjects of its high-minded objective.

The mass of events in our lives which seem to be without point have a purpose. It may be a bed of pain or a thwarted love or a frustrated ambition or a calamitous tragedy or just mediocre success. But if all that men see is the event that happens, there is something unseen behind it. Back of the event is the loom and the framework of God's great purpose. And on this great loom He weaves, according to His great pattern, the fabric of character that shall be the eternal clothing of the Christian.

One thing that needs to be recovered from the limbo of forgotten truths is the truth of the sovereignty of God. We have come to trust so much in the modern religion of science that we have long since ceased to think of a sovereign God whose decrees and decisions have necessarily affected the whole framework of life and history. If His divine decrees of natural law are still necessary to hold our physical creation together, is it not equally necessary that there be the divine decrees of spiritual law to hold our spiritual creation in a state of fixed purpose and progress until it shall reach its consummation in the image of His Son?

If the natural man needs the support of the law of gravity to hold him to the earth, the spiritual man needs the law of continuity to hold him to Christ and holiness. One guarantees the security of the creature while the other guarantees the security of the Christian. The Christian's salvation is not reduced to something you get and try to keep. It is a life-bond with God. It is wrapped up in the eternal purpose of God. It is not merely your choice of God but it is God's choice of you. It is not only God's choice but God's call. And then when faith responds to that call, it is the creation of God's child. And then what? Is it luck, chance and fate? After that, it is "all things working together for good." And then with this law operating in the events of daily life, everything is made to bear on the safety and security and certainty of these children of God who must live in the midst of all kinds of dangers.

II. Chosen in Him. Verses 29, 30.

    1. We Are Foreknown. Verse 29.

    "For whom he did foreknow. . ."

This is to know beforehand. We are not, therefore,

as the heirs of life, God's afterthoughts, but God's forethoughts. Here is the divine prognosis and it removes the scheme of Christianity far from the human pantheons of artificial gods. This is not a scheme competitive to human religions and philosophies. It is a divine and eternal forethought, having been born out of the genius of God and bearing a stamp of authenticity that recommends it to any thinking person. It is not a Lutheran plan, or a Presbyterian plan, or a Catholic plan, or a Jewish plan. It is God's plan. No one can gather it into the circle of his sect and say this is mine. If we are in the plan it is not because of the patronizing nod of some ecclesiast, but by virtue of the foreknowledge of God. Sects and creeds may keep us out, but they can never put us in. This is a prerogative belonging only to God. Go the Bible way and you go the only way, and by that token, the right way and the sure way.

2. We Are Predestinated. Verse 29.

". . . he also did predestinate to be conformed to the image of his Son, that he might be the first-born among many brethren."

What God foreknew was not merely what man would do but rather what God would do for them. On this basis he proceeds to mark out a certain outcome. The outcome He marked out for those whom He foreknew is that they should be "conformed to the imagine of his Son."

Way's translation of this verse reads, "Long ere this he knew our hearts, long ere this he claimed us (as a man claims property by setting his landmarks thereon) as those whom he should mould into the very likeness of his own Son, so that he should have many brothers, himself the firstborn."

In the thought of predestination, there is no thought of an arbitrary predetermination of men to heaven or hell. Here is a sacred mystery which encompasses both God's choice of us and our choice of God. Where the sovereignty of God ends and the freedom of the human will begins, we cannot tell. But both the divine choice and the human choice are found here.

The consummation of God's choice is to be in our conformation to His Son. We are destined to be "conformed to the image of his Son." The word conformed means, in its most proper and direct sense, "to be sealed." It is to be moulded into a likeness of character with Christ. This likeness is not merely to be like Christ but to be as Christ. It is to be what He is, both in character and body.

This conformation has as its final purpose the creation of a new society of men and women among whom Christ is to be known as the firstborn. He was born the only begotten of God. And from Him comes a new begetting of new men who ultimately come into an image-likeness of Him and form an eternal race of men and women.

The process of the conformation into the image of Christ is both spiritual and physical. It is both present and future. It is spiritual now. It will be physical later. Now as Paul states in II Corinthians 3:18, "But we all, with open face beholding as in a glass the glory of the Lord, are changed into the same image from glory to glory, even as by the Spirit of the Lord." Later at the rapture He "shall change our vile body, that it may be fashioned like unto his glorious body,

according to the working whereby he is able even to
subdue all things unto himself" (Phil. 3:21).

3. We Are Called. Verse 30.

"Moreover whom he did predestinate, them he
also called. . ."

The order of the statement is very important. God's
calling was not before His predestining. He did not
wait to see what our reaction was going to be before
He acted. Before all else, this procession of events
is led by a divine foreknowledge steeped in a divine
sovereignty and issuing at last in a gratuitous call
of grace.

Calling means to be invited. But it means more.
It means an effectual invitation. It means that with
the call comes an ability to respond. There is a solemn
sense in which no person can become a Christian when
he or she chooses to. He can only be such when the
effectual calling of God operates in his life through
the Holy Spirit. We are urged to "exhort one another daily, while it is called today: lest any of you
be hardened through the deceitfulness of sin."

4. We Are Justified. Verse 30.

". . . and whom he called, them he also justified."

Having become the object of the divine call, its
acceptance now makes us the subject of a work of
grace in which we are brought into a new standing
before God. In this new standing lie all the potential-
ities of the new life. The resources of grace and life
become the present possession of the believer who
is enabled to live as before he could not live.

Having reached this place in the progression of

grace, the Christian has reached a place of new power and privilege. He must recognize it and move in to his new situation with all of the daring of faith. He is now upon the verge of the greatest adventure of life. And if he is seeking a new adventure in living, he has it in his grasp. It is not in geography. It is not in leisure or pleasure. It is not in dollar chasing. It is in grace. It is in Christian living. Let us dare to find it where we are because of what we are. Let us dare to defy mediocrity and misery. Let us challenge the dominion of sin. Let us move on and up because God has moved into our lives.

While we are riding high in the realms of such overwhelming truths as this chapter affords, we must never forget the practical implication and application that necessarily go with all Bible truth. The Scriptures are revealed in this book of Romans in order that they might be re-lived in our lives. There is a Bible bound in skin as well as leather. That Bible is the Bible in our daily lives.

5. We Are Glorified. Verse 30.

"And whom he justified, them he also glorified."

There are two things you are asked to notice about this matter of glorification.

(1) *What it is.*

The word itself means honor. It is in that sense the same honor which God bestows on His Son. But this honor is more than homage. It is something far more than applause and acclaim. It is, at long last, the completed redemption of the children of God. It is the end of a process of salvation which began with our justification and now ends with our glorification.

The extent of this glorification is our conformation to the image of Jesus Christ. It is, therefore, in a sense, the restoring and retrieving of what man lost in the fall, for, in creation, the pattern was the image of God, while in the new creation the pattern is the image of God's Son.

The exact process of this glorifying is not indicated. But regardless of that, we know most certainly that it is not to be construed as some mystical and artificial religious halo that is placed upon us as a sort of medal of honor or badge of merit. It is fundamental change in the status of life. It is the reproduction in the physical, of the present spiritual work of regeneration. It will affect our whole physical experience, transforming body and mind upon the basis of the new life for the new world of which this glorification is but the prelude and the preparation.

For this reason, glorification is God's remedy for corruption in creation. It is, in fact, the process of a new creation. It is the time and means by which all the disabilities of our bodies shall disappear. It will mean life without the handicap of the present phase with its disease and death. In a word it will mean a new creation.

(2) *When it is.*

This great process is future, of course. It is not now going on in a process of gradual betterment any more than the orginal creation was the gradual collection of chemical materials and their progressive assembly into a created order.

But here the future is taken for a fact. It is stated in the past tense, "them he also glorified." Here is one of the most daring statements of faith in all the

Bible. It is stated as an accomplished fact, and what is so stated is to be so considered. And as far as God is concerned, those whom He has foreknown and predestinated and called and justified are, by the same token, glorified.

Here the Christian is seen, not as he may seem to be, but as God sees him. To God, "the pilgrim is already in the Immortal Country; the bondservant is already at the day's end, receiving his master's 'Well done, good and faithful.' "

The picture of the Bible's great program of world rehabilitation through the salvation of Christianity is like a five-link chain. To begin with, that chain is anchored and secured to a great divine purpose. Proceeding from that purpose are five links. The first is *foreknowledge;* the second is *predestination;* the third is *calling;* the fourth is *justification;* and the fifth is *glorification.* Here is a salvation which began in the eternity of the past and ends in the eternity of the future. It began in a divine purpose and is consummated by a divine process and leaves at its end a divine product; a race of those who are glorified in the image of God's Son.

Every link in this chain is a divine act. Therefore, they are inseparable. Their welding is by the hand of God and their security lies in the heart of God. It is not left to human chance of frail behavior. It is rather the product of a process begun in the eternal and unchangeable purpose of Almighty God.

To all this, there is both a present and a practical implication. If all this is true, as it is, then what have we to fear? What force, what power, what adversity can harm us? What is there and who is there whose intervening and interfering evil can thwart a purpose so grand as this? The answer follows in the next section.

Now we will see how certainly God has secured us to the completion of His great two-world purpose.

III. KEPT BY HIM. Verses 31-36.

For the sake of keeping the continuity of the dominating thought of this chapter in our mind, let us review its outline. Proceeding from the key thought expressed in the first verse, which is "in Christ Jesus," we have nine related facts which are as follows: Union with Him, Living with Him, Adopted by Him, Heirs with Him, Suffering with Him, Sustained by Him, Chosen in Him, and now Kept by Him which is to be followed by the last of these nine things, namely, Conquerors through Him.

We now look upon language whose riches of truth far exceed anything to be found elsewhere. These verses begin with a question, "What shall we then say to these things?" To what things? Why, to the five things just completed. To those things which began in divine foreknowledge and ended with our glorification. What shall we say concerning their reliability? Shall we say about them, we hope they are true? Shall we say about them, we trust that they will come to pass? No, we dare not, for their accomplishment is not left to probability, or chance, or fate. They are securities which rest their ultimate end in divine certainties. Seeing that this is so, let us garnish the chamber of our hope with these verities of faith. Let them be the food that nourishes our courage for the present conflict. Let us go forth to the day's duties with the knowledge that each seemingly insignificant task has its part in the great purpose.

We address ourselves to a question. It is this opening sentence of verse 31, "What shall we then say to these things?" Way's translation of this question reads, "In face of all this, what remains for us to say?" Yes, what shall we say? We dare not offer any refutation, for all these things will gainsay our argument. There is but one thing to do. Let us accept the assurances that these things offer and pursue our lives in the securities wherewith Christ surrounds us. Let us not go on in our decrepit and disgraceful way, but go on in the assurance of these certainties.

Four questions dominate this section. They proceed from its basic thought found in verse 31, "If God be for us."

1. Who Shall Oppose Us? Verses 31, 32.

"If God be for us, who can be against us? He that spared not his own Son, but delivered him up for us all, how shall he not with him also freely give us all things?"

*This is our protection.* In verse twenty-six we find the Holy Spirit "for us." In verse thirty-one we find God "for us." And then in verse thirty-four we will find Christ to be "for us." Here is the Trinity "for us," and they add up to a great conviction of security. Here, indeed, is a formidable source of protection. Here are forces and influences calculated to meet, measure and master every foe. Here is a sufficiency of divine power actively engaged in our direction. In no case is it divine help awaiting our call but God taking the initiative and helping us even before we call.

The Holy Spirit is "for us" as our intercessor to help our infirmities. The Father is "for us" in working all things together for good. The Son is "for us" as our intercessor at the right hand of God. Because this is so, who can be against us? There remains no condition and no person formidable enough. "A man in the right, with God on his side, is in the majority, though he be alone" (H. W. Beecher).

Let this conviction settle itself in our thoughts and we become unconquerable. God is "for us" in our weakness. God is "for us" in our sickness. God is "for us" in our moment of depression. When we doubt, God is "for us." When we fall, God is "for us." When we fail, God is "for us." There is no time, no place and no condition in which God is not "for us." Let us take courage in this conviction and press on to conspicuous living and serving. Let us allow no thought to disarm us and defeat us because the prevailing attitude of God toward us is that He is "for us." Therefore, from this moment, do not let it be the thought of who or what may be against us. Strength does not rise out of either the inferiority or the superiority, the presence or the absence of our adversaries. It is not who is against us but who is "for us."

How do we know that God is for us? The evidence is found in verse thirty-two, "He that spared not his own Son, but delivered him up for us all, how shall he not with him also freely give us all things?" The evidence of God's favor is in the exhibition of His love to us. What was true of the past is the measure of the present. What God has already done is proof of what He will continue to do. The persuasion lies in God's performance. If He delivered Christ to meet our sins while we were sinful; it is much more true that with Christ He will give us all things necessary to keep us now that we are His children. In other words, God's greater gift ensures God's lesser gifts.

In this, God has established both a precedent and a proportion. The precedent is in *what He gave.* Having given Christ in crucifixion for our sins, He will surely give with Him all the necessary means of grace for our security. The proportion is in *how He gave.* God gave Christ without stint or measure and the proportion of His historical gift is the proportion of His personal gifts of grace to each of us now.

2. Who Shall Accuse Us? Verse 33.

"Who shall lay anything to the charge of God's elect? It is God that justifieth."

*This is our perfection.* The expression before us has been gathered out of legal language. The words, "lay anything to the charge of," literally mean to arraign, as an officer of the courts would arraign a person before the judge. In this case, it is accusation before God and it is such accusation as might be brought either by Satan to attempt to discredit the efficacy of the atonement or by man to attempt to discredit Christianity.

The argument is that no one can successfully accuse a Christian. First, because of who is being accused. It is an accusation against "God's elect." Such accusation is of no consequence, for in the believer's position he has been previously shown to be foreknown, predestinated, called, justified, and glorified. Second, because of the One before whom the accusation is made. It is made before God. But if God is the judge, He is also the justifier. God has already decided in our favor. God has already put us on His side and declared Himself to be "for us." God has already declared us just, therefore, His decision for us is both final and irrevocable.

But all this being true is no reason for the relaxing of responsibility for our own acts. Because God is for us is no reason or excuse why we can be for anything we choose to be. God's justification of us commits us to righteousness in every act of life. Hence, the position of the believer is fundamentally secured and established.

3. Who Shall Condemn Us? Verse 34.

"Who is he that condemneth? It is Christ that died, yea rather, that is risen again, who is even at the right hand of God, who also maketh intercession for us."

*This is our vindication.* The case of the Christian cannot be reopened nor can a further charge of condemning delinquency be brought before the tribunal. God has already ruled in our favor. It is a ruling that not only covered all past sins, but of provisional necessity covers all future sins. Therefore, it is a closed matter.

There are four reasons for the finality of the believer's judicial position. All of these four things are found in the work of Christ, and before any flaw can be found in our position, a flaw must be found in Christ's person and work.

(1) *Christ's death*—*"Christ died."*

It was both final and sufficient. It was accepted of God as having met every requirement and condition.

(2) *Christ's resurrection — "Yea rather, that is risen again."*

His resurrection was the proof of the sufficiency and efficiency of His death and the visible and historical evidence of our justification.

(3) *Christ's ascension—"who is even at the right hand of God."*

This means a place of authority at which Christ exercises Himself in our behalf. His present place is not a tomb but a throne.

(4) *Christ's intercession—"who also maketh intercession for us."*

This duplicates what was said of the ministry of the Holy Spirit in verse twenty-seven. The Holy Spirit's intercession can properly be said to be *in us.* while Christ's intercession can be said to be *for us.* This is so because the Holy Spirit is in us on earth while Christ is for us in heaven.

Now "what shall we then say to these things?" It is a question for each of us to answer. Shall we say: this is my assurance? Shall we say: this is my life? Shall we say: this is my security? Let us not only say it but act on it and live by it.

4. Who Shall Separate Us? Verses 35, 36.

"Who shall separate us from the love of Christ? shall tribulation, or distress, or persecution, or famine, or nakedness, or peril, or sword? As it is written, For thy sake we are killed all the day long; we are accounted as sheep for the slaughter."

*This is our security.* Here the question concerns our circumstances as the previous three concerned our character. The others had to do with what we are while this one has to do with where we are. Three questions inquired about the security of our relationship to God, while this last one deals with our social and physical security in the midst of an environment of calamity and adversity.

The instant answer follows the previous answers to the effect that since there is no successful opposition, no just accusation, and no true condemnation, neither can there be any effective separation. Add up these spiritual facts and you have the sum of a fourfold assurance of the Christian's security.

Three things appear in the subject matter of the thirty-fifth verse.

(1) *Who attempts the separation?*

As in the previous question, it is the personal pronoun "who." Following the pronoun, however, are seven impersonal events. There is no mistake here. This is not an accident of rhetoric. It is correct, for the source of evil is never impersonal, although the events of evil may be. To explain evil in the world you never deal merely with events and things. The Bible reveals the presence of evil in the world in the person of an evil one. There is a law of evil as well as a law of good. There is a realm of evil, as well as a realm of good. If good is from God, evil is from the opposite of God. We have the divine and the diabolical. We have the Holy Spirit and the evil spirit. We have the Son and Satan. And this "who," as in each previous case, refers to him—Satan.

(2) *What is the attempted separation from?*

It is "from the love of Christ." The bond that binds a believer to his Lord is not only a bond of life, but love. This love is not a transient affection in the heart of Christ. It was tested in the death of the Cross. Therefore, it is something that will not yield to the pressures or oppressions of life. Since it is a link with the heart of God and since its security is in the very highest manifestation of God, we can be sure that nothing can separate us from that love.

If a believer's destiny is moored to his own feelings, then he has a frail and changeable anchor indeed. If it is moored even to his own behavior, he has a very fluctuating security. But it is anchored to neither, for here it is declared to be linked by an inseparable bond to the love of Christ. Let us take new courage and gather renewed assurance from this truth and enter life's arena determined to be winners.

(3) *How is this separation attempted?*

Seven things are listed as constituting the array of weapons employed against us. Let us lift them out one by one and examine them.

    a. "Tribulation."

This refers undoubtedly to the multitude of afflictions that are common to life. Because they are common to life, they are common to the Christian except where God's providence may decree otherwise.

    b. "Distress."

Here is a word with a very suggestive meaning. It means a very narrow place where one is crammed and pressed in by oppressive circumstance. It is to be, as we say, "in straits." In such dilemma one could not go forward. There was no way to go around. And one could not even beat a retreat. But always in such distress the Christian can look up. If we have no promising outlook, we always have a reassuring uplook.

c. "Persecution."

This refers to any adverse opinion and treatment of us because of our Christian faith. To persecute literally means "to pursue." Are we pursued by the tongues of those who hate us for Christ's sake? Does a designing enemy seek occasion to denounce us and injure us for Christ's sake? Then be assured of this that never has persecution ever separated anyone from the love of Christ.

d. "Famine."

Here the weapon becomes economic. It reaches into kitchen and cupboard. It touches purse and bank account. It emaciates the body and shrinks the stomach. How can this be? Is it not true that God will always provide liberally for His children? Not always. Here, want and hunger and pinched faces and aching stomach and craving appetites come into the scope of the permissive will of God. But even such a state of affairs cannot alienate and separate us from the love of Christ.

e. "Nakedness."

How in the economy of divine grace and love can nakedness and rags contribute to character and enhance the Christian life? It seems irreconcilable, but it is a factor God can use effectively and to lasting good. He must sometimes divest us of everything to give us the best. It is not clothes but character that counts. And should God see fit to permit this to come upon us, remember that we will then be a companion with Paul. He said, "even unto this present hour we both hunger and thirst and are naked and buffeted and have no certain dwelling place." Yet Christ's love abounds

even in the absence of every physical luxury and
sometimes in the presence of physical necessity.

f. "Peril."

The meaning is self-evident. This mechanical civilization increases our perils and we are in imminent
danger each day of our lives. But even on the most
precarious occasions we are safe, for nothing can
sever us from the love of Christ. Your peril, seen or
unseen is impotent to harm though it may look tragic
and monstrous.

g. "Sword."

When organized government uses the sword of execution, even this is impotent to separate us. It is so
because the ties that eternally secure us to Christ
are impervious to all such assaults and methods. There
is no weapon so cleverly devised but what fails when
used on a Christian. It may even carry out its apparent purpose but its real purpose is thwarted because
nothing alienates us from Christ.

Here were people who, according to their own testimony in verse thirty-six, were ready any moment to
surrender their lives for their faith in Christ. What
they believed, they believed in sight of the gallows
and the arena. They knew the price of discipleship
and they gladly paid it. They paid it with their
life blood. And when Paul wrote this to Rome, he was
preparing them for coming events when many of
the very ones he addressed died at the claws and
mouths of wild beasts in the Coliseum. "Do you
want a relic?" asked a Pope of some visitors to Rome.
"Gather dust from the Coliseum; it is all the martyrs'."
The days of martyrdom are destined to return. They
come now on swift feet. Europe has them and we

may in America. Let us saturate our souls with such truths as these that we may wear an armour nothing can pierce. We may have need of it sooner than we think. Let us be wise and prepare for the evil day while good is present. Let us get ready for adversity in the days of prosperity.

We see now a man of triumph standing upon the summit of the heaped-up adversities and complexities of life. With his head bared to the heavens, he is uttering a never-to-be-forgotten cry of victory. Hear him, "Nay, in all these things we are more than conquerors through him that loved us."

IV. CONQUERORS THROUGH HIM. Verses 37-39.

The eighth chapter of Romans leads us out of condemnation and into conquest. Its presentation of the Christian message does not leave us with a negative godliness in which we live in a holy vacuum. It leads us, instead, into a life of aggressive victory and to the place where we can face any of the many foes of life and declare ourselves to be "more than conquerors."

Notice four things about the believer's superlative conquest.

1. The Extent of the Conquest. Verse 37.

"In all these things. . ."

Here is an extent which encompasses every human and earthly condition. It embraces every possible contingency. Nothing is omitted from the scope of the believer's area of victory. It does not modify its message by saying "in some things," or "in most things," but completes the range of conquest by saying "in all these things." And "all these things" goes back to the things mentioned in verse thirty-five where it speaks of tribulation, distress, persecution, famine, nakedness, peril, and sword.

We must remember that conquest always presupposes a contest. There can never be any victory without a battle nor can there be any conquest without a contest. The battles and the contests are sure to come in a believer's life. Christianity never promises to shield us but it does promise to sustain us. There is no immunity to a Christian so far as life's problems are concerned. He must suffer what the sinner suffers. Many people come to great grief because they think that God is going to make cosmic pets out of them and provide them with a sheltered life. It will not be so. But what God does grant the Christian is a way of life which is not only superior but superlative. He provides the Christian with an inner life which can meet and master every circumstance in the outer life. This is the glory of the gospel. Let us be sure that we do not underestimate its provisions and under-live its possibilities.

2. The Degree of the Conquest. Verse 37.

"We are more than conquerors. . ."

Here is Christianity's superlative result. It is not only success but more success. It is not only conqueror but more than conqueror. It is not only victory but more victory. There is not adequate language to describe it or standards by which to measure it.

Just what is it to be "more than conquerors"? It is difficult to comprehend. Someone has said that "a conqueror is one who wins by fighting; a 'more than conqueror' is one who wins without fighting." But that is not sufficient, for the Christian is a constant factor in every victory. And it is right here where the more than conquering comes in. To conquer may gain a victory over the foe, but to more than conquer is to gain an advantage out of victory for the victor. There is nothing so empty and depressing as a normal victory. Hitler had dreamed for years of victory over France but when it came, we dare say it was very depressing. It was Wellington, the Iron Duke, who, viewing Waterloo, was heard to remark that "the saddest thing next to a great defeat is a great victory." It is only when the victory does something for the victor that it means what it ought to mean.

In ordinary circumstances, to conquer tribulation would be to end it and the same with distress, persecution, famine, nakedness, peril, and the sword. But to more than conquer these seven enemies is as Chrysostom suggests, "to conquer by means of our adversary," that is, to use the adversity which the adversary employs against us for our own good. It is to learn from our foes of life the lessons that could never be learned in the ordinary things.

To be more than conqueror over "tribulation" is to become patient through it. In Romans 5:3, Paul says, "We glory in tribulations also; knowing that tribulation worketh patience." In this way the adversity is used for an advantage. The thing that is designed for our evil becomes our good. We not only conquer it but more than conquer it by making it serve in us a good purpose.

To be more than conqueror over "distress" is to become master over the most straitened circumstances. It is to rise above the restrictions that life may place about us. It is not only to endure them but to use them.

To be more than conqueror over "persecution" is to become Christlike toward the persecutor. Instead of employing the weapon of hate, use love. Instead of using force, use faith. Instead of descending to the lower levels of carnal fighting, use the weapons of warfare which are spiritual. To be more than conqueror here is to keep from being mean and low, and to be aggressive and positive in grace.

To be more than conqueror over "famine" and "nakedness" is to let economic adversity teach one the wealth of spiritual things. It is not merely to be in the place of legalism where "thou shalt not covet," but to be in the place where the absence of these things enhances character.

To be more than conqueror over "peril" is to have a confident dependence upon God that gives poise in the midst of impending calamity. Paul knew what it was to be more than conqueror over peril when he reported his own experience in these words of II Corinthians 4:8-10, "We are troubled on every side, yet not distressed; we are perplexed, but not in despair; Persecuted, but not forsaken; cast down, but not destroyed; Always bearing about in the body the dying of the Lord Jesus, that the life also of Jesus might be made manifest in our body."

This is what it means to be more than conquerors in the situations which have been set before us. It is not merely putting down the enemy but rising to higher heights upon his prostrate form.

3. The Source of the Conquest. Verse 37.

". . . through him that loved us."

It is important to notice who are the conquerors and how. It is "we" who conquer "through Him." Christ does not conquer for us but we conquer through Him. Paul said, "I can do all things through Christ which strengtheneth me." It is our battle, but His resources. It is the assertion of "the law of the Spirit of life in Christ Jesus." It is the resident power of the indwelling Christ. It is our walk after the Spirit.

This means more than assistance; it means association. It is not the case of an artificial religious assistance given to us because we say our prayers and perform our religious duties. It is not striking a bargain with God so that for so much human affection we receive so much divine assistance. It is the association of life with Christ's life. This association begins by birth and continues by growth. The birth is the new birth and the growth is the result of our spiritual association in the organic union of the new life with Christ.

4. The Completeness of the Conquest. Verses 38, 39.

"For I am persuaded, that neither death, nor life, nor angels, nor principalities, nor powers, nor things present, nor things to come, Nor height, nor depth, nor any other creature, shall be able to separate us from the love of God, which is in Christ Jesus our Lord."

These words are led by that majestic phrase of personal confidence and assurance, "I am persuaded."

This is a wonderful place to come to. Too many are in the place of equivocation and vacillation. They have not reached the place of spiritual maturity and are "like a wave of the sea driven with the wind and tossed."

When Paul says that he is persuaded he means that he is convinced. To be convinced means to have a belief beyond doubt. Such a belief is not founded on emotional ecstasies. It may bring tremendous and moving emotional experiences but it does not have such a foundation. It is something founded on proof and the argument of this proof Paul has presented hitherto in a long procession of declarations. Paul is persuaded because a divine law of intercession and another divine law of intervention operate in his behalf. He is persuaded because a five-link chain anchors him to an eternal purpose of God. He is persuaded because no valid accusation and condemnation and no effective separation can operate against him. And, furthermore, because he is in Christ and because Christ is in him, he is supported in all the changing and fluctuating fortunes of life with this great conviction.

The conviction Paul has is enhanced and strengthened, and in fact it is demonstrated to be valid and genuine, because it is both intelligent and demonstrable. Someone has reminded us that there are only two ways of getting through this world of ours; one is to stop thinking and the other is to stop and think. Paul did not stop thinking when he became a Christian but, as is the normal effect, thought processes that he never knew he had before, and never used before, even while he was Gamaliel's honor student, came into play. Now he really thought for the first time in his life. His mind was released from the confining restrictions of the bondage of sin. Instead of that cloudy atmosphere of the Adamic nature, he was able to think God's thoughts after Him. Hence, this conviction.

Just what did Paul's persuasion consist of? It lists ten things that he is convinced can never separate him from the love of God. Let us examine them and see how formidable they may be.

(1) *"Death."*

Death in its natural setting is a penalty. As such, it separates. It separates not only body and soul, but the spirit and God. But in Christ death is met and the penalty removed, consequently, it cannot separate.

(2) *"Life."*

Surely, life cannot be considered in the category of enemies. But it is. Life is more dangerous than death. It sets up a thousand conditions that might seriously affect our lives. It is full of perils. As near the most beautiful of desert blooms there lurk the deadliest vipers, so in life's most alluring and attractive situations are the gravest dangers. But even so, to the Christian who is secured to God's great and eternal purpose, there can come no separation.

(3) *"Angels."*

Here, undoubtedly, are hostile forces of another world who, sight unseen, are parts of a vast organized body of spirit beings. There can be no demonstration of them on the basis of our present experience, but both revelation and our intuitive reasoning confirm their existence. Surely, it is enough that they are mentioned here and that their reality is declared to be just as definite as either death or life.

(4) *"Principalities."*

These are spirit beings of a higher rank. They may be properly classed as spirit sovereigns existing as a celestial hierarchy. They are mentioned by Paul in Ephesians 6:12 in company with "spiritual wickedness in high places" and "the darkness of this world." As such, these principalities no doubt constitute the reigning order of the evil world which is all around us as well as above us.

(5) *"Powers."*

These powers are undoubtedly linked with the previous principalities. The word power comes from a word which means "energy." Here it is the evil influence of the evil personalities called principalities. It is a statement of their evil working. There is a realm of this evil working in our modern world. It includes all kinds of sorcery, necromancy, and bewitchment which is pawned off on a gullible public as spiritism. On the borderland of this dangerous evil working lie such seemingly harmless practices as fortune telling and their kindred shady arts. These we ought to shun and remember that what may be the remnants of superstitution and witchcraft are but a faint and indistinct pointing to a realm of evil working and an energy of demonic malignity. Let us shun it and have nothing to do with it. But, in any case, we should remember that even such evil energy as this cannot separate us from the love of God.

(6) *"Things Present."*

This means the present world order. Whatever the

arrangement may be, it cannot affect the essential relationship of believer and Lord. If it is totalitarian or democratic; if it be individual or institutional; if it is some enticing thing of present fancy, it cannot sever us from Christ. We are secured to Him against any foe.

(7) *"Things to Come."*

Here is the future. What an uncertain quantity this is unless we have a well-founded life! Whatever is not now in existence and that may arise cannot touch the Christian. Whatever a fertile imagination can invent and whatever undreamed of event can arise, has no power to sever the ties which bind us to Christ.

(8) *"Height."*

If things present and to come speak of time, we now have something which speaks of space. Though its distances are vast and we live in an infinite universe, there is nothing so vast about it that can rob a Christian of his consciousness of God. Space cannot separate us from Christ because He is intimately present among His people. In the flesh, He was limited to a bodily manifestation. Now He is so near as to never be absent and so close as never to be separated.

(9) *"Depth."*

Depth is, after all, a relative thing. It is not so much depth in relation to the earth but in relation to all the universe. But it may be spiritual as well. The Psalmist said, "Whither shall I go from thy Spirit? or whither shall I flee from thy presence? If I ascend up into heaven, thou art there: if I make my bed in hades, behold thou art there. If I take the wings of the morning, and dwell in the uttermost parts of the sea; Even there shall thy hand lead me, and thy right hand shall hold me. If I say, Surely the darkness shall cover me; even the night shall be light about me" (Ps. 139:7-11). No condition of space or time can sever the life and love-bound ties that secure us to Christ.

(10) *"Any Other Creature."*

Here is a summary and a gathering of any contingency and every condition that might possibly have escaped our notice. In it is implied anything and everything that could possibly act in the capacity of an enemy to the Christian. The conclusion arrived at now is that neither one nor all, either separately or collectively, "shall be able to separate us from the love of God, which is in Christ Jesus. Here is inseparable love in the midst of every conceivable enemy.

But there is a prescribed sphere wherein this inseparable love operates. It is declared here to be "the love of God, which is in Christ Jesus our Lord." It is not the love of God as a principle, but in a Person. It is not the love of God which is a feeling but which is the result of fellowship. Here, then, is something definite. It is "in Christ Jesus our Lord." Meeting this condition, we will enter into that significant place of security and blessing which adds divine joy and blessing to our lives.

With this security, the pen of the divine writer brings its message to a close. He spans the distance from an Inexcusable Man in sin to an Inseparable Man in security. Having dipped his pen in the blackest colors of sin, he now dips his pen in the brightest colors of glory and triumph.

# 13

## THE PAST ELECTION OF THE JEW
### *Romans 9*

ROMANS eight left us upon lofty heights of truth
while Romans nine leads us into practical channels for the application of that truth.   There is
found here a different treatment of that which is under
consideration throughout the entire book, namely, the
righteousness of God.   In the first eight chapters it
was the righteousness of God in respect to individuals.
But here it is the righteousness of God in respect to
nations.   To be more precise, in respect to one nation,
the nation of Israel.

We enter now the second phase of our study of the
book of Romans.

This section divides into three smaller sections, each
one embracing a complete chapter.   It deals with the
Jew in Rejection.

1.   The Past Election of the Jew   Chapter 9.
2.   The Present Salvation of the Jew.  Chapter 10.
3.   The Future Restoration of the Jew.  Chapter 11.

We have then to examine the first section which
deals with the divine purpose of God as it concerns
the nation of Israel.

I. PAUL'S PASSION. Verses 1-3.

"I say the truth in Christ, I lie not, my conscience also bearing me witness in the Holy Ghost, That I have great heaviness and continual sorrow in my heart. For I could wish that myself were accursed from Christ for my brethren, my kinsmen according to the flesh."

Here is the vicarious passion of Paul showing the genuineness of his faith. Jesus showed the genuineness of His deity by His vicarious passion for us. It is given to us to show the genuineness of our Christianity by our vicarious passion for others. Jesus died vicariously for others; we must live vicariously for others. It is only by this sort of living that Christianity can be given its proper demonstration. It is essentially a vicarious life.

If we spoke as Christians, we would speak the mind of Christ. His mind was one of honesty, purity, love and peace. It was the speech of Jesus that called forth the amazement of His enemies. And it is in the speech of Christians that we can reflect the significance of our faith. One thing is sure, we will reveal the depth of our experience.

Paul not only spoke according to a pattern of thought, but he spoke with the witness of his conscience, for he said, "I lie not, my conscience also bearing me witness in the Holy Ghost." What a difference it would make if we were constantly conscious of this inner witness! It would act as a monitor to our speech which would then flow out of our lips in gracious blessing.

The depth of Paul's attitude is expressed with great

feeling as he says, "I have great heaviness and continual sorrow in my heart." This does not mean that Paul was continually mourning. It does mean, however, that his life was motivated by deep feelings and purposes. He was not a selfish consumer but rather a selfless contributor. He was not living an empty life of sham that could only end in shame. Ah, no! He was a man of purpose and it was reflected in a great yearning desire for his fellow man.

Do we ever sigh for the souls of man? Are we ever burdened and troubled about the spiritual welfare and eternal destiny of our fellows? A selfish Christianity is a travesty. Its very purpose is reproduction. God intends that every Christian shall reproduce Himself in other Christians. It is no different in the spiritual world than in the natural world. In nature the law of reproduction was "after its kind." And there is an identical law of reproduction in Christianity where Christians are to multiply after their kind. This is normal to a true experience, and when Paul expresses himself in the terms of heaviness and sorrow, he is mentioning the travail and birth pangs of his soul for the salvation of others.

Notice to what lengths Paul was willing to go in order that he might help his countrymen. "For I could wish that myself were accursed from Christ for brethren, my kinsmen according to the flesh." Who of us have ever so completely negated ourselves and our feelings and personal ambitions that we were willing to take the place of cursing that others might find the place of blessing? Who of us wish ourselves a place in hell that someone might have a place in heaven? Consider the self-effacement that was necessary for this man to take such a place as this. Its equal is never found except on the Cross.

If this world and its humanity are ever to have an adequate witness for Christ some of us will have to make some such vicarious sacrifice as Paul made. It seems that the church has hit a high center on the highway of world evangelization. It is hung up on selfishness. It is consuming its energy in heresy hunting and membership fighting. Instead of fighting on a common front, it is divided into separate camps to satisfy personal grudges and exploit particular doctrines. But where today will we find the vicarious travail of Paul?

We wish you to notice that the logical effect of truth as found in Romans eight is the living that is found in Romans nine. It demands a conscientious honesty and it leads to a passionate concern for others. No true Christian is an introvert who finds his satisfaction in himself.

II. ISRAEL'S PORTION. Verses 4, 5.

"Who are Israelites; to whom pertaineth the adoption, and the glory, and the convenants, and the giving of the law, and the service of God, and the promises; Whose are the fathers, and of whom as concerning the flesh Christ came, who is over all, God blessed for ever."

Paul had two conflicting relationships. He was spiritually related to Jesus Christ and he was naturally related to Israel. Between Israel and Christ was a wide gulf and a great antipathy. Paul's consuming desire was to bring his brethren to a fellowship with his Christ. Just what was the great obstacle? Was it the case of Israel being stiffnecked, bigoted unbelievers? That is the characteristic Christian way of looking at the Jewish problem. But that is not the fair way, nor is it the way of the Scriptures. There may be individual cases which could be multiplied many times over, but there is a more fundamental problem here.

We have to deal with the Jew's relation to Christianity. It is introduced by Paul's passionate desire that they might know Christ. Just why was the Jew holding back? Paul enumerates a great heritage that attached to the Jews that should have made it easy for them to see the naturalness and perfect conformity of both an individual and national faith in Christ. Yet they held back, and the reason for this holding back lay largely in the Gentilizing of Christianity. Some Jews were guilty in Paul's day of Judaizing Christianity. This prevented Gentiles from embracing Christianity. But, on the other hand and to an equal detriment, some Gentiles were Gentilizing Christianity and this prevented Jews from embracing Christianity. This Gentilized Christianity claimed God as its own and in its pronouncements of the future it left the Jew out of the coming events. Therefore, when the Jew saw this, he held back because when he read his Old Testament he found everywhere promises about a universal kingdom of the seed of Abraham. Yet he saw in the church neither a Kingdom nor anything comparable to world-wide dominion.

Paul proposes now to set aside the Jew's objections to Christianity by pointing out that Christianity was not antagonistic to Judaism. Neither was it the same as Judaism. Christ introduced a new order. It was the church, separate and distinct from the nation of Israel, in which one was not considered by national ties; for in the church there is neither Jew nor Greek. The church was not intended to displace Israel but in a proper sense to temporarily supersede Israel. The church is not the Kingdom. It will never fulfill the Old Testament promises of world-wide dominion. Its purpose is spiritual and not national. It is evangelistic and not political. It is to be a witness to individuals and thus to gather a body of believers, both Gentile and Jewish. In the church is to be seen God's great purpose of bringing the world to Christ. This will not be consummated, however, until Israel as a nation is brought to Christ.

With this view of Christianity Paul overcame the prevalent objection of the Jew to Christ. He left them no valid reason for their rejection of Him and gave them a compelling reason for their acceptance of Him, for in Him all their nationalistic hopes would ultimately be realized.

Notice the question, "Who are Israelites?" It does not merely ask who are Jews. It goes back to the historic beginnings of the nation and in its answer enumerates eight excellencies of that nation. What is more, it declares a truth which we, sadly enough, have left out of our perspective of world policy and statesmanship. It speaks of that great Bible fact of a world destiny which is associated with the nation of Israel. Our diplomacy ignores this. Our nationalistic ideologies are endeavoring not only to minimize the Jew, but to obliterate him. So long as this is true, just so long will we frustrate all our hopes and plans for world peace and world prosperity. For all such in the Scriptures are tied up to a Kingdom which goes back for its beginnings to historic Israel.

This Kingdom is not exclusively Gentile nor is it exclusively Jewish, but is based upon the regeneration of both. It will never be born out of modern Judaism any more than it will evolve out of modern Christianity. It is to be in a new era, at a new time, and of a new order. This order will not be a church order nor will it be based on modern Jewish thought, commerce, or education. It involves a great national regeneration. But its beginnings go back to the nation of Israel. Paul answers his own question even before he asks it. In the fourth verse he asks, "Who are Israelites?" but in the third verse he has said, "my kinsmen according to the flesh." These Israelites were Paul's kinsmen after the flesh. He identifies them as the Jews of the first century who have and do continue to our own times. But he also describes them in terms of a great heritage. They may have been dispersed into all quarters of the world but what they are is not to be estimated by where they are. Their present plight in the world as they flee the heel of the tyrant from one nation of Europe to another, is neither the past nor the future picture of the Jew.

Notice the great heritage which describes him.

1. "The Adoption." Verse 4.

This refers to national Israel and not to spiritual Israel. And it further signifies a time of national adoption when the nation, as a nation, was brought into a special relationship to God in distinction from all other nations. This adoption was national, whereas, the adoption of Romans eight is individual. This adoption was for the purpose of producing redemption while the individual adoption is the result of redemption. One is the national cause while the other is the individual effect.

2. "The Glory." Verse 4.

This was that special and particular manifestation of God to this nation in token of His presence among them.

3. "The Covenants." Verse 4.

These covenants were more particularly divine promises rather than co-operative contracts. They were declarations of God's' great intention consonant with His redemptive plan.

4. "The Law." Verse 4.

The obvious thing here is the Law of Moses. It was the divine standard of national righteousness.

5. "The Service of God." Verse 4.

This referred to the sacrificial and ceremonial system of Tabernacle and Temple, all of which were foreshadowings of the person and work of the Messiah. Their portrayal and possession were peculiar to Israel and belonged to no other nations whose religious practices were usually revolting and idolatrous.

6. "The Promises." Verse 4.

Particularly Messianic and millennial promises which disclosed the divine intention to extend blessing to all the nations through this one nation. But in both scope and detail they set forth the program of a new life and a new earth, all of which would come into fulfillment through the Messiah.

7. "The Fathers." Verse 5.

Here was a national heritage of great characters. No nation could boast of such choice ancestry as the patriarchs of Israel. They were links in a great redemptive plan that unfolded from generation to generation.

8. "The Christ." Verse 5.

Notice the wording as between the reference to the fathers and this reference to Christ. It says previously, "whose are the fathers." But now "of whom as concerning the flesh Christ came." The one is possessive for the Fathers belonged to them. But the reference to Christ is simply a statement of production. They were the national means of being the physical channel in producing the Messiah. He is not merely of them. He is out of them. The Fathers were distinctively and exclusively Jewish, but not Jesus. He came the Jewish way but He belongs to the world. The Jewish lineage of Jesus goes back through Abraham to Adam, and is therefore racial as well as national. You cannot compress Christ into a small national mould since, in the intention of God, He came for a world service.

You will be careful now to notice who Christ is. It says "Of whom as concerning the flesh Christ came, who is over all, God blessed forever." Here we see the twofold character of Jesus Christ. He was both human and divine. He is associated with man by our flesh—"Of whom as concerning the flesh." He is associated with God by His name—"who is over all, God blessed forever." Our flesh and God's nature link in one personality, the Redeemer.

For this reason, and all the foregoing items of their heritage, Israel should embrace the Christian faith because it is the progressive consummation of a great divine plan which began with Israel's adoption.

So here, we do not have a humanly devised sect, nor a humanly invented creed. It is a revelation of God and it fits the need of all nations and all men. No wonder Paul, by the Holy Spirit, puts an emphatic and convincing "Amen" at the conclusion of his argument.

We are at present in a time of the history of the nation of Israel when the great purpose of these people has been suspended. The nation is no longer the redemptive channel for the world. Now that channel is the Church. All the previous dispensations of priests and prophets, law and promise are set aside. The whole trend of prophecy, so far as the nation of Israel is concerned, has temporarily ceased. During this age it largely concerns the Christian church and the Gentile nations. Of course, the dispersion of Israel continues and to that extent Jewish prophecy continues to be fulfilled. But this is the period of divine rejection and the age of national dispersion. During this time, God's dealings with Israel are not national but individual. And the basis of those dealings is the same with the Jew as with the Gentile. They are not on the basis of law but grace; not the Temple but the Cross. Whatever hope the Jew has is an individual hope, not as an Israelite, but as a sinner. He must not come boasting his heritage but loathing his bankruptcies.

It is this which Paul now endeavors to make the Jew see. He does it by beginning where the Jew is thinking. If all this is so, the Jew is thinking that God's Word has failed. Others are thinking that God has changed His mind and altered His plans. But that is far from the case, for Paul says in verse six, "Not as though the word of God hath taken none effect." In other words, he is saying that God's Word has not failed. God's purposes and His plan for world redemption still go on. He has not diverted or deferred a single intention. What has failed is not His promise but His people Israel. But in spite of that national failure, the great racial objectives of God go on to completion. Just how they will go on we shall see. Let us be sure that we see here the far-reaching and broad presentation by Paul, of the fact that the Christian faith and the Christian gospel are not human inventions or a narrow human sect. It is the present part of God's great plan for world rehabilitation. God is behind these things in the spiritual world just as surely as He is behind the continued existence of the physical world. Therefore, the Christian fellowship into which we invite both Jew and Gentile is not a temporary refuge for a few deluded fanatics. It is God's plan of preparing a people for a coming new age and a coming new world. It is as old as the councils of God and it is as certain as the character of God. Let us, therefore, rejoice in who we are and where we are, for we are now in a procession of events whose ultimate destiny will bring us into divine perfection.

III. GOD'S PURPOSE. Verses 6-24.

Here we find two things dealt with (Dr. W. Griffith Thomas).

1. Israel's Rejection and God's Faithfulness. Verses 1-13.

Here two proofs of this faithfulness are submitted in connection with two separate sets of brothers.

(1) *In Isaac and Ishmael.* Verses 6-9.

"Not as though the word of God hath taken none effect. For they are not all Israel, which are of Israel: Neither, because they are the seed of Abraham, are they all children: but, In Isaac shall thy seed be called. That is, They which are the children of the flesh, these are not the children of God: but the children of the promise are counted for the seed. For this is the word of promise, At this time will I come, and Sarah shall have a son."

The apostle sets out to show that failure has not come to God's Word but has, instead, developed in God's people.

His statement in the sixth verse is to this effect, just because a person was born an Israelite does not mean that they automatically reap Israel's blessings and inheritance. It is still an individual responsibility within a national opportunity. "The real Israel is within the limits of the natural Israel." Because they were from Israel was not proof that they were of Israel.

Just how were their place and privileges determined? Just the same as it is with us. First, individually; second, of grace; third, by faith. Notice the seventh and eighth verses, "Neither, because they are the seed of Abraham, are they all children: but, In Isaac shall thy seed be called. That is, They which are the children of the flesh, these are not the children of God: but the children of the promise are counted for the seed." Here is a radical distinction of two kinds of children. One kind are the children of flesh and the other are the children of faith. It states distinctly that the children of flesh "are not the children of God." On the other hand, "the children of the promise are counted for the seed." That is, the great purposes of God are going to be fulfilled not through the children of flesh but the children of faith.

Just who are these children of flesh and faith? Notice the ninth verse, "For this is the word of promise, At this time will I come, and Sarah shall have a son." To Sarah was born the child of promise. His name was Isaac. But to Hagar was born the child of flesh. His name was Ishmael. And in Genesis you read the genealogical records of two family lines of Abraham. One, the generations of the children of his flesh, and the other the generations of the children of his faith. Who succeeded to the heirship and the promises of Abraham? The children of faith. This has been God's policy always. It still is and it always will be. And if any claim priority by national heritage, he is making an unallowable claim.

Here is a great treatment of a consistent Bible truth. It is this. God's children are not merely of human generation. They are that plus divine generation. They are not the product of the natural, but the product of the spiritual. And the case cited is Isaac of whom the seventh verse says, "In Isaac shall thy seed be called." His birth was the type of the Christian's birth which is both natural and spiritual; both human and divine.

(2) *In Jacob and Esau.* Verses 10-13.

"And not only this; but when Rebecca also had conceived by one, even by our father Isaac: (For the children being not yet born, neither having

done any good or evil, that the purpose of God
according to election might stand, not of works,
but of him that calleth;) It was said unto her, The
elder shall serve the younger. As it is written,
Jacob have I loved, but Esau have I hated."

As we go back to the historical incident referred to
here, it recounts the birth of Jacob and Esau. One was
chosen to carry on the spiritual succession. In this
case, the choice of God is something we cannot humanly explain. It was a choice made before either of
the twins were born. It was made without either
having done good or evil. It had nothing to do with
character. It was not a matter of works, good or
bad. It is solely and simply a matter of divine choice.
And there is but one reason as expressed in verse 11,
"that the purpose of God according to election might
stand."

Here is a majestic statement. Here is the mightiness
of Almighty God set forth in a great purpose. Here
is deity standing out in principle. Let man and his
finiteness defy God and His infiniteness if he will. Let
man bash his brains upon the impregnable rock of
divine sovereignty if he chooses to. But there is
reserved for God the prerogative of choice. It is a
prerogative that is His by right of priority and integrity. It stands back of all the fluctuating course of
human events as the bulwark of continuity. It is the
one thing that guarantees all things a good and righteous and proper consummation.

In the light of this we behold the mystery of such
a statement as verse thirteen, "As it is written, Jacob
have I loved, but Esau have I hated." Is it possible
for divine love to hate? Does it mean only that God

loved Esau less than He loved Jacob? Or does it mean, so far as He is concerned, that it is a matter of principle in which He will recognize Jacob and ignore Esau? Surely whatever is meant we have confidence to know that God did the right thing. In a world of righteousness and unrighteousness, God must be on one side. He cannot be on both sides. Consequently, He must be "for" some and "against" others. But whatever side God is on, it behooves us to get on that side. It ill became these Israelites to stand by in a national pout. It would not be the part of wisdom for them to lose their individual blessing because God's national purposes for this people were set aside.

Wherever there is either a Gentile or a Jew, today, let him remember that God has extended to him great blessings. They are not blessings for creatures but for children. They are not through the natural world but the spiritual world. They are not to be received by religion but by life. They are placed to our credit in Christ and finding the simple way to Him we find our way to emancipation and enlargement such as we never dreamed.

There stretches before us in the verses from fourteen to twenty-four a discussion which contains one of the most profound mysteries of this world. It deals with the second fact found in God's purpose concerning Israel. The first one was Israel's rejection and God's faithfulness.

2. Israel's Rejection and God's Justice. Verses 14-24.

"What shall we say then? Is there unrighteousness with God? God forbid."

This question is as new as it is old. In moments of personal doubt most of us have thought it even if we have not asked it. We ask why and how? Pharaoh's case is summoned for review and we inquire into the dealings of God with this king. But it must resolve itself to one conviction, that to think of God as being unrighteous and unjust in His dealings with any human being is unthinkable. We, as human beings, have no right to summon God before the bar of justice. Who are we to judge? What prerogative do we possess? Yea, verily, "Hath not the potter power over the clay; of the same lump to make one vessel unto honor, and another unto dishonor?" We must ascribe to God some rights which we do not possess.

In proof of God's justice in His rejection of Israel, Paul cites here the contrasting cases of Moses and Pharaoh as previously he had cited the contrasting cases of Isaac and Ishmael as well as Jacob and Esau. Here Moses was a vessel of mercy while Pharaoh was a vessel of wrath. Now, the question is resolved to this consideration found in verses 22 and 23, "What if God, willing to shew his wrath, and to make his power known, endured with much longsuffering the vessels of wrath fitted to destruction: And that he might make known the riches of his glory on the vessels of mercy, which he had afore prepared unto glory."

We say how can God create responsible human beings for the deliberate purpose of destroying them? How can God deliberately harden a man's heart and then damn him? Well, He cannot and He does not.

Go back to the twentieth verse where Paul cites the case of a human potter and by comparison likens him to the Divine Potter. The potter takes two pieces of clay. He has taken them from the same lump. They are similar, identical. Out of one piece of clay his left hand fashions a vessel unto honor. It may serve the king as a cup. But out of the other piece of clay he fashions a vessel of dishonor. It becomes a crock or a jar that performs a menial service in the house. Does anyone deny the potter the right to choose what he will make? So likewise, are two lives. Both come from the same sinful humanity. The Divine Potter is not responsible for their sinfulness. He did not create them so. But in His divine providence one is used for an honorable service and one for a dishonorable service. Shall we deny Him the right of choice?

A further question arises. Does God actually fit one man for mercy and another man for wrath? Does He arbitrarily prepare one man for glory and another man for destruction? Most people mis-read the facts in these verses. It does not say that God fits and prepares anyone for destruction. When it speaks of "vessels of wrath," it simply says of them that they are "fitted to destruction." It carefully and correctly avoids saying that God fitted them for destruction. Yet notice in the twenty-third verse where it speaks of "vessels of mercy," that it does definitely say that God personally fitted them unto glory—"which he had afore prepared unto glory." The fitting for destruction in the "vessels of wrath" was a self-accomplished thing. It was the result of their own choices and actions. And God accommodates His purposes to these vessels which are what they are by their own desire.

We do not believe that God in any case, elects or predestines any human being to destruction, wrath and death. If it is so, that in the final judgment of all things, some shall have a destiny of death instead of life and wrath instead of mercy, it comes in consequence of their rejection of the only means of life.

When God chose to emancipate Israel from Egypt and brought them across the Red Sea upon dry sand, it resulted in two opposite consequences. For the Israelites it was life, while for the Egyptians it was death. The salvation of the one meant the destruction of the other. It was, however, God's will that saved the Israelites. But, on the other hand, it was Pharaoh's will to pursue that destroyed the Egyptians. And when the Egyptians were destroyed, it was by the very means which saved the Israelites. But notice that the initiating cause here was God's decree to save and not destroy. He decreed to save the Israelites through the Red Sea. He did not need to decree the destruction of the Egyptians. Their death was the result of self-destruction. It was not their fate which had been predetermined, but a fate which they chose in consequence of their sin. And whoever suffers a destiny of wrath does so because of his own free will and volition. He is not fated nor forced into it. To refuse the way of life is to accept the way of death. Neither is neutrality, so-called, a way of escape. We are dealing with facts and not fancies. We deal with the words of God and not the whims of God. Here is something as consistent, as reasonable and as justifiable as the law of gravity in nature.

There is a spiritual world that is higher than the physical world. We live in the higher as really as we do the lower. There is death in the one as certainly as there is death in the other. To have the destiny that belongs to God we must be born with the nature of God. This is a spiritual birth which is subsequent to our natural birth. And this is a birth which comes through Christ. We dare not deny these facts for they conform to the laws of nature and the laws of nature are nothing less than the laws of God made available to our eyes and ears.

Paul brings this matter to a practical conclusion. He says in verse twenty-four, "Even us." Who was he referring to? They were "not of the Jews only, but also of the Gentiles." He was referring to God's new order of the Church of Christ. It was made up of Jews and Gentiles. But notice what kind. It is not any Jew or any Gentile. It is not all Jews or all Gentiles. It is made up of some of each and they were those who, it is said, God "hath called." They are not of blood but of the Spirit. They are not in it because of accident but by atonement.

Here we stand upon the threshold of the beginnings of Christianity and behold the goodness of God. We stand to see His sovereign purposes and remember that we do not belong to the transient dream of some religious dreamer. We belong to God through a process of life that guarantees to us His unchangeable purposes. Let us thank God afresh and face our days with a new sense of kinship with big and eternal things. Let us dare to live beyond the petty and the trivial. Let us choose to lend our lives to the fulfillment of God's purpose no matter who we are or where we are.

IV. GENTILE'S POSITION.   Verses 25-33.

In spite of our increasing conflicts and in spite of our multiplying armaments, the final issues of the world will not be resolved by nations as such. Great international problems are never going to be settled by war. Their settling is not of that kind. They belong instead to a biology of life which we find in the Bible.

There are three divisions in this section, the two of which are summarized in the third.

1. Hosea's Citation Concerning the Gentiles. Verses 25, 26.

> "As he saith also in Osee, I will call them my people, which are not my people; and her beloved, which was not beloved. And it shall come to pass, that in the place where it was said unto them, Ye are not my people; there shall they be called the children of the living God."

The immediate application of this prophecy, so far as the Prophet Hosea was concerned, belonged to the ten tribes of Israel. But because of their apostasy, they placed themselves on somewhat the same level as their Gentile neighbors. Therefore, it became consistent for God to treat them as He did the Gentiles and the Gentiles as He did Israel. So, then, they who did not belong to the ranks of Israel came to be known as His people.

The fulfillment of this prophecy did not take place until Paul's day when, as a result of the gospel message, multitudes of Gentiles embraced the Cross and were now the people of God. Thus, it had come to pass, "that in the place where it was said unto them,

Ye are not my people; there shall they be called the children of the living God." Notice particularly that it says, "The children of God" as distinguished from "my people." This is indicative of the new relationship. It is no longer racial but family. It is no longer a bond of law but life. Here "children" point to a new family and a new order entirely different from the previous relationship.

We have passed from the national Jew to the individual Gentile. God's dealings with men are no longer through movements and masses. It is back to the first biological and spiritual basis of individuals. It is not nation by nation, clan by clan, nor family by family.

2. Isaiah's Citation Concerning the Israelites. Verses 27-29.

> "Esaias also crieth concerning Israel, Though the number of the children of Israel be as the sand of the sea, a remnant shall be saved: For he will finish the work, and cut it short in righteousness: because a short work will the Lord make upon the earth. And as Esaias said before, Except the Lord of Sabaoth had left us a seed, we had been as Sodoma, and been made like unto Gomorrha."

Here is the contrary case of those who are intended to be His people failing to become His people. Here is a vast multitude encompassed in the divine intention. It is a multitude "as the sand of the sea." They had been presented with great opportunities. Yet, in spite of these things, we find that only "a remnant shall be saved." There were Gentiles outside who were now inside. Here were Israelites inside who were now outside. What a change has taken place in these relationships! A new day has arrived in God's dealings with men.

Whoever finds himself on the inside and in favor with God, does so on the basis of individual acceptance. Here were great national privileges, but individual responses. Here was a sand-numerous nation rejected and a handful-remnant accepted. Yet, when the acceptance took place, it was the acceptance of the remnant as individuals.

A great change of thought has taken place. It is the change from divine sovereignty to human responsibility. It is true that God has decreed but it is equally true that man must decide. God has predetermined but man must determine. If God has a gift to give, there must be an empty hand to receive it and that must be man's willing hand.

3. Paul's Conclusion Concerning the Way of Salvation for Both Gentile and Israelite. Verses 30-33.

> "What shall we say then? That the Gentiles, which followed not after righteousness, have attained to righteousness, even the righteousness which is of faith. But Israel, which followed after the law of righteousness, hath not attained to the law of righteousness. Wherefore? Because they sought it not by faith, but as it were by the works of the law. For they stumbled at that stumblingstone; As it is written, Behold, I lay in Sion a stumblingstone and rock of offence; and whosoever believeth on him shall not be ashamed."

This scripture begins with the question, "What shall we say then?" That is, how is it that this great reversal has taken place? How can the favored Jew be rejected and the alien Gentile be accepted?

Certainly not on the old basis of the law or the covenants. It can only be so on a new basis of grace and faith. The acceptance of the one was because of faith. The rejection of the other was because of works. One found righteousness through the law of faith while the other failed of righteousness because he sought to establish it by the works of the law.

Here, indeed, is a profound change in God's dealings with men. It is no longer a matter of law but life; no longer works but faith. The time of this change indicates the reason for the change. It did not come gradually but suddenly. It came when Christ came and died. He is described here as the stone of stumbling. His coming marks the change from the old era to the new era and from the old law to the new life. Henceforth, all men as individuals are to be considered in their relation to Him. He stands now at the head of a new race of twice-born men and women. Here is a spiritual new beginning which would retrieve all that was lost in the old beginning. Here is the fountain-head of a new biology, the biology of the Spirit. Here is the genesis of an era which would end in a consummation of perfection.

Henceforth, then, there is a new question. Not, What does the law think of me? But, "What think ye of Christ?" It is no longer the sin question but more properly the Son question. It is no longer our righteousness but His righteousness. It is no longer our work but His work. Indeed, it is exactly as Paul states it to be in verse thirty, "What shall we say then? That the Gentiles which followed not after righteousness (according to the Jewish pattern) have attained to righteousness, even the righteousness which is of faith." And this is the fundamental New Testament precept of salvation, namely, that it is a personal and individual righteousness by faith.

The chapter closes with a straightforward reference to Christ. To us, and not only to the Jews of Paul's day, He is one of two things. He is either a stumblingstone or a steppingstone. As a stumblingstone He becomes our hindrance but as a steppingstone He becomes the means of never ceasing advance and ascent. To Israel, Christ was a national stumblingstone. They could not reconcile their Old Testament prophecies with His New Testament program. And, ever since, they have stumbled over Christ. So does the intellectual who worships his wisdom. So do the rich who trust in their wealth. So does the moralist who depends on his personal excellence. But, on the other hand, we see Christ as He ought to be in every life, a steppingstone, for "whosoever believeth on him shall not be ashamed." In Him, there is the increasing joy of eternal life. In Him there is the mounting life that is without separation. In Him there are the higher altitudes of the Spirit. Yea, verily, in Him we go from faith to faith, strength to strength and from conquerors to more than conquerors.

# 14

## THE PRESENT
## SALVATION OF THE JEW
### *Romans 10*

THE Christian's approach to the Jewish problem is not nearly so difficult as the Jew's approach to Jesus Christ. Back of him are centuries of misunderstanding, abuse, and persecution. All of which are, to him, identified with Christ. But the genuine Christian has never been a party to any such anti-Semitism. He has a profound and deep respect for the Jewish heritage. He has tried to understand the Jewish position. Having passed through the precincts of the ninth chapter where that position is so plainly stated and the way is cleared for an understanding by the Jew of the Lord Jesus Christ and the Christian gospel, we are ready to listen to another passionate plea for his salvation.

Paul sets the present salvation of the Jew before us in the very first verse. "Brethren, my heart's desire and prayer to God for Israel is, that they might be saved." He assumes that they are not saved. No less an authority than Paul sets forth the need of every Jew for personal salvation. It is not now a national heritage. It is not a cherished creed. It is an imperative need.

It would be an imposition for any of us, from Paul down, to seek to make a convert of the Jew if that conversion was merely a change from one set of ideas to another, or from one religion to another. But it is not, therefore it is no imposition to seek his conversion for Paul has shown us how the eternal purposes of God run through both Jewish and Christian eras. And, furthermore, it is clearly pointed out that the Jewish system has been set aside by the Cross for the gospel of the Christian Church. This is not the Christian's doing. He did not invent his faith nor decree its requirements. It is God's doing and the gospel message gives ample reason why it should be embraced by both Jew and Gentile. Therefore, Paul rises up in the passion of his heart to say, "Brethren, my heart's desire and prayer to God for Israel is, that they might be saved."

The chapter divides itself into two equal sections:

I. THE WAY OF SALVATION. Verses 1-11.

Paul goes immediately into the historic position of the Jew by saying in verse two, "For I bear them record that they have a zeal of God, but not according to knowledge." Here was religious zeal to call forth the heartiest commendation. But it was in error. Zeal is good but it must be well founded. No man is ever to be saved because of his good intentions. Salvation is a matter of life and life is the effect of a cause. Find the cause and you will have the effect.

Two things are then dealt with.

1. The Righteousness of the Law. Verses 3-5.

"For they being ignorant of God's righteousness, and going about to establish their own righteousness, have not submitted themselves unto the righteousness of God. For Christ is the end of the law for righteousness to everyone that believeth. For Moses describeth the righteousness which is of the law. That the man which doeth these things shall live by them."

Here is the thing that the Jew was continually seeking, but his was a mistake of tradition. He was doing now what was without point and purpose. What he was doing was in ignorance. What did this ignorance consist of? It was the failure to recognize the fact stated in verse four. "For Christ is the end of the law for righteousness to everyone that believeth." That is to say, that the law was consummated in Christ and, as a result of our faith in Him, we possess the righteousness of God. This is God's way. It means that Christ absorbed the law. Its truth continues in His truth but its legalistic regulations cease to be. There is now a new order. It is an order of life and when we are organically united to Christ, we possess the source of righteousness and the means of life which satisfy God. There is no reason why we should read this to say that since Christ has come and is the end of the law, we may lie, steal and murder as we will. It does mean that we have all of these things in a new form, the form of grace.

Under the law it was, do and live. But under Christ it is, live and do. How different!

2. The Righteousness of Faith. Verses 6-11.

"But the righteousness which is of faith speaketh on this wise, Say not in thine heart, Who shall ascend into heaven? (that is, to bring Christ down from above:) Or, Who shall descend into the deep?

(that is, to bring up Christ again from the dead.)
But what saith it? The word is nigh thee, even in
thy mouth, and in thy heart: that is, the word
of faith, which we preach; That if thou shalt confess with thy mouth the Lord Jesus, and shalt believe in thine heart that God hath raised him from
the dead, thou shalt be saved. For with the heart
man believeth unto righteousness; and with the
mouth confession is made unto salvation. For the
scripture saith, Whosoever believeth on him shall
not be ashamed."

In verses five and six a contrast is made between
the righteousness of the law and the righteousness of
faith. "For Moses describeth the righteousness which
is of the law, That the man which doeth those things
shall live by them. But the righteousness which is
of faith speaketh on this wise, Say not in thine heart,
Who shall ascend into heaven? (that is, to bring Christ
down from above.)"

One righteousness is abortive. It declares in verse
five that whoever seeks righteousness by law must find
life in such righteousness. It was an abortive effort
because it was an impossible endeavor. Paul said in
Galatians 3:11, "But that no man is justified by the
law in the sight of God, it is evident: for, The just shall
live by faith."

The other righteousness is completed and attained
by an act of faith. For as it says in verses six to
eight, it is not something to be sought after. It is
finished. We do not need to find someone who will
do it. It has been done. We do not need to storm
heaven and achieve it. Christ has already come down
from heaven in incarnate form. We do not need to

raise the dead. Christ has already been raised to give ample attestation to His completed redemption. In fact, the way of salvation is not some mysterious thing far from us. It is so accessible as to be what is described in verse eight, ". . . nigh thee, even in thy mouth, and in thy heart: that is, the word of faith, which we preach." No magic phrases are needed. No conquests are required. All that is necessary is the word of faith. And all of us, no matter who we are, have that word right now. We have it at the tip of our tongue if we wish to say it. We have it in the depths of our heart if we wish to express it. It is simple, artless, and withal impressive and sufficient.

The experience of salvation requires but two things. They are found in verses nine and ten. "That if thou shalt confess with thy mouth the Lord Jesus, and shalt believe in thine heart that God hath raised him from the dead, thou shalt be saved. For with the heart man believeth unto righteousness; and with the mouth confession is made unto salvation." Here we have *consent* and *confession*. It is our consent to God and our confession to man. By our consent we give admission of personal sin and delinquency, but also acknowledgment of Christ's adequate salvation to meet that sin. By our confession we identify ourself before men as belonging to Christ. It is an open avowal of His cause. It is a public espousal of His way of life. And it is by these two acts of self-submission that the new birth and the new life come.

Consent to God involves a particular faith. It does not say to believe that Christ died on the cross but it directs our faith to the one event which was demonstrable beyond doubt, the resurrection. Its effect was retroactive. For if He was raised it was proof He had died, and if He had died it was also certain that He died for sin. Therefore, our salvation rests finally in His resurrection. But consent without confession is not enough. "The mouth without the heart might be hypocrisy, while the heart without the mouth might be cowardice."

Here is an experience within reach of all. It is not beneath the reach of the moralist or the intellectual. Nor is it beyond the reach of the reprobate or the simple. It is divinely designed to meet all men on a common ground, the ground of a sinner's needs. And it is divinely calculated to be of such sufficiency as to satisfy the needs of universal man.

II. THE APPLICATION OF SALVATION. Verses 12-21.

There are to be found in these verses four things that describe the practical application of salvation.

1. The Universal Need. Verse 12.

"For there is no difference between the Jew and the Greek: for the same Lord over all is rich unto all that call upon him."

This scripture frankly states that "there is no difference." Truth is a great equalizer. The traditionally religious Jew and the religious Gentile were in the same category. There was no difference between the Jew with his one God and the Gentile with his many gods. Of course, this statement does not overlook the fact that there were individual differences between Jew and Gentile as well as between Jew and Jew and Gentile and Gentile. One man may have been more upright than another. The degree of difference might have been very great but not the kind of difference. As to kind they were all alike. It made no difference whether one was a philosopher and the other a farmer, or whether one was a moralist and the other a profligate. There was no difference before God as regards the fundamental need of personal salvation.

And this "no difference" status went even further than this. It meant that there was no difference in the means of salvation. In other words, when Jew and Gentile are summoned to this place, it is to point out that salvation is not for one a Jewish salvation and for another a Gentile salvation. The message of Christianity has nothing to do with class or race distinctions. It offers one means for all men. There is no difference in the way men are saved any more than in the way men are born. When we see that salvation, as such, is neither ritual nor creedal, but a birth into a new life, we will then see how vain are these artificialities of ecclesiastical religion.

Humanity is here reduced to a common level. This is accompanied by an equally important companion fact. If there is a sameness in humanity, there is also a sameness in deity. It is "the same Lord." He is not the exclusive property of the Jew nor is He the exclusive property of the Gentile. We treat God too often as we do property. This arises out of that unspeakable conclusion that man made God. Here begin all the vicious perversions of life. Make God the product of human hands and minds and you have lost the dignity of life. What difference is there between the savant who makes God with his mind and the savage who makes God with his hands? Only a difference of degree but no difference in kind. Until our modern intellectuals cease their blasphemous god-making, we will have little right thinking and right living in the leadership of the world.

The need of man rises in his need of God. It is not merely his selfish need of what God can do for him. Here lies the fallacy of so many of our modern emergency appeals for revivals of religion. We reach a period of depression or a great war crisis. Men see liberty being threatened by totalitarianism and when these things come on apace, they send up a cry for a return to God. But why do they want us to return to God? It is not for the sake of deity but utility. It is the "why not try God?" philosophy. Everything else has failed, let us try God. But God is never a divine means to a human end. We do wrong to think of Him as a means to prosperity, or peace, or health, or liberty. God is to be desired for Himself. He is to be the end and not the means.

And it is because we are so fundamentally wrong in our principles that we are so woefully wrong in our practices. If we had the Lord we would have the Lord's riches, for "the same Lord is continually wealthy to all those who are continually invoking His aid."

Here is our wrong, let us right it and we will then put ourselves in the place of great blessing. If we have been .spiritually poor and live dissatisfied lives, we have only our selfishness and ignorance to blame for it. If we will seek the Lord for the Lord's sake and confess our sins and not be religious merely for the consideration we think we may get out of it, our whole spiritual outlook will be different.

Notice the striking contrast between this verse and the twenty-third verse of the third chapter. In 3:23

it declares that all have sinned, there is no exception. Whereas, here it states that all may be saved, there is no distinction. In the first case it has to do with sin while in the second case it has to do with salvation. There is no exception in the fact of sin and no distinction in the need of salvation.

2. The Simple Condition. Verse 13.

"For whosoever shall call upon the name of the Lord shall be saved."

Notice it states here that "whosoever shall call." The promise is as broad and inclusive as the plight of man. If all men need to be saved, then all men may be saved. It does not say that all will be. There is considerable difference between may be and will be. Salvation is a provision but it is also provisional. It has been provided but it must be appropriated. The provision is historical and has been true for nigh on to twenty centuries. But the appropriation is individual. One is a fact. The other is by faith. One is by an act of God. The other by an act of man. It states here that "whosoever shall call upon the name of the Lord shall be saved." This puts the matter upon a personal basis. The Jew would not be saved because he was a Jew. This was his false boast. The day of national promises had passed and the day of personal faith had come.

Here is a specific condition. It was not to all that fall, but all that call. The sinner was not to be saved merely because he was a sinner and needed salvation. Salvation did not automatically apply to all that fell. It was not on the basis of creation but calling. It was not a promiscuous provision to the race. It was not to all who were sincere, moral, religious, or kind, but to all who "call upon the name of the Lord." Here is divine redemption plus human responsibility. In chapter eight is to be found God's call to man. In chapter ten is to be found man's call upon God. A true experience requires both calls.

Notice the object of man's call. It is "the Lord." He is to be saved directly through the Lord, not through the intermediate agencies of ritual or ceremony or his own personal morality. He is not to call upon his own excellencies and be saved by what he is, but to call upon the Lord. In other words, the essence of the Christian salvation is a Person. This is fundamental. Man was originally made in the likeness of that Person and he must be re-made into that Person's likeness. He was made to be mastered by God and only as he submits to the mastery of the Son of God will he have peace.

The gospel offers salvation by another and not salvation in ourselves. This is offensive and objectionable to many. And yet our daily lives are only possible by what others do for us. Others gave us the life we now live. Others cook our meals; others supply our food; others drive our cars; others make our clothes; others mould our thinking. Every opinion we have is the opinion someone has contributed to us. Our whole life is a vicarious contribution by someone else. It is so with salvation. It is provided for those who could not and cannot provide it for themselves. It is ethically correct. It is morally perfect. It is biologically sound. It is divinely authentic.

It is true here as it was stated of one of our prominent

public men, "That is why so many active men, when they want to learn something, say 'Don't give me a book, give me a man.'" God has given us both a book and a man. One is the Bible and the other is Christ. One is the Word in letter and the other is the Word in flesh.

But the fact is that salvation rests in a man. God has not given us a set of rules but a man who was the truth and who lived the truth. It seems that the whole matter is summed up in this story. In New York City a few years ago a man became known in some circles for his zeal in being helpful in as many ways as possible. He had a strange knack of being on hand when need arose in the lives of others; when he could help he did so; when he needed more help he knew how to ask it of others. He was asked one day how he came to be so active in helping other people. He replied, "A man once died for me." It came out that in an emergency when his life was in danger a man had thrown himself into the breach and saved him from death, though in doing so the other man lost his own life. He had always felt he owed double duty to the world for that. A Man died for us once, the Man Christ Jesus. After that, we cannot be our own. We owe double duty of courage, obedience, and service. We are not our own; we belong to Him.

3. The Human Means. Verses 14-17.

"How then shall they call on him in whom they have not believed? and how shall they believe in him of whom they have not heard? and how shall they hear without a preacher? And how shall they preach, except they be sent? as it is written,

How beautiful are the feet of them that preach the gospel of peace, and bring glad tidings of good things! But they have not all obeyed the gospel. For Esaias saith, Lord, who hath believed our report? So then faith cometh by hearing, and hearing by the word of God."

Notice the four questions which are asked.

(1) *"How then shall they call on him in whom they have not believed?"*

We notice that the process of the application of salvation points always to a person. It is never to a set of rules or ideas. Here calling and believing are connected events. Believing in God is something passive. Calling on God is something active. Believing is an act of mind. Calling is an act of will. Believing is what we think about it. Calling is what we do about it. It is not enough to say we believe. It is only enough when we have acted on our faith.

(2) *"How shall they believe in him of whom they have not heard?"*

Here believing is linked with hearing and hearing is linked with a person. It is "in Him of whom they have not heard." Belief is therefore made something definite and tangible. It is not some wandering religious feeling that creeps into our minds out of nowhere. It is not anything that we consider acceptable to our own judgments and standards. It is a specifically placed conviction in a personal God.

(3) *"How shall they hear without a preacher?"*

Here is the human agency. If calling requires believing and if believing requires hearing, then hearing requires telling. This all means that the gospel's message of salvation is not a discovery. It is not something we dig out for ourselves. It is, in a sense, traditional although it is not a tradition. It is something we receive not from another but from God through another.

Notice that God does not use impulses to transmit the message but personalities. He never committed the message to angels but to men. Man is an important link in the great plan of redemption. Being redeemed, he is responsible to see that others share what he has. Herein lay the phenomenal success of the early church. Its tremendous influence on the pagan life of the first centuries did not lie in its education, social prestige or wealth. Without any of these things they become personal propagators of the message of redemption.

We must be careful not to draw our conclusions too close, for while it says "How shall they hear without a preacher" this hearing is not to be construed as audible hearing alone. Literature is as much God's agency as lecturing. Literature is the lecture in print, behind which we still see the preacher. But, even so, we must not carry this too far and suppose that the world can be won by campaigning with leaflets. Tracts and books all have their place, but that place never supersedes the preacher.

Little did Paul suspect the coming of radio whose magic flings the voice of the preacher into miles of space where it is available to all within its reach. Now it is possible to multiply the voice and scatter the message to unbelievable proportions. It is possible to reach the sinner in the very midst of his sin and the sufferer upon the bed of his affliction.

(4) *"How shall they preach except they be sent?"*

What does it mean by being sent? We believe it is twofold. First, by divine authority. Second, by human assistance. There is no question but that preaching of the true sort is to be by divine commission. It was under divine commission that Paul went forth from Antioch. In Acts 13:2 it says, "The Holy Ghost said, Separate me Barnabas and Saul for the work whereunto I have called them." Thus, they went out under divine authority. But they also went with human assistance. Those at home or those who received the benefits of this ministry were expected to contribute of their means for the assistance of these workers. For this reason Paul wrote to the Galatians, "Let him that is taught in the word communicate unto him that teacheth in all good things" (Gal. 6:6).

If we are not called to go, we are called to let others go and lend them all necessary assistance. In this way the sending would become an effectual means of world evangelization. It would put in motion a chain of both human and divine circumstances that would extend from time to eternity. The sending would result in telling, the telling in hearing, the hearing in believing, the believing in calling, and the calling in God's answer.

The apostle concludes his four questions in an exclamatory statement concerning the mission of the preacher. It is in verse fifteen, "How beautiful are the feet of them that preach the gospel of peace, and bring glad tidings of good things!" It does not mean to extol the physical members of the messenger but rather to extol his spiritual mission. You cannot divorce the messenger from the mission. If the mission is beautiful, the messenger is to be also. Therefore,

"How beautiful are the feet of them that preach." The accompaniments of preaching are no small part of the accomplishments of preaching. Here was a task that was to be performed with a technique that was described as beautiful. Are we as careful to merit this description as we ought to be? Is the man we know as our preacher like this description? In dress and speech, manners and character, is he attractive and winsome? Is he honest and straightforward and clean? Is he a recommendation of his message? It seems that the messenger needs beautification as well as education.

We point out two things about the gospel.

a. Its glory.

It is a gospel of peace and glad tidings. The gospel has charm and attraction because its character is that of peace. But we must not lose its benefits by our neglect. It is, as someone has pointed out, "a great mercy to enjoy the gospel of peace, but a still greater one to enjoy the peace of the gospel."

b. Its tragedy.

The tragedy is stated in verse sixteen, "they have not all obeyed the gospel." The tragedy does not of course, belong to the gospel but, because of it, to those who do not obey it. Great opportunity means great responsibility. Glory spurned means tragedy earned.

Now, the summary of this recital of facts about the gospel's application is that it is in the first and last place a matter of faith. How do we get faith? The answer is in verse seventeen: "So then faith cometh by hearing and hearing by the word of God." We do not get faith by asking, but by hearing. We do not get it by reasoning but by revelation, for it is a product of the Word of God.

The faith that is mentioned here, is of course, saving faith. It has an equal application to any other function of faith. The origin of faith is in the Word of God. Just as the red corpuscles of the blood stream are manufactured in the marrow of our bones, so faith is produced in the heart of the Bible. Out of these divine truths rises our strength. If you are weak or lacking in faith, saturate yourself with the truth of this Book. They are the sources of all spiritual energy and ability.

4. The Divine Patience. Verses 18-21.

> "But I say, Have they not heard? Yes, verily, their sound went into all the earth, and their words unto the ends of the world. But I say, Did not Israel know? First Moses saith, I will provoke you to jealousy by them that are no people, and by a foolish nation I will anger you. But Esaias is very bold, and saith, I was found of them that sought me not; I was made manifest unto them that asked not after me. But to Israel he saith, All day long I have stretched forth my hands unto a disobedient and gainsaying people."

This is revealed particularly in the twenty-first verse where it says, "All day long I have stretched forth my hands unto a disobedient and gainsaying people."

Here is an attitude of extended patience. Try to stretch out your hands and see how soon they become too heavy to hold. Here the picture does not mean physical hands but rather an attitude of great patience. It is God's attitude to the world. In this specific case it was Israel, but in its widest meaning it embraces the entire race.

Notice to what kind of a people this patience is extended. They are "disobedient and gainsaying." That is to say they refused to be persuaded. It was a willful attitude. Let none of us be imitators of these people. Let us flee to the open and inviting arms of God and there find surcease from life's alarms and preparation for life's duties.

# 15

## THE FUTURE RESTORATION OF
## THE JEW
### *Romans 11*

HOW true it is that change is the only thing in this world that remains unchanged! It is so in the fortunes and affairs of men. Through the brief lifetime of each of us we have witnessed change in all about us. Today's dominant forces will be gone tomorrow and a new set will arise. But one thing we can be sure of in the affairs of this changing world is the future of Israel. It looks doubtful today with anti-Semitism raging throughout the world, but there is a divine destiny which shapes the course of this people and will restore them to a place of national blessing. That restoration is emphatically declared in this chapter.

The two parts of this chapter are introduced by an identical phrase. The phrase, "I say then," is found in verse 1 and verse 11.

I. Has God Cast Away His People?  Verses 1-10.

This question inquires as to the completeness or extent of the dispersion. By the dispersion we mean the present scattered condition of the Jew. This is at the same time one of the world's greatest phenomena and one of the Bible's greatest proofs.

Here is a nation which in dispersion reveals the evident hand of God upon its destiny. It is the wonder of the world that being scattered, murdered, robbed, beaten, and the object of a maniacal and demonic hatred, it should continue to exist.

At the beginning of the final phase of their dispersion, Paul asks this question, "Hath God cast away His people?" In other words, is God through with the Jew? Used prior to this to produce the world's greatest literature, the Bible, and the world's greatest life, Jesus Christ, are they now just a castaway nation? Has their glory been consumed in their shame? Has their great heritage been lost in their great apostasy? To this question Paul gives an emphatic answer. "God forbid." Away with the thought. Yea, shame on the thought.

Before we pursue the argument that follows, let us first determine who these people are. Who does it mean when it says "His people?" We have a lot of fantastic theories to complicate our understanding of this matter. Here, for instance, is the novel idea that the Anglo-Saxons are the people through whom these promises are to be fulfilled as if they were now certain of the tribes of Israel. There is also the idea that the church is to inherit the promises and lead the world into a new era.

Neither fits the case. And no matter how finely and carefully we distinguish between one word and another in an effort to build up some theory of interpretation, we are thrown back continually to one conviction. It will be a national Israel that will be brought out of dispersion into restoration, through whom international blessing will come to all the world. But national restoration also means national regeneration. And this national regeneration is of significance for the Jew as well as for the Gentile.

It will be statecraft and diplomacy and government and economics built on a new pattern. In fact, it will mean a new geography and a new economy, and a new biology and a new geology. It is not a narrow Jewish question, or a narrow Gentile problem. It will be begun in those categories but it will be changed into a new status by the coming regeneration which will affect the nations.

God has a program and He is working to that program. For that reason, He has not cast away His people. World interest will center on them yet and world attention will focus on Palestine. This land which has been lying in obscurity and barrenness for these many centuries is destined to play a dominant part in the world's future. It is the strategic pivot of the earth. It is not merely sacred soil for contending sects who are blinded by bigotry. It is strategic to the world's destiny. It is strategic geographically, politically, and prophetically, even as it has been strategic spiritually.

From this land came our Bible and our Christ. From it will yet come our world peace and world prosperity. It will be the seat of a great millennial government under the sovereignty of Christ. It will bring liberty to the beleaguered peoples of the world. It will bring plenty to the world's poverty. It will bring civilization and culture to the world's slavery and savagery. Here on the same soil where sacred blood was shed for a world's redemption, human blood will be shed in streams in the world's greatest battle. But the key to the situation is this people. No, God has not cast away His people.

Paul answers the question he raises by an assurance of a threefold election or remnant.

1. It Is Personal. Verse 1.

> "I say then, Hath God cast away his people? God forbid. For I also am an Israelite, of the seed of Abraham, of the tribe of Benjamin."

Paul points to himself as proof of this. God by His grace had retrieved Paul out of a brilliant yet bigoted religious career and transformed his life and given him a place in divine service. This was proof to Paul that no Israelite was irretrievably cast away, and that any Israelite might find a large and abundant place of blessing in God's present program for the world.

2. It Is Historical. Verses 2-4.

> "God hath not cast away his people which he foreknew. Wot ye not what the scripture saith of Elias? how he maketh intercession to God against Israel, saying, Lord, they have killed thy prophets, and digged down thine altars; and I am left alone, and they seek my life. But what saith the answer of God unto him? I have reserved to myself seven thousand men, who have not bowed the knee to the image of Baal."

In these verses Paul cites the instance of Elijah's career when he had to flee for his life. Under the stress of this circumstance, Elijah was sure that his cause was lost and considered himself the only one left who had not apostatized. But in his complaint to God, he received this reminder, the reminder of a remnant, "I have reserved to myself seven thousand men, who have not bowed the knee to the image of Baal." Even in that wicked and diabolical day when spiritual decay had set in so generally there was a preserved remnant. Upon such a remnant God would build a new day and a new nation. It was proof to Paul that in historic days God had not completely cast away His people.

3. It Is Spiritual. Verses 5-10.

"Even so then at this present time also there is a remnant according to the election of grace. And if by grace, then is it no more of works: otherwise grace is no more grace. But if it be of works, then is it no more grace: otherwise work is no more work. What then? Israel hath not obtained that which he seeketh for; but the election hath obtained it, and the rest were blinded (According as it is written, God hath given them the spirit of slumber, eyes that they should not see, and ears that they should not hear;) unto this day. And David saith, Let their table be made a snare, and a trap, and a stumblingblock, and a recompence unto them: Let their eyes be darkened, that they may not see, and bow down their back alway."

God's purposes were not merely historical, for Paul saw a remnant in his own day that would continue until our day through which the great blessing of God would come. He says, "Even so, then at this present time, there is a remnant."

These remnants are the minorities of righteousness that reside through the centuries to keep God's purposes alive and the redemptive machinery intact. They are isolated islands of the faithful through which truth remains pure and uncorrupted. They are the seemingly insignificant communities of the godly who are despised by their contemporaries but jealously guarded by God. They are the salt of the earth and its sole saving element. Without them civilization would have long since ceased to exist and man would have been swallowed up by his sinful folly.

Yes, God has always had a remnant and He always will. Noah was the remnant saved out of Cain's godless age. Lot was the remnant saved out of Sodom's godless city. Here and there, uncounted and unclassified, is God's godly remnant continuing through all ages. But the particular remnant spoken of here is Jewish, and it has to do with the coming national restoration. It exists to prove that Israel is not in the discard.

Notice what the origin of this remnant was. In kind it was Jewish but in origin it was of grace. As Paul states in verse 5, "There is a remnant according to grace." That is most significant. The truth of Romans is built on two great things, grace and faith. Regardless of nationality or culture, it is all of grace through faith. Grace is the God-ward aspect of salvation. Faith is the man-ward aspect. Grace originates and faith appropriates. But notice that it is grace not only for regeneration but for restoration. Grace not only for the individual but for the nation. While the election of grace mentioned here has its individual aspect, it also refers to the great coming day of national restoration. Herein lies the germ of all hope for humanity and the future.

The titanic struggle of democracy and the threatened collapse of civilization will not make the world safe even if these struggles succeed. Science and its kindred crafts cannot remake our world into a safe and secure place by its human tools. It requires something more than this. When we have sifted the nations and watched the struggles, we must end our search for a panacea at this place. It goes back to the divine purpose of grace. Here lies humanity's hope.

Paul is advancing the idea that the presence of a remnant is pledge of Israel's future recovery. That fact produces another one, namely, that any recovery whether national or individual must begin at the center. It must begin on the inside and not the outside. It must be spiritual and not merely cultural, political, social or intellectual. Plato said, "If the head and body are to be well, you must begin by curing the soul."

But where does spirituality begin? We dare not follow our own ideas or desires or we will be forever wrong. In God's order, spirituality begins in faith. It brings life to the place of birth and out of a new birth a spiritual life is born to grow and develop under the tutelage of divine agencies. Here is the secret of recovery. We will do well to learn it and live it.

A serious problem is raised in verses seven to ten. It cannot be ignored for no honest mind will be comfortable without at least a decent inquiry. In verse seven Israel appears in two groups. First, there is "the election," apparently a small remnant. Second, there is "the rest," ostensibly a large majority of people. The election had entered into the present blessings

of God through Christ and the Cross.  But the rest
were remaining in abysmal blindness.  The election
had come into their blessings by grace.  But as for the
rest they were in a state of confirmed unbelief.

The clue to the problem lies close at hand.  It is
in verse 7.  It says, "The rest were blinded" or as it
might be more correctly rendered "hardened."  The
verb hardened comes from a noun which was used
medically.  It described the formation of a callous in
the fractures of broken bones.  It was a case of
calcifying; a condition common in arthritis.  The
thought here is well put in Arthur S. Way's translation,
"The rest have been callously indifferent."  The
thought then is this, while it is true that they have
become hardened like stone, and unable to make any
moral and spiritual movements, but are satisfied and
rebellious, it is the natural result of their own indifference.  And if it is said that God did it, He only
did it as a judicial act.  He declared them such because and after they made themselves such.

These people are said to have had "the spirit of
slumber (stupor)."  Their senses were stupefied.  It was
a condition which rendered them insensible to divine
promptings.  But such a condition was acquired.  It
was not imposed arbitrarily upon them.  It was of
their own doing.  It was the result of moral laws
which exist in the moral world.  By such laws human
unbelief, resistance, disobedience and even indifference
cause us to become hardened and stupefied and in a
moral coma.  In all of this, not one word intimates that
God "meets a soul tending upward and turns it downward; that He ignores or rejects even the faintest
inquiry after Himself; that He is the author of one

particle of the sin of man." Instead, it is evident
here that these are "no helpless victims of an adverse
fate, but sinners of their own will." In this case, God
judges and confirms what man has desired.

Here is an illustration of that scripture which says,
"How shall we escape if we neglect so great salvation?"
Neglect does not merely result in a negative state, but
a positive state of degeneration and destruction. It
is so in the natural world and it is equally so in the
spiritual world. In the matter of personal salvation,
faith is vital but unbelief or neglect is fatal. This
fatality of neglect or unbelief not only causes one to
miss salvation but to actually spoil the capacity for it.

The soul has a capacity for God. It is like a curious
chamber added on to being, and somehow involving
being, a chamber with elastic and contractile walls,
which can be expanded, with God as its guest, illimit-
ably, but which without God shrinks and shrivels until
every vestige of the divine is gone, and God's image
is left without God's Spirit. One can scarcely call
what is left a soul. It is a shrunken, useless organ, a
capacity sentenced to death by disuse, which droops
as a withered hand by the side, and cumbers nature
like a rotted branch. Nature has her revenge upon
neglect as well as upon extravagance. Misuse, with
her, is as mortal a sin as abuse.

II. HAS ISRAEL GONE BEYOND RECOVERY? Verses 11-32.

The question asked in verse 1 was concerned with
the completeness and extent of Israel's dispersion. Now
the question asked in verse 11 is whether it is something that is irretrievably lost. The emphatic answer

is the same as before. "God forbid." The assurance is in their coming restoration, a fact which is discussed at considerable length from this point on to the conclusion of the chapter.

Three things comprise his contention in these verses.

1. The Jewish Fall and the Gentile's Salvation. Verses 11-15.

> "I say then, Have they stumbled that they should fall? God forbid: but rather through their fall salvation is come unto the Gentiles, for to provoke them to jealousy. Now if the fall of them be the riches of the world, and the diminishing of them the riches of the Gentiles; how much more their fulness? For I speak to you Gentiles. inasmuch as I am the apostle of the Gentiles, I magnify mine office: If by any means I may provoke to emulation them which are my flesh, and might save some of them. For if the casting away of them be the reconciling of the world, what shall the receiving of them be, but life from the dead?"

Paul never loses sight of the fact that the hope of the present is in the future. If Israel has fallen, she will rise again. And, if when she fell, because of her own sin and unbelief, it led to the presentation of the gospel to the Gentile and the consequent salvation of multitudes of them, it is also true that her recovery is to result in even greater blessings. It is argued that if Jewish adversity brought blessing, then how much more would Jewish prosperity bring blessing.

Here are found two things. Israel's fall which is past and Israel's fulness which is future. By her fall the world was enriched. A great national tragedy resulted in a great international blessing. This is

strange but true, for the persecutions instituted by
the Jew on the early church resulted in her scattering
and the consequent spreading of the gospel in all the
world.   But there is coming the time of her fulness.
It is a divine promise, and with that fulness will be
a far greater blessing to all the world for her restoration will be the means of blessing the entire world.

2. The Jewish Branches and the Gentile's Grafting.
Verses 16-24.

"For if the firstfruit be holy, the lump is also
holy: and if the root be holy, so are the branches.
And if some of the branches be broken off, and
thou, being a wild olive tree, wert graffed in among
them, and with them partakest of the root and fat-
ness of the olive tree; Boast not against the branches.   But if thou boast, thou bearest not the root,
but the root thee. Thou wilt say then, The branches were broken off, that I might be graffed in. Well;
because of unbelief they were broken off, and thou
standest by faith.   Be not highminded, but fear:
For if God spared not the natural branches, take
heed lest he also spare not thee.   Behold therefore
the goodness and severity of God: on them which
fell, severity; but toward thee, goodness, if thou
continue in his goodness: otherwise thou also shalt
be cut off.   And they also, if they abide not still in
unbelief, shall be graffed in: for God is able to
graff them in again. For if thou wert cut out of the
olive tree which is wild by nature, and wert graffed
contrary to nature into a good olive tree: how
much more shall these, which be the natural
branches, be graffed into their own olive tree?"

Here is a figure drawn from a garden or grove.   It
refers to a common practice among orchardists.   It is

the practice of grafting. A selected branch of a particular fruit is joined, by grafting, onto a parent stock. But here the process is the reverse of the usual one. In any ordinary case of grafting, the good or selected stock is grafted onto the ordinary stock. The superior is grafted into the inferior for it is the trunk that insures the nourishment while the graft insures the quality of the fruit. But this process of grafting is described in reverse. It was the inferior graft onto the superior trunk. When this is done, the reason is always to "invigorate the fruitful stock and not to fertilize the wild shoot."

To point out the specific details of the illustration, we notice that "the root" mentioned in verse 16 refers to the parent olive tree which is here typical of Israel as a nation. "The branches" are the individual members of that nation, some of whom were broken off through unbelief and no longer shared in the blessings God had promised to that nation. The "wild olive tree" of verse 17 is the graft and refers to any Gentile who participates by faith in the blessings of salvation. After all, we are forced by facts to admit that whatever salvation any Gentile enjoys is essentially of Jewish provision. While not of Jewish origin, it is of Jewish production. Both the Bible and the Redeemer came through this nation. Being grafted into this association is not to indicate that Gentiles become Jews in order to become Christians. What is portrayed here, is not so much the nationalizing of Jew or Gentile but their spiritual transformation. All God's blessings to the world come through a particular channel. In this case it is pictured as an olive tree into which individual branches are grafted. It is not a new organism of life but rather an origin of life. It refers, without question, to the great and extensive spiritual blessings which flow through this natural source to whoever will permit themselves to be united.

In any case, it bears out the fact that we have endeavored to stress throughout the whole book, namely, that the salvation offered the world in the Christian gospel is not some artificial or manufactured religious exercise that we engage in like we would a parade or calisthenics. It is a life-union with Almighty God, the beginning and source of all life. Without organic union with Him, we are spiritually and eternally dead. Here that union is under the figure of a graft which is the union of one kind of life with another, and their ultimate union and fusion as a single unit of existence. It is something thoroughly logical and biological, and when applied to Christianity it is thoroughly spiritual and scriptural.

We must always remember that this is not the usual way. It refers to an emergency. It refers to something which some day will pass away for Israel will be saved. It will pass through a purging and a purification.

In permitting some branches to be broken off, as in the case of unbelieving Jews, and in permitting other branches to be grafted, in the case of believing Gentiles, God exhibits two contrasting qualities. One is goodness and the other severity. Notice verse 22, "Behold therefore the goodness and severity of God: on them which fell, severity; but toward thee, goodness, if thou continue in his goodness; otherwise thou also shalt be cut off." While these divine qualities are contrasting qualities, they are not contradictory to the character of God. They balance His perfection. They are as proper in the spiritual world as they are in the natural world. We must remember that with God there is both grace and government. There is both love and law, both mercy and justice. And, because these are so, there is with Him both goodness and severity.

God cannot abandon the world to the whims of finite men and women. If He did, we would long since have destroyed ourselves. We can thank God for His severity in government as much as His goodness in grace. And we can also take warning as well. Let flippant sinners beware. Let them have a care. Let them ponder their folly as they not only despise God's grace manifest in the Cross, but flaunt God's government. This is a world where it is still true that "Whatsoever a man soweth, that shall he also reap." Sow a thought and you reap a deed. Sow a deed and you reap a habit. Sow a habit and you reap a character. Sow a character and you reap a destiny. Let these consider the Cross and remember that it is God's answer to a world's need. It is God's law revealed in love and as it has been wisely said, if any man stumbles into hell, he must do so over the heart of God.

You will notice that God speaks of a wild olive tree and a good olive tree and that the wild olive tree is grafted into the good olive tree. There existed in Paul's day in Palestine, a species of olive tree known as the oleaster. It looks like the genuine fruit-bearing tree but it yields no fruit. It consumed space, sunshine, soil and rain, but yielded nothing in return. It was a counterfeit. It needed revitalizing

and a new nature. It got it by grafting. We are all by
nature like the wild olive tree. We are consumers
but not contributors. We need a life-union with the
good olive in order to possess the life that blesses.

3. The Jewish Blindness and the Gentile's Fulness.
Verses 25-32.

"For I would not, brethren, that ye should be
ignorant of this mystery, lest ye should be wise in
your own conceits; that blindness in part is happened to Israel, until the fulness of the Gentiles be
come in. And so all Israel shall be saved: as it is
written, There shall come out of Sion the Deliverer, and shall turn away ungodliness from
Jacob: For this is my covenant unto them, when
I shall take away their sins. As concerning the gospel, they are enemies for your sakes: but as touching the election, they are beloved for the fathers'
sakes. For the gifts and calling of God are without repentance. For as ye in times past have not
believed God, yet have now obtained mercy
through their unbelief: Even so have these also
now not believed, that through your mercy they
also may obtain mercy. For God hath concluded
them all in unbelief, that he might have mercy
upon all."

The rehabilitation of our world and its establishment
in peace and righteousness will never be the product
of the mind. Instead, it will come from the heart.
When the heart is right, the head will be right. We
have not begun to explore the possibilities that lie
either in the mind or in the world outside. The discoveries of the twentieth century are what Job said,
but "parts of His ways." The revised version of Job
26:14 reads thus, "Lo, these are but the outskirts of

his ways: And how small a whisper do we hear of him!" But the thunder is yet to come. The liberated heart will mean a liberated mind. And the liberated mind will mean a liberated world. But, mark it, when it comes, it will not come out of a laboratory, but from the Cross. It will not be intellectual but spiritual. Being spiritual of origin it will result in the emancipation of all life.

No doubt, we stand on the threshold of that great day. Wars bring the shift of nations that set the stage for the final act. Science, with its false worship of force, is moving in the outskirts of God's way. This is the only way to account for the phenomenal and unprecedented discoveries of the past generation. They are the whispers that precede the thunders.

One of the most important and strategic phases of the coming day of world liberation concerns Israel. We are in danger of misunderstanding the future by judging it in the light of the present. This is what Paul meant in verse 25, "For I would not, brethren, that ye should be ignorant of this mystery, lest ye should be wise in your own conceits; that blindness in part is happened to Israel, until the fulness of the Gentiles be come in." There is a present blindness over Israel. That blindness or, more properly, hardness, is one of the most apparent facts there is about the modern Jew. He does not appreciate our saying it, but he stiffens into stone at the mention of anything pertaining to Christianity. Yet, wrapped up in that Christianity, Paul has pointed out, is the continuation of God's great historic and prophetic purposes that date from Abraham.

Notice three things concerning this blindness.

(1) *It is with a limitation—"in part."*

It says in verse 25 "that blindness in part is happened to Israel." That blindness is not true of all Israelites for there are exceptions where some, here and there, have embraced Christ.

(2) *It is with an end—"until."*

This blindness will not always be. It is only to a given point. It is "until the fulness of the Gentiles be come in." Note that the destiny of Israel depends on the Gentile just as does the destiny of the Gentile depend on Israel. The time of Gentile fulness is without question the close of the present Gentile dispensation in which we now live. Jesus said in Luke 21:24 that "Jerusalem shall be trodden down of the Gentiles until the times of the Gentiles be fulfilled." The fulfilling of these times will mark the end of a phase of history which began with Babylon. It will be concluded with a revived and rebuilt Roman Empire. At the conclusion of that age will commence a new age. The empires of men will be succeeded by the Kingdom of God. The Kingdom of God will mark the coming of the King. And, in line with these tremendous events, will be the end of the national blindness of Israel.

(3) *It is with a recovery—"all saved."*

In verse 26 it says, "And so all Israel shall be saved." This can only mean that at the close of our present dispensation, grace will be extended to the nations as it is now extended to individuals. Its outcome will result in the existence of the first truly Christian nation. As paradoxical as it sounds now, the first Christian nation will be Israel. Nations are only nominally Christian now, but then there will be one nationally so.

Here, "all Israel" does not necessarily mean every individual. There will be irreconcilable individuals then as now. It means "all" without distinctions. Nor does it mean merely a spiritual Israel or a tribal Israel. It means Israel as a nation in contradistinction to the Gentiles as nations. If it is national for the Gentiles, it is national for the Jews.

Just how will all this be accomplished? Will it be a process of religious evolution? It will not. It will come rather through a great spiritual revolution. It will come simultaneous to a great coming. That great coming is mentioned in verse 26, "There shall come out of Zion the Deliverer." His coming will mean their restoration. It is true that Christ, the Messiah, has come, but it is also true that He is coming again. He has come in grace. He will come for government. He has come for the redemption of the individual. He will come for the redemption of the nation. He has come as a Saviour. He will come as a Sovereign. He has come for the Cross. We will come for the crown. He has come in shame. He will come in glory.

His coming will have specific results. Notice verses 26 and 27, ". . . and shall turn away ungodliness from Jacob: For this is my covenant unto them, when I shall take away their sins." Blindness is apparently the effect of ungodliness. When this is removed, then normal spiritual perception returns. And when this blindness is gone, the ancient basis of the covenant will return. But only, "when I shall take away their sins." Here again is proof that the basic cause of human disorder is sin. When it is gone, a life normal in its relation to God returns. And here God puts into force once more the long suspended covenant. So long as sin prevailed, that great contract remained invalid. But the lifting of sin meant the reinstatement of the contract. Israel will at that moment stand to receive the magnificent blessings promised to Abraham and the rest of the world through them, for "in thee shall all the families of the earth be blessed."

This is all in the future. What of the present? Its responsibilities are found in verses 28 to 32. Notice particularly verse 28: "As concerning the gospel, they are enemies for your sakes: but as touching the election, they are beloved for the fathers' sakes." Here are contrasts, the gospel and the election; enemies and beloved; your sakes and the fathers' sakes. What do they mean? Just this. We live today with the future before us. That future has a definite cast. We know what it will be. Israel is destined to a great future, but is inglorious today. She is scattered and dispersed, blinded and hardened. When viewed through her attitude to the gospel, she is an enemy. But we should consider her through the election as being beloved. We should be tolerant and forgiving. We should be tender and considerate. We should consider what she will be and not judge her for what she is. If she misjudges us, let us not misjudge her. Remember that "blindness in part is happened to Israel." If she considers us an enemy, let us consider her a friend. Here is real Christianity in its attitude to Jewry. This may not be the attitude of political Christianity, but it is the attitude of spiritual Christianity.

# 16

## THE CHRISTIAN AS A MEMBER
### *Romans 12*

WE COME now to the third and final section of
the book of Romans. It deals with "The Christian in Experience," and sets forth the practical
effects and expressions of a normal Christian experience.

It is the most logical and proper kind of conclusion,
for it thus gives order and meaning to truth.

Here we find that duty follows doctrine; responsibility follows revelation; and practice follows principle. Unless these things appear in the course and
conduct of our daily living, we give the lie to our
faith. Their absence tells us that the presence of
Christianity in us is only a fiction and a pretense.
"All our professions, our desires, our ideals, our hopes,
our intentions, will count for nothing unless we manifest holiness in thought, word, and deed in all the
circles of daily life and activity." Here is the fact
of privilege following precept. And we must remember with care that Christianity contains the preaching
of privilege as well as precept.

As a sainted servant of God once remarked, if he
had to choose between preaching precepts and preaching privileges, he would preach privileges. He believed

that the privileges of the gospel tend by their very nature to suggest and stimulate proper action, while the precepts standing alone tend to become academic. We need both. And with both we need to be constantly bearing in view two things. One is appropriation and the other is application. We must not only appropriate the truth but apply it. And in these two functions, we will automatically share in the life and fellowship of Christ, thus bringing to bear on our daily problem all the mighty energy and force of His divine life.

We have been led up to this point in the book of Romans through the processes of a personal Christian experience. We have been led out of sin into salvation. We have been led through justification into sanctification. We are now to be led through surrender into service. Let us lose neither the perspective nor the prospective. Let us not be lost in a passive religious contemplation but consider the reason why we are here.

We observe the Christian as a member of a great body of believers. Whether this has in view the body of Christ composing all believers, or whether it is a body of related and organized life is not made clear. At any rate, the believer is not an isolated unit of life. He belongs to a great community of spiritual life and his life must be lived in respect to the whole.

The chapter divides into four sections:

## I. THE CHRISTIAN'S CONSECRATION. Verses 1, 2.

Five facts appear concerning the Christian's Consecration.

1. The Appeal to Consecration. Verse 1.

"I beseech you therefore, brethren, by the mercies of God."

How significant that the appeal to consecration is mercy! It is neither force, authority, nor fear that prompts our consecration; it is mercy. Mercy received in salvation is the source of our response in consecration.

How important it is to remember that "we work from, not for salvation!" If conduct is to be right, it must begin with the right character. Whatever life the Christian lives must be lived by the dynamic of the indwelling Christ. In such a life, Christ not only comes to indwell us but we yield and surrender ourself to Him so that His indwelling becomes an outworking of all the traits and abilities of His divine life.

There is a distinction we need to make between salvation and consecration. One is the appropriation of life and the other is the application of life. One is getting something and the other is giving something. One is what God does for us and the other is what God does through us. Consecration is necessary, not to enhance or add to the character or quality of our salvation, but rather to enhance our enjoyment of it and produce the practical use of it.

2. The Act of Consecration. Verse 1.

". . . that ye present your bodies a living sacrifice, holy, acceptable unto God . . ."

The act of consecration includes three things.

(1) *It is voluntary—"present."*

Here is an act that suggests the giving of a gift and is a term used in the temple. It is exactly what we do when we make a present to someone. It is not forced by compulsion but prompted by voluntary convictions. This voluntary presenting of ourself to God is the first willful act in the process of consecration. But in no case can we consecrate ourself. That is a prerogative which belongs to God. We do the presenting, or giving, and God does the consecrating.

(2) *It is personal—"your bodies."*

This indicates something which is complete and entire. It is neither partial nor temporary. It is wholly and solely. It does not mean our bodies so much as our lives and yet, of course, God cannot have our lives without our bodies. It is through the body that we give both action and expression to our character, and God desires, yea demands, this to be the instrument of divine service.

Whatever else it means, above everything the presenting must be complete. God never consecrates the part, only the whole. When the High Priest was consecrated, the anointing oil went from the head to the feet. It included hands, feet, heart and head. It was all of the man or none of the man.

While this scripture tells us to present our bodies, it omits saying to whom these bodies are to be presented, but the answer is obvious. The presentation is not to God for He is in heaven; not to Christ for He has His own glorious body and has no desire nor need of our sinful one. It is to be to the Holy Spirit who has come to earth without a body and is seeking such that He might make them temples of His abode. This was the intention of redemption, for "Know ye not that your body is the temple of the Holy Ghost which is in you, which ye have of God, and ye are not your own?"

Consecration is not inviting the Holy Spirit to infill you. He is in you if you are in Christ. But it is yielding your body to His instrumentality and His use. He is in you by right of new creation. Let Him be in you also by right of consecration.

(3) *It is sacrificial—"a living sacrifice, holy, acceptable unto God."*

It is to be, as it were, an altar offering. The day of the physical altar is gone but the day of the spiritual altar has come. The sacrifice of blood has passed but the sacrificial surrender of body is here. The obligation and privilege is as great today as ever in the history of God's dealings with man. Let us then recognize the unspeakable opportunity which is ours. Let us make glad the heart of God and offer Him that which is without blemish and that which is well pleasing. Let us not wait to give God our age but our youth; not our poverty but our wealth; not our sickness but our health; not our days but our years; not our blindness but our sight. And in doing this, we will find our way to unspeakable happiness.

3. The Argument for Consecration. Verse 1.

". . . which is your reasonable service."

The argument that requires and rationalizes our consecration is the preceding subject matter of Romans. If we are the subject of such a redemption as it sets forth, and if we are to be the object of such a program planned for the future, then, by all the rights of reason we should belong to God with every fibre of our being. Here is Christianity at its intelligent best. Intelligent Christianity lends itself to service. It does not consume itself in a meaningless mutter of words but is an intelligent application of Christianity to the world about us.

4. The Attitude in Consecration. Verse 2.

"And be not conformed to this world: but be ye transformed by the renewing of your mind . . ."

(1) *The negative attitude—"Be not conformed to this world."*

To be conformed means to be made like. And in this case, it means to take shape, so far as our conduct is concerned, from the ideals and practices of the world.

Every Christian has a new center of activity in Christ. He is to change his circumstances, and not allow his circumstances to change him. It is impossible to be divided in our loyalties and to be happy with our Lord. There must be a forsaking of the world or there will be a forswearing of the Lord.

There are a great many people who are afflicted with a mental condition called a divided personality. This personality causes them to shift from one character to another and to live in two different worlds. But they are neither normal nor happy. There are Christians like that. They are trying to give a Dr. Jekyl and Mr. Hyde character to their religion. It is folly and gives them nothing but a weary heart.

The secret of Christian joy and victory and contentment is from within. It is folly to seek it in the externalities of the world. They are but bursting bubbles. Goethe said long ago, "He who is plenteously provided for from within needs but little from without."

(2) *The positive attitude—"but be ye transformed by the renewing of your mind."*

A reasonable service and a transformed mind are proper companions. He who has them has the secret of a good and a great life. Transformation is the remedy for conformation. If we wish to prevent conformation from without, we must submit to transformation from within. To be transformed means to be transfigured. It means more than a change in our manners. It is a change in our mind. Christians are not merely to be negatively unlike the world; they are to be, in a real sense, like the Lord. An artificial legalism falls far short of this expected change. We are not transformed by restrictions but by a renewal. That renewal is of the inner man, the mind. Here is the seat of his thinking and acting. If it is renewed, the whole man will be renewed. The face will reflect the heart. No man or woman can reach the thirtieth year without having the past sculptured on the face. The sculptor that fashions our face is greater than Angelo or Rodin. This sculptor is thought.

This transformation as we find it here, is not the transformation of salvation but consecration. It is not the transformation of regeneration for that has already taken place. It is the transformation of "renewing." This "renewing of the mind" refers to "the adjustment of our moral and spiritual vision to the mind of God." This adjustment is not instantaneous but gradual. For that reason consecration is a process following a crisis. We present our bodies in the crisis of decision. The transformation takes place in the process of the renewing of our minds. The renewal is in fact the continuation of regeneration. Regeneration is the initial and single act, done once for all. Transformation is the continuation of regeneration so that "we all, with open face beholding as in a glass the glory of the Lord, are changed into the same image from glory to glory, even as by the Spirit of the Lord" (II Cor. 3:18).

This renewal is accomplished from within. It is accomplished by the Holy Spirit to whom we have yielded or presented our bodies. It is not a process of mental culture but of spiritual change. We do not change our mind by our thoughts. Our thoughts are the children of the mind. Therefore, the parent must be right in order that the child might be right. And the cause of a right mind is the renewing by the indwelling, possessing, directing and mastering Holy Spirit.

5. The Achievement of Consecration. Verse 2.

". . . that ye may prove what is that good, and acceptable, and perfect will of God."

The attainment of a practical consecration will result in a new way of life. That way of life is the will of God. This will come freely and naturally from the renewal of our minds. We will be harmoniously united with our Lord in thought and deed.

We will find God's will to have a threefold characteristic.

(1) *It is "good."*

It will always be beneficial in its effect upon us. We need never fear the consequences of obeying God.

(2) *It is "acceptable."*

This means that with our minds adjusted to God's mind we will never find God's will an obnoxious thing.

It will be acceptable to us. This balances the other "acceptable" in the first verse. There what we did was acceptable to God. Now what He does is acceptable to us.

(3) *It is "perfect."*

It is a flawless and mature way of life. There is nothing lacking and nothing wrong.

These three add up to make a happy, joyous, and victorious Christian experience. We may have that kind of life if we will follow the pattern of this truth.

Immediately following the fact of consecration, which is the devoted employment of what we are and have in consistent life service, comes the reminder of the channel through which this consecration is to be exercised.

II. THE CHRISTIAN'S RELATIONSHIP. Verses 3-5.

We should recognize and observe our relationship in a twofold attitude.

1. In Humility. Verse 3.

"For I say, through the grace given unto me, to every man that is among you, not to think of himself more highly than he ought to think; but to think soberly, according as God hath dealt to every man the measure of faith."

This is only another way of saying that we should not become overimpressed with our own importance. After all, whatever success we have in the place we occupy, whether considered significant or insignificant, is due to the faith which God gives us. There is the proper place for human ability, but only when that ability is employed through this "measure of faith." Our capacity for both intelligence and usefulness is determined by the measure of faith. We are not indispensable to God, but rather God is indispensable to us. It is not our effort but His equipment. But after the preparation, comes the performance and the need for industry and fidelity in the task and the place we have.

2. In Unity. Verses 4, 5.

> "For as we have many members in one body, and all members have not the same office: So we, being many, are one body in Christ, and every one members one of another."

Christians collectively are likened to a body. Each body has many members with different functions. These functions are not interchangeable. The eye will never be able to do the hearing for the ear. The lungs will never be able to perform the functions of the heart. Each member must do its own work. The seemingly insignificant part must not aspire or desire the prominent place. Every one is important and indispensable in his Creator-given task. So it is with the Christian. Our lives must be lived in the light of our connection with our fellow Christians. There can be no free-lancing. We can not go on our own. Because it is the life of union, it must be labor in unison.

Not long since, we read an article entitled, "The Most Important Job in the World." Who do you think has it? Most of us would like to have it. But if we realized it and if we are living in God's will, we have it right now and just where we are. The writer said this: "Naturally, all of us want to do something important, but few of us realize that we are probably doing it in our everyday lives. We have fallen into the habit of thinking that the only important jobs are the 'glamour' jobs. But the essential work of the world isn't done by jazz band leaders and radio and movie stars . . . It is done by the man with the hoe or the hammer, by the women who care for those men and their children and homes." And someone adds that "we may live without books, but civilized man cannot live without cooks." Few of us understand what a big job a little job may be.

Our place in life may be made a big place if we will fill that little place in a big way. This does not mean to feel big or important, for all our labor must be in the spirit of the preceding verse. But the person who has presented himself to God has a big reason for doing small things in a large way. He has both the ability and the aid that would not othewise come. It is not your place that is so important. It is the way you fill it.

III. The Christian's Duties Through Gifts. Verses 6-8.

"Having then gifts differing according to the grace that is given to us, whether prophecy, let us prophesy according to the proportion of faith; Or ministry, let us wait on our ministering: or he that teacheth, on teaching; Or he that exhorteth, on exhortation: he that giveth, let him do it with simplicity; he that ruleth, with diligence; he that showeth mercy, with cheerfulness."

It is led off with the statement, "Having then gifts . . ." These are to be thought of as special gifts as in the following section we will hear of general duties. Here, they are official while later on they are personal. This applies in a more or less direct way to those whose lives have been given over completely to Christian service, such as minister and missionary. Each are to minister on the basis of these gifts, for we recognize that in God's economy of grace, all are not alike.

Here are seven things, four of which are special and three general. Notice these gifts in their order:

*"Whether prophecy."* It is to be with carefulness that the truth may be symmetrically presented. And this prophesying is not so much foretelling as it is forthtelling. It is to declare the whole counsel of God and is to be done without hobbying.

*"Or ministry."* This is undoubtedly administrative work. It should be done wholeheartedly.

*"Or he that teacheth."* Here is the gift of exposition. It is in contrast and distinction from prophesying and while it was not more important it was probably less spectacular and therefore many times neglected. But, oh how needed it is today! Thrill saturated moderns find it difficult to keep their seats long enough to use their brains.

*"He that giveth."* How strange that this should be mentioned as a gift! But it apparently is a gift to be able to give wisely, properly, and spiritually. It is to be done "with simplicity," or more properly with liberality.

"*He that ruleth.*" It means supervision or presiding. It is official duty done with discretion and devotion.

"*He that showeth mercy.*" Religious service seems so often to wrap itself in an unreasonable and unnecessary gloom. Of all the services in the world, Christian service should be rendered with cheerfulness.

The word, cheerfulness, means hilarity. It is to be a hilarity in keeping with the dignity of decency. Surely, we are not to make a burlesque out of Christianity. It dare not become a religious vaudeville. Let us not demean the gospel by a false hilarity which will only cheapen and disgrace it. Anyone who has presented himself to the Holy Spirit will have an inner recognition of what is proper. In any other case, he is clearly not under the Spirit's control, for God never led anyone to be a religious clown. Let us strike a happy medium and recommend our Christian life to others by its cheerful godliness. Here is an attractive translation of this statement, "If you come with sympathy to sorrow, bring God's sunlight in your face."

Since we make a gift of ourselves to God, He in turn gives gifts of ability to us. Our gift results in His gifts. Give Him what you have and He will return it furnished for a better and a larger life.

We are prone to shut up our Christianity in the Temple and leave it there until we come back a week hence. The sphere of precept is in the Temple but the sphere of practice is in the home and the community. If we have any notion that Christianity is not practical, we ought to abandon it. If it is not practical, it is not true. If it is not true, it is not worth having.

IV. THE CHRISTIAN'S DUTIES THROUGH GRACE. Verses 9-21.

The things mentioned previously were special. These are general and have application to the usual and common circumstances of everyday life.

They are led off with an exhortation. "Let love be without dissimulation." Love was to be without hypocrisy. The hypocrite, as Paul knew and used the term, was an actor who wore a costume and acted a part other than his own character. In the same way hypocrites passed under religious robes and acted out what they were not. This was particularly abhorrent when it came to love, the highest and noblest virtue. It should be transparent and sincere.

This, then is how love is not to be manifested. But we have another treatment of it, for there follow from this point numerous qualities and characteristics of love. It shows us what love is to be like and how it is to act. It sets the tempo of Christian living. It explains to us how the exhortation, "Let love be without hypocrisy," is to be fulfilled.

1. Love Is Discriminating. Verse 9.

"Abhor that which is evil; cleave to that which is good."

Love is of such a nature that it can only be attached to what is clean. Lust is impure but love is pure. Lust is loathesome but love is attractive.

2. Love Is Fraternal. Verse 10.

"Be kindly affectioned one to another with brotherly love . . . "

It is in fact a "brother love." The extent of our

manifestation of this love is not limited to our families. It is "one to another." It belongs to the spiritual brotherhood as well as the physical brotherhood. It belongs to the wider family of faith. It makes the real brotherhood. There is a brotherland more real than this fictitious thing we call the brotherhood of man. It is of faith and not of flesh. It is of love and not of hate. It is of peace and not of war. It is the brotherland of Christian fellowship.

3. Love Is Humble. Verse 10.

". . . in honor preferring one another."

Place seeking is a curse to Christians. The lust of it creeps into our affections before we realize it has taken root. There should be, instead, a courteous preference and recognition of others. Love is willing to vacate rather than occupy; to descend rather than ascend.

Humility does not mean that we must undervalue ourselves any more than we are to overrate others. We should not have an inferiority complex any more than a superiority complex. We are simply to be what we are in Christ.

4. Love Is Practical. Verse 11.

"Not slothful in business; fervent in spirit; serving the Lord."

Notice the things that are given together. One is "business" and another is "spirit." And the implication of the whole verse is that we may serve the Lord in secular life as well as spiritual life. In fact, there is an erroneous and entirely unwarranted distinction in too many things between the secular and the sacred. There is a good sense in which all secular things should be sacred.

The man who is truly fervent in his spiritual life will be diligent in his business life. In fact, he should be as Way translates this verse: "Your spirit should be fairly seething with enthusiasm while you are toiling as the Lord's bondmen." Here is practical and plausible and workable Christianity. The Christian "must not only mind heaven, but attend to his daily calling. Like the pilot, who while his eye is fixed upon the star, keeps his hand upon the helm." His head may be in the heavens, but his feet must be kept on the earth. And whatever he does, of science or craft, let him do it unto the Lord. Let him do as well as Jesus must have done in Nazareth's carpenter shop. There is an old saying that "he who does well, will always have patrons enough."

5. Love Is Exultant. Verse 12.

"Rejoicing in hope . . . "

Love is the most optimistic thing in all the world. It may sometimes be falsely so, but true love has a true hope. It looks on the bright side and not so much on the bleak side.

6. Love Is Enduring. Verse 12.

". . . patient in tribulation . . . "

This means any kind of affliction and adversity. It should be impressed upon us that it will come. It is a part of life. Neither can we choose our afflictions. We can not be sure that even God chooses them, but He does often permit them for purposes of sovereign grace. And there are none without their value.

This endurance of love is more than enduring affliction. It is outlasting it in patience. It is defeating it by becoming better through it.

7. Love Is Prayerful. Verse 12.

". . . continuing instant in prayer."

This is not possible merely in an act of prayer but rather in an attitude of prayer. The attitude should always be the atmosphere of the act. Prayer moves more than our moods—it moves mountains. It does not merely influence our emotions. It profoundly influences and changes external events in the world about us.

8. Love Is Helpful. Verse 13.

"Distributing to the necessity of saints; given to hospitality."

The object of love's help is "the necessity of the saints." There is a special preference here. It is one Christian's preferred help for another Christian's preferred need. We are to "do good unto all men but especially to them that are of the household of faith."

This does not tell us how to help; it just tells us that love is helpful. Benevolence, of course, should always be with intelligence. But by far the greater danger in our benefactions is not that we will do it unwisely, but rather that we will not do it at all.

And then it says here, "given to hospitality." This would make of every Christian home a Christian inn where love extends the blessings of our board and bed.

9. Love Is Blessing.  Verse 14.

"Bless them which persecute you: bless, and curse not."

Here love steps up rather than stoops down to the carnal place of contention. Love blesses instead of curses. It places no imprecations on the head of its persecuting pursuer. It does not merely suffer and endure this ill-treatment but actually counterbalances it by wishing well those who are engaged in their hurt. We must recognize how superior this is to the ordinary attitude.

10. Love Is Sympathetic. Verse 15.

"Rejoice with them that do rejoice, and weep with them that weep."

Love has an interest in others. Love interests itself in others not only in sorrow but also in success. Here opposite sympathies are mentioned. We can easily share our brother's sorrow, but do we as joyously share his success? We may find it difficult to congratulate with the same feelings as those with which we console. But when love exists without hypocrisy it rejoices in the joy of others.

11. Love Is Unifying. Verse 16.

"Be of the same mind one toward another. Mind not high things, but condescend to men of low estate. Be not wise in your own conceits."

Love unifies. It never divides or separates. A normal effect of this unification among those who love is condescension toward others and the right estimation of ourselves. Way's translation reads, "Do not be exclusive, but walk hand in hand with the lowly." Christianity does not classify men by station and rank, but by character. It does not partition us into sections of class rivals but bids us participate with one another in Christian love.

To condescend means to give oneself to such as are here described as "men of low estate." We can be sure it does not mean low-minded men but men and women in the lowly walks of life. We place too much emphasis on our artificial social classifications.

At the same time, we hold this opinion of others, we should be careful to have the right opinion of ourselves and "not be wise in our own conceits." Being wise in our own conceits means to overestimate our wisdom. It means to have nothing to learn and everything to teach.

12. Love Is Without Retaliation. Verse 17.

"Recompense to no man evil for evil . . ."

Love does not engage in cheap retaliation; neither does it lend itself to the common tactics of ordinary men.

13. Love Is Provident. Verse 17.

". . . Provide things honest in the sight of all men."

This has in it the thought of propriety as well as provision. Whatever means we employ to provide ourselves with life's needs must be honorable and carry with it the respect of decent man. Way's translation says, "Be careful to conform to the proprieties, the decencies of human society." The Christian should be ethical as well as spiritual. In fact, if he is spiritual, he will be ethical.

14. Love Is Peaceful.  Verse 18.

"If it be possible, as much as lieth in you, live peaceably with all men."

The nature of love is that of peace.  But even love has its principles.  And when it states, "as much as lieth in you," it means that as far as you can without sacrificing your principles.  It is not peace at any price.  It is to be peace by principle.  But it is to be the exercise of every effort and the exhaustion of every means.  Then, such an one is guiltless if peace cannot be achieved.

15. Love Is Without Vengeance.  Verses 19, 20.

"Dearly beloved, avenge not yourselves, but rather give place unto wrath: for it is written, Vengeance is mine: I will repay, saith the Lord. Therefore, if thine enemy hunger, feed him; if he thirst, give him drink: for in so doing thou shalt heap coals of fire on his head."

This scripture distinguishes between vengeance and wrath.  Vengeance is an act while wrath is a feeling. It is better to give place to the feeling than to indulge in an act of revenge.  Vengeance is the right and prerogative of God.  If we want a just and full compensation for an injury done us, let us not seek it ourselves.  We will never get it.  God will give it in His own good time and when He gives it, it will be right and just.  There is nothing so hollow and empty as getting revenge.  It leaves one flat and unhappy.

There is another side to this.  It is not merely to negatively step aside and wait the day of God's reckoning upon our enemy.  It is more.  It is to step out and help him. It is to serve his hunger and his thirst. In so doing "thou shalt heap coals of fire on his head." The cause of our good should be love and not the satisfaction of seeing our enemy squirm under our benefactions. We may sometimes act like the Indian did who had been taught this kind of treatment of his enemies. When he practiced it on one of them, the missionary asked him why he did it. He replied that he liked to see his head smoke.

16. Love Is Victorious. Verse 21.

"Be not overcome of evil, but overcome evil with good."

Victory is achieved contrary to all accepted standards of life. It does not retaliate with the kind of treatment it receives. It returns the opposite. Good is sent for evil. When did we last do this? Dare any of us be courageous enough to review our lives to see whether this is our practice? It is to be the practice of Christianity here and now. It is the activity of love—a love which is without hypocrisy.

# 17

## THE CHRISTIAN AS A CITIZEN
### *Romans 13*

HERETOFORE, in the previous chapter, the Christian lived in relation to his fellow believer. Now his life is seen in relation to his fellowman. Before it was to the church. Now it is to the state. Once it was his relation to love, Now it is to law. Once it was as the member of a body of believers. Now it is as the part of a commonwealth. There are important duties and opportunities in each. What they are in this sphere we shall presently see.

I. THE CONSTITUTION OF AUTHORITY. Verses 1-4.

"Let every soul be subject unto the higher powers. For there is no power but of God: the powers that be are ordained of God. Whosoever therefore resisteth the power, resisteth the ordinance of God: and they that resist shall receive to themselves damnation. For rulers are not a terror to good works, but to the evil. Wilt thou then not be afraid of the power? do that which is good, and thou shalt have praise of the same: For he is the minister of God to thee for good. But if thou do that which is evil, be afraid; for he beareth not the sword in vain: for he is the minister of God, a revenger to execute wrath upon him that doeth evil."

Political and patriotic organizations use this chapter as a means to stimulate political and patriotic loyalty. But the approach is not political. It does not belong to the average citizen but to the Christian citizen. It is spiritual not political.

The reason assigned to good citizenship goes back of government to God. Five times in these four verses the phrase "of God" occurs. It indicates the origin of government. That origin is God's authority. It is expressly stated for "the powers that be are ordained of God." This means that God is back of the principle of government. And it is significant to observe that while God has decreed governments, He has not declared what form they shall have.

There is something about all governmental authority that carries with it an instinctive respect. Wherever such authority is set up, it creates a sense of respect that goes back of the office and the officeholder to God, for "there is no power but of God." What is the authority of law? Is it in the policeman's club or badge? Is it in the judge's robes? Is it in the king's crown? Authority, and respect for it, goes back of these symbols to God, for there is created in every agency of law and civil authority a sense of divine investment. Without this, there would be no respect for government. We may write our constitutions, elect our congresses and pass our laws, but they would all be without enforcement except for the God behind government.

A new appreciation and understanding of this might assist governmental rulers and officers to appreciate the authority of their office and the people to realize whence the strength of civilization comes.

There is an intimation in the second verse that people may sometimes be at variance with their governments. It says "whosoever therefore resisteth the power, resisteth the ordinance of God." Can a Christian be a revolutionist or a reactionary? Can a Christian oppose the officers of the law? Can a Christian resist regulations? Or is it blind obedience and an abject slavery to any system that is enjoined here?

Let it be clearly in mind that nothing is said about forms or rules of government. What is said here is merely the fact that God has established authority. Whoever there be then who would rebel against authority or the power of being governed, is in reality revolting against God's arrangement.

Any Christian has a right to question the motives and principles and deeds of his government. He is a citizen with certain rights under the constitution or the crown of his country and within those limits he may consider his own conscientious responsibility. If he recognizes God behind government, then he has a right to require God in that government to the point where his government shall not do anything contrary to God's law.

If the Scriptures were to give minute regulations as to our actions in all given circumstances, it would contain an interminable number. It does not, therefore, give us a code of citizenship, but reminds us of the character of the citizen and lays down the principal fact that all government goes back to God.

Just how far back does this go? Genesis 9:5 and 6 gives the first intimation of human government. This is our first democracy. It is the institution of capital punishment for the protection of human life which is the sacred trust of all government. We have later on a theocracy and still later, a monarchy. Among the nations, there has been every form of government from tribe to empire, from democracy to autocracy. But wherever authority is vested in rule, that authority is "ordained of God." And again we say that this in no manner gives Bible sanction to all the deeds of governments. It merely states that the essence of authority back of all order and decency in the world is God. And if this is so, we ought to have a new sense of reverence for God in our nations.

There is an interesting question asked in the third verse, the answer to which extends down into verse 4. The question is, "Wilt thou then be afraid of the power?" Another way of saying it is this, "Do you wish to have no reason to dread authority?" What is the answer? "Do that which is good." If we want to be comfortable citizens, then be good citizens.

Within recent time a fugitive from justice was arrested because of this very thing. He was about to cross a street in Los Angeles when he saw a police car, and so instinctive was his reaction to guilt that he darted back and tried to evade the officers who noting his suspicious actions arrested him. He then began to protest innocence of a particular crime. Only the guilty have reason to fear. Under ordinary circumstances, this verse means that if we will respect government, government will respect us. If we are good, government will be good to us, for it says, "Do that which is good, and thou shalt have praise of the same." But this will only be true where and when we recognize God back of our government and govern in that respectful reverence that fits us.

## II. THE CONSCIENTIOUS OBEDIENCE. Verses 5-7.

"Wherefore ye must needs be subject, not only for wrath, but also for conscience sake. For this cause pay ye tribute also: for they are God's ministers, attending continually upon this very thing. Render therefore to all their dues: tribute to whom tribute is due; custom to whom custom; fear to whom fear; honour to whom honour."

Obedience is enjoined for a moral reason as well as a civil reason. The Christian citizen has a Christian conscience, therefore, let his citizenship not only be because he fears civil consequences, but because of his conscience.

In these days of grave national and international distress, we need a new attitude toward both God and government. God has been ignored by rulers and the governing classes of the nations, and as a result, nations are facing the very extremity of their existence. It is still true that "God reigneth" and man had better recognize it.

The day after the great earthquake and fire at San Francisco, a newsboy was showing a dazed man the way through the city, and as they walked, the lad philosophized: "It took men a long time to put all this stuff up, but God tumbled it over in a minute. Say, mister, 'tain't no use for a feller to think he can lick God."

## III. THE CHRISTIAN'S PRACTICE. Verses 8-10.

"Owe no man anything, but to love one another: for he that loveth another hath fulfilled the law. For this, Thou shalt not commit adultery, Thou shalt not kill, Thou shalt not steal, Thou shalt not bear false witness, Thou shalt not covet; and if there be any other commandment, it is briefly comprehended in this saying, namely, Thou shalt love thy neighbor as thyself. Love worketh no ill to his neighbor: therefore love is the fulfilling of the law."

We are largely interested in the first statement of the eighth verse which says, "Owe no man anything." Is this to be taken literally or figuratively? It does not convey the meaning that we cannot contract an obligation. It does mean that we must pay every obligation we contract. It literally means that we must not leave a debt unpaid.

Notice where this verse is placed. It follows what has been said in verse 7, about tribute and custom; about our civil obligations as citizens. These we must pay. Christians must meet their obligations.

This thought of paying and not the restriction against owing is what this verse chiefly teaches. It is not the contracting of an obligation which is spoken against but the keeping of it unpaid. There is nothing unchristian or unethical in assuming a debt. What is unchristian is to assume more debts than one can pay or to ignore the payment of them. It has a meaning which is first determined by the text, which Way translates, "Do not leave a debt to any man unpaid." And second, by the context to which we have already called attention. No conscientious Christian citizen will take more obligations than he can properly care for, nor take advantage of another by refusing to acknowledge his debts. He will in all things be frugal and provident, faithful and honest.

While there are these debts that can and should be paid, there is a debt which can never be paid. It is our debt "to love one another." This is a perpetual debt to which we stand in constant obligation. No matter what payment we have made heretofore, we are continually in debt to one another. What a magnificent obligation!

Is love really an obligation? It is. The reason it is, the apostle says, is because it fulfills the law, for "he that loveth one another hath fulfilled the law." The law is then cited and salient commandments are given, all of which are declared to be comprehended by the one commandment to love thy neighbor. Does this mean that we are being linked once more with the law? Not at all. Christianity is never life by regulation but by principle. Here we love not because a law says we must, but because our life has that kind of a nature. When he is living normally, the Christian does not love because he has to, but because he can not help it. Therefore, love is more than an obligation. It is an opportunity.

Love has a primary motive. That motive is "good," for "love worketh no ill to his neighbor, therefore, love is the fulfilling of the law." And so in the normal expressions of a life of love, freed from the confining restrictions of this prohibition and that, we find the principle of the law fulfilled. It is fulfilled by Christians because it was fulfilled in Christ.

IV. The Crisis of Service. Verses 11-14.

"And that, knowing the time, that now it is high time to awake out of sleep: for now is our salvation nearer than when we believed. The night is far spent, the day is at hand: let us therefore cast off the works of darkness, and let us put on the armour of light. Let us walk honestly, as in the day; not in rioting and drunkenness, not in chambering and wantonness, not in strife and envying. But put ye on the Lord Jesus Christ, and make not provision for the flesh, to fulfill the lusts thereof."

The crisis which is presented to us here is not so much what we are to do; but when we are to do it. It is to be done now. This scripture says "it is high time." Yes, this is the "high time" of Christian privilege and opportunity, and it is like high tide when affairs are at the full force of their strength. It is the time to take advantage of and do the things Christian citizens ought to do.

It is high time:

1. To "Awake Out of Sleep." Verse 11.

This is the only place in the Bible where it speaks of soul sleep and it is of the soul sleep of those who are alive. They are sleeping while they are living. Theirs is the sleep of spiritual lethargy. Awake thou that sleepest, for these are momentous days. It is not fitting that Christians should be dullards any more than drunkards.

It is high time:

2. Because, "Now is our salvation nearer than when we believed." Verse 11.

Distinction is one of the secrets of interpretation. Here salvation is not the present spiritual phase of our regeneration. It is the future physical phase. It is the salvation of the body and the consequent redemption of the universe and the Christian's deliverance from the present conditions which so limit his activities.

It is nearer, but how near is it? It is nearer than we think. Let us awake and arise and be about our Father's business; not dreaming about the future, but doing something about the present.

It is high time:

3. Because, "the night is far spent, the day is at hand." Verse 12.

Here night and day stand in contrast. Of course, they are not physical night and day, but refer to this "whole period of alienation from God." As for the night, it is "far spent." It is far advanced. In Paul's day it was so. How much further has been its advance in our day? As for the day, it is "at hand." This means that it has drawn near. It was near when Paul wrote and it is much nearer today. If the crisis of the times was great to Paul, how much greater to us?

It is high time:

4. To "Cast Off"—to "Put On." Verses 12-14.

Time is of the essence of our holiness. Consideration demands our Christlikeness. We are to "cast off the works of darkness" which is anything that is unchristian, be it a practice or a principle.

We are to "put on the armour of light" which includes all the weapons in the arsenal of grace and faith. We are engaged in conflict with spiritual forces of darkness and can only hope to succeed when we possess the spiritual weapons of light.

John Bunyan said, "Religion is the best armour that a man can have; but it is the worst cloak."

The result of such putting off and putting on will be seen in the way we walk. It will not be "in rioting and drunkenness; not in chambering and wantonness, not in strife and envying." It will be in the practices of daylight living. The full blaze of divine publicity is upon every thought and deed. And anything short of such decent and decorous living is unworthy of Christians.

Observe here the two things we are charged to put on. It is, first, "the armour of light" in verse 12. And, second, "the Lord Jesus Christ," in verse 14. The first is armament. The second is clothing. The first is for protection. The second is for perfection. The first is defensive. The second is offensive. The one provides us with the abilities of Christian warfare. The other provides us with the attributes of the Lord's nature. One is for the Christian as a soldier. The other is for the Christian as a saint.

# 18

## THE CHRISTIAN AS AN EXAMPLE
### Romans 14

SINCE the book bears a united message, there is a connection between its chapters. It is no less true here, for in the thirteenth chapter we saw the Christian in relation to his fellow-citizen, while in this chapter we see the Christian in relation to his Christian brother. In the previous chapter it was his life in regard to civil duties while here it is his life in regard to conscientious conduct. It is a question in this chapter of how we should live in view of the differences of opinion concerning personal conduct. What Paul has in mind are not the great questions of spirituality and morality but the minor matters of detail that might arise in daily life.

The problems dealt with might have been occasioned by a local difficulty but they are certainly of general application. The same differences of opinion prevail today. What we should be careful to avoid is that these differences of opinion do not cause divisions in fellowship. We may differ, but we must not divide.

I. THE PROBLEM AND THE SOLUTION. Verses 1-13.

1. The Problem. Verses 1-5.

"Him that is weak in the faith receive ye, but not to doubtful disputations. For one believeth that he may eat all things: another, who is weak, eateth herbs. Let not him that eateth despise him that eateth not; and let not him which eateth not judge him that eateth: for God hath received him. Who art thou that judgest another man's servant? to his own master he standeth or falleth. Yea, he shall be holden up: for God is able to make him stand. One man esteemeth one day above another: another esteemeth every day alike. Let every man be fully persuaded in his own mind."

The problem is suggested in the first verse and it is the problem of the weak brother. His problem is not that he is weak in faith but rather weak "in the faith." He is not defective in his character but he does not know as yet, because of lack of growth and understanding, how to regulate his conduct. It is not the case of being weak morally or mentally, but the necessity of maturing in faith.

Way speaks of him as "a man who overlays his faith with tender scrupulosities." Therefore, he may be described as a person who is under-spiritual and over-scrupulous. But here he is—what are we going to do with him? We must move with caution because unless we do, these differences of opinion about our conduct are going to result in divisions in our fellowship and we will be found by the world to be quarreling and quibbling over things that have no moral or spiritual consequence. The weak brother is liable to become critical of the strong brother's indulgence. The strong brother is liable to abuse his liberty when he sees the weak brother's abstinence.

The thing to do is quickly given. It is this, "receive ye, but not to doubtful disputations." In other words, we are to consider ourselves in the light of an example rather than as a critic. These "doubtful disputations" literally mean judgments of reasonings or decisions of doubts or deciding mere matters of opinion. It is the mistake of trying to regulate the conduct of others by reason rather than revelation. It is trying to enforce the law of the mind rather than "the law of the Spirit of life in Christ Jesus," and it amounts to nothing more or less than Phariseeism. There is that sort of thing among doctrinally scrupulous Christians. In an attempt to avoid Phariseeism in doctrine many people today are unconsciously becoming Pharisees in conduct.

The problem presented by this weak brother was twofold. With him it was a question of diet and observances.

(1) *Diet.* Verse 2.

"For one believeth that he may eat all things: another, who is weak, eateth herbs."

It appears that the one referred to was a vegetarian, for it says that he "eateth herbs" and had a conscientious scruple against doing what the other man did who ate "all things." This was more than a question which was common in that day of distinguishing between meat bought in the markets and meat bought at the pagan temples which had been offered to idols. It was a question of conscience about eating any meat and living exclusively on vegetation.

What should be done about it? The answer is in verses 3 and 4. "Let not him that eateth despise him that eateth not; and let not him which eateth not judge him that eateth: for God hath received him. Who art thou that judgest another man's servant? to his own master he standeth or falleth. Yea, he shall be holden up: for God is able to make him stand."

We are not to despise this man's conscientious behavior. We are not to become unbrotherly and consequently unchristian. We are not to fling the charge of narrowmindedness at someone who is doing something which is not specifically regulated by the precepts of the Scriptures and which does not agree with our opinion.

In cases where the Scriptures do not make specific regulations or offer particular details, the arbiter and judge is to be conscience enlightened by the Holy Spirit and not our critical attitude. Christian liberty, within our spiritual position in Christ, is the inviolate right of every Christian and only a bigoted Phariseeism will deny it.

The admonition works both ways. Not only is it true that the strong are not to despise the weak but it is equally true that the weak are not to judge the strong. And here the admonition is based on the fact that "God hath received him." This refers to conversion, and if God has received him on the basis of his faith in Christ, who are we to judge him on the basis of his conduct? After all, Paul says, "Who art thou that judgest another man's servant? to his own master he standeth or falleth." This man's conduct is something he is accountable for to God and not to man. If God has His hands on a man, we must leave our hands off.

Then Paul adds at the end of verse 4, "Yea, he shall be holden up: for God is able to make him stand." That is, what this man does before God, with God as the guide of his conscience, is going to merit God's approval. He is not turned loose to live like the devil in filth and corruption. His liberty is not license. It is a godly conscientiousness. What God has not condemned, we have no right to condemn.

After all, the secret of contented Christianity is life in the will of God. We can be turned loose within the limits of that will and like Chrysostom said, "Love God and do as you like." What we like will be His will, and what we do will be His pleasure.

(2) *Observances*. Verse 5.

"One man esteemeth one day above another: another esteemeth every day alike."

Paul may have had in mind the case of a Jewish convert who was still clinging to his Sabbath worship and feast days. With him it was the virtue of feasting and fasting at appropriate times. Paul does not make an issue of this. He does not even say he should not do it. He just ignores it.

But then there is the other brother who "esteemeth every day alike." It does not mean that there are no sacred days in this man's calendar. It means that they are all sacred to him. It does not mean that this man flaunts all standards to act as he likes. It means that it is his policy to consider all time sacred and every duty divine.

Who is right about these days? The answer is close at hand. "Let every man be fully persuaded in his own mind." The thing to govern a Christian is conviction and not custom. He is to act in accordance with convictions of his own, which he has arrived at on the basis of his responsibility to his Master. He has no obligation to another man's opinion or custom. And when he lives enlightened by the Holy Spirit, he has no responsibility to act the way other people think. He is responsible for himself alone and accountable to God alone.

But we dare not overstep the truth that is dealt with here any more than we should understate it. Does it mean that there are no days sacred for worship in a Christian's calendar? Is there nothing he dare not indulge in? Can he live and act like any godless soul just because he thinks he can? As far as the day is concerned, he has one. It is the Lord's day. To him it will be sacred for the Lord's sake. But it does not mean that we can take the Christian first day and make it over into a Jewish seventh day. The Christian has a day and he will keep it.

As for indulgences, amusements and recreations, there is no list of what is prohibited or proscribed. The Christian's behavior is going to be instinctively managed by the Christian's character. And the Christian's character has been laid in a Christlike pattern.

We go back to the closing verses of the previous chapter where the admonition is to "put ye on the Lord Jesus Christ." Whoso does this will live in the light and not in the dark. His deeds will conform to his character. His criterion of behavior is not, can I do it? but would He do it? He will not walk according to the "faith of the faddists," but to the "faith of our Fathers." He will remember that "those whose eyes are raised to the stars should not crawl on their bellies." His life will be intelligent and spiritual. It will be free and happy. It will be clean and conscientious. It will be godly and Christlike. It will, in consequence, be a benediction and blessing.

One of the most perplexing and constantly recurring problems among earnest Christians is their behavior in respect to the world about them. We ask ourselves, may we do this? or should we go there? What is to be the pattern of our lives? This is exactly the problem dealt with in this fourteenth chapter. It is not stated in so many words. It does not use our modern terminology. It does not give names. It does not, even in its answer, set up a list of do's and don'ts. This makes us realize once more that the practice of the Christian is not regulated by rules but by principles. We are not considered children under a regime of law but adults who are given grace. Thus, we walk by grace through faith in a sphere of life that is in the heavens and which determines the character of our earthly life.

The second half of the first section of the chapter deals with:

2. The Solution. Verses 6-13.

"He that regardeth the day, regardeth it unto the Lord; and he that regardeth not the day, to the Lord he doth not regard it. He that eateth, eateth to the Lord, for he giveth God thanks; and he that eateth not, to the Lord he eateth not, and giveth God thanks. For none of us liveth to himself, and no man dieth to himself. For whether we live, we live unto the Lord; and whether we die, we die unto the Lord: whether we live therefore, or die, we are the Lord's. For to this end

Christ both died, and rose, and revived, that he might be Lord both of the dead and living. But why dost thou judge thy brother? or why dost thou set at nought thy brother? for we shall all stand before the judgment seat of Christ. For it is written, As I live, saith the Lord, every knee shall bow to me, and every tongue shall confess to God. So then every one of us shall give account of himself to God. Let us not therefore judge one another any more: but judge this rather, that no man put a stumblingblock or an occasion to fall in his brother's way."

When the question arises concerning what another man does in something that is not specifically regulated by the Scriptures, Paul reveals that first of all it was to be a matter of personal conviction—"let every man be fully persuaded in his own mind." Now he adds another consideration to this solution. If, in the first place, it was to be personal conviction, then that personal conviction was to be arrived at in the light of his connection with and responsibility to his Lord. And so he states in verse 6, "He that regardeth the day regardeth it unto the Lord; and he that regardeth not the day, to the Lord he doth not regard it." That is to say, when a Christian is walking not only with intelligence but reverence, not only in faith but fellowship, he will respect his Lord's opinion.

We have here a standard of behavior. It does not say we must or we must not. It sets up before us, instead, the person of our Master. And when we are "walking honestly as in the day," and when we have "put on the Lord Jesus Christ," we are going to regard our actions and habits and pleasures and companions and all else in one light, "the Lord."

Here is the individualism of verse 5 made subject to the mastership of Jesus. We are not little gods to set our own course as we please. Our new pattern of thought is within God's will. Our new pattern of life is with God's Son. What shall I do? The answer is, What would He do? Where shall I go? The answer is, Where would He go? The solution is simple and final, for there was no one who lived so beautifully correct and noble and righteous as He.

We next notice the seventh verse where it says, "For none of us liveth to himself, and no man dieth to himself." In understanding the principles of Christian behavior, we must not miss the connection between this verse and verse five. In the fifth verse we might ask the question, do we think for ourselves? Yes! In the seventh verse we might ask the question, do we live for ourselves? No! Why not? The answer is in verse eight, "For whether we live, we live unto the Lord; and whether we die, we die unto the Lord: whether we live therefore, or die, we are the Lord's." Our pattern of thought is the Word but our pattern of life is the Lord.

One of the glories of our Christian faith can be justly said to be its individualism. We have a right to think for ourselves. We are not required to parrot some other person's religious sayings. We do not have to pray other people's prayers. We do not have a religion handed down to us as cut and dried as a set of recipes. Our faith is not fabricated by a ruling class of ecclesiasts. We do not have to follow a unison laid down by men. Ours is Christian individualism, although it is not a new deal in religion. It is a new life in Christ. It is a new liberty in grace. It is a

new adventure in faith.  As there can be no liberty
and freedom except by law, so here our great liberty
is in the law of our new life, "the law of the Spirit
of life in Christ Jesus."  Here we think and act not
because of regulations but because of a nature that has
partaken of the divine nature so that our lives are
synchronized to His life.

When it comes to the matter of living, no Christian
can arrogantly say, I am going to live as I please.  None
can say I will do what I want with my life.  The law
of the land would not let us do what we pleased with
our life, much less the law of God.  Try to commit
suicide and the law would arrest us for it.  Try to
commit spiritual suicide by doing what we please and
God's law steps in to arrest us.  The Scriptures say
to every Christian, "Ye are not your own."

If then, we possess an individuality of thought, we
possess, equally a responsibility of action.  We are to
live "unto the Lord," or as it might be put "after the
Lord."  All things are to be done or left undone in
the light of this.  If we differ about what the Lord
says, we cannot differ about what the Lord does or
would do.  His Spirit within us and His example
before us are sufficient to any given case that may arise
in our lives.

There is something else here.  It says, "Whether we
live or die, we are the Lord's."  When we live, we are
conscious; but when we die, are we not unconscious?
How can a person "die unto the Lord"?  The answer
follows in verse nine, "For to this end Christ both died,
and rose, and revived, that he might be Lord both of
the dead and the living."  Christ is the Lord of both
the living and the dead, therefore, the dead are alive

in their death.  They go right on living and if they go right on living, they go right on serving.  Even death does not cause our service or influence to cease.  Our influence is left behind and our service goes on ahead and continues in another sphere.  For here there is a present continuous tense that suggests not only what we are, but what we continue to be after death.

When some promising Christian young man or some beautiful Christian young woman is cut off from a useful life by death, remember that, in reality, life is not cut off for them.  Its sphere of experience has changed.  There are occupations in yonder world of heaven for young hands and young hearts.  It is so for all ages, and if this is so then let us consider how earnestly we should live and serve while in this present life.  Indifference and indolence and half-heartedness are not going to be suddenly succeeded by angelic service over there.  We do not know how it can be or will be, but we believe what we are we will be.  This is a solemn thought and it ought to lead us to scrutinize our lives.  We have been living too carelessly and thoughtlessly, and what is worse, we have been living too Christlessly.  If we lived "unto the Lord," we would "die unto the Lord."

Three great things should be cherished by all men: How to love, how to live, and how to die.  Having learned the love of God in the Cross, we will learn how to live and how to die.  But to learn love, we must learn God's love.  All of this makes necessary that we not only own Bibles, but also that we possess them.

Paul urges another consideration in this matter of Christian behavior.  He has already told us that we ought to live with our brother in view and with our

Lord in view. Now he turns to the future and tells us that we ought to live with the judgment in view. Consequently he says in verse 10, "But why dost thou judge thy brother? or why dost thou set at nought thy brother? for we shall all stand before the judgment seat of Christ." Notice that in one case one brother condemns another, while in the other case one brother holds the other in contempt. It is neither Christian to be either condemning or contemptuous. Why? One reason is that "to his own master he standeth or falleth." And the other reason is that this standing or falling, this approval or disproval will not be according to our judgment; but God's. Futhermore, it is not apparent in this life but later, for some day we shall all stand before the judgment seat of Christ.

The principle here is that because God will judge us and determine what has been right or wrong, because we will all come to a place where all our differences will be resolved, and all the divisions among His people will be straightened out, we should refrain from passing judgment now. Thus, the exclamatory question, "Why dost thou judge thy brother?"

This does not mean that our minds have to be like a vacuum and utterly blank and empty of opinion, or that we should not possess a sense of fitness or rightness. If we see something which is self-evidently wrong, we can have a decided and positive opinion about it. But what is denied us here is the right to pass *judicial judgment.* We have no right to make it a closed case, for God is going to open the case of each of us at the Judgment Seat of Christ.

There will be another great judgment known as the Judgment of the Great White Throne mentioned in Revelation 20:11. These are two diversely different occasions. The Judgment Seat of Christ is at the close of this present dispensation of grace. It follows the Rapture of the Church. The Great White Throne is at the close of the Millennial Age. The Seat of Christ is for Christians alone. The White Throne is for sinners alone. The first one is in respect to life-work. The other has to do with sin. The Christian at the Seat of Christ is judged solely for "the things done in the body." The sinner at the White Throne is judged solely because his name "was not found written in the Book of Life." One has to do with faithfulness and the other with faith.

The word, Judgment Seat, is, in its original language, *a bema*. This was a raised place to be mounted by steps on which the magistrate sat to hear legal cases. It was a tribunal or, as the original word indicates, a footprint. Our footprints through life will be examined to see where we have walked and how. At this footprint tribunal, "Every man's work shall be made manifest: for the day (this day of the tribunal) shall declare it, because it shall be revealed by fire; and the fire shall try every man's work of what sort it is. If any man's work abide which he hath built thereupon, he shall receive a reward. If any man's work shall be burned, he shall suffer loss: but he himself shall be saved; yet so as by fire" (I Cor. 3:13-15).

When we quote the verse from Isaiah which is recorded here in verse 11, "Every knee shall bow and every tongue shall confess to God," we invariably apply it to the ungodly, recalcitrant and rebellious sinner, but God uses it here of the believer. It means that if in any particular instance of our belief or our behavior we have not been in full agreement and accord with the Lord, that we will come to agreement at the Judgment Seat of Christ. It will not come by force but because there will be such a complete airing and adjustment of all mysteries and misunderstandings that we will all see the inerrancy and the righteousness of all God's doings. Then we, in a last great display of homage and honor, will bow and confess His sovereignty and Lordship. We should be glad for the prospect of such an adjusting day. Then, and then only, will heaven be able to be heaven and all things be in harmony and unity.

As if to re-emphasize the importance of this consideration, Paul adds in verse 12, "So then every one of us shall give account of himself to God." It will be everyone for himself. It will not be the whole body but the individual member. It will be an individual inquiry with individual responsibility. Therefore, if we want that day to be right, let us make this day right. If we want to give a good account of ourself before the Lord, let us give a good account of ourself before the world. Eternity is made today and each day adds its favors or disfavors to the record that will be reviewed. For this reason, we are admonished not to be judging others, but to be setting our own house in order and living our own lives in the light of a sanctified reason and an everpresent Master and a coming judgment.

The sum of the whole matter under consideration is given in the thirteenth verse. "Let us not therefore judge one another any more: but judge this rather, that no man put a stumblingblock or an occasion to fall in his brother's way." It is the example of being helpful instead of critical; not to judge or condemn and get out of microscope of the Pharisee to see whether others have conformed to our opinions or even to the opinions of God. This is none of our business. God is the Judge and He will do the judging. But we have a business, "that no man put a stumblingblock or an occasion to fall in his brother's way." Let us, instead, put steppingstones that our brother might rise higher by our help rather than see him fall lower and lower. Our delight should be to help rather than hinder, and if we remember to live in character as an example, this is what we will do.

What is the greatest stumblingblock that one can put in the way of another? It is what is implied in these verses we have been dealing with. It is a professing Christian who has not been living Christ's life and who is constantly sitting in condemnation and judgment upon others, but making no effort to square his own behavior with his Master's. This accounts for far more outrages of faith and discouragements and offenses than probably anything we could mention. Others may be bad, but this is worse.

From classic history there comes the remembrance of an incident in the life of a Macedonian emperor. It goes as follows: "A painter was commanded to sketch the monarch. In one of his great battles, he had been struck with a sword upon the forehead, and a very large scar had been left on his right temple. The painter, who was a master-hand in his art, sketched him leaning on his elbow, with his finger covering the scar on his forehead; and so the likeness of the king was taken, but without the scar." Let us put the finger of charity upon the scar of the Christian as we look at him, whatever it may be,—the finger of a tender and forbearing charity, and see, in spite of it and under it, the image of Christ notwithstanding.

II. The Precept and the Practice. Verses 14-23.

Here are to be found four sets of precepts and practices. They come in sets of two each with a corresponding precept and a practice in each set. They are presented to encourage and assist the Christian in his life as an example. It is notable to observe that the precept explains the practice and that the practice demonstrates the precept. And, furthermore, here you will find no list of taboos. It is entirely free of any such thing. If it were not, it would be no different than the legalism out of which grace seeks to deliver us. Let none of us, then, in our zeal to be correct and proper, put in what Scripture leaves out. Let us be governed by what it says and not by what we want it to say. There would be less fanaticism if we followed the Scripture as is.

1. First Set of Precepts and Practices. Verses 14-16.

(1) *The Precept.* Verse 14.

"I know, and am persuaded by the Lord Jesus, that there is nothing unclean of itself; but to him that esteemeth any thing to be unclean, to him it is unclean."

This is the principle by which we are to act. It is twofold: First, Paul says, "I know." This is reason and he is here following the previous principle of verse 5 where it says, "Let every man be fully persuaded in his own mind." Second, Paul says, "I . . .

am persuaded by the Lord Jesus." This is revelation. Thus he acts by both reason and revelation. He is in life-union with Jesus Christ and this union is one of intelligence, reason, persuasion, conviction and consequently confidence. Thus in union with Christ, Paul found a reasonable way to live because it was His Lord's way.

He now arrives at the precept that "there is nothing unclean of itself." Let us not lose the connection and we will not lose the meaning. Paul is not speaking of moral uncleanliness but rather ceremonial uncleanliness. It is a religious question. To say that nothing is unclean of itself, no matter if it is in the bawdy house or the sanctuary, is to pervert the meaning of this scripture. The Bible speaks in no uncertain terms about lots of things which are morally impure. To these we should be violently opposed. But when it came to matters that applied to ceremonial law, this was to be decided by personal attitude.

To begin with, the grace-saved Christian was not living under the dictum of ceremonialism and therefore to him there could be no purity or impurity by priestly decree. He was living under the sensitized conscience of a new Lordship and to him "there is nothing unclean (or as the margin says, common) of itself." Rather it was the practice that made things clean or unclean. If one ate with knowledge and persuasion, it was not unclean. But if one ate under the legalism of the law, then, of course, to him it would be unclean.

And so Paul says, "But to him that esteemeth anything to be unclean, to him it is unclean." Let us be sure that we do not pervert this scripture by going away from its sanctity and purity to say that it does not make any difference what we do and where we go, since as Christians the only wrong is in the attitude, or to say that everything is clean and therefore everything is permissible. This is not so. Instead of this low-minded and false idea, there is the high place of spiritual opinion. The Christian's life is above the gutter. It is also above the ridiculous fanaticism of traditionalists and legalists. It is pure, high, lofty and beautiful. But we cannot run away with it. Notice the practice that is enjoined upon us in respect to this precept.

(2) *The Practice.* Verses 15, 16.

> "But if thy brother be grieved with thy meat, now walkest thou not charitably. Destroy not him with thy meat, for whom Christ died. Let not then your good be evil spoken of."

The precept said, "there is nothing unclean of itself." The practice is to be with consideration and caution, for we are constantly dealing with life situations that involve people who do not have as high a view as we may possess. For this reason it is prudent to refrain from doing what we might legitimately do because "if thy brother be grieved with thy meat, now walkest thou not charitably." Let us remember that even though we are delivered from the law, we have an even higher responsibility in love. And love will cause us to refrain from doing those things which will injure another.

We understand by the phrase "with thy meat," that it does not refer to the use of meat in our ordinary diet. It has become now a question of ceremonialism;

of blessed and unblessed meats; of temple and market meats. It is the question which troubled so many in that day, whether it was right to buy meat offered to pagan gods. Therefore, it was a religious question rather than a moral one. But, in this case, practice should conform to love. It might mean that our example sometimes required abstinence for the sake of love. The precept said, "there is nothing unclean of itself." But in the practice there was to be the remembrance of love and the consideration of our brother's conscience.

Does this mean that my brother's weakness is to be the measure and the limit of my strength? Must I limit the enjoyment of my knowledge to his ignorance? Must I, in my fellowship, circumscribe my liberty to his legalism? These are difficult questions. To answer them we dare not transgress the spirit of the counsel given in these scriptures. The answer here is that love must decide and dictate. The question of habits, amusements, etc., is not decided by a list of taboos but a law of love.

In deciding the course of our action, let this consideration weigh heavy in the balance, "Destroy not him with thy meat for whom Christ died." It is possible, if we were to exercise the fullest liberty of our conscience, that we might by our example lead someone else into spiritual disaster. We might lead someone who was not as yet fitted with moral and spiritual strength of character to withstand temptation, into paths of evil consequence. Seeing us, they might say it must be right because so-and-so is doing it.

Thus, we might nullify Christ's death by our life. So, in our practice, we should be careful to "let not then your good be evil spoken of." That is, do not allow actions which are thoroughly and spiritually reliable to us, be open to misconstruction and evil example by others. At any rate, the greatest happiness does not come from doing the things we want to do, but rather the things we ought to do. Happiness does not come from selfishness but helpfulness and godliness. To go our willful way will be to defeat the purpose of our Christianity.

2. Second Set of Precepts and Practices. Verses 17-19.

(1) *The Precept.* Verses 17, 18.

"For the kingdom of God is not meat and drink; but righteousness, and peace, and joy in the Holy Ghost. For he that in these things serveth Christ is acceptable to God, and approved of men."

After all, this says, the essence of the Christian life and the spirit of the Kingdom are not in eating and drinking. It has higher and greater, deeper and broader joys than come from physical indulgence. Its joys are of the heart and the spirit. They are righteousness, joy, and peace. The organ of life's richest delights is not the stomach but the heart. Christianity's greatest enjoyments are not external but internal. It is not the nourishment of the body, but the soul. For this reason the precept is telling us that we can forego much that an Epicurean world considers essential to its pleasure. We have meat to eat that the world knows not of.

If this is followed, Paul says in verse 18, we will be serving Christ and the result will be twofold, we will be both acceptable and approved. We will be "acceptable to God." How desirable this is! If our lives please God, what else matters, for in that very conformity is life's greatest satisfaction. But what does it mean when it says, "approved of men"? This sort of thing is precisely what they do not approve of. This does not mean popular approval, for neither Christian principles nor practices are scaled to that kind of a pattern. But wherever men will understand the precept, they will approve the practice. And so to lots of people we are bound to be misunderstood, but so long as we are intelligent in our precept practice and enjoying the smile of our Father's approval, we can afford to let all others misunderstand.

(2) *The Practice.* Verse 19.

"Let us therefore follow after the things which make for peace, and things wherewith one may edify another."

There are two things here that our practice includes. *"The things which make for peace."* These are the things that do not create strife and division so far as others are concerned, for, after all, ours is a community life among other Christians and in the midst of a non-Christian world. The Christian bears a very great responsibility.

*"And things wherewith one may edify another."* These are the things which contribute to the upbuilding and strengthening of the fabric of our Christian fellowship. They are of the nature of constructive rather than destructive actions. They build up and do not tear down.

There was once a party of tourists who employed an Indian guide to take them into the Canadian wilds.

Before starting, the Indian went alone to the top of a nearby foothill. The tourists were eager to be off, and became impatient with the Indian as he stood silent and motionless for a long time gazing at the mountains and forests all about him. "Why are you delaying so long?" called out one of the men to the Indian. But the Indian paid no attention. Finally he came down to the tourist party. All day long the party wound its way along narrow trails around mountains, over rugged crags, and into mysterious valleys, and never once did the Indian guide hesitate. He had located his marks from the top of the foothill, which guided him in the day's exploration of the mountain wilderness. And, we, too, who travel the trails of life will reach our goal successfully if we establish well-defined guide marks. This should be done early in life and it is particularly urgent early in our Christian lives.

3. Third Set of Precepts and Practices. Verses 20, 21.

(1) *The Precept.* Verse 20.

"For meat destroy not the work of God. All things indeed are pure; but it is evil for that man who eateth with offence."

Here is a very high-minded thing. It is not that selfish idea so commonly heard, "I'll do what I please." But here is declared the purpose of never undoing God's work in another's life, for the sake of gratifying some selfish whim or appetite. Instead, we are to consider ourselves in the light of others and cause our deeds to contribute to their credit and to refrain, for their sake and the sake of God's cause, from anything that would be destructive.

This precept says, "All things indeed are pure." It parallels what was said before that nothing is unclean. And again it is not a question of moral purity, but ceremonial purity. To a matured Christian, living in all the high privileges of grace, there was no ceremonial impurity in these meats that troubled the conscience of the novice. To him, eating such with a weak and offended conscience, made them impure and thus wrong. For that reason this novice should refrain from them until his conscience was educated and strengthened by grace.

(2) *The Practice.* Verse 21.

> "It is good neither to eat flesh, nor to drink wine, nor anything whereby thy brother stumbleth, or is offended, or is made weak."

Here is a course of action that is described as "good." It is something which is morally noble to exercise self-denial in the things one might do in order to be helpful to another. What a better thing, what a finer thing, what a Christlike thing to set limits about our own practice for the sake of considering our brother's welfare!

How far should we carry this? If the stronger Christian has all this self-denying consideration for the weaker Christian, should not the weaker Christian be charitable in return? Should he not in return respect the liberty of the fellow-believer? Should he not also yield himself to the means of grace by which he will grow in strength and character? Most surely, for the precept works both ways but, irrespective of this, the heavier burden is on the stronger of the two. Let us be resigned to it with joy. Let us be clean not only for example's sake but for cleanness sake. Let us be without reproach as far as in us lies.

Certainly, the profession of the Christian faith and the production of the Christian life should have everywhere about them the atmosphere of cleanness both of character and conduct. At the Ford Motor Company plant in Detroit, Michigan, five thousand men are assigned to the one task of keeping that plant clean. It must be spic and span. If the production of automobiles is carried on with such careful cleanness as this, what about the conduct of Christian lives?

What is the character of our self-denial to be? It is moral and not physical. We are not to torture our bodies and afflict ourselves with pain; nor make long and tortuous pilgrimages; nor live on mountain-tops or isolated in deserts. Our self-denial is not to be for our sake particularly, but for the sake of others. It is "good neither to eat flesh nor to drink wine, nor anything" that might not be prejudicial to another's well being. Here is a high, lofty, noble and beautiful purpose in living.

Beecher said wisely that "no man need hunt among hairshirts, no man need seek for blankets too short at the bottom and too short at the top, no man need to resort to iron seats or cushionless chairs, no man need shut himself up in grim cells, no man need stand on the top of towers or columns, in order to deny himself. There are abundant opportunities for self-denial. If a man is going to place the higher part of his nature uppermost, he will have business enough on hand. He will not need to go into the wilderness to deny himself." Our denials are at home; they are within us.

4. Fourth Set of Precepts and Practices. Verses 22, 23.

(1) *The Precept.* Verse 22.

"Hast thou faith? have it to thyself before God. Happy is he that condemneth not himself in that thing which he alloweth."

If, with us, it is the case of being persuaded of the lawfulness of a thing so far as our action is concerned; if we have faith to do a certain thing, which to others is doubtful, then we ought not parade it before them so as to cause offence. We are to have that faith before God. We are to do what we are going to do with God as our guide and the monitor of our conscience. But we are not to flaunt the feelings of others.

Here is Way's translation, "as for the liberal faith which you have, keep it to yourself, displaying it only to God."

In doing anything at all, happiness does not come from indulgence. It comes from the spirit of the act and the principle and faith that prompt it. Yea, "happy is he that condemneth not himself in that which he alloweth." Happy is the man "whose practice does not go beyond his convictions." This happiness comes to the stronger Christian who does not have to condemn himself for doing something that harms another. It may be his liberty but it is not his choice; and in refraining from it there is a happiness that knows no bounds. Yes, there is many times far more happiness in abstinence than in indulgence; in saying no, rather than yes; in being a so-called narrow-minded person than a broad-minded one. For, in these things, one's movements are dictated by the highest and holiest principles of life.

(2) *The Practice.* Verse 23.

"And he that doubteth is damned if he eat, because he eateth not of faith: for whatsoever is not of faith is sin."

Whoever acts out of faith falls into condemnation for his act. The word damned is not final judgment involving his salvation, but self-judgment which brings condemnation. It is the condemnation of Romans 8:1. This comes from living by faith and under the operation of "the law of the Spirit of life in Christ Jesus." But whoever does not walk by faith and does those things which his conscience disallows is going to walk in condemnation and unhappiness.

Every act of our lives should be in the light of the final sentence of this chapter, namely, "whatsoever is not of faith is sin." The basis of our Christian life was faith. We should proceed from faith with faith so that the whole process of life is one of faith. All our motives, all our actions, should result from this faith union with Christ. Apart from this, if we act from selfishness, from public opinions, from custom, from popular standards: it is an act of sin. Let us be prompted then by our life and fellowship with Christ, and all our acts will be those of faith and consequently the most fruitful and joyful.

# 19

## THE CHRISTIAN AS A WORKER
### Romans 15

I T IS interesting to notice how consistently the the Scriptures tie works to faith. It never ties faith to works but it does declare that doing must follow believing. This is so as we enter another phase of Christian experience.

Six things are set forth as belonging to every good and efficient Christian worker.

I. The Interest of the Worker. Verses 1-4.

"We then that are strong ought to bear the infirmities of the weak, and not to please ourselves. Let every one of us please his neighbor for his good to edification. For even Christ pleased not himself; but, as it is written, The reproaches of them that reproached thee fell on me. For whatsoever things were written aforetime were written for our learning, that we through patience and comfort of the scriptures might have hope."

Notice how these verses are led off—"We then that are strong." Way translates this, "We of the robust faith." Do we have a robust faith? Or, is it pale and sickly, stooped and weak? We cannot have a healthy and strong Christianity without a robust faith. Neither can we have a robust faith except by observing the diet of truth in the Word and the hygienics of holiness. A robust faith is not picked off trees. We cannot buy it in books. A weekly trip to the temple will not get it. It is a process of life which is not only weekly but daily, not only daily but momentary.

Is a Christian to have no interest in himself? When it says in verse 2, "Let every one of us please his neighbor for his good to edification," just what does this mean about our own interests? The Christian should have a very great interest in himself but it must not remain there. We cannot neglect the trees and expect the fruit.

There are two extremes to avoid. With some, there is the extreme of always cultivating the tree and looking out for personal interests with neither care nor concern for others. With others, it is forever expecting fruit without taking time for spiritual culture. There are people who rush from one activity to another with scarcely a moment's meditation. It is better that we attend fewer religious meetings and engage in fewer activities and take time for meditation and preparation so that what we do is well done. Remember, that while you are worshipping you are not working, and while you are working you are not worshipping. There must be time for both.

The Christian's interests lie in others. This interest is described as "the infirmities of the weak." This reference to the weak may carry over from the preceding chapter where it dealt with the one who was weak "in the faith." But here it is a different phase of weakness. It is here the inability to perform all the duties of life. It may be limited economics or physical disabilities, or one of many infirmities. But whatever it is, it will be quickly recognized by every alert Christian whose affections are not for himself alone.

One of the best ways to promote our own happiness and growth is to seek the good of others. Water without an outlet becomes a place of filth. A life without an outlet becomes unlovely. Even worldly success demands the spirit of doing for others. The man who succeeds in the world and rises to the top of the crowd is the man who gives something extra of his service.

In communities where apples are grown, there will occasionally be a tree which gives all its energy to producing wood and leaves and bears no fruit. When that occurs, the orchardist makes a deep gash with an ax across the trunk of the tree and close to the ground. The result of the gash is such a shock to the selfish tendencies of the tree that a change is brought about and the next year it bears lots of fine fruit. Sometimes we are like that and need to be "gashed" out of our selfishness. Let us learn the lesson of the suffering tree.

There is a worthy precedent for this sort of living. It is the example of Christ in verse 3, "For even Christ pleased not himself." This is suggested for the purpose of inspiration and imitation. He is to be our inspiration and we are to be His imitation. But this is suggested with reservation. No one can grow *into* the likeness of Christ though all may grow *in* that likeness. You cannot walk around in a room until you have walked into it. The natural cannot imitate the spiritual. The human cannot even approximate the divine. It requires a new birth to possess God's nature and the development of that nature will proceed according to the principle of imitation. It will be our life into His likeness.

If we became sincerely solicitous for the welfare of others, it would not only transform our own existence but change the whole world around us. Think what a difference this would make if we considered the infirm, the cripple, the sick, the needy, and the timid. How long since we stopped at the home of the crippled man in our neighborhood? How long since we looked in on the widow who works so hard to gain a living for her children?

The statement of verse 4 concerning the learning of the Scriptures brings before us an important consideration. These things "written aforetime were written for our learning." This makes all of the Bible valuable for all of us all of the time. While the Scriptures are to be rightly divided in the sense of interpretation and application there is a dangerous extreme to which it can be carried. Perhaps the greatest danger we face is non-application rather than misapplication.

The learning gleaned from the Scriptures is for life. It is not the learning of science or other branches of knowledge. It is for the creation of a great hope through "patience and comfort." Patience is the power of endurance and comfort is the inspiration of encouragement. These will develop a Christian life which will be stedfast in the midst of many adversities.

II. The Mind of the Worker. Verses 5, 6.

"Now the God of patience and consolation grant you to be like-minded one toward another accord-

ing to Christ Jesus: That ye may with one mind
and one mouth glorify God, even the Father of
our Lord Jesus Christ."

In verse 5 it speaks of "the God of patience"; in
verse 13 "the God of hope"; in verse 33, "the God of
peace." God's character is expressed in terms of His
manifestation toward us. It is not who He is in Himself, but what He is toward us. These reveal what He
will do for us, and what we may find in Him. He is,
in this threefold capacity, the *source of our endurance,*
the *security of our hope,* and the *secret of our peace.*
How intimate this makes God! We usually think of
Him as an unapproachable Creator wrapped in thunder
and mystery and surrounded with angelic and cherubic
courts. But here He comes down to our life to supply
its necessities.

The worker's mind is to be the mind of unity. This
is what is said in verse 5, "grant you to be like-minded
one toward another according to Christ Jesus." It is
necessary that workers be united. That union is not
to be arranged by an agreement arrived at in our
minds. We are possessed of too much diversity. It is
to come by all possessing Christ's mind. It is to be
another phase of our imitation of Christ. The workers
are to possess their own minds within the pattern
of His mind. This is not religious regimentation;
neither is it mental limitation. It is the highest sort of
liberty.

The effect of this unanimity will be a unanimous
witness of mind and mouth to the glory of God.
"That ye may with one mind and one mouth glorify

God, even the Father of our Lord Jesus Christ." Thus, relieved of our foolish differences and our petty frictions, we will lend our faculties to divine praise. One is led to wonder how much earth suffers, and how much God is robbed of praise and adoration, by all our petty controversies. Freed from these, we would find our minds and mouths filled with glad songs and our lives enriched by a happy fellowship.

The problem of the work is the problem of the worker. It is the worker, all other things being equal, that is the key to any given situation. God does not indwell the work; He indwells the worker. God does not bless the work; He blesses its workers. God's plan has always comprehended the man. Whatever deficiency that may exist in Christian service is not in the message, but the messenger. What is needed is the full power of Pentecost to be turned on the worker. It is not more organizations endowed with enthusiasm, but more organisms indwelt by the Holy Spirit.

III. THE ATTITUDE OF THE WORKER. Verses 7-12.

"Wherefore receive ye one another, as Christ also received us to the glory of God. Now I say that Jesus Christ was a minister of the circumcision for the truth of God, to confirm the promises made unto the fathers: And that the Gentiles might glorify God for his mercy; as it is written, For this cause I will confess to thee among the Gentiles, and sing unto thy name. And again he saith, Rejoice, ye Gentiles, with his people. And again, Praise the Lord, all ye Gentiles; and laud him, all ye people. And again, Esaias saith, There shall be a root of Jesse, and he that shall rise to reign over the Gentiles; in him shall the Gentiles trust."

His attitude is to be that expressed in verse 7, "Wherefore receive ye one another, as Christ also received us to the glory of God." This does not raise a question of social intercourse but it refers rather to the matter of unity which preceded, and the racial prejudices between Jew and Gentile which follow.

Our cordial and considerate reception of another is to be on the basis of Christ's reception of us. Here, at last, is a place where bitter racial and social differences may dissolve. That place is Christ. Whatever the differences that divide us racially and which stood between Jew and Gentile, exist no more in Christ. No true Christian has a right to raise them. What a person was before is no basis for judgment or treatment after. In Christ "there is neither Jew nor Greek, there is neither bond nor free, there is neither male nor female: for ye are all one in Christ Jesus." And that mystical oneness should forever exclude differences and distinctions that would grievously divide God's people.

Here is the law of Christian brotherhood that marks the gathering of a great family from all the ends of the earth. Nations will rise and fall; kingdoms will come and go. But the nucleus of an eternal race is in this great Christian brotherhood. It is not a brotherhood by Adam's blood but Christ's. It is not a brotherhood of flesh but faith. It is not a brotherhood of the first birth but the second birth.

IV. THE EQUIPMENT OF THE WORKER. Verses 13-16.

"Now the God of hope fill you with all joy and peace in believing, that ye may abound in hope, through the power of the Holy Ghost. And I myself also am persuaded of you, my brethren, that ye also are full of goodness, filled with all knowledge, able also to admonish one another. Nevertheless, brethren, I have written the more boldly unto you in some sort, as putting you in mind, because of the grace that is given to me of God, That I should be the minister of Jesus Christ to the Gentiles, ministering the gospel of God, that the offering up of the Gentiles might be acceptable, being sanctified by the Holy Ghost."

This does not mention a formal education as one of the equipments of the worker. For one reason there was none to be had in that day that was particularly useful for this kind of a worker. This lack of mention is not a denial of its desirability. It is rather dealing with the worker's spiritual equipment which in many ways transcends any other equipment. What he receives from God is far more valuable and essential than what he receives from man. If he is going to do God's work, he ought to be God's worker equipped with God's power. Let the worker wisely take advantage of every opportunity to enrich himself, but let him also be sure that in this gain he has not neglected what God can do personally in him and through him.

Paul prays that the God of hope may fill us with joy and peace because of our faith. If the worker does not have these, he has a poor basis on which to begin helping others to find joy and peace. What the worker knows must not take the place of what the worker has. He is to be someone as well as to do something.

The source of this equipment is not only inward but continuous. Our hopes are not pinned on the present state of the world, nor the temperature of our feelings, nor the attitude of our friends. All the spiritual factors are "through the power of the Holy Spirit." It is because of His indwelling that we can have this outpouring. What we do for others is because of what He does in us.

Here is His unction for our action. It is because we have not waited for this unction that so much of our action is of sounding brass and tinkling cymbal. It is beautiful but not fruitful. It has what we call technique, but it does not have the pull of power. And no amount of secular training for the individual, and no amount of brightly-polished organizational machinery, will take the place of this unctionizing of action.

Why is this enduement of divine power necessary? For the reason that it conforms to the divine plan. In the creation God made man in His image and indwelt him by breathing in him His own Spirit. This fitted man for service. It was a partnership between God and man. It was a co-operative endeavor. Man could only govern the earth, subdue it and extract from it its deep-locked secrets, as he co-operated with God and remained in fellowship with Him. Our present scientific discoveries are only an insignificant item of what we shall know when man is once more restored to fellowship and partnership with God.

As it was in the creation, so it is in the redemption, man becomes indwelt once more by God in the person of the Holy Spirit. His service is to be rendered in the light of a partnership or a corporation. God is now seeking co-workers. As Paul said in I Corinthians 3:9, "We are laborers together with God." God supplies us with the message and the spiritual enablement, but we must go to work. God did not hand man a finished electric light bulb or a luxurious airplane or a completely assembled radio and say, enjoy yourself. The materials and laws and secrets were tucked away in the embraces of nature to await their discovery by man. And there is likewise stored in the vastness of Himself and in the truth of the gospel enough material and power to make this a new world. It waits on two things—we as laborers together with God and the coming day of physical and universal redemption through Christ.

V. The Sufficiency of the Worker. Verses 17-21.

"I have therefore whereof I may glory through Jesus Christ in those things which pertain to God. For I will not dare to speak of any of those things which Christ hath not wrought by me, to make the Gentiles obedient, by word and deed. Through mighty signs and wonders, by the power of the Spirit of God; so that from Jerusalem, and round about unto Illyricum, I have fully preached the gospel of Christ. Yea, so have I strived to preach the gospel, not where Christ was named, lest I should build upon another man's foundation: But as it is written, To whom he was not spoken of, they shall see: and they that have not heard shall understand."

Paul's sufficiency was not in himself. He did not, of course, minimize the worker, but he exalted the Master. And so he says in verse 17, "I have therefore whereof I may glory through Jesus Christ in those things which pertain to God."

Does he have anything to take pride in or glory in? Much in every way. But he will never do it apart from his Master. It will always be "through Jesus Christ." Paul never injected his personality into his message. To be sure, the message came through his personality, but Paul always retired to the covering of the Cross.

Notice how frankly Paul puts it in verse 18, "For I will not dare to speak of any of those things which Christ hath not wrought by me." Way's translation to this is very helpful. He says, "Of course, I shall not presume thus to speak of any work, except what has been actually done by himself as an instrument in the hands of Messiah." This is not the false humility that you so often hear in this respect. Paul magnifies the Master, yet he does not minimize the instrument. After all, even God is helpless without the instrument. But it is not the instrument alone; it is the instrument in proper hands. A chisel may be of the finest tempered steel and sharpened to a surgical precision, but unless it is in the hands of a skilled master, it is nothing. And our attitude and preparation and God-given abilities are as important to God as a fine tool is to a craftsman. We must not go to the opposite extremes and say on the one hand that the worker is nothing and on the other hand say that God is nothing. There is a place where the worker and the Master meet for useful and fruitful service. That place is in these paths of truth which we now traverse and their secret will be our success.

We notice what magnificent and conspicuous use God made of Paul. God made use of Paul to change lives, yea, whole communities. In one city, the effect of God's use of Paul was so great that multitudes turned from the idoltrous worship of Diana and so thoroughgoing was their change that they collapsed the silvermaker's craft because they no longer used their idols. In the same city "many of them also which used curious arts brought their books together, and burned them before all men: and they counted the price of them, and found it fifty thousand pieces of silver." This was the mighty use God made of Paul. But it is not necessary to lead such mass movements and have such notoriety to be used of God. The wind that comes in a cyclone also comes in a zephyr. God does not always work in a cyclonic fashion.

When Elijah was in the cave on Horeb, "Behold, the Lord passed by, and a great and strong wind rent the mountains, and brake in pieces the rocks before the Lord; but the Lord was not in the wind; and after the wind an earthquake; but the Lord was not in the earthquake: And after the earthquake a fire; but the Lord was not in the fire: and after the fire a still small voice" (I Kings 19:11, 12). God was in the still small voice. We can be a still small voice for God. He needs voices. Some people want to be loud-speakers and we need them, but not exclusively. There is sometimes more persuasion in a small voice than in a large one. There is more moving in a whisper than a roar. But remember God has use for us. Do not deny Him that use, for if we will give Him full access to our personality, He may use us to transform lives and homes. It may not be as spectacular as finding a cure for cancer, but one thing is sure, it will have more eternal value.

When Paul mentions that his service is rendered "by the power of the Spirit of God," we have the secret not only of strength but efficiency. The Holy Spirit is the supervising director of Christian service, and when we are led by Him, we will engage in an efficient service. Our service will be both intensive and extensive. This is exactly what it was with Paul.

1. It Was Intensive. Verse 19.

"I have fully preached the gospel of Christ."

He mentions that this full preachment had a geographical completeness. But the important part here is its intensiveness. It was fully done. Not a truth was omitted. Not a note was left unsounded. Not a principle was undeclared. The completeness of his message resulted from the supervising direction of the Holy Spirit. If we had it today, we would have a more proper selection of sermon materials in our pulpits.

About fifty years ago, during a sensational political storm in Canada, a pastor in Winnipeg announced this subject for his forthcoming sermon: "The Topic of the Day." As a result, the church was crowded and, among the rest, the attorney general of the province. All were expecting a sensational discussion of the political situation. But when the preacher arose, he announced this as his text, "What must I do to be saved?" Here, indeed, was the topic of *the* day and it is never out of date.

2. It Was Extensive. Verse 20.

"Yea, so have I strived to preach the gospel, not where Christ was named, lest I should build upon another man's foundation."

Paul's aim was as extensive a coverage as possible with the gospel. He would not duplicate other's labors. His foundations would not be laid on the work of others. His aim was to get the gospel to the most people in the briefest time. This was sensible and another evidence of the intelligent direction of the supervising Holy Spirit. When we labor under Him, we will not go to the wrong place, speak to the wrong person, or say the wrong thing. If we had such direction today, inefficiency would disappear, and the greatest good would come from the least of our efforts.

## VI. THE MOTIVES OF THE WORKER. Verses 22-33.

One of the great needs of the worker is to learn how to discern his way. The art of spiritual discernment and guidance is so generally lacking. Upon its development among the rank and file of Christians, as well as the leaders of Christian work, there would come a renaissance in our service. Can we imagine hundreds and thousands going forth fortified with the conviction of being God-sent? It was no little part of the tremendous success of the first Christians. It was this which led them through such manifold difficulties to such conspicuous success.

The motives and ideals of Paul reveal themselves in the course of his daily life and labors. They do in ours also. It is not what we shout from the street corner that proclaims who we are. It is what is revealed in the things we do. We proclaim ourselves by our lives. With this fact in mind and with the other fact also in mind, that Paul is before us as an example of the Christian as a worker, let us look at the motives and ideals that he sets forth.

1. The Christian and His Difficulties. Verse 22.

"For which cause also I have been much hindered from coming to you."

The hindrances which kept this worker from the immediate achievement of his desires were not only adversities, of which he had many, but also his opportunities. The opportunities for preaching Christ where He had not been named were so numerous and so urgent that Paul's long-delayed visit to Rome had to be postponed time after time. It is a great thing when our opportunities become our hindrances and a greater thing when we recognize it, and suspend our own desires and ambitions to do the thing God gives us to do.

Here is proof that Christians do not always get their desires. God does not bend to our whims. Life is not all play. There is work to do and for God to be constantly gratifying our desires would be to destroy our usefulness. There is an old saying which runs like this, "Whom God curses, he gives them the desire of their hearts."

Not all of Paul's difficulties arose out of his opportunities. He had many adversities. Here were some of them listed in II Corinthians 11:23-27, ". . . in labors more abundant, in stripes above measure, in prisons more frequent, in deaths oft. Of the Jews five times received I forty stripes save one. Thrice was I beaten with rods, once was I stoned, thrice I suffered shipwreck, and a night and a day I have been in the deep; In journeyings often, in perils of waters, in perils of robbers, in perils by mine own countrymen, in perils by the heathen, in perils in the city, in perils in the wilderness, in perils of the sea, in perils among false brethren; In weariness and painfulness, in watchings often, in hunger and thirst, in fastings often, in cold and nakedness." Here was a Christian who knew what difficulty was, but in spite of it and many times because of it, he was able to accomplish a glorious service.

Storms which have sometimes blown with destructive fury and menaced sea craft have been responsible for driving birds off their accustomed courses and thus have populated remote islands with bird life. Storms have thus filled barren places with life. In a similar manner adversities have been the means of bringing blessings to us which would otherwise not have been ours.

In traveling through the Redwood Empire of northern California and lower Oregon, one becomes familiar with the attractive souvenirs which are made from the redwood burls. The beauty of these burls lies both in the grain and color of the wood. But where and how did the burl come? It is the result of adversity to the tree. It was born in a wound to the giant Redwood. It may in one case be a bruise which came by the branches of another tree falling on or rubbing against it. Or perhaps an animal by claws or teeth had bruised the tree. It may be the result of lightning or even a parasite. But as the years pass, the tree produces a special growth of wood around the wound. Thus, it makes a thing of beauty out of an ugly wound.

How suggestively this befits our lives! Grace makes wounds into objects of beauty. It takes our gashes and pours the growth of godliness into them and builds around them the attractions of beauty.

Archibald Rutledge wrote an article a number of years ago in which he spoke of the manner in which God covers up nature's disasters. It may be vines draping the fracture of a limb from a lightning stroke. Or, it may be a new growth of grass or shrub over the blackness of a fire. And here it is the burl that hides the gash. What tragedy or wound has come to us? Let God make a burl out of it. Let Him drape the fire that has scarred your soul with a growth of grace.

2. The Christian and His Service. Verse 23.

"But now having no more place in these parts . . ."

What constitutes a call to Christian service? We have many notions. We wait for some strange feeling to possess us as if that was to be our call. It may come that way. As for the apostle, his call was the world's need. He had wanted for a long time to minister to these people in the capital of the world's greatest empire. Now, the opportunity came. It came because he had finished his service in one place and looked abroad to see opportunities in another place. Although he had finished the work he was given to do, he was not through. Its completion in one place led to its commencement in another place. Our work is never completed. It goes on and on, and not always in the same place, for it leads us many times into far places as it led Paul to Rome.

3. The Christian and God's Will. Verse 23.

". . . having a great desire these many years to come unto you."

Paul was greatly influenced in his decision not only because of the circumstances that surrounded his immediate labors, but by his "great desire." We have, of course, good and bad desires. Some are purely selfish and quite out of line with the larger purpose of life. These, God finds necessary to deny. But the desires of a God-surrendered life are not to be considered as will-o-the-wisp whims. In a thoroughly consecrated mind they are the indications of the divine will. God can work as much through our desires as He can through our convictions. And when Paul found himself in this state of mind, he found himself in the way of divine guidance and leadership.

4. The Christian and His Friends. Verse 24.

"Whensoever I take my journey into Spain, I will come to you: for I trust to see you in my journey, and to be brought on my way thitherward by you, if first I be somewhat filled with your company."

Paul recognized a friendship which extended beyond the bounds of geographical location. His friends were the friends of Christ. There is in that relationship a bond that many times is closer than the ties of blood. Here was a vast family scattered throughout Rome's great domain, and wherever members of this family existed there was a port of call and a haven of rest.

We need to cultivate the grace of Christian friendship. There is strength in union. The bonds should be more closely drawn. Although our world is not as hostile and inhospitable as was the world of Paul's day; yet it has perils and dangers and animosities that would be easier met in the strength of a Christian friendship.

There is a beautiful touch of personal deference in the closing sentence of the verse, where it says, "if first I be somewhat filled with your company." It literally means "filled with you." Although Paul had not seen many of these Christian friends in person, he held them in such high regard that their presence would give him the utmost satisfaction. Their presence would be his inspiration. Who can measure the consolation and encouragement that comes through the fellowship of a Christian friendship? We doubt not that Paul's great labors would have been quite impossible, were it not for the friendship of these who harbored him in place after place. In Corinth it was the home of Gaius. In Philippi it was the home of Priscilla and Aquila. Who is our house guest of grace? Whom do we help on the way? Is there a prophet whose way is made easier because of our friendship? Is there a lonely soul for whom the day is brighter and the night less drear because we have said to him, "I will come to you" and he says, "if first I be somewhat filled with your company"?

5. The Christian and Human Needs. Verses 25, 26.

> "But now I go unto Jerusalem to minister unto the saints. For it hath pleased them of Macedonia and Achaia to make a certain contribution for the poor saints which are at Jerusalem."

Paul's projected extensive journey to Spain was to be preceded by an errand to Jerusalem. Then, at a later date, he would discharge his obligation of friendship to the Christians at Rome. Why was he going to Jerusalem? The reason for his errand was "to minister unto the saints." The ministry was possible according to the generosity of other Christians, "For it hath pleased them of Macedonia and Achaia to make a certain contribution for the poor saints which are at Jerusalem."

Here is a Christian in relation to human needs. Paul did not minimize physical needs while magnifying the gospel that met man's spiritual needs. Nor dare we. There is a proportionate consideration to be given to the earthly needs of others. This is everywhere enjoined upon us. If every Christian obeyed the Scriptural order of giving, which was given in I Corinthians 16:1 and 2 in connection with this very journey of Paul's to Jerusalem, there would be enough means to care for all the needs of all Christians. If we were faithful, there would never be the spectacle of a child of God dependent on the state. If "upon the first day of the week . . . everyone . . . lay by him in store, as God hath prospered him," there would be a sufficiency and a surplus for every bit of Christian work and every case of Christian need. There would be created automatically a benevolent society of such ability that no case of the smallest or greatest need would fail to be met. Thus would be removed any possibility of a scandal on the Christian church as it is today.

And in this connection we should be careful to remember that if our need is produced by our indolence, it is automatically out of the realm of another's responsibility. There cannot be any shirking of our responsibility in the expectation that others will assume what we willfully neglect. We do not believe that there is any provision in God's care for this sort of action. The thing that produces the need is that which governs the answer. When it says in Philippians 4:19 that "My God shall supply all your need," you will find that the need was produced by the benevolence of the Philippian Christians in caring for Paul. It was their benevolence and not their indolence which created the need. This would determine the answer.

6. The Christian and His Spiritual Debts. Verse 27.

"It hath pleased them verily; and their debtors they are. For if the Gentiles have been made partakers of their spiritual things, their duty is also to minister unto them in carnal things."

We are familiar with financial debt but here is another kind of debt in which we stand with constant obligation. Here it was the case of Jews ministering spiritual things to Gentiles and the Gentiles in return ministering physical things to the Jews. Paul concludes it to be the duty of those who have received liberally of spiritual things "to minister unto them in carnal things." This is God's order. Those who minister the gospel are to be sustained by the gospel. Those who receive the spiritual benefits of the gospel are in material debt to their ministers. There is a parity of exchange here that will solve all spiritual and physical problems in relation to Christian work.

7. The Christian and His Dependence on God. Verses 28, 29.

"When therefore I have performed this, and have sealed to them this fruit, I will come by you into Spain. And I am sure that, when I come unto you, I shall come in the fulness of the blessing of the gospel of Christ."

Notice how sacred Paul considers this task of ministering to the physical needs of these dependent Christians. It was no light matter with him. It was not a condescending charity. It was not crumbs for a beggar but bread for a brother. It was a sacred task that he would discharge with as much fidelity as any spiritual mission he had ever performed.

Furthermore, not only this errand, but the extension of his visit to Rome would be in the fulness of the gospel's blessing. Paul was not going merely as a social worker. He was going as a gospel messenger. But what he did at Jerusalem was as important to the gospel as what he would do in Rome. Wherever Paul went and whatever Paul did, his dependence was upon God through the medium of the gospel he carried.

That gospel was not a gospel of Christian ethics, neither was it a gospel of Christian socialism nor a gospel of Christian education. It was the gospel of the Cross. It was the gospel of Christ and Him crucified. And it was always sufficient for it has a social aspect as well as a spiritual. If we are spiritually right, we will be socially sensitive. And with this constantly before him, Paul could expect abundant success in whatever he undertook. God is bound to make the gospel succeed. If we wish to come to our tasks of life in "the fulness of blessing," let us come to them in the principles and power of the gospel.

8. The Christian and Prayer. Verses 30-32.

"Now I beseech you, brethren, for the Lord Jesus Christ's sake, and for the love of the Spirit, that ye strive together with me in your prayers to God for me; That I may be delivered from them that do not believe in Judaea; and that my service which I have for Jerusalem may be accepted of the saints; That I may come unto you with joy by the will of God, and may with you be refreshed."

Paul asks here for a partnership in prayer. He recognizes the spiritual nature of his ministry. The engagement to which he invites these Christian friends is not some dilettante farce of religion. It was to be a battle royal. It was to be a "striving" and this striving was an agonizing wrestling with unseen spiritual forces.

After all, the Christian's enemy is not defeated on the battlefield but in the closet. D'Aubigne said, "In Luther's closet we have the secret of the Reformation." And it was the secret of Paul's triumph as it will be of ours.

Roger Babson, whose ability as a statistician has given him a first-rate place in the economic world, made this observation: "I have not been able to find a single useful institution which has not been founded by either an intensely religious man or by the son of a praying father or a praying mother."

Paul asked for prayer in three particulars:

(1) *For deliverance from his enemies.*

"That I may be delivered from them that do not believe."

He did not ask for protection from their presence nor freedom from their nuisance. He did not ask to be shielded. He asked for deliverance from their evil consequence. God never promises a shielded life, but He does grant a delivered life.

(2) *For understanding by his fellow-Christians.*

"That my service which I have for Jerusalem may be accepted of the saints."

He feared lest motives might be misunderstood and that prejudice might prevail. Prayer would create an atmosphere of understanding.

(3) *For a prosperous and happy journey to Rome.*

"That I may come to you with joy by the will of God and may with you be refreshed."

He did come to Rome by the will of God. However, he came with joy. But the actual journey was undoubtedly of a different character than either Paul or his prayer-partners anticipated. It was as a prisoner that Paul finally went to Rome. It was with the suffering of almost every adversity that could happen to a traveler. Yet, it could be said that Paul went in the will of God. It was not as Paul might have desired. But remember our wishes and God's will are ofttimes very different. Yet the divine purpose was accomplished and it was this that Paul desired. Contentment lies not in the gratification of our wishes but the accomplishment of God's will. When this is the object of our staying or going, then it will be in joy. In prayer we may find that we get all that we pray for, yet nothing we ask for.

9. The Christian and Peace. Verse 33.

"Now the God of peace be with you all. Amen."

Here is the completion of the triad of characteristics of God. He is spoken of in this chapter as "the God of patience," "the God of hope," and "the God of peace." To possess any of these things we must possess God. There can be no peace apart from His person. This is not peace in an emotion, for an emotional peace may depend either on the inward temperament or the outward circumstance. This is the peace of personality resident in us.

# 20

# THE CHRISTIAN AS AN INFLUENCE
## Romans 16

ONE OF earth's greatest forces is the power of a Christian influence. That power is a privilege within our reach. We need not be talented, wealthy, educated or socially prominent. All we need is to be what we are in Christ. It may mean being different than what we are in ourself, but if we will be what we are in Christ, there will proceed from our Christian character and conduct an influential effect upon others which will prove a great boon to mankind.

The appearance of the Christian as an influence is presented in this chapter under a considerable list of names. They are the names of Christians, who, for the most part, resided at Rome.

I. SALUTATIONS TO THOSE IN ROME. Verses 1-16.

"I commend unto you Phebe our sister, which is a servant of the church which is at Cenchrea: That ye receive her in the Lord, as becometh saints, and that ye assist her in whatsoever business she hath need of you: for she hath been a succourer of many, and of myself also. Greet Priscilla and Aquila my helpers in Christ Jesus: who have for my life laid down their own necks: unto whom not only I give thanks, but also all the churches of the Gentiles. Likewise greet the church that is in their house. Salute my well-beloved Epaenetus, who is the firstfruits of Achaia unto Christ. Greet Mary, who bestowed much labour on us. Salute Andronicus and Junia, my kinsmen, and my fellowprisoners, who are of note among the apostles, who also were in Christ before me. Greet Amplias my beloved in the Lord. Salute Urbane, our helper in Christ, and Stachys my beloved. Salute Apelles approved in Christ. Salute them which are of Aristobulus' household. Salute Herodion my kinsman. Greet them that be of the household of Narcissus, which are in the Lord. Salute Tryphena and Tryphosa, who labour in the Lord. Salute the beloved Persis, which laboured much in the Lord. Salute Rufus chosen in the Lord, and his mother and mine. Salute Asyncritus, Phlegon, Hermas, Patrobas, Hermes, and the brethren which are with them. Salute Philologus, and Julia, Nereus, and his sister, and Olympas, and all the saints which are with them. Salute one another with an holy kiss. The churches of Christ salute you."

1. Salutations to Those in Rome.

These salutations are introduced by a word of commendation passed on to the Christians at Rome concerning a distinguished Christian lady named Phebe. She it was, you will remember, whom we discussed at the beginning of these studies. She bore this letter for Paul from the city of Corinth to Rome.

What immediately arrests attention is the first two words, "I commend." Paul's commendation is a recommendation first of this lady's character and also that she be helped in her business by the fellow Christians at Rome. We wonder why Christian courtesy seems to have become such a lost art. In its place is an altogether too eager willingness to harass rather than help. But Paul, true Christian gentleman that he was, extends his hand to meet the extended hands of the Roman Christians. This is as it should be. It should be an attitude of courteous helpfulness.

Phebe's name at the head of this extensive list of Christian names is a reminder of the place of women in Christian life and work.

She is described by three words:

(1) *"A sister."*

This was, of course, a notation of her place in the family of faith. She was a sister by ties of faith, not of flesh. This gave a family association which extended far beyond the bounds of her home. And here, also, was a family which has union with all ages and all races. It is that "general assembly and church of the first-born." It is to be gathered "out of every kindred, tongue, and people, and nation." But until that gathering there is this interim of fellowship. Let it be as courteous in its consideration of others as was Paul's for Phebe.

(2) *"A servant."*

It might sound out of place to some to have this lady called a servant. There is no indication that she was a preaching or teaching servant. We have here the only reference to a woman as this kind of a servant. The word, "servant," is one which means deacon, which in turn means, "a minister." Whatever her duties were, she was evidently an active and faithful servant of the Lord in her particular church.

She who had ministered to others was now being recommended to the ministration of others. How fitting, and how proper and just! What we do for others we deserve for ourselves. The law of the harvest works in human life just as much as it does in the field. Sow kindness and you will reap kindness. Sow helpfulness and you will reap helpfulness. It is the old truth of casting your bread upon the waters and finding it after many days. If the harvest of our years is bitter, it is because the sowing of our days has been with the tares of evil. Phebe proves that it pays to be a sower of good things.

(3) *"A succourer."*

This means a "patroness" or a "champion." Phebe had been a patroness and a champion of many an obscure cause and person. She had stood by the poor man in his adversity. The name of "succourer" was a title given to Greek officials who looked after the rights of aliens. And Phebe was constantly solicitous of those who could not defend themselves. She was a worthy woman. Moreover, she was worthy of all the help that the Roman Christians could extend her. And here, again, is her realization of a dividend on her investment. The interval of waiting might be long but the interest is good.

There is a notable thing here that reminds us of the sphere and character of this life with its gilt-edge investment and assured interest. The sphere is described in verse 2 as being "in the Lord." Notice how many times that phrase and similar ones occur throughout this chapter. In every mention of a person, it is almost invariably with this description. It indicates the sphere of their lives and consequently the scope of their blessing. They were citizens of Rome but they were in Christ. One had to do with geography and the other with godliness. To be of Rome might have described their handicap, but to be in Christ meant their advantage. What they were in Christ far outweighed whatever else resulted from their Roman residence.

But it was more than a name. It was the mark of a union of life and carries us back to the underlying principle of success in the Christian life. It is "the law of the Spirit of life in Christ Jesus." This law gave them a union of power with Almighty God whom Rome's vaunted power could not conquer. Furthermore, it gave birth to spiritual characteristics which moulded and shaped life along the lines of both strength and beauty.

The book of Romans began with its very first chapter showing men in sin. It ends with men belonging to a nobility of faith and being found in Christ. What a vast change has come! There is no mystery about it. It follows the course of a divine re-creation wherein lives of sin are changed by a process of regeneration. Their destiny has been completely altered. Their lives show a new usefulness. Here is the power not of eugenics or euthenics but the power of the gospel to change human lives.

To link arms with such nobles of faith and life as walk out of the pages of this book is to stand in the midst of a refreshing company. It is good to be able to retreat to the company of such noble men and women. To go through the names and deeds found in a daily newspaper is to want some kind of a refuge other than what earth can afford.

Here were people who had been won by Christ out of the depths and darkness of paganism. They had lived in all the shameful practices and orgies of evil. Their conduct knew none of the refinements of grace. But now we behold them in the Lord. They have not left the places of their former living but they have left the practices. Some of them are undoubtedly members of Caesar's vast household. But their offices are filled with a new fidelity. Their lives are lived with a new purpose. All of this is because they serve a new master, the Lord Jesus Christ.

As one reads the list and notes the characteristics of these Christians at Rome, there creeps over him an amazement of wonder when he reflects that here in the seat of the mightiest empire on earth with its power steeped in the most vicious cruelty, there is to be found this colony of Christ-loving men and women. All the former spirit of their pagan philosophy is gone. All the malignity of their former practices has vanished. They are now a gentle, pure, and righteous remnant of grace situated in the midst of a vast and corrupting society of evil. Whence did they come? Who planted this garden in the midst of such a wilderness? Who founded the Church at Rome? The credit goes to no man. It was not Peter and certainly not Paul. The fact is that Christianity planted itself. It may have been some obscure soldier who, touched by the inevitable consequences of Pentecost, going home on leave, carried the seeds that grew into such a glorious harvest. Who planted the Cedars of Lebanon? No man but God through winds and birds. Who planted the redwoods of California? No man. Christianity is of such a self-propagating nature that in its beginnings it needed no committees, organizations or commissions. It needed only the spontaneity of its own life. Beyond that point of beginning, there were such as Paul who carried the seeds to other lands and church colonies sprang into existence.

2. Phases of Christian Service.

The next whom Paul mentions are Priscilla and Aquila. The mention of these two, whom we recognize as husband and wife, is in connection with certain facts that reveal the nature of Christian life and service.

(1) *The unity of husband and wife.*

They are mentioned together in connection with their Christian faith and their Christian service. Their marriage union was in a Christian unity. This is as it should be. If it is otherwise, its mending should be the primary and paramount concern of whatever party is now Christian.

Priscilla and Aquila were old friends of Paul who now resided at Rome. Apparently, Rome was their original home although Paul was acquainted with them at both Corinth and Ephesus. They had been driven from Rome by the violent persecutions of the Emperor Claudius Caesar. During the time of their exile, they lived at both Corinth and Ephesus. They were now back in Rome. But wherever they were, they were that together. You never hear their names mentioned apart from each other. This association of names was an evidence of the nearness of their lives. They worked together. They worshipped together. They were social together. They travelled together. They suffered adversity together. They planned together. And all of this was because they were "in Christ Jesus" together. One could desire and wish and pray for nothing better than the kind of Christian comradeship between husband and wife like that which was true of Priscilla and Aquila.

(2) *The place of women workers.*

The mention of Priscilla along with that of Phebe reminds us of the prominence of women in Christian service. That place was not in the seat of official leadership. It was not as apostles or prophets. But, even so, there was a large place for the exercise of her gifts. She apparently had a large place in the affairs of the early church, for here her mention is more numerous than that of the men. She did not dominate in official capacity but she apparently predominated in zeal and fervor for the Lord. For this she has always been noted. We remember her throughout all ages of the church for her courageous and persistent zeal for Christ.

"Priscilla" strangely enough means "old-fashioned." But what does old-fashioned mean? Does it mean to wear the costumes and observe the styles of the previous century? Some think so. To be old-fashioned does not mean to be unattractive. It does not mean to be odd, queer or peculiar. To be old-fashioned means to be true to virtues and ideals that have passed out of current use. In this respect, the Christian is in constant demand. He or she must sponsor the forgotten virtues of righteousness. Putting on an old dress is not espousing godliness. Wearing out-moded styles is not the height of Christlikeness. But to take the things for which Christ died and dare to live these in a streamlined age is being old-fashioned. And yet it is not as old-fashioned as we think, for the fashion of the day in morals and mentality is constantly changing, while the one who is consistently Christian is perennially up-to-date.

In the mention of Priscilla we have a contrast with Phebe. Here were two types of Christian womanhood. Phebe was an unmarried woman while Priscilla was a married woman. Phebe was a business woman while Priscilla was a domestic woman. Their careers were diverse, yet their service was similar, no matter where the sphere of life. It was dominated and controlled by a similar passion to serve Christ. Their Christianity was not merely identified with the temple. It was taken into the world as well as into the home. It was something public as well as private. It governed the conduct of commerce as well as the rearing of children. Yes, Christianity in the hearts and hands of noble women was taken abroad into every conceivable life situation.

(3) *The character of Christian service.*

Paul called Priscilla and Aquila "my helpers." This meant, in reality, his co-workers. This association of service probably grew out of the days they spent in Corinth as weavers. There they engaged in the making of tents. But the making of tents was only their avocation. Their vocation was spreading the gospel.

Their service was as "helpers." They were not officials, yet their place was indispensable in the scheme of the divine Master. We must not despise our place; nor consider ourself either dispensable or indispensable. It is as great a sin to be too retiring as it is to be too forward. Do not forget that it was the man with the one talent who hid it. Dare to dignify your present place with God-honoring service!

A housemother in a Children's Home in Alaska relates that after an unusually busy morning, when the last little boy had said, "Goodbye" and trotted off to school, she stood at the front door with a broom in her hand. She looked out at the majestic mountains, the rolling sea with its many small islands dotted all about her own small one: beauty beyond compare! She thanked God for leading her there, placing a broom in her hand and love in her heart for the children in that home, His little ones for whom she swept each day. With brooms in our hands and His praise on our lips we can live for the Lord today.

(4) *The hazards of discipleship.*

Paul spoke of these two disciples as those "who have for my life laid down their own necks." The incident is obscure, but the noble and heroic act is faithfully remembered. It is also a reminder of the grave dangers which surrounded the early Christians. They espoused Christ at the expense of great sacrifice and suffering. In our day it is less hazardous, but none the less with its price. It costs friends, position, the opinion of others' approval. Its suffering is more mental and spiritual than physical. But the fact still remains that "all that will live godly in Christ Jesus shall suffer persecution."

(5) *The Christian home life.*

Paul's final reference to Priscilla and Aquila is in verse 5. "Likewise greet the church that is in their house." It seems quite certain that there was no church building in Rome at this time. In fact for the first three centuries the Christian church met usually in the homes of Christians. Public assemblage was not permitted but this did not prevent Christians from assembling together. They met in the homes of believers where accommodations were suitable for such a gathering.

One wonders if the neglect of the modern church in the matter of public worship may not lead to a return to the original practice of the church "in thy house." The liberty of our day to enter beautiful churches is neither appreciated nor accepted. It is one of the marks of our appalling indifference to spiritual things. The peak of church attendance in the United States was reached as far back as 1887. Since then, the attendance in ratio to population and church facilities has steadily declined until today the average pastor in the average church on an average Sunday has an average audience that is only 30 per cent of the capacity of the church. What a travesty and what a tragedy!

But here is an opportunity. While not neglecting the worship of God's house, let each family make a church in its house. It is the most fitting use we can make of it. Where is it more logical and practical to worship God than in the home? It was the original church of the Old Testament and the original church of the New Testament. Here our problems are to be solved. Here the major portion of our lives are to be spent. Here we entertain our friends. Here life is born and life departs. Here is life's most strategic place. Why should it not also be the place of God's abode?

3. Four Observations in Workers.

We have begun the examination of a list of names found on a roster of friendship. These names are of people living in Rome. We are not to suppose that since Paul had not been to Rome that he was not acquainted with these people through personal contact. Rome was the gravitational center of the whole empire and many of Paul's companions in labor, and acquaintances of faith had found it necessary for one reason or another to reside at Rome. Paul, therefore, reads the roll of old friends and as he does, we observe at least four things.

(1) *Variety and unity.*

What a variety is to be found among these names! They were men and women from all walks of life. Their abilities and personalities ranged the whole gamut of human experience.

With all of this variety, there existed a most remarkable unity. They had blended their differences into a common likeness. That likeness consisted of a state of life. It was "in Christ." No matter whether it was master or servant, man or woman, they were all brought through the common identity of discipleship into this unity of place and position. It must have been a beautiful thing to behold and even more delightful to experience.

(2) *Obscurity and opportunity.*

Not all whose names are listed here filled prominent places. Here was Mary whom Paul mentions in verse 6 and of whom he said she "bestowed much labor on us." Here was a mission in obscurity. But in that obscurity she saw an opportunity. She seized it and made the best of it. Whatever it was that she did for Paul, it was with extreme faithfulness and untiring fidelity.

Whoever else the apostle called out of obscurity into public and eternal mention were so honored because of their faithful service. We can be sure they were neither unbelieving nor slothful. They glorified opportunity with action. They dignified obscurity with faithfulness.

(3) *Humility and honor.*

In this mention of names, there is nothing said of distinguished leaders. Paul does not parade pompously-dressed ecclesiasts before public gaze. Except for one mention and that in verse 7 where it speaks of "my fellow-prisoners who are of note," it says nothing about distinction and favor. Their chief distinctions are in their faith and faithfulness. After all, what other distinctions are worthwhile? What else matters? A man's faith takes care of character and a man's faithfulness takes care of conduct. Neither character nor conduct are accidents. They do not happen; they occur.

Such as these were preferred to honor. Self-effacing, they became immortal. We have all read with interest the list of names to be found on public buildings and federal projects. Why are they there? By virtue of an office. How long will they last? As long as the building stands. Yet, here is a roster of names as immortal as the Throne of God. And its immortality lay in its identification. They were such as were "in Christ Jesus." His name will outlast the stars, and ours with His if we belong to Him. We must go back to Christ if we would go on into the future.

(4) *Friendship and fellowship.*

Here is a well-beloved company whose friendship supplied a beautiful fellowship.

"This page is no mere relic of the past; it is a list of friendships to be made hereafter, and to be possessed forever in the endless life where personality indeed shall be eternal, but where also the union of personalities, in Christ, shall be beyond our utmost present thought." Here is a thrilling prospect; the beginning of a far more satisfying fellowship than is now possible by earthly ties.

Paul was bound by ties of faith, which had grown stronger than any ties of blood, to a great company of friends that extended into a never-ceasing experience of fellowship. The secret of this friendship and fellowship was "in Christ Jesus."

Can you imagine what these bonds meant to Paul in that alien world of pagans and that bitter world of angry Jews? While our world is not as hostile as Paul's, we need the refuge of friendship's fellowship and the encirclement of love's protecting embrace. Cultivate a Christian friendship and we have found the shaft of a mine of golden joys and memories. We must be sure it bears the real friendship formula "in Christ Jesus."

4. Roster of the Faithful.

All of this unity out of variety, opportunity in obscurity, honor through humility, and fellowship in friendship are found in this list of some two dozen names extending from verse 5 to verse 16. Out of their faith and faithfulness, can be found a beautiful, satisfying and solid philosophy of life, if we will be careful to read their biographies as they are recorded ever so briefly.

All of them speak of faith and life in Christ who is the object of all true faith and the source of all real life. They are not identified in any case with human geneological records. Their geneology is one of faith. It proceeds from a new birth. It is a new order of life in Jesus Christ and not an old order of life in Adam. In Adam all die but in Christ all live. What an important thing it is to have this kind of a new beginning! If our biology is right, our destiny will be right. If our birth is right, our death will be right. If our beginning is right, our ending will be right.

Proceeding from this fact of the new geneology are characteristics of distinction.

(1) *Epaenetus.*

Here is a first-fruit triumph from Paul's labors in distant Achaia. How we remember our first things! Epaenetus was the earnest of a great harvest which has not ceased to be gathered.

(2) *Mary*

Then comes one who is not forgotten because "she bestowed much labor." Are we remembered or forgotten? Social climbers and idle dissipaters are never lifted to the level of this kind of remembrance.

(3) *Andronicus and Junia.*

They shared Paul's family and Paul's experience and were doubly endeared. Andronicus means to "excel others" and points to ideals of Christian perfection that should seek to be the best and do the best.

(4) *Amplias*

Here is a name which means "enlarged" or "ample" and speaks to us of that amplitude of growth in grace to which we are enjoined by the Scriptures. Many lack spiritual vitamins and remain pitiful skeletons of possible giants.

(5) *Urbane.*

This means "belonging to the city," with special

reference to politeness, civility, and courtesy. Christians are not at their best in the backwoods of ill-breeding and discourtesy. They should show the culture of Christ.

(6) *Aristobulus.*

Here was a name meaning "wise or excellent counsellor," and it indicated that maturity of wisdom and prudence and good judgment which should rest upon the brow of the Christian.

(7) *Phlegon.*

This spoke of "zeal" which meant intensified and applied earnestness. It was directed into channels of productive service and spared one from a wasted life. People are busy going nowhere. The world is on its way but where it is going it knows not.

(8) *Philologus.*

Here is a name quickly recognized as pertaining to learning. It meant a "lover of learning." Faith is the beginning of wisdom. Christ is the alphabet of a new language of learning. It speaks of "the wisdom of God in a mystery, even the hidden wisdom, which God ordained before the world unto our glory: Which none of the princes of this world knew: for had they known it, they would not have crucified the Lord of glory. But as it is written, Eye hath not seen, nor ear heard, neither have entered into the heart of man, the things which God hath prepared for them that love him. But God hath revealed them unto us by his Spirit: for the Spirit searcheth all things, yea, the deep things of God" (I Cor. 2:7-10).

Make a composite of these names and we find the character of Christianity in the characteristics of its disciples. It is born of God, industrious, excelling, enlarged, courteous, prudent, zealous and learned.

Here stands a list of men and women whose lives made a magnificent contribution of faith and influence to a needy world. May we be as influential as they.

II. FINAL EXHORTATION. Verses 17-20.

It seems very significant that this particular exhortation should be given as the very last admonition of Paul's message. May that fact not be an indication of both its urgency and importance?

1. Our Attitude to Dissenters. Verse 17.

"Now I beseech you, brethren, mark them which cause divisions and offences contrary to the doctrine which you have learned; and avoid them."

It seems so tragic that into the midst of this scene of unity there should be sown the seeds of discord and dissension. But it is almost inevitable. Jesus said, "It is impossible but that offences come; but woe unto him through whom they come."

The first thing to do is to "mark them which cause divisions." They were to be on their guard and in a state of intelligent awareness. They were not to be gullible children willing to give anxious ear to every preachment and argument. It i. just such alertness and guarded caution that we need today. Anyone who raises a voice can get a hearing, no matter how wild or extreme his talk may be. Discernment is the precious possession of discriminating ears. Let us grow up in our faith as well as our mind. Let us grow up in our mind as well as our body. One of the most difficult things there is today is to get people to think.

They want to feel and that means mostly they want to be fooled. The challenge of the Bible is "think on these things."

What are we to be on our guard against? ". . . them which cause divisions and offences contrary to the doctrine which ye have learned." The starting place was "the doctrine which ye have learned." The age might change but not the truth. Here is an unchanging doctrine as the premise of all wisdom. Here is an unchangeable doctrine as the foundation of the temple of truth. It was to be the test of all forthcoming ideas. It was to be the judge between apostle or apostate. It was to declare the difference between disciple or heretic.

The particular recognition of these dissenters was in the fact that they would "cause divisions and offenses contrary" to this doctrinal standard of New Testament truth. In Paul's language a "division" was a separation while an "offense" was a scandal or stumblingblock. One was brought about by what these dissenters taught and the other by how they lived. Anything that tends to divide and segregate and disintegrate the body of Christ and everything that offers a substitute for this truth is a scandal to Christianity.

There was one gratifying fact about these Roman Christians. Paul intimates that they were learned believers in doctrinal truth. He says, "the doctrine which ye have learned." Our security lies in our learning and knowledge of truth. Feelings never build walls of security about anyone. Again, Paul tells us in verse 19 that they were obedient as well as proficient, "For your obedience is come abroad unto all men." They lived what they learned. They practiced the precepts. They became possessors in fact and act. If we will live what we learn, our knowledge will never be in jeopardy of sabotage.

Here were fifth columnists who were infiltering the ranks of believers and carrying on their espionage and subversive activities. What was the strategy to employ against them? Paul simply says, "avoid them." He is telling them to turn away from these subverters. Notice that he does not say turn them out, nor does he say to turn on them. We would do either of the two. But to contend with dissenters is only to add contention to dissension and this would result in confounding confusion. Paul was extremely wise. He believed in giving a positive declaration of the truth, but to engage in debate would have served to advance the aims of these fifth columnists.

An unnamed philosopher, wise in the ways of men, offers the following as a means of permanent peace: "If a man cheats you, quit dealing with him; if he is abusive, quit his company; if he slanders you, take care to live so that nobody will believe him. No matter who he is, or how he misuses you, the wisest way is to let him alone; for there is nothing better than this cool, calm, quiet way of dealing with the wrongs of persons or nations."

2. The Reason for Dissension. Verse 18.

Two things are revealed in connection with these subverters.

(1) *Their motives.*

"For they that are such serve not our Lord Jesus Christ, but their own belly. . ."

Their motives were for selfish gain. They were not subject to the Lordship of Christ. They were not surrendered to the will of God. They were both false and fleshly. They were both base and selfish. They saw advantage in religion and they set out to make the best of it. Here false doctrine was linked with false living. They are always cause and effect. They are the reason for rebels in the ranks of Christ's soldiers. They serve "their own belly" which means base interests.

Let us not be surprised at the existence in our day of the remnants of these fifth columnists. A traitor is always the proof that there are patriots. Counterfeits mean that there is genuine currency. Apostates prove the reality of apostles. Hypocrites tell us that Christians live. Error proves truth. And if we find a continuing company of espionage workers who market the gospel for gain, they only serve to prove the reality of the gospel. The New Testament is full of statements to arouse suspicion and set up precautions against these who are ready to take advantage of the gospel for the sake of gain. And, furthermore, it states that "evil men and seducers shall wax worse and worse."

(2) *Their methods.*

". . . by good words and fair speeches deceive the hearts of the simple."

Arthur S. Way describes this as "sanctimonious cant." But it goes deeper than that. In the very first place, it means a voluble mouth. It is clever and smooth speech which presents plausible arguments of personal convictions.

Watch out for the man who flatters his audience by "good words and faith speeches." That man is more interested in what his audience thinks of him than what God thinks of his audience. Flattery is one of the surest baits to catch, what Paul described here as, "the simple." It does not mean simple-minded, for gullibility is not confined to those whose mentality is listed in the lower brackets. It refers to those trusting souls who never suspect people and never expect evil. They are due for a very rude awakening. The false parade under the banners of truth exist today as well as yesterday. All who handle the truth are not necessarily truthful. Those who preach the Word are not always true to the Lord as this passage clearly tells us. They "that are such serve not our Lord Jesus Christ." Let us cast aside this childish simplicity and remember that safety lies in a knowledge of and obedience to the Word of God.

Someone points out very cleverly the difference between a thermometer and a thermostat. The thermometer registers the temperature of a room while the thermostat regulates the temperature. They look very much alike, but are very different. The thermometer is a separate instrument while the thermostat is connected with the heating unit. One indicates what the temperature is while the other determines what it shall be. And there are people like these two instruments. Some are like thermometers, merely reflecting their environment, thermometers hanging by themselves and living in themselves. Others are like thermostats, actually reforming their environment. They are connected with the source of energy and power. The difference between people is the difference between these instruments. Here is the secret of life. It is living alone or living with God.

3. Our Philosophy of Success. Verse 19.

"For your obedience is come abroad unto all men. I am glad therefore on your behalf: but yet I would have you wise unto that which is good, and simple concerning evil."

There are here the opposite faculties of being wise and simple. Here is a faith which is first of all to be spiritually intelligent. We all know the old charge made against Christianity that it is superstitious and ignorant. Its contrary is true. It neither glorifies nor genders ignorance or superstitution. As is true here, it seeks for its own an intelligent spirituality.

Here it means wisdom in goodness. To be "wise unto that which is good," means exactly what it says. But there is a hidden truth here that we must not miss. No wisdom apart from God can be good. We must remember that "the world by wisdom knew not God." Wisdom is being made the goal and the end. But there is such a condition as glorifying wisdom and damning the wise. And, here, no one can be "wise unto that which is good" until he is first of all good and none can be good without God. Wisdom begins in the fear of the Lord.

It is also true that good is never gained out of evil. One does not need to practice evil in order to be wise in it. Purity never comes out of impurity. All of this means that if we are wise in good things we will be good in our wisdom. We will then bless the world with something more than knowledge. We will bless it with a practice of good things. And this it sorely needs. If we paid more attention to goodness and godliness in our curricula we would be blessed with a wisdom which would not now be applied to the destruction of cities and the slaughter of men as in modern warfare.

The other part of this philosophy says that we are to be "simple concerning evil." The maxim of the world is the opposite. It says to be wise in the evil and simple in the good. And that is exactly what is wrong with the world. To be simple in this way is not merely to be harmless or guileless or ignorant. It is a state of mind and life wherein the springs of our strength do not come out of the sources of evil thoughts and evil practices.

To be wise and simple in these things is to be made strong and secure. Let us be sure to guard both the weak spots and the strong spots. Jesus called our attention to the fact that Peter failed at his strong point. He boasted of his loyalty to Christ. He was sure he would not fail Christ there. Others might but he would not; yet he did.

The hurricane which laid waste so much of New England some years ago uprooted many thousands of trees. In the terrific wind, elms, maples, birches, and oaks went crashing to the ground with apparently little resistance. The prevailing winds in that region are from the northwest and in consequence of that usual condition the trees sent out sturdy roots in that direction in order to hold the tree steady against those prevailing gales. But along came a hurricane from a different direction, the southeast. There were no roots in that direction to hold the trees and down they came. Many of the fatalities of life result because trouble comes from the opposite direction and we have not sent out roots of protection. It is well to be prepared for the unexpected and never to leave unguarded the outposts of our strength. To be prepared, we should carefully adhere to this philosophy of spiritual success.

4. The Assurance of Victory. Verse 20.

"And the God of peace shall bruise Satan under your feet shortly. The grace of our Lord Jesus Christ be with you."

Even though paganism surrounded them and dissenters invaded them, the Christian's cause was a winning one. It had a pre-determined issue of success. Here is the recognition of a spiritually evil source behind all the moral, mental and physical evil of the world. Back of the visible enemy is the invisible foe. It is not a battle of ideologies or nationalities, but of spiritualities arising from a Satanic source.

The ultimate and final victory will come when Satan is conquered beneath the heel of Christ as predicted in Genesis 3:15. But the immediate victory may come when by the power and authority of the God of peace, we may "tread Satan" under our feet. This is a promise of the Christian's supremacy over evil. It indicates his personal triumph over the invisible forces that seek both his dominion and downfall. And this conquest is through all the weapons of warfare of the new life which are set forth heretofore in the teaching of Romans. Here is God's way of life for men beset by all sorts of adversity and a Satanic adversary. It is a spiritual way that dares to assault the very citadel of the adversary. It is the only way that has assurance of success. It is so because it deals with the fact of evil on its own grounds. Let us take courage and dare to live in the privilege of our faith.

For the battle that faces us there is a good measure of grace to furnish us with the necessary strength for that conflict. Paul says, "The grace of our Lord Jesus Christ be with you." Without this furnishing we are ill-prepared to meet the great adversary.

III. Salutations from Those in Corinth. Verses 21-24.

> "Timotheus my workfellow, and Lucius, and Jason, and Sosipater, my kinsmen, salute you. I Tertius, who wrote this epistle, salute you in the Lord. Gaius mine host, and of the whole church, saluteth you. Erastus the chamberlain of the city saluteth you, and Quartus a brother. The grace of our Lord Jesus Christ be with you all. Amen."

Previously, Paul extended his individual greetings to friends at Rome. Now he conveys the greetings of his compatriots who are with him at Corinth where he wrote his Epistle. These now send greetings through Paul.

The names of these Corinthians mean little to us except as reminders of their place in the founding of our faith. Each played his part. Timothy had a large part. He was a valuable companion to Paul. But of the others we know little. Yet, we are not to suppose that their influence was little. Here, for example, was Tertius, Paul's amanuensis, who transcribed this letter. Then there was Gaius, Paul's host, who so generously and graciously gave him living quarters. All of these contributed their part to a great cause.

Finally, we have reference to two men. One was Erastus and the other Quartus. Notice the one is mentioned because of his position as city chamberlain and the other because he was a brother. We may not be a city treasurer and occupy such a trusted office, but we can be a brother or a sister to someone. Usefulness to Christ's cause varies. How noble of this city official that he should lend his influence for Christ! Would God that we had more of them today. But do not despair. If we do not have a position, we still have a privilege. Use it in humility, even in obscurity.

We look now upon the last words of this great document. They breathe the spirit and passion of the entire letter. They sum its truth into a brevity of expression that sets the whole letter before us in a few words. They link the ending with the beginning and remind us of the consistent continuity that persists from its opening statement to its closing words.

Here is a document delivered to enhance the knowledge and establish the faith of a small colony of Christians who lived in Rome, seat of the world's mightiest and most ruthless empire. Rome was the exponent of the imperial philosophy that might makes right. Here was a contrary truth. It was the teaching that right makes might. It dared to face man with a true picture of his real character and demand his capitulation to Christ. Its secret was not in new ideas but a new life. That new life was heaven-born and earth-changing. It not only required a change in character and conduct, but what is more important, it produced it.

A noted political reformer in England who had labored ceaselessly for world peace through disarmament and arbitration, saw the folly of trying to change the nations without a change in the citizens. He said in consequence of his new conviction, "As I near eighty, and look back across my life, I see that I have not been successful, but if I had it to do over again, I think I would give my whole life to the changing of men, for without that change, nothing can be changed.

IV. FINAL BENEDICTION. Verses 25-27.

> Now to him that is of power to stablish you according to my gospel, and the preaching of Jesus Christ, according to the revelation of the mystery, which was kept secret since the world began, But now is made manifest, and by the scriptures of the prophets, according to the commandment of the everlasting God, made known to all nations for the obedience of faith: To God only wise, be glory through Jesus Christ for ever. Amen."

This benediction is in the form of a doxology. It is a doxology which has a twofold content. It carries with it the divine and the human element. It is not just a wordy ascription to deity but a sincere expression of praise to God which would react to the blessing of these Roman Christians.

It is a doxology of desire. It is the expressed desire for the establishment and security of these believers. Paul sees no benefit to the world in weak and vacillating Christians. He sees no good in compromisers who nullify their profession by wrong conduct. He seeks now the final security of a band of believers who dare to challenge Rome's might and dare to stand counter to the current of Rome's way of life and dare to deny Rome's false philosophy of force.

How can granite be put into the soul of such? How can character be fabricated with the steel of strength that never wavers though all else fails? How? Paul knew the answer. He gives to these as his parting message an assuring up-look. He opens heaven for them. He swings back the separation of sense and leaves these believers, not to stand in Rome alone, but to stand in the company of God while they live in Rome. And so he says, "Now to Him that is of power to stablish you."

We could desire nothing better for you who have walked through the pages of this book of Romans, than that you too should begin this new life in Christ Jesus; that you should feel the strong underpinning of eternal truths; that you should feel the grip of everlasting arms.

The beginning of such security is in a birth and its continuing is in a growth. The birth is one that begins with a personal faith in Jesus Christ. The growth is one that continues in daily contact and communion with the means of grace He puts at our disposal, one of which we are engaging in right now—meditation on His Word.

In this doxology of desire, Paul gives the agencies for the establishment and security of Rome's Christians. They follow in these verses.

1. The Precept—"to establish you according to my gospel."

The gospel is precept by doctrine. This doctrine Paul has very brilliantly set forth in this Epistle. But what is doctrine? It means a teaching. Every chemist has a doctrine of chemistry. Every architect has a doctrine of architecture. Every doctor has a doctrine of medicine. Here is a doctrine of life. It is the setting forth of God's new law of life in our lives. When we have received this doctrine, we become the recipients of its life.

Just what are the elements of this doctrine as found in Paul's gospel? In the first place, Paul said "that the gospel which was preached of me is not after man" (Gal. 1:11). It is a doctrine of human inability; a doctrine of divine justification; a doctrine of complete salvation; a doctrine of ultimate consummation. It is the doctrine of a Divine Word and a Divine Lord. It is the doctrine of a personal faith and a practical life. There can be no missing the way if one follows the landmarks of truth Paul sets out for earth's travelers.

If this doctrine of Paul's gospel was a workable way of life for Christians of the first century in Rome, is it still a workable way for Christians of the twentieth century? Indeed it is. Time has not abrogated it nor outmoded it. Whatever progress and change has come in man's knowledge of the material world has not affected man's spiritual and moral world. In the physical world there is vast change and increasing progress. But when we move into the moral and spiritual world, there is no change. The laws of truth, honesty, morality, and prayer have not changed. The laws that support the material world are the same as at the creation. The laws that support the spiritual world are the same as at the redemption. The gospel does not change. It operates on the same principles. It advocates the same precepts. It produces the same results. And we say with Paul, "I am not ashamed of the gospel of Christ: for it is the power of God unto salvation to every one that believeth; to the Jew first, and also to the Greek."

2. The Person—"to stablish you according to . . . the preaching of Jesus Christ."

The proclamation of this person is "according to the revelation of the mystery." A mystery in the ordinary sense is something where knowledge is withheld, but here it is the disclosing of a truth. The mystery of this person was found in type and symbol throughout the Old Testament. It was a secret, except to faith, "since the world began." But it was revealed to faith in Adam's coat of skins, in Abel's acceptable offering, in Abraham's offering of Isaac until at last it came into full bloom in the birth, life, and passion of Jesus Christ. And so Paul could say, "But now is made manifest (unveiled)." It is made manifest in His virgin birth, His virtuous life, His vicarious death and His victorious resurrection.

It is made manifest—

| | |
|---|---|
| In His humanity | Romans 1:3 |
| In His deity | Romans 1:4 |
| In His redemption | Romans 3:24 |
| In His resurrection | Romans 1:4 |
| In His Lordship | Romans 7:25 |
| In His intercession | Romans 8:34 |
| In His inseparability | Romans 8:35 |
| In His salvation | Romans 10:9, 10 |
| In His consummation | Romans 8:29, 30 |

Here is a full-orbed and completely proportionated Saviour. Here is one of adequate stature and consummate power. He is the subject of this book and the object of our faith. He is the means of our life and the end to which we move with unerring certainty.

Out of gratitude for His grace; out of devotion to His cause, let us gladly lend Him the facilities and the faculties of our lives, our homes and our businesses. And let us do it in such a self-forgetful way that no one will question the sincerity of our motives.